THE DECLINE OF INFANT AND CHILD MORTALITY

Carlo A. Corsini and Pier Paolo Viazzo (editors)

THE DECLINE OF INFANT AND CHILD MORTALITY

The European Experience: 1750–1990

United Nations Children's Fund
INTERNATIONAL CHILD DEVELOPMENT CENTRE
Florence - Italy

SIDES
Società Italiana di Demografia Storica

ISTITUTO
DEGLI INNOCENTI
DI FIRENZE

MARTINUS NIJHOFF PUBLISHERS

Published by Kluwer Law International
P.O. Box 85889
2508 CN The Hague, The Netherlands

Sold and distributed in the USA and Canada by
Kluwer Law International
675 Massachusetts Avenue
Cambridge, MA 02139, USA

Sold and distributed in all other countries by
Kluwer Law International
Distribution Centre
P.O. Box 322
3300 AH Dordrecht, The Netherlands

A C.I.P. catalogue record for this book is available from the Library of Congress

The contents of this book are the responsibility of the contributors, and do not necessarily reflect the policies or views of the United Nations Children's Fund (UNICEF).

Cover photograph: Sogno della Madre del Beato Sorore in the Pellegrinaio dell'Ospedale di Santa Maria della Scala, Siena
by Lorenzo di Pietro detto il Vecchietta (1420–1480)
© Cover photograph: Fabio Lensini

Printed on acid-free paper

Cover design: Robert Vulkers

ISBN 90 411 0466 6

© 1997 UNICEF

Kluwer Law International incorporates the publishing programmes of Graham & Trotman Ltd, Kluwer Law and Taxation Publishers and Martinus Nijhoff Publishers

Foreword

The Decline of Infant Mortality: Child Survival—Indicator or Symbol?

Thanks to the efforts of the many actors in the international community, child survival has become one of the principal objectives of social development programmes through-out the world, especially during the past 15 years. This is particularly the case in the health field, where IMR (infant mortality, or the rate of mortality under 1 year of age) and U5MR (mortality under 5 years) are actually the key indicators for evaluating the success of programmes. Concentrating on improving infants' and children's chances for survival is in some ways an obvious choice and indeed should be a clear priority in countries where IMR and U5MR exceed 50 and 70 per 1,000 live births, respectively.

At the historic 1990 World Summit for Children, heads of state adopted a Plan of Action setting goals for children and development that were to be reached by the year 2000. First on the list was the reduction of IMR and U5MR by one third. Today the United Nations Convention on the Rights of the Child has been approved by virtually every country in the world (187 as of the end of 1996, with only 5 countries still un-committed). Although the Convention must be considered as a whole and the rights it defines are indivisible, the fact that the child's right to survival appears among its early articles (Article 6) is significant. *Primum vivere*: first life, and then all the rest can follow, including speculations on the quality of the lives that have been saved.

Since the end of the Second World War, world trends in infant and child survival have been steadily improving. This in itself is evidence that focusing on this issue can yield good results. The extraordinary advances in health technologies have of course played an important role. In addition, it has been shown that spectacular results can be obtained by lowering the costs of these technologies and making them widely available. However, the issues involved in the reduction of infant and child mortality are not just technical and financial, but also—and primarily—moral. Precisely because of the advances that have been made, countries and the international community now have an irrefutable duty to use the means that are available to save as many young lives as possible.

However, as the different chapters of this book highlight, the causes of infant and child mortality reduction are complex—much more so than one might suppose. Certainly, medical advances have been a key factor, but in some circumstances breast-feeding practices appear to have been even more important. Reductions in IMR documented during periods of severe economic crisis, for instance, have been attributed to higher rates of unemployment among women resulting in more mothers choosing to breastfeed. Similarly, the link between the per capita income of a population and infant and child mortality is not so clear as one might expect. One study finds that the avail- ability of new technologies can be more important than income, and that these two factors can act independently of each other. Other findings are that a mother's working status may have a positive rather than negative influence on infant survival, and that breastfeeding can be a greater determinant of survival than legitimacy or illegitimacy.

Each of these conclusions is tentative and conditional on many factors. However, although this volume does not arrive at hard truths, it makes a very important contribution to the literature on this subject by showing that an understanding of infant and child mortality trends requires the simultaneous use of diverse techniques and an analytical effort that is multidisciplinary in nature. This is a crucial point not just because it will help policy makers to avoid supporting decisions that are based on simplistic analyses, but also because we have here the proof that infant and child mortality is an essential entry point in attempts to set different processes in motion to promote systemic changes in a society.

Avoiding unnecessary infant and child deaths is not only a humanitarian action. From another perspective, child survival is emblematic of the way societies assemble and prioritize their basic values. When children die for preventable reasons, when their deaths could have been avoided, it is not merely a sad event but also a symptom of a complex malaise affecting the entire society.

A better understanding of the causes of infant and child mortality and their inter- relationships is the first step to saving more children's lives in the future. At the same time, this understanding enables us to use the emotional power that children universally generate to promote a model of development based on the improvement of the quality of life—a model that children's well-being can fully symbolize.

Paolo Basurto, *Director*
UNICEF International
Child Development Centre

Acknowledgements

This volume contains revised versions of the papers presented at the Second Innocenti Seminar on the Decline of Infant and Child Mortality in Europe, held in Florence on 5–6 December 1994 in the unique setting provided by the Spedale di Santa Maria degli Innocenti, a magnificent Renaissance building designed in the first half of the fifteenth century by Filippo Brunelleschi to serve as a refuge for foundlings and other needy children. The Seminar was very appropriately organized and hosted jointly by the Istituto degli Innocenti of Florence—one of the first institutions in the world to be specifically devoted to the welfare of children, and the oldest in continuous operation—the UNICEF International Child Development Centre and the Italian Society of Historical Demography (SIDES).

A previous meeting, also promoted by the Istituto degli Innocenti and attended by scholars from 12 European countries, had been held in Florence in the spring of 1992, with the twofold aim of reviewing the state of the art in the study of infant and child mortality in Europe and laying the foundations for a coordinated effort to shed light on the many elusive aspects of its historical decline, most of which occurred between the middle of the nineteenth century and the Second World War. The encouraging results of that meeting convinced the participants that an international project on the decline of infant and childhood mortality in Europe during the last two hundred years was feasible and timely. The project was launched in February 1993. The Second Innocenti Seminar provided an ideal opportunity for the participants in the project to present and discuss the results achieved in the first two years and to plan the further development of the project.

As conference organizers and editors, we want to express our gratitude to the administrative and secretarial staff of the Istituto degli Innocenti and to the publication staff of the UNICEF International Child Development Centre. We are especially indebted to Maria Bortolotto, Richard Dunbar, Sveva Fedeli and Patricia Light. We owe a great deal to other participants in the meeting who did not present papers but greatly contributed to the discussion: in particular, Professor Karl Eric Knutsson and Stuart J. Woolf played a crucial role in ensuring the success of the meeting. We were exceptionally fortunate in having available the skill and secure judgement of Jason Pearce, who so ably edited the text of this volume and watched over all phases of its production. We were also lucky that Eugene Grebenik, the distinguished demographer and editor of *Population Studies*, agreed to translate the two chapters on France.

C. A. Corsini
P. P. Viazzo

Contents

Notes on Contributors

JOSEP BERNABEU-MESTRE, Associate Professor of the History of Science, Department of Public Health, University of Alicante, Spain, and President of the Iberian Society of Historical Demography.

MARIA BORTOLOTTO, Research Officer, Istituto degli Innocenti, Florence, Italy.

PATRICE BOURDELAIS, Directeur d'Etudes, Ecole des Hautes Etudes en Sciences Sociales, Paris, France, and Editor of *Annales de Démographie Historique*.

ANDERS BRÄNDSTRÖM, Associate Professor, Department of Historical Demography, Umeå University, Sweden.

CARLO A. CORSINI, Professor of Historical Demography, Department of Statistics, University of Florence, Italy, and President of the Italian Society of Historical Demography.

MICHEL DEMONET, Maître de Conférences, Ecole des Hautes Etudes en Sciences Sociales, Paris, France.

CHRIS GALLEY, Research Fellow, Department of Geography, University of Liverpool, UK.

VIOLETTA HIONIDOU, Lecturer in Social Statistics, University of Southampton, UK.

JAN KOK, Research Officer, International Institute of Social History, Amsterdam, The Netherlands.

ELLEN KRUSE, former research assistant, Netherlands Interdisciplinary Demographic Institute, The Hague, and currently a student of history, Leyden State University, The Netherlands.

PAOLA MANCINI, Research Fellow, Department of Demographic Sciences, University of Rome 'La Sapienza', Italy.

GODELIEVE MASUY-STROOBANT, Chercheur Qualifié du Fonds National de la Recherche Scientifique, and Professor, Institute of Demography, Catholic University of Louvain, Belgium.

VICENTE PÉREZ-MOREDA, Professor, School of Economics, Universidad Complutense de Madrid, Spain.

ANTONELLA PINNELLI, Professor of Social Demography, Department of Demographic Sciences, University of Rome 'La Sapienza', Italy.

FRANS VAN POPPEL, Senior Research Associate, Netherlands Interdisciplinary Demographic Institute, The Hague.

DAVID S. REHER, Professor, School of Political Sciences and Sociology, Universidad Complutense de Madrid, Spain.

ALICE REID, Ph.D. student, Cambridge Group for the History of Population and Social Structure, University of Cambridge, UK.

CATHERINE ROLLET, Professor of Demography, Population History and the History of Childhood, University of Versailles Saint-Quentin-en-Yvelines, France.

PIER PAOLO VIAZZO, Associate Professor of Social Anthropology, Department of Anthropology, University of Turin, Italy, and Director of Historical Research, Istituto degli Innocenti, Florence.

JÖRG VÖGELE, Senior Lecturer and Deputy Director, Institut für Geschichte der Medizin, Heinrich-Heine-Universität Düsseldorf, Germany.

NAOMI WILLIAMS, Research Fellow, Department of Geography, University of Liverpool, UK.

ROBERT WOODS, John Rankin Professor of Geography, Department of Geography, University of Liverpool, UK.

ANDREA ZANOTTO, Ph.D. student in economic history, University of Naples, Italy.

Introduction
Recent Advances and Some Open Questions in the Long-term Study of Infant and Child Mortality

CARLO A. CORSINI AND PIER PAOLO VIAZZO

Of all the changes that have taken place in European society during the past century, few have been as significant as the steep decline in both birth and death rates. Europe was transformed from a society in which women bore large numbers of children and saw many of them die into one in which only one, two or three children were typically born to each woman and the death of an infant or a young child became a rarity. Identifying the factors responsible for this 'secular' and seemingly irreversible decline in both fertility and mortality is clearly a major task for research. Despite its importance, however, the decline of infant and child mortality has been the subject of far less systematic inquiry than has the fall of fertility.

Some basic facts about the long-term decline of infant mortality in Europe are, of course, well established. Vital registration series are available for most European countries from the 1870s, and for virtually all of Europe from 1900. They show that in the late nineteenth century levels of infant mortality were still extremely high and could vary quite markedly from one country to another, ranging from around 100 per 1,000 live births in Norway and Sweden to 200 or even 250 per 1,000 in such countries as Germany, Austria and Russia (Mitchell 1980, 140–141). At the turn of the century, infant mortality began to fall almost right across the continent. Since the decline was steeper in the countries with higher mortality levels, a certain degree of convergence towards lower levels can already be detected in the first decades of the twentieth century. By 1950, most national infant mortality rates ranged between 20 and 80 per 1,000. In the second half of the twentieth century, further and fast decline in infant mortality has been recorded all over Europe. Around 1985, infant deaths ranged between less than 10 per 1,000 in northern and western European countries to rates in the region of 20 to 30 per 1,000 in Portugal and in several countries of Eastern Europe, which represents a reduction of around 90 per cent since 1900 (United Nations 1989; Keyfitz and Flieger 1990).

One problem with these figures is that, while leaving no doubt about the magnitude of the decline, they told a story so obviously successful as to blunt the analysis of the factors contributing to the fall of mortality. Economists and social scientists were keen on hailing the sharp decline in infant mortality in Europe and in the rest of the industrialized world as the epitome of a golden age of social development. They emphasized the fact that chances of surviving the dangerous first months and years of life had increased in parallel with rapid improvements in the nutritional status of children,

C.A. Corsini and P.P. Viazzo (eds.) The Decline of Infant and Child Mortality, xiii–xxxi.
© 1997 UNICEF. Printed in the Netherlands.

steady growth in household incomes, control of major infectious diseases and the spectacular results of the use of antibiotics. In the late 1980s, however, it became painfully clear that progress in child welfare was slackening off in a number of European and other industrialized countries, and that in some of them the slow-down was alarmingly pronounced (Cornia 1990). Among other things, this unexpected situation led both analysts and policy-makers to realize that surprisingly little was known about the precise reasons for infant mortality decline and that the available data did not offer a reliable guide to understanding even its most recent phases.

A brief examination of the evidence conveniently assembled by Nathan Keyfitz and Wilhelm Flieger in 1990, and presented here in tabular form, immediately lays bare some serious limitations in the data and invites a few reflections. Table I.1 is, first of all, a reminder that infant mortality (that is, the probability of dying under one year of age, or q_0) is not the only mortality indicator to be taken into account when studying improvements in child health and child welfare. The probabilities of dying between 1 and 5 years of age ($_4q_1$) and between 5 and 10 years ($_5q_5$) are also important, if often underrated, indicators. So, too, are such measures of adult life expectancy as e_{10} (the average number of years children aged 10 can expect to survive), which are assumed to be influenced by variations in young-age mortality experience.

In a different vein, it is relevant to observe that some European countries are absent owing to lack of comparable information, and that at least some of the figures provided for the 22 countries included in the table are rather dubious. It seems difficult to believe, for instance, that in Bulgaria, Hungary and Poland the steep fall in q_0 recorded between 1970 and 1985 was accompanied (for males, but not for females) by a substantial decline in e_{10}. Nevertheless, such traces of gender-related differentials in the recent evolution of e_{10}, along with numerous other data contained in the table, bring out another highly significant point, namely that overall figures may easily hide marked differences not only between countries but also between males and females. Finally, even a cursory glance at the table is enough to realize that the various indicators have not moved together. A closer analysis reveals that the relationship between q_0 and e_{10}, which was very weak or virtually non-existent in 1970 ($R = -0.19392$ for males, -0.42333 for females), had become stronger in 1985 ($R = -0.52969$ for males, -0.60019 for females). On the other hand, the relationship between q_0 and $_4q_1$ appears to have weakened: for males, the value of R declines from a very strong positive association of 0.95542 in 1970 to 0.70139 in 1985; for females, from 0.93105 to 0.75724.

These data and the relationships that can be detected between them point, on the one hand, to the uneven and often disappointing quality of the evidence that was available to the students of infant mortality decline in Europe as late as 1990, and, on the other, to the complexity of their task. The very fact that even multiple regression fails to bring out any significant and unambiguous pattern of relationships (as shown in the lower panels of Table I.1) underscores the need for better data, more subtle indicators and more astute analytical and comparative strategies. As we have already noted, the unexpected slowing down of improvements in child welfare, first experienced in several European countries in the late 1980s, demonstrated that such improvements (including

Table I.1. Europe: Infant and childhood mortality indicators for 22 countries,
by gender, 1970 and 1985

(*a*) *Males*

	1970				1985			
	q_0	$_4q_1$	$_5q_5$	e_{10}	q_0	$_4q_1$	$_5q_5$	e_{10}
Austria	28.1	4.3	3.3	58.9	11.8	2.5	1.0	61.6
Belgium	24.6	3.9	2.7	60.0	11.6	2.5	1.4	62.0
Bulgaria	30.8	5.2	3.0	61.8	15.6	4.3	2.6	59.7
Czechoslovakia	25.3	4.2	2.5	58.3	15.7	2.2	1.8	58.6
Denmark	17.1	3.4	2.5	62.5	9.0	1.7	1.8	62.4
Federal Republic Germany	25.9	4.3	3.1	59.5	10.0	1.9	1.2	62.5
Finland	14.8	3.7	3.2	57.6	6.3	1.5	1.4	60.8
France	17.1	3.6	2.4	60.2	9.8	2.0	1.4	62.2
German Democratic Republic	20.3	3.8	2.5	60.3	10.6	2.8	1.7	60.6
Greece	39.7	4.2	2.4	64.0	17.4	2.2	1.4	63.9
Hungary	39.7	4.6	2.3	59.5	22.8	2.4	1.5	56.9
Italy	31.6	4.1	2.6	61.5	12.9	2.0	1.2	62.6
Netherlands	14.1	3.7	2.9	62.3	8.9	1.8	1.1	63.9
Norway	14.9	4.1	2.8	62.6	10.2	2.1	1.3	63.6
Poland	38.9	4.7	2.6	59.6	20.2	2.8	1.8	58.2
Portugal	118.8	14.9	4.9	59.6	19.5	4.6	2.6	61.4
Republic of Ireland	20.7	3.6	2.5	61.1	9.3	1.9	1.6	61.7
Spain	31.5	4.2	2.7	62.1	11.7	2.5	1.7	64.1
Sweden	12.8	2.6	2.2	63.5	7.4	1.2	1.0	64.5
Switzerland	30.3	5.3	3.4	62.2	12.5	3.3	1.0	65.0
United Kingdom	21.0	3.3	2.0	60.5	10.4	2.0	1.1	62.6
Yugoslavia	56.1	9.4	3.3	59.8	30.1	4.4	2.3	60.6
Mean	30.6	4.8	2.8	60.8	13.3	2.5	1.5	61.8
Standard deviation	22.4	2.6	0.6	1.7	5.7	0.9	0.5	2.1

Regression results: Dependent variable e_{10}

	1970	1985
R	0.2768	0.6664
Intercept	62.991	65.473
F	0.498	4.9989
Beta values		
q_0	0.0075	−0.2215
$_4q_1$	−0.0601	1.3367
$_5q_5$	−0.7633	−2.6236

Table I.1. (*cont.*)

(*b*) *Females*

	1970				1985			
	q_0	$_4q_1$	$_5q_5$	e_{10}	q_0	$_4q_1$	$_5q_5$	e_{10}
Austria	21.3	3.8	1.6	65.5	8.1	1.9	0.8	68.4
Belgium	18.2	3.0	1.7	65.9	8.2	1.6	1.0	68.8
Bulgaria	22.6	4.5	1.8	65.7	13.1	3.8	1.8	65.6
Czechoslovakia	19.6	3.4	1.7	64.8	12.1	1.8	1.3	65.9
Denmark	11.0	2.1	1.9	67.2	7.0	1.4	1.0	68.3
Federal Republic of Germany	19.5	3.4	2.0	65.5	7.8	1.7	1.1	69.0
Finland	11.9	2.2	1.7	65.6	5.6	1.0	0.9	69.2
France	13.2	2.7	1.6	67.5	7.3	1.6	1.0	70.4
German Democratic Republic	16.3	3.0	1.6	64.9	8.3	2.0	1.6	66.3
Greece	31.9	3.8	1.8	68.1	13.4	1.5	1.0	68.8
Hungary	31.2	3.8	1.7	64.9	18.6	1.9	1.1	64.8
Italy	25.6	3.7	1.6	67.0	10.8	1.7	1.0	69.0
Netherlands	10.9	2.8	1.6	67.7	7.2	1.5	0.7	70.6
Norway	10.3	2.6	1.4	68.5	6.7	1.6	1.2	70.4
Poland	30.0	3.7	1.8	65.7	15.5	2.3	1.2	66.2
Portugal	60.7	13.8	3.6	65.3	14.8	3.1	1.4	68.1
Republic of Ireland	15.9	2.8	1.3	65.5	7.9	1.5	0.8	67.2
Spain	24.6	3.4	1.8	67.2	9.6	2.0	1.1	70.2
Sweden	9.5	1.6	1.8	68.3	6.4	1.1	0.5	70.5
Switzerland	22.0	4.2	2.1	68.1	10.4	2.5	0.7	71.8
United Kingdom	16.0	2.6	1.4	66.5	8.3	1.6	0.9	68.3
Yugoslavia	52.9	10.2	2.3	64.6	25.4	4.2	1.8	66.2
Mean	22.5	4.0	1.8	66.4	10.6	2.0	1.1	68.4
Standard deviation	13.0	2.8	0.5	1.3	4.8	0.8	0.3	1.9

Regression results: Dependent variable e_{10}

	1970	1985
R	0.4892	0.7675
Intercept	65.467	72.706
F	1.888	8.598
Beta values		
q_0	−0.0345	−0.2399
$_4q_1$	−0.2391	1.3947
$_5q_5$	1.4485	−4.1907

Source: Keyfitz and Flieger 1990.

mortality decline) could not be taken for granted—as part and parcel of vaguely defined processes of modernization—but required precise explanation. What we would like to add is that this realization went hand in hand with a growing awareness that cross-sectional analyses, or such relatively short-term comparisons as the ones allowed by the data presented in the table, were hardly sufficient. A correct understanding of the causes and mechanics of the historical decline of infant mortality seemed essential to shed light on the unforeseen predicament of contemporary Europe, and might have implications for those parts of the world where high birth and death rates continued to have such a great impact on social welfare, health and the economy.

THE STATE OF RESEARCH IN THE EARLY 1990S

The research agenda for the 1990s was set by two major books, both published in 1991. The essays contributed to *The decline of mortality in Europe* (Schofield, Reher and Bideau 1991) provided an authoritative report into the state of research on the historical decline of mortality and, at the same time, made a powerful plea for more systematic investigation. As Roger Schofield and David Reher pointed out in their introduction to that volume, nothing similar to the Princeton Project, launched in the 1960s by Ansley Coale to chart the course of the fall in marital fertility throughout Europe since the mid-nineteenth century (see Coale and Watkins 1986), had been attempted for mortality. As a consequence, they complained, 'it would be only a small exaggeration to say that our understanding of historical mortality patterns, and of their causes and implications, is still in its infancy' (Schofield and Reher 1991, 2). Progress had been hampered both by the methodological and substantive complexities inherent in the study of mortality decline and by severe data problems. The study of mortality at young ages, in particular, had largely remained a piecemeal affair. This was especially lamentable, since it was well-known that falls in infant and child mortality had been responsible for much of the overall decline. It was in this area that a coordinated research approach along the lines of the Princeton Project was most urgently needed.

In the same year, important new perspectives for the historical study of infant and child mortality came from across the Atlantic. In their pathbreaking and influential book *Fatal years: child mortality in late nineteenth-century America*, Samuel Preston and Michael Haines emphasized that, although most Western European countries had good vital registration systems by the mid- or late nineteenth century, these systems 'produced data for large geographic aggregates, not for individuals or families or classes' (1991, p. xv). The resultant lack of a detailed portrait of the mortality conditions of different individuals and groups explained why our understanding of the causes and timing of decline was still tenuous and vague. The novelty of Preston and Haines's work was that they had been able to use a data set that had recently become available and that offered 'unparalleled opportunities' to depict mortality conditions in the late nineteenth century. The US Population Census of 1900 had asked married women how many children they had ever given birth to and how many of those children were still living at the time of the census. By constructing a large sample of individual answers to these questions, and applying the techniques of indirect estimation developed by William Brass (1975) for use in situations where there is no vital registration system to provide numbers of births and deaths, Preston and Haines had managed to produce improved estimates of the levels of child mortality in the United States during the last decade of the nineteenth century.

Fatal years demonstrated not only that individual-level data extracted from national censuses could be exploited to great effect by historical demographers through the use of certain *methodological* tools, but also that these data made it possible to tackle previously forbidding *substantive* issues and gave modern scholars a chance to disentangle the complex skeins of causality that had baffled many a contemporary observer. In particular, such data allowed a more satisfactory assessment of the weight of class and other factors (including cultural ones) in affecting levels and trends of infant and child mortality. As indicated by the amount of discussion and controversy it immediately raised (see Caldwell *et al.* 1991), *Fatal years* made a strong impression on those who were working on infant and child mortality in both contemporary and past societies. It greatly contributed to drawing their attention to the deficiencies of the 'old' official sources, to the necessity of searching for new ones, and especially to the crucial importance of collecting and analysing individual-level data. Much attention was also attracted by Preston and Haines's contention that, in the late nineteenth century, the effect of parental occupational differences on infant and child mortality was far less pronounced in the United States than in England, where early industrialization had probably created an unusually differentiated class structure. In America, differentials by ethnic group, presumably reflecting different customs in infant feeding and child raising, appeared to have been more significant. In addition to its substantive merits, this contention had important methodological implications, since it suggested that progress in the study of infant mortality decline could come not only from the use of better data and more refined statistical tools, but also from cultural analysis. In this respect, Preston and Haines were in agreement with Schofield and Reher's (1991, 16–17) conclusion that 'in the long run, cultural factors were essential for the breakthrough in the fight against high mortality' and that any thoroughgoing understanding of the mortality transition would necessarily be an interdisciplinary one, with demographic knowledge helping to define the dependent variable 'in a complex equation including social, economic, cultural, geographical, and even climatological variables'.

THE INNOCENTI PROJECT

The idea of starting an international European research project on the decline of infant mortality was spurred by the feelings of urgency and excitement embodied in the two major books published in 1991. A 'launching' seminar, focused on the period when decline was known to have been at its sharpest (1850–1950), was held in Florence, at the Istituto degli Innocenti, on 9–11 April 1992. The seminar had the threefold aim of reviewing the state of the art in the study of infant mortality in the various European countries, surveying the available sources and, rather more ambitiously, laying the foundations for a coordinated research enterprise along the lines of the Princeton Project.

The review of the state of the art proved very instructive and revealed the existence of significant 'national' differences in terms of the levels, trends and timing of decline. One immediate outcome of the seminar was the publication of a volume containing four of the papers presented in Florence (Corsini and Viazzo 1993). The four papers were selected for publication in that volume primarily because they were based on unusually long national time-series, stretching back to 1818 for Austria (Kytir and Münz 1993), 1750 for France and Sweden (Rollet and Bourdelais 1993; Brändström 1993), and as early as 1550 for England (Woods, Williams and Galley 1993). They unmistakably showed that, before the end of the nineteenth century, trends could vary widely and the presumed uniformity of the 'secular' decline of infant mortality in Europe was more apparent than real, the result of a sort of optical illusion caused by the insufficient chronological depth of most national series.

Indeed, the Florence meeting confirmed that the data that formed the basis of current views on the decline of infant mortality could not provide satisfactory answers to many fundamental questions. In order to understand the timing and the causes of mortality decline better, it seemed especially urgent and important to promote the construction of long-term series, extending both national and geographically disaggregated series as far back as possible without disregarding post-transitional developments. The survey of the published and manuscript sources available in the various European countries suggested that in some cases good returns could still be obtained through a more systematic sifting of official statistical documentation. In other cases, however, progress could be ensured only by producing entirely new and more flexible data sets capable of taking the analyst as close as possible to the individual level.

Fine-grained information and flexible data sets were a prerequisite to any attempt to deepen our understanding of mortality differentials related to gender, socio-economic circumstances and environmental diversity. The Florence meeting made clear, in particular, that much work was still to be done on urban–rural differentials and, even more importantly, that a careful exploration of the relationships between infant and child mortality was badly needed. Contrary to widespread assumptions, it emerged that infant mortality (defined as mortality under 12 months of age) was not always paralleled by mortality among young children aged between 1 and 5 years. The two trends actually departed so markedly from one another at times that there seemed to be some justification for treating infant and child mortality as almost unrelated phenomena. It was very likely, on the other hand, that largely the same factors affected mortality in the months before and after the first birthday. An important step forward in the exploration of the blurred boundaries between infant and child mortality would consist in extending to the second year of life some of the infant mortality measures conventionally limited to the first year (Breschi and Livi Bacci 1994). Such an advance was, however, very difficult to achieve in the study of large populations owing to the fact that the overwhelming majority of the statistical documentation available in print follows the conventional distinction between infant mortality (q_0) and child mortality ($_4q_1$).

The main indications offered by the Florence meeting are reflected in the differences between the title of the seminar, which focused on the decline of infant mortality between 1850 and 1950, and the title of the research project that originated from the seminar itself, the purpose of which was to study the decline of both infant and childhood mortality over the last two hundred years (Woods, Kertzer, Viazzo and Brändström 1993). It is worth noting that the Innocenti Project, while drawing its inspiration from the Princeton Project and taking very seriously its methodological lessons, had no ambition of covering the whole territory of Europe (as the Princeton Project had done) or even of Western Europe. Rather, its aim was to bring together specialists not only from different countries but also from different disciplines, and to provide a common framework for their research activities. The scholars who attended the First Innocenti Seminar in 1992 already came from a diversity of disciplinary backgrounds, and this multidisciplinary orientation was further strengthened in the following years. When the members of the research network met again in Florence in December 1994 for a second plenary meeting, papers were given by scholars from a wide range of disciplines: demography, social and economic history, geography, epidemiology, anthropology, and the history of medicine.

THIS VOLUME

This volume contains revised versions of the twelve papers presented at the 1994 seminar. The reader will probably still sense the dominant feelings experienced by those who took part in the meeting—especially the realization that in the two intervening years considerable advances had been made, that new sources had become available and some old ones could still yield significant returns when properly exploited, that brand-new data sets were being created and that new methods were being used and not simply talked about. It should be stressed that the chapters of this volume do not emerge from final research reports, but reflect work in progress, which explains a certain emphasis on methodology. Yet, it seems fair to say that these essays do not indulge in methodology for its own sake. They are all rich in substantive results and even touch on numerous issues of considerable relevance to current debates on the policies to be adopted to curb infant and child mortality in both developed and developing countries.

Methodological issues

A distinctive and, we hope, useful feature of this volume is that virtually all types of sources, data sets and methods appear to be represented, from the comparative analysis of official aggregate statistics for 27 European countries (chapter 1) to the use of family reconstitution to collect individual-level data for a tiny Greek island population (chapter 8).

When the first meeting was held in 1992, a somewhat 'iconoclastic' mood prevailed among the participants. There was a widespread feeling that it was high time to move away from official statistics and aggregate data and to concentrate on individual-level analysis. In essence, this meant that systematic work was to be conducted using unpublished archival material, mostly at the local level, and that research strategies bordering on social and cultural anthropology could also be used (Kertzer 1992, 1994). It was nevertheless agreed that it was important to assemble a set of improved national series of infant mortality measures, since it appeared that, although these measures were very often used for international comparisons, they were probably not as reliable as commonly believed, either because of the quality of the vital registration systems or because of differences in the legal definitions of the registered events (stillbirths, late foetal births, live births, deaths).

It was also suggested, in a rather different vein, that new insights could be expected if official aggregate statistics were analysed at the regional or subregional level in order to detect spatial variations in the patterns of infant mortality. Thus it was decided that aggregate figures and published sources deserved a last chance, so to speak—and this decision has paid off. Five of the chapters in this volume show that official statistics are still far from yielding diminishing returns.

This is most impressively demonstrated in the opening chapter, by Godelieve Masuy-Stroobant, who has created a database where vital registration statistics published at the national level have been stored for 27 European countries from 1900 to 1990. National-level statistics are also used by Antonella Pinnelli and Paola Mancini in their analysis of gender mortality differences from birth to puberty in Italy (chapter 4), which illustrates how progress can be achieved in the study of mortality differentials when data are disaggregated by gender, age and cause of death. Utilizing the tools of geographical analysis and following the Princeton Project precept that spatial variations should be studied at the most detailed scale available, Robert Woods, Naomi Williams and Chris Galley investigate the relationships between infant and child mortality at the registration district level and demonstrate that national averages for England and Wales disguise considerable geographical differences (chapter 3). Finally, aggregate data are used both by Patrice Bourdelais and Michel Demonet (chapter 5) and by Jörg Vögele (chapter 6) to shed light on urban patterns of infant mortality in France and Germany, respectively. Where Bourdelais and Demonet construct cross-sectional life-tables for 71 French towns and cities in the early 1860s, drawing on official statistics that have recently surfaced from the Paris archives, Vögele overcomes some serious limitations of aggregate statistics on urban and rural infant mortality by focusing his analysis on the ten largest cities of Imperial Germany, in order to bring the 'urban effect' into sharper relief.

From a methodological point of view, the remarkable study of childhood mortality patterns in Spain from 1800 to 1940 conducted by David Reher, Vicente Pérez-Moreda and Josep Bernabeu-Mestre (chapter 2) occupies an intermediate position between the chapters based on official aggregate data that have just been mentioned and most of the other chapters in the volume, which rely predominantly on individual-level data. The admittedly unusual potentialities of Spanish parish archives have enabled Reher,

Pérez-Moreda and Bernabeu-Mestre to generate long-term series of young-age mortality indicators for 49 different communities located in the central areas of the country and in the eastern province of Alicante. This chapter provides a striking demonstration of the advantages to the study of infant and child mortality of being able to collect aggregate data in such a way that they can be rearranged into age groups and categories, escaping the straightjacket of official statistics.

Although the Spanish study is a salutary reminder that flexible data sets can be produced without necessarily descending to the individual level, and that aggregate data can still open excitingly new perspectives on the study of the decline of infant and child mortality, the value of approaches using individual-level data can hardly be doubted. It should be observed that a variety of such approaches exists, and that very different research strategies can be devised and tailored to the questions to be tackled and to the specific characteristics of the sources. This volume contains examples of several different 'styles' of individual-level analysis. Alice Reid (chapter 7) applies Brass's method of indirect estimation to a sample of individual returns from the 1911 census of England and Wales. On the other hand, both Anders Brändström (chapter 9) and Jan Kok, Frans van Poppel and Ellen Kruse (chapter 10) use cohort data to analyse the life-courses of illegitimate children in two areas of Sweden and the Netherlands, respectively, and to compare their fates to those of legitimate children. The reader will, however, notice some differences between the two approaches, and also a few similarities between Brändström's study, which deals primarily with local communities rather than with samples of larger populations, and the study carried out by Violetta Hionidou on the Greek island of Mykonos (chapter 7), where the classic microdemographic method of 'family reconstitution' is supported by quasi-ethnographic fieldwork. A mixed research strategy, combining the use of aggregate data and the in-depth analysis of individual-level information, is illustrated by the last chapter of the volume, which follows the evolution of infant mortality among nearly 200,000 foundlings admitted to Florence's Spedale degli Innocenti from 1750 to 1950.

Substantive issues

The chapters in this volume provide a valuable demonstration of the variety of the sources as well as of the versatility of the methods, but their substantive results are no less interesting and important. Indeed, they are so rich as to make any summary very difficult.

The painstaking investigation conducted by Masuy-Stroobant marks a significant step forward from the provisional generalizations arrived at during the launching seminar of 1992, and casts serious doubts on some crucial aspects of the 'convergence' theory of infant mortality decline. It is commonly assumed that in the course of the twentieth century the differences in infant mortality patterns originally exhibited by the countries of Europe have disappeared through a gradual process of convergence leading to essentially similar and very low levels of mortality. Masuy-Stroobant's comparative analysis of infant mortality trends from 1900 to 1990 reveals that, although Europe-wide differences in levels were of course much higher at the turn of the century, the *ranking* of the various countries and regions displays unexpected and remarkable stability.

However strange this may appear to scholars accustomed to much shorter time-series, one limitation of the data assembled and analysed by Masuy-Stroobant is that they start *only* in 1900. The study by Reher, Pérez-Moreda and Bernabeu-Mestre demonstrates that perspectives and conclusions can be radically modified when the time-span is expanded. Contrary to commonsense notions, it shows that pre-transitional mortality in Spain did not reach a plateau but went through a number of major fluctuations: had only published official data been used, a correct understanding of the childhood mortality transition would have been impossible. The other limitation of Masuy-Stroobant's data is, of course, that they concern only *infant* mortality, that is mortality under 12 months. Again, the Spanish study is illuminating in showing that the various components of young-age mortality behaved quite differently. Indeed, it will be noticed that most of the studies included in this volume deal with both infant and child mortality and explore their relationships from various disciplinary angles.

Besides vindicating the potentialities of official statistics when subjected to sophisticated geographical analysis, the chapter by Woods, Williams and Galley shows, with reference to nineteenth-century England and Wales, that infant mortality (q_0) and early childhood mortality ($_4q_1$) did not necessarily trend together. The overall picture presented by this chapter is, however, further complicated by intriguing gender differences and, even more importantly, by a marked contrast between rural areas and urban settings, where infant mortality tended to be lower than child mortality, thereby violating one of best-known 'rules of thumb' in the demographic literature.

The question of gender differences is taken up by Pinnelli and Mancini, who note that historical or contemporary cases of excess female mortality are attracting increasing interest, since they are seen as exceptions to the rule that women outlive men. Two kinds of hypothesis have been put forward: biological–structural hypotheses suggest that gender mortality differences are constant, whereas social hypotheses maintain that such differences are variable over time. These alternative hypotheses are tested by Pinnelli and Mancini with reference to the evolution of mortality at young ages in Italy from 1887 to 1940, a period of great economic, social and political change. The conclusion they reach is that social explanations are to be favoured. The fact that females ceased to be at a social disadvantage played up the only real biological disadvantage, that of males, which slowly worsened as social transformations took place.

Urban mortality is the subject of Bourdelais and Demonet's chapter on France, of Vögele's on Germany and, to some extent, also of Reid's chapter on England and Wales. Bourdelais and Demonet wonder whether it is possible or correct to speak of 'urban' mortality irrespective of the size, function and location of towns and cities, and also whether mortality between 1 and 4 years, or even between 5 and 9, may prove a better indicator of difference than infant mortality. Some interesting, if provisional, conclusions emerge from their construction and analysis of separate life-tables for 71 French towns. Towards the middle of the nineteenth century, survival at 10 years of age (l_{10})

tended to vary with the size of towns. No less importantly, urban rates of infant and child mortality were *not* always higher than rural rates; it appears that it was only in industrial environments that the urban disadvantage could be unambiguously detected. For his part, Vögele remarks that one major reason why recent research in Germany has concentrated on urban–rural differentials is that, in the late nineteenth century, regional disparities in infant mortality were diminishing, whereas social differentials were increasing. 'Since these were not identical to class formation, mortality change cannot be exclusively explained in terms of differences in wealth' (p. 109). Changes in the 'healthiness' of towns or cities, possibly related to sanitation and other public health campaigns, might provide the clue.

The problem of wealth vs. locality is at the core of Reid's analysis, which focuses on the short period (1895–1911) that encompasses the sharp downturn in infant mortality in England and Wales. The debate about the relationships between socio-economic differences and mortality is a long-standing one. Thirty years ago, Antonovsky (1967) argued that in the remote past there were no class-related mortality differentials. In another influential paper specifically devoted to infant mortality, Perrenoud (1981) contended that differentials (what he called 'inegalité sociale devant la mort') did exist, but sometimes in the unexpected direction, as shown especially by Scandinavian evidence that infant mortality was higher among prosperous farmers and landed peasants than among the poorer cottars. As we have noticed, this debate has recently been rekindled by Preston and Haines's *Fatal years*, and the exchange is currently very lively (Rollet 1994; Haines 1995; Sundin 1995; Woods and Williams 1995). Much of the recent debate centres on the case of England around the turn of the nineteenth century and, in particular, on the information provided by the 1911 census of England and Wales. So far, however, only aggregate data have been available. Reid's chapter makes a decisive contribution to this debate, since she has been able to take advantage of privileged access to a set of anonymized individual returns to the 1911 census. These data are essentially similar to the ones analysed by Preston and Haines (1991) for the United States, and allow Reid to use the same methods to explore the interrelationships between locality, class and other variables measurable from the census. Her conclusion is that location appears to be more important than class: 'To a fairly large degree, infant mortality differentials by social class are observed because environment is not controlled for' (p. 138).

Whereas Reid's chapter deals with a large national sample of 102,752 individuals, Hionidou's contribution is a fascinating in-depth study of the tiny Greek island of Mykonos, the population of which ranged from just under 5,000 inhabitants in 1861 to about 3,500 in 1961. Her main findings are that the rapid fall in infant mortality on Mykonos started in the 1930s, that it was mainly accounted for by a decline in postneonatal mortality and, quite interestingly, that pre-transitional levels of infant mortality were relatively low, probably as a result of long breastfeeding periods. Although still very little is known about levels and trends of infant mortality in Greece, Hionidou is inclined to believe that the Mykoniati pattern was fairly representative of that of the whole country if the major urban centres are excluded.

It is worth noting that one of Hionidou's recommendations for future work in Greece is that 'research concerning illegitimacy and foundlings should be an essential part of the study of infant mortality in urban centres because of their potential for inflating rates of mortality to excessive levels' (p. 170). In fact, and rather surprisingly, until recently the mortality patterns of illegitimate children, foundlings and other children belonging to similar 'high-risk' groups have been the subject more of emotional debate than of serious historical–demographic investigation. The reasons for their higher rates of mortality, and the exact extent of their disadvantage, have been left undetermined. The last four chapters of this volume, all of which are devoted to illegitimate or abandoned children, mark a significant step towards redressing this state of affairs.

Brändström's study of the fate of illegitimate children in the industrializing Swedish region of Sundsvall and Kok, van Poppel and Kruse's multivariate analysis of mortality differentials between legitimate and illegitimate children in mid-nineteenth-century The Hague show how better data and sophisticated statistical techniques can lead us beyond vague and unsupported generalizations. A number of assumptions still holding sway in the literature on child abandonment in European history are challenged by the case of Florence's Spedale degli Innocenti. Using what is arguably the longest infant mortality curve ever reconstructed for large foundling homes, Viazzo, Bortolotto and Zanotto (chapter 12) reveal that decline was by no means linear and monotonic, and that the medical and scientific advances of the late nineteenth century had little, if any, impact. On the other hand, a series of provisions intended to ensure a constant and sufficient supply of wet nurses had major beneficial effects. Along with Catherine Rollet's broader discussion of the measures taken in France to curb mortality among foundlings and other children in care (chapter 11), the case of the Innocenti is a reminder that the study of foundling homes provides a unique vantage point from which to assess the effects of medical, organizational and legislative innovations aimed at improving the survival chances of infants and young children.

Policy issues

The main reason why the study of foundling homes provides such a unique vantage point is, ultimately, that it was among foundlings that the waste of human lives was at its most visible and most urgently called for public intervention. Measures to reduce what was patently *excess* mortality were, therefore, taken at an early historical stage. Moreover, the effectiveness of these measures (for instance, changes in the duration of breastfeeding) was relatively easy for contemporary observers to ascertain and can be checked again by modern scholars. It would seem, on the other hand, that before the late nineteenth century both governments and parents regarded serious illness and the ensuing mortality of infants and young children as inevitable. The first great successes scored by medical science appear to have contributed to creating a widespread awareness that many deaths were preventable, and public health programmes to combat infant mortality were eventually started in earnest.

Whether, and to what extent, such programmes were really successful is a different matter. Vögele's chapter provides a thorough discussion of the varying degree of success and failure of the campaigns launched in Germany to reduce infant mortality, especially in urban areas. His conclusion is that the impact of health-securing measures has been overestimated. By the late nineteenth century many municipalities had established their own management system to deal with the supply and distribution of milk, which should have contributed to a decline in mortality from tuberculosis and digestive diseases. However, the potential benefits were not realized, owing to the absence of a corresponding improvement in personal hygiene. The success of infant-care facilities was also limited. Despite house visits and financial support for breastfeeding, many mothers could not be dealt with by the local advisory centres, and the whole approach was based on serious misconceptions of working-class living conditions. (A similarly negative judgement is passed by Hionidou, when she writes that it seems unlikely that public health measures could have initiated the decline of infant mortality on the Greek island of Mykonos.)

Rather surprisingly, the German evidence strongly suggests that significant reduction in infant mortality was achieved not so much through health campaigns as through the *deprivation* of the First World War years, which resulted in increased numbers of women choosing to breastfeed. Interestingly enough, this unforeseen conclusion reached by Vögele's investigation is strikingly reminiscent of what has recently been reported for Eastern Europe. Contrary to most expectations, the massive health and mortality crisis experienced by Eastern European countries over the last few years has not hit the groups that are traditionally most vulnerable. In five of the nine countries monitored in a UNICEF study directed by Andrea Cornia (1994), infant mortality has continued to decline, and even in the others the upswing in mortality among infants has been substantially less dramatic than among adults and the elderly. The likeliest explanation is that worsening economic and social conditions, and in particular the growing rate of unemployment and inactivity among women, are having a positive impact on the incidence and duration of breastfeeding and, as a consequence, on the health and nutrition of infants. The remarkably similar results that emerge from Vögele's historical study of Imperial Germany and Cornia's analysis of current mortality trends in Eastern Europe are both unexpected and paradoxical, and invite reflection on some issues concerning past and present policies to fight infant and child mortality.

LESSONS FROM THE PAST AND CHALLENGES FOR THE FUTURE

It is still customary to take the level of infant mortality as the best indicator of health care. It is very often used for international comparisons or to evaluate progress over time within specific countries. Yet, as Masuy-Stroobant points out in the opening chapter of this volume, there are several reasons why infant mortality rates and other measures of young-age mortality should be treated with great caution. For one thing, it has become apparent that past and present vital statistics are often less accurate than might be expected. Second, all young-age mortality measures are increasingly affected by classificatory and definitional differences in the vital registration rules followed by the various countries. Third, and no less significantly, the recent advances in obstetrics and perinatal care are producing not only a decline in neonatal mortality rates but also an extension of the period during which preterm infants remain at risk, thereby altering the very context of dying in the early days or months of life.

In a sense, the first lesson to be learned from a long-term study of the evolution of infant and child mortality is that any comparison with the past may easily prove misleading. Nevertheless, it would seem that such comparisons are almost inescapable. In particular, policy-making inevitably entails—explicitly or implicitly, purposefully or inadvertently—a search for 'precedents', which is just another way of saying 'lessons from history'. In a period in which it appears that very real and vexing social and economic difficulties might soon be threatening the survival and proper development of children not only in Eastern Europe but also in the richer Western countries, it is sensible to pay renewed attention to the policies enacted in the decades that saw the beginning of the 'secular' decline of infant and child mortality. The danger of learning the wrong lesson is, however, very serious.

However crude and inadequate they were in many respects, the statistical data available at the time were sufficient to signal that infant mortality was falling. Medical practitioners, administrators and child-welfare campaigners looked for proof that health programmes were yielding satisfactory results, and were prepared (sometimes too quickly) to believe that their favourite programme was responsible for a good deal of the decline. Rollet's exemplary analysis of the work of Dr Pierre Budin, one of the pioneers of the movement to use demographic criteria to assess public welfare measures, demonstrates that many of the methods he suggested were imperfect. Nevertheless, at the time, the results obtained by Budin and others seemed sufficiently convincing to provide the motive force for the adoption of new laws and the creation of infant-health consultancy centres. Both Rollet's and Vögele's chapters show very clearly how faulty measurements can produce inaccurate assessments, which in turn may easily generate policies whose ineffectiveness is masked by the direct or indirect effects of other forces at work in the same period.

It should be recognized that assessing the causes of infant and child mortality decline is a complex and tricky task, since the fall in mortality typically tends to occur simultaneously with many other changes, social and economic as well as specifically in the health sector. Even for those scholars who study historical declines, and can therefore benefit from hindsight, disentangling the diverse influences may prove difficult. As Rollet rightly stresses, much depends on our ability to create better data sets and develop better analytical tools. Indeed, this has been the primary aim of our research project, as testified by virtually all of the chapters in this volume. They provide several demonstrations that historical studies using richer sources and more refined methods can show that some of the demographic rules of thumb that guide or influence policy-making do not hold true. Woods, Williams and Galley argue that mortality in infancy and early childhood need to be differentiated in all populations with low life expect-ancy. They also suggest that findings about the different timing of the declines of child mortality and infant mortality may have important implications for the long and often simplistic debate on the relationship between mortality and fertility decline. In fact, the case of England and Wales reveals that if fertility decline was spurred by decline in mortality at young ages, the determining factor was child mortality ($_4q_1$) not infant mortality (q_0). Similar indications come from the Spanish material, which also shows the importance of *gradual* mortality decline for family demography and family eco-nomics (see also Reher 1995). To give another example, Reid reports that the Registrar General of England and Wales believed the 1911 census data to have established the 'evil results of maternal employment' with regard to child health. Like Reid, Kok, van Poppel and Kruse in their study of The Hague are quick to point out that the relationship between the working status of women and infant health and mortality is by no means obvious and unilateral. What is more, Reid's evidence, far from demonstrating that women's work is necessarily detrimental, actually suggests that in some environments the children of working women had slightly better survival prospects than those of non-working women.

The historical question of greatest potential relevance to current problems sur-rounding childhood mortality, in both the developing and industrialized world, probably remains the one raised by Preston and Haines in *Fatal years*. 'In 1900', they remarked, 'the United States was the richest country in the world . . . On the scale of per capita income, literacy, and food consumption, it would rank in the top quarter of countries were it somehow transplanted to the present. Yet 18 percent of its children were dying before age 5, a figure that would rank in the bottom quarter of contemporary countries. Why couldn't the United States translate its economic and social advantage into better levels of child survival?' (1991, 208).

The high levels of childhood mortality that existed among the relatively affluent American population were taken by Preston and Haines as proof of the inadequacy of the thesis proposed by the British physician and historical demographer Thomas McKeown in his controversial book on *The modern rise of population* (1976), and more generally of those explanations of twentieth-century mortality that emphasized im-provements in material resources. It is worth noting that over the past twenty years these explanations have played a major role in shaping programmes aimed at reducing child mortality in Africa, Asia and Latin America. Many policy-makers have been impressed by McKeown's assertion that, historically, both therapeutic and, to some extent, preventive medicine had been ineffective, and that the reduction of infant mor-tality was primarily an economic issue. Thus, instead of investing money in sophisti-cated medical technology, or perhaps even in public health measures, it seemed preferable to promote programmes capable of increasing the nutritional level of the whole population and enhancing the resistance of its younger members to the aggres-sion of germs and parasites (Boulanger 1980). Similar dilemmas are re-emerging today in Europe, where complex medical techniques have been developed in order to improve infant survival. However, these techniques demand an enormous amount of human and financial investment, and it is doubtful, as emphasized by Masuy-Stroobant, whether the Eastern European countries in particular can afford such costs in view of 'the adverse effects of structural changes and possibly long-term economic crisis, which bring about a lowering of public health expenditure and a widening of social inequalities' (p. 28).

Preston and Haines (1991, 209) contended, on the basis of the lack of social-class differentials in child mortality in the United States around 1900, that 'lack of know-how rather than lack of resources was principally responsible for foreshortening life'. As we have briefly noted above, this argument has given rise to a heated debate. In particular, Woods and Williams (1995, 130) maintained that 'know-how influenced the sharp downward trend of mortality, but resources conditioned the persistent differentials and social class gradients'. And Reid, in her contribution to this volume, adds the important qualifier that 'superior knowledge and resources only secured survival benefits in the most unhealthy environments. Where the threat to infant and child life was smaller, any differences in behaviour between the classes paid few dividends' (p. 152). This is not the right place to review a debate that revolves mostly around one historical phase of infant and child mortality decline but whose wider implications are not hard to see. These cursory notes are merely intended as a reminder that a number of crucial questions are still far from being settled, and a number of related practical problems are far from being solved. Much further work is required in order to specify, for different contexts and historical periods, the relative weight of medicine and the economy in affecting child survival, and to clarify the relationships between mortality and socio-economic differences. Nevertheless, the studies collected in this volume offer at least some answers to these and other questions. It is hoped that the empirical information they add to the record and the methodological refinements they propose will make a useful contribution both to our understanding of the past and to our planning for the future.

References

ANTONOVSKY, A., 1967. 'Social class, life expectancy and overall mortality', *Milbank Memorial Fund Quarterly* 45, pp. 31–73.

BOULANGER, P. M., 1980. 'Les grandes orientations de la lutte contre la mortalité des enfants', in P. M. BOULANGER and D. TABUTIN (eds.), *La mortalité des enfants dans le monde et dans l'histoire*, Liège, Ordina.

BRÄNDSTRÖM, A., 1993. 'Infant mortality in Sweden, 1750-1950: past and present research into its decline', in CORSINI and VIAZZO 1993.

BRASS, W., 1975. *Methods for estimating fertility and mortality from limited and defective data*, Chapel Hill, NC, Carolina Population Center.

BRESCHI, M. and LIVI BACCI, M., 1994. 'Le mois de naissance comme facteur de survie des enfants', *Annales de Démographie Historique*, pp. 169–185.

CALDWELL, J. C. *et al.*, 1991. 'Forum: Fatal Years', *Health Transition Review* 1, pp. 221–244.

COALE, A. J. and WATKINS, S. C. (eds.), 1986. *The decline of fertility in Europe*, Princeton, NJ, Princeton University Press.

CORSINI, C. A. and VIAZZO, P. P. (eds.), 1993. *The decline of infant mortality in Europe, 1800–1950: four national case studies*, Florence, UNICEF and Istituto degli Innocenti.

CORNIA, G. A., 1990. 'Child poverty and deprivation in industrial countries: recent trends and policy options', Innocenti Occasional Papers no. 2, Florence, UNICEF International Child Development Centre.

—— (ed.), 1994. 'Central and Eastern Europe in transition: crisis in mortality, health and nutrition', Economies in transition studies, Regional monitoring report no. 2, Florence, UNICEF International Child Development Centre.

HAINES, M. R., 1995. 'Socio-economic differentials in infant and child mortality during mortality decline: England and Wales, 1890–1911', *Population Studies* 49, pp. 297–315.

KERTZER, D. I., 1992. 'The role of culture in historical–demographic explanation', paper presented at the First Innocenti Seminar on the Decline of Infant Mortality in Europe, Florence, 9–11 April.

—— 1994. 'Political–economic and cultural explanations of demographic behaviour', in S. GREENHALGH (ed.), *Situating fertility: anthropology and demographic inquiry*, Cambridge, Cambridge University Press.

KEYFITZ, N. and FLIEGER, W., 1990. *World population growth and aging: demographic trends in the late twentieth century*, Chicago, IL, University of Chicago Press.

KYTIR, J. and MÜNZ, R., 1993. 'Infant mortality in Austria, 1820–1950: trends and regional patterns', in CORSINI and VIAZZO 1993.

McKEOWN, T., 1976. *The modern rise of population*, London, Edward Arnold.

MITCHELL, B. R., 1980. *European historical statistics, 1750–1975*, 2nd rev. edn, London, Macmillan.

PERRENOUD, A., 1981. 'Les aspects socio-économiques de la mortalité différentielle des enfants dans le passé', in *Proceedings of the International Population Conference (Manila 1981)*, vol. 2, Liège, Ordina.

PRESTON, S. H. and HAINES, M. R., 1991. *Fatal years: child mortality in late nineteeenth-century America*, Princeton, NJ, Princeton University Press.

REHER, D., 1995. 'Wasted investments: some economic implications of child mortality patterns', *Population Studies* 49, pp. 519–536.

ROLLET, C., 1994. 'La mortalité des enfants dans le passé: au-delà des apparences', *Annales de Démographie Historique*, pp. 7–21.

—— and BOURDELAIS, P., 1993. 'Infant mortality in France, 1750–1950: evaluation and perspectives', in CORSINI and VIAZZO 1993.

SCHOFIELD, R. and REHER, D., 1991. 'The decline of mortality in Europe', in SCHOFIELD, REHER and BIDEAU 1991.

SCHOFIELD, R., REHER, D. and BIDEAU, A. (eds.), 1991. *The decline of mortality in Europe*, Oxford, Clarendon Press.

SUNDIN, J., 1995. 'Culture, class, and infant mortality during the Swedish mortality transition, 1750–1850', *Social Science History* 19, pp. 117–145.

UNITED NATIONS, 1989. *World population prospects 1988*, New York, United Nations.

WOODS, R., KERTZER, D., VIAZZO, P. P. and BRÄNDSTRÖM, A., 1993. 'International Project on the Decline of Infant and Childhood Mortality in Europe During the Last Two Hundred Years: A research agenda and proposal based on the findings of a workshop held at the Istituto degli

Innocenti, Florence, 9 to 11 April 1992'. [Available from the Istituto degli Innocenti di Firenze, Information and Documentation Centre.]

—— and WILLIAMS, N., 1995. 'Must the gap widen before it can be narrowed? Long-term trends in social class mortality differentials', *Continuity and Change* 10, pp. 105–137.

—— —— and GALLEY, C., 1993. 'Infant mortality in England, 1550–1950: problems in the identification of long-term trends, geographical and social variations', in CORSINI and VIAZZO 1993.

1

Infant Health and Infant Mortality in Europe:
Lessons from the Past and Challenges for the Future

GODELIEVE MASUY-STROOBANT

In Europe, progress in reducing infant mortality since the late nineteenth century has been and still is impressive. From a very high level throughout the nineteenth century, with about 1 out of every 5–6 newborns dying within their first year of life, infant mortality rates (IMRs) today concentrate around the 1 per cent mark in most countries. As a result of the widely observed association between socio-economic factors and infant mortality at both the individual and the aggregate levels, the infant mortality rate is one of the most sensitive and commonly used indicators of the social and economic development of a population (Basch 1990). Although it is very often used for inter-national comparisons or to evaluate progress over time within specific countries, in view of the quality of the vital registration systems, this indicator is probably not as accurate as might be expected.

Vital statistics offer many advantages for the production of mortality indicators, but they are still a by-product of legal obligations and therefore depend closely on the legal definitions of the vital events to be declared: stillbirths (or late foetal deaths), live births and deaths. Despite a tendency towards harmonizing definitions, comparability over time and between countries continues to be affected by differences in data-processing methods, administrative registration rules and declaration practices. When infant mortality was high in Europe and mainly post-neonatal, these differences could not result in gross misclassification of countries according to their IMRs. However, the present situation is dramatically different: infant mortality is very low in Europe and tends more and more to occur in the very early days or even hours of life. Accordingly, the impact of differences in legal and administrative vital registration rules, which chiefly concern babies who die shortly after birth, is increasing (Gourbin and Masuy-Stroobant 1995).

The efficacy of medical intervention during the reproduction process has recently increased in several ways: at conception (many assisted reproduction technologies lead to an increased incidence of multiple pregnancies), during pregnancy ('therapeutic'

I am grateful to my colleagues, Ms A. Burban, Mr M. Debuisson, Ms L. Guéret, Ms C. Gourbin and Mr J. P. Sanderson for their technical help. A French version of this chapter was presented at the 1994 'Chaire Quetelet' on 'Child health and mortality in Europe: social inequalities yesterday and today' held in Louvain-la-Neuve (Belgium).

C.A. Corsini and P.P. Viazzo (eds.) The Decline of Infant and Child Mortality, 1-34.

abortions to prevent the birth of handicapped children), during the prenatal period (induced preterm delivery when foetal distress is detected) and during the neonatal period (where the impressive performance of neonatal intensive-care techniques during the 1980s led to a redefinition of the *de facto* viability criteria). These advances probably exert a very specific and sometimes controversial impact on infant health and mortality (Lantoine and Pressat 1984; Friede *et al.* 1987).

Therefore, to compare the evolution of infant mortality in different countries, one has to take into account the legal definitions and registration practices, the nature and frequency of common medical interventions, and the age-at-death patterns of infant mortality risks, which definitely offers a better foundation for comparative studies than the overall infant mortality level (Masuy-Stroobant 1995).

The programme of research that remains to be done is wide. The international comparability of administrative and legal definitions has been the subject of research for some time (United Nations 1954; Mugford 1983; WHO 1985). The most recent study refers to the 1991 situation in Europe (Gourbin and Masuy-Stroobant 1995). Although the practice has been studied in detail, this research has tended to be conducted at the local level (Keirse 1984; Hertoghe *et al.* 1987; Gourbin 1991).

Since we do not have at our disposal exhaustive and comparable information at a national level on the nature and frequency of medical interventions during the reproduction process, it is on some of their consequences—the frequency of multiple deliveries and the recorded incidence of low birthweight children (less than 2,500g) and of very low birthweight children (less than 1,500g)—that we will focus the analysis.

Since 1900, the evolution of infant mortality in European countries has been accompanied by very significant shifts in the age-at-death distribution and in the pattern of its medical causes. With these similarities in secular tendencies, we contrast the persistence of differences in the level of mortality between countries and even a surprising stability in the geographical pattern of European infant mortality during the twentieth century. The comparative analysis of the evolution of risks of infant mortality by age should allow for the identification of the modalities for different countries and possibly lead to better understanding of the inequalities between countries that still remain.

MATERIAL AND METHODS

A database called 'Infant Mortality in Europe, 1900–1990' is being created as a result of a Concerted Action Research Program of the Institute of Demography of the Catholic University of Louvain.[1] The database represents a systematic compilation of vital registration statistics published at the national level. To complement this information countries were asked to complete a detailed questionnaire on the modalities of vital event registration, including legal definitions and administrative registration rules.

---

[1] It is part of a larger programme on 'The social and regional inequalities in health and mortality in Europe', funded by the Ministère de la Communauté Française de Belgique, A.C. Grant number 89/94-138.

Some of the results of this survey have already been published (Gourbin and Masuy-Stroobant 1995; Gourbin 1995; Masuy-Stroobant 1995). A total of 27 countries participated actively in the survey; the database also concerns 27 countries.[2]

The use of primary sources for the compilation of the database was a fundamental choice given the inconsistencies found in the infant mortality figures published in such international statistical yearbooks as the *United Nations Demographic Yearbook* and the *World Health Statistics Annual*. It is especially important when long-term series are sought: the figures in such secondary sources are sometimes provisional or standardized according to certain criteria. The search for consistency over time also led us to prefer the most recently reconstructed time-series produced by each country's national statistical institute (when available), especially in cases where the political borders of the country have undergone significant changes during this century. In such cases, figures refer to the 1990 territory. For other countries, additional information is provided in Appendix 1.1.

Vital registration data are necessarily limited by the current definitions of declared events and by the contents of the vital registration forms. A further shortcoming is linked to the way the collected information is made available, either through publication or by granting access to the individual data files. At the beginning of this century, the range of comparable information collected at birth (either live or stillborn) and death registration was limited to the sex of the child, its legitimacy (born within or outside marriage) and its date of birth. Age at death was calculated from the difference between the date of death and the date of birth, both of which recorded on the death form. Multiple deliveries were usually recorded on the birth certificate from the very beginning of the organization of vital registration systems, but were and are still rarely recorded at death. Around the Second World War, an increasing interest in fertility analyses and family policies led to a significant enrichment of the birth records through the addition a variety of information on the socio-demographic characteristics of the parents, although infant deaths were still registered on general death forms. In an important step in the late 1970s a number of European countries decided to include medical information (weight at birth or length of gestation) on their birth records and, simultaneously, to introduce either a specific form for infant or neonatal deaths or to add specific information about infant deaths to the general death form. Nevertheless, in the overwhelming majority of countries, the birth registration form is far more informative than the death form. Consequently, comparable information for deceased infants can only be obtained through record linkage, the results of which are rarely extensively and systematically published. Access to such data is usually limited to very specific research programmes. Although available to us for some countries and for very short periods, these data were not included in the database because of their exceptional character.

---

[2] Bulgaria is included in the database, but until recently no Bulgarian correspondent could be identified for the survey phase of this research. The former USSR participated in the study on definitions, but no data could be obtained for inclusion in the database.

The database is thus presently limited to the information that is considered to be comparable across countries and is available from the very beginning of the twentieth century. Since our objective is the study of infant mortality, only characteristics recorded (and published or accessible) at birth and death, allowing for the calculation of specific mortality risks, were selected. Thus, the database includes the total number of live births (including the 'présentés sans vie'[3]), stillbirths and infant deaths; infant deaths by age at death; and illegitimate live births, stillbirths and infant deaths. Multiple deliveries were also included, distinguishing twins and higher-order multiple births. This section of the database is today almost complete for 27 countries from 1900 to 1990. Based on crude figures, it is organized to be as comparative as possible: one has, however, to be aware of the problems linked to differences in the definition of vital events, the late introduction of the compulsory registration of stillbirths in several countries (1920 in Greece, 1924 in the Netherlands, 1927 in England and Wales, 1933 in Poland, 1939 in Scotland, 1956 in the Republic of Ireland and 1961 in Northern Ireland), and the procedures for the publication of the age-at-death groupings, which were highly variable across countries in the first half of this century.

A second section of the database is devoted to the more-recently registered information on birthweight. Published birthweight categories differ from country to country and the data could not be organized into a comparable data base. Figures were thus included in the form in which they appear in the sources, country by country for all the available years: that is since 1956 for Hungary, 1965 for Czechoslovakia, 1975 for Poland, and more generally from the early 1980s for the Western European countries.

The age-specific mortality risks are calculated with reference to the survivors at the beginning of each age interval under consideration. For the stillbirth rate, total births are taken into account (that is, live births and stillbirths). The rates have not been 'adjusted' for birth cohort: they refer to births and deaths occurring during the same calendar year. Since most of the comparative analyses make use of rates calculated over five-year periods, annual variations in number of births are smoothed and do not bias the figures. Age-specific mortality rates were produced distinguishing first-day mortality, the remainder of early neonatal mortality (that is, mortality from 1 to 6 completed days), late neonatal mortality (from 7 to 27 completed days) and post-neonatal mortality (from 28 to 364 completed days). Early neonatal mortality was split into two distinct measures because of the increasing importance over time of the first-day mortality rate in the global risk of infant mortality, and because of the sensitivity of the first-day mortality indicator to international differences in vital-event definitions and registration practices. Even though the majority of European countries employ the WHO definition for the registration of a live birth, some countries still impose legal or

---

[3] The 'présentés sans vie' or declared-dead births usually take two forms: 'true' stillbirths and live-born infants whose death occurred before their birth registration, also called 'false stillbirths'. They formed a special category in the published statistics at the beginning of the century and were often not counted in the figures for live births and infant deaths, which caused the published infant mortality figures to be underestimated in some countries (including France and the Netherlands). For Belgium, published figures that allow us to make the correction have been kept since the late nineteenth century.

administrative restrictions for live-born children who do not meet a given minimum gestational duration or birthweight. In Spain until 1978, and still (in 1991) in several countries (France, the Netherlands, the former USSR, former Czechoslovakia, Poland and Romania), the usual additional requirement for these out-of-range live-born children was their survival over a defined period, often 24 hours. The strict application of the definition of live birth proposed by WHO could, therefore, lead to an inflation in the figures for first-day mortality. Even in those countries where the WHO definition is adopted, the 24 hours' survival criterion is far more common in everyday practice than might be supposed (Gourbin 1991; Keirse 1984). As far as the accuracy and comparability of neonatal or infant mortality figures are concerned, the most worrying fact is that if preterm infants are not registered as live births, they usually also fail to meet the minimum requirements to be considered as stillbirths and are thus not registered at all.

As health indicators, the usual measures of incidence of low birthweight (less than 2,500g) and very low birthweight infants (less than 1,500g) have been calculated for live births according to the available information. The frequency of multiple deliveries (twin deliveries per 1,000 deliveries, and triplet and higher-order deliveries per 10,000 deliveries) has been calculated in order to evaluate some consequences of the use of medically assisted reproduction technologies.

LATE FOETAL MORTALITY AND INFANT MORTALITY IN EUROPE SINCE 1900

Infant Mortality

As a result of a hierarchical cluster analysis (Ward method)[4] five homogeneous (according to their general level of infant mortality and its evolution over time) clusters of countries were identified. The clustering retained about 90 per cent of the initial variance of the data.[5]

The five clusters are ordered on a continuum that goes from countries with low mortality levels over the whole study period to those with relatively high mortality levels. The differences in mortality levels were, of course, much higher at the turn of the century, but the ranking of countries stays the same throughout the observation period, with remarkable stability (Appendix 1.2 and Figure 1.1). With the exception of a few cases, the clustering corresponds to the classical geography of European infant mortality along a North–South axis followed by a West–East axis.

---

[4] A description of this statistical technique can be found in Everitt 1980. The application was made using the sixth version of the SAS/STAT program, published in 1994.

[5] Owing to the incompleteness of age-at-death information for the period preceding the First World War in several countries and the poor data quality of the published statistics produced during the Second World War period, we limited the analysis to the years 1921–1940 and 1946–1990.

- The lowest mortality levels (Cluster 1) over the whole period are observed in the Scandinavian countries, the Netherlands and Switzerland;
- Next follow almost all the Western European countries (Cluster 2), including the former German Democratic Republic, where the levels of infant mortality have always been very close to the former Federal Republic. Austria does not join this cluster: Austrian mortality levels have, until recently, stayed closer to those of the Southern European countries;
- Austria and Czechoslovakia join the Mediterranean countries to form Cluster 3;
- Bulgaria, Hungary, and Poland form Cluster 4;
- with their very high mortality levels over almost the entire study period, Yugoslavia, Romania and Portugal form Cluster 5.

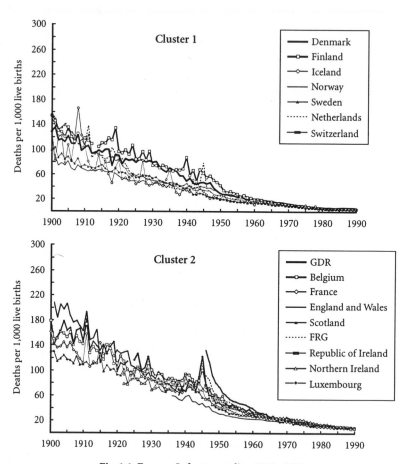

Fig. 1.1. Europe: Infant mortality, 1900–1990

Source: vital registration.

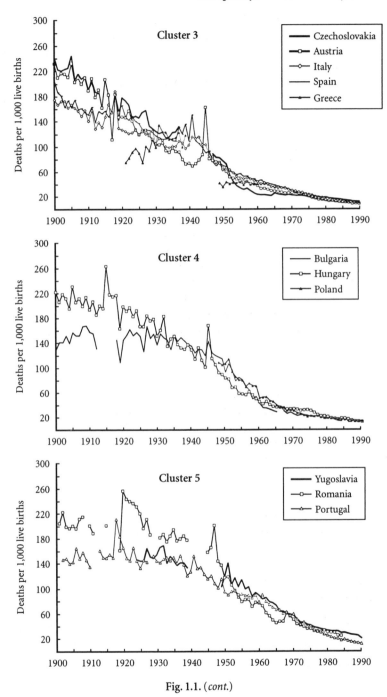

Fig. 1.1. (*cont.*)

Portugal and Austria probably do not belong to a single cluster throughout the period considered: their infant mortality rates declined much faster during the last decades than did those of the other members of their clusters. Membership to a single cluster is otherwise the rule for all countries.

A feature of twentieth-century Europe has been the continuous decline of the infant mortality rate. Crisis periods such as the two world wars, which affected the countries and regions of Europe differently, were the only exceptions to this general tendency. This tendency departs dramatically from the relative stagnation in the level of infant mortality observed during the nineteenth century in many countries that nevertheless experienced a reduction in their childhood (1–4 years old) mortality. However, there were a few notable exceptions to this nineteenth-century trend: Northern countries, like Sweden, registered a continuous decrease in infant mortality throughout the century. On the other hand, in the Western European countries that experienced rapid indus-trialization during the nineteenth century (France, Belgium and Great Britain), the first signs of improved survival in early infancy (at a national level) were only notice-able at the turn of the century. The causes of this decisive evolution, which is part of the epidemiological and demographic transition of the populations of Europe, have been studied in detail elsewhere (Imhof 1981; Masuy-Stroobant 1984; Woods, Watterson and Woodward 1988; Rollet-Echalier 1990). However, we must emphasize that it is difficult to analyse the subject in a similar fashion for the whole of Europe given the lack of reliable statistical data in some cases, or even the absence of national-level figures in others, for the centuries preceding this century.

Although it declined overall before the years 1940–1945, infant mortality still fluc-tuated highly, which indicates that it was not entirely under control. The decline has continued at a more stable pace since the 1950s. The end of the 1980s was marked by a slowing down of the decline, if not a stopping of it in the Northern and Western Euro-pean countries. The countries with higher infant mortality levels (Clusters 3, 4 and 5) continued their decline at least until 1990 (Table 1.1).

Late Foetal Mortality

Late foetal mortality has benefited from a renewed interest, especially over the last two decades. Having been very stable for a long time, late foetal deaths or stillbirths[6] seem to be avoidable in an increasing number of situations. The improvement of obstetric techniques, the capacity to detect foetal distress during pregnancy, and the decrease in the occurrence of serious or lethal congenital anomalies as a result of preventive meas-ures (such as vaccination against rubella and genetic counselling) or voluntary (thera-peutic) abortion have certainly contributed to the reduction in foetal mortality.

The great variety of medical interventions, from before the conception to delivery, coupled with a significant reduction in the risk of death during the early neonatal period (first week of life) have increased the interest of doctors, epidemiologists and

---

6 Late foetal deaths are, according to the WHO definition, which is shared by the majority of European countries, those that occur after 28 weeks of gestation. See Gourbin and Masuy-Stroobant 1995.

Table 1.1. Europe: Infant mortality, 1986–1990 (deaths per 1,000 live births)

	1986	1987	1988	1989	1990
Cluster 1					
Norway	7.92	8.42	8.29	7.89	7.02
Sweden	5.93	6.12	5.82	5.77	5.96
Iceland	5.41	7.15	6.21	5.48	5.87
Denmark	8.19	8.31	7.60	7.97	7.39
Finland	5.82	6.17	6.08	6.09	5.61
Switzerland	6.83	6.85	6.85	7.34	6.84
Netherlands	7.74	7.55	6.83	6.78	7.06
Cluster 2					
England and Wales	9.55	9.20	9.04	8.45	7.88
Republic of Ireland	8.88	7.94	8.86	8.13	8.18
Northern Ireland	10.16	8.68	8.93	6.90	7.47
Scotland	8.83	8.50	8.20	8.73	7.73
France	8.04	7.84	7.84	7.54	7.34
Belgium	9.60	9.66	8.97	8.53	7.97
Luxembourg	7.89	9.44	8.69	9.86	7.29
Federal Republic of Germany	8.55	8.28	7.50	7.44	—
German Democratic Republic	9.24	8.71	8.07	7.58	—
Cluster 3					
Italy	10.18	9.76	9.31	8.69	8.18
Spain	9.20	8.88	8.05	7.78	7.60
Greece	11.99	11.62	10.90	9.66	9.67
Austria	10.27	9.83	8.13	8.31	7.84
Czechoslovakia	13.37	12.87	11.91	11.31	11.25
Cluster 4					
Bulgaria[a]	14.66	14.70	*13.60*	*14.40*	*14.80*
Hungary	19.05	17.31	15.83	15.74	14.82
Poland	17.51	17.51	16.22	15.96	16.01
Cluster 5					
Portugal	15.92	14.25	130.60	12.18	10.99
Romania	—	—	—	—	—
Yugoslavia	26.72	25.15	24.50	23.52	19.27

[a] Provisional figures in italics.

Source: vital registration.

demographers in perinatal mortality. The idea of combining late foetal mortality and early neonatal mortality into a single index called *perinatal mortality* goes back to an article published in 1948 in *Population Studies* (Peller 1948). It is around this period that the stillbirth rate began a sustained and irreversible decline all over Europe.

In all countries and throughout the period under consideration, late foetal mortality levels are lower than general infant mortality rates. But the decline started much later than the decline of infant mortality: for some countries the first signs of improvement

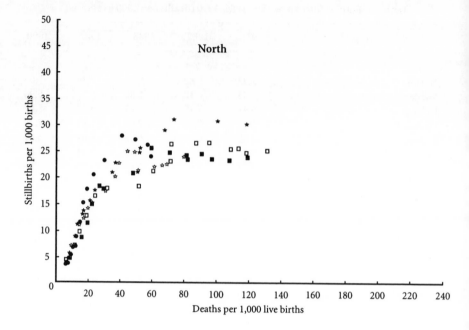

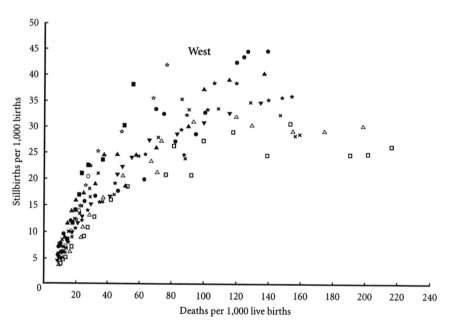

Fig. 1.2. Europe: Stillbirth rates by infant mortality, by region, 1900–1990
Source: vital registration.

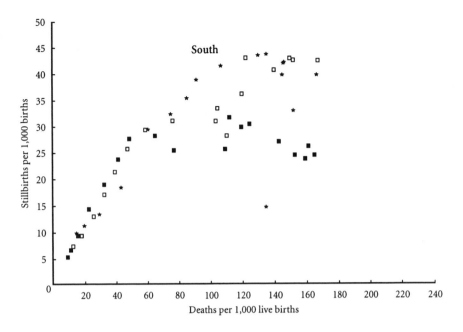

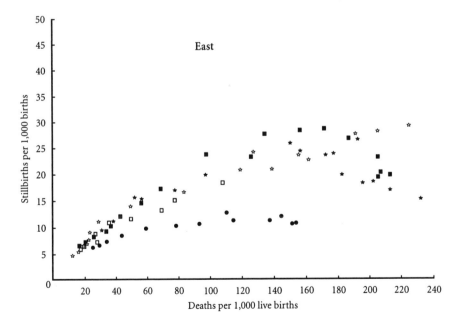

Fig. 1.2. (*cont.*)

appeared in the 1930s; for others it began only after the Second World War. The evident underregistration of this type of birth in some countries (Greece, Bulgaria, Portugal at the turn of the century), where even an increase in the rate of stillbirths is observed at the beginning of the study period, is quite striking. Also noticeable is the late decision of England and Wales (1927) and Scotland (1939) to organize the compulsory registration of stillbirths.

Moreover, the very low level of late foetal mortality in the Eastern European countries is surprising given their (high) level of infant mortality (Appendix 1.3 and Figure 1.2). In terms of comparable infant mortality levels, the rate of stillbirths in Yugoslavia is not even half of that in Portugal. Since 1950, Yugoslavia has used the criterion of 28 weeks of gestation to define foetal deaths that should be registered, which implies that the two countries shared the same definition of stillbirth from 1955 to 1980. Compared with Austria, Czechoslovakia also has a particularly low stillbirth level. Even the Finnish levels were higher than those of Czechoslovakia until 1975. The same remarks could be made for Hungary, which until the early 1970s had a significantly lower level of stillbirths than most Western European countries.

The relationships established between the stillbirth rate and the infant mortality level were evaluated using the Pearson correlation coefficient (Table 1.2) and their values were plotted according to four major geo-political regions (Figure 1.2). Owing to the poor quality of the available stillbirth figures, Greece and Bulgaria were excluded from the analysis; the former German Democratic Republic was also excluded, because it was part of the German Republic before the Second World War and showed very similar levels to those of the former Federal Republic thereafter.

Within each region, the correlation between infant mortality and the rate of stillbirths is consistently very strong (above 80 per cent) and statistically highly significant for the period following the Second World War. No relationship could be established for the preceding decades. The correlation calculated over all the countries for the postwar period (1946–1990) reaches only 65 per cent, which confirms the presence of distinct regional models.

The graphical representation of this relationship (Figure 1.2) shows that a generalized stagnation in the rate of stillbirths accompanied the rapid decline in the level of infant mortality at the start of the century. The first signs of a decline in the stillbirth rates took place at differing levels of infant mortality across the regions: when a threshold of 60–40 deaths per 1,000 live births was reached in the Scandinavian countries, 80–60 deaths per 1,000 births in the Western region, 120–100 per 1,000 in the South of Europe, and 140–120 in Central and Eastern Europe. Despite this, there is a striking simultaneity in the decline of the late foetal mortality rate across Europe: it started either in the years immediately preceding the Second World War (Scandinavian countries) or in the years immediately following it.

A puzzling fact is that, despite their extremely different levels of infant mortality, the Northern and Eastern European countries share the lowest stillbirth rates. This seems paradoxical given the situation observed in the other two regions, where the rate of stillbirths is relatively higher.

Table 1.2. Europe: Correlation coefficients of
stillbirth and infant mortality levels, 1900–1940 and 1946–1990

Region	1900–1940		1946–1990	
	Correlation coefficient (number of observations)	Significance	Correlation coefficient (number of observations)	Significance
North (Denmark, Finland, Iceland, Norway, Sweden)	0.24 (36)	n.s.	0.86 (42)	0.001
West (Belgium, England and Wales, Federal Republic of Germany France, Republic of Ireland, Luxembourg, Netherlands, Northern Ireland, Scotland, Switzerland)	0.19 (16)	n.s.	0.81 (94)	0.001
South (Italy, Spain, Portugal)	0.05 (23)	n.s.	0.96 (26)	0.001
East (Czechoslovakia, Hungary, Poland, Romania, Yugoslavia)	0.14 (28)	n.s.	0.82 (44)	0.001
Total (23 countries)	0.06 (165)	n.s.	0.65 (231)	0.0001

Note: n.s. = not significant at the 5% level.

Source: vital registration.

RISKS BY AGE AT DEATH: ARE THERE POSSIBILITIES FOR FUTURE PROGRESS?

It has been repeatedly shown that progress in the field of infant survival during the twentieth century has been associated with rising living conditions and improvements in nutrition, hygiene, medicine and levels of education. Infectious diseases and malnutrition, the primary causes of post-neonatal mortality, were the first factors to be brought under control. It is primarily to the decrease in the mortality of infants aged 1 month or more that the decline in the level of infant mortality in European countries during the first half of the twentieth century should be attributed. This decline implied an increase in the relative weight of early deaths, which at the time were less able to be affected by either preventive or curative action.

The generalization of prenatal care after the Second World War and the acceleration of the hospital delivery process certainly induced closer medical attention for mothers and infants during the perinatal period.

The emergence of neonatology, which established itself as an autonomous discipline in the 1960s (Duc 1982), permitted the development of dedicated intensive-care units. There is no doubt that the impressive efficacy of neonatal intensive-care techniques is partly responsible for a recent shift in the *de facto* viability criteria, given the still increasing survival chances of even more preterm and of even lower birthweight infants. Today, the concept of very low birthweight tends to replace the previous concept of low birthweight in the evaluation of high-risk infants.

This evolution is far from negligible. Infants with very low birthweights will more often be considered viable and thus registered. An increased registration of those high-risk infants may even be responsible for a future (slight) increase in the infant mortality figures of the most advanced countries, given their relative weight in the total number of infant deaths (around 20 per cent).

The number of countries for which it was possible to trace comparable evolutions of mortality risks by age for the whole period 1900–1990 is rather small. The way age-at-death figures were published varied enormously from country to country during the first part of the century. They only exceptionally followed the age categories considered standard today. Nevertheless, for Belgium and France in the period before the First World War, early neonatal mortality can be approximated by mortality occurring during 0–4 (completed) days. Other countries made only a distinction between deaths occurring within the first month and deaths occurring after 30 days (Iceland, Austria, Luxembourg, Switzerland, Greece, Czechoslovakia). For Denmark and Hungary it is possible to trace the evolution of deaths occurring within the first 24 hours or first day of life from the beginning of the century. This figure appeared more often in publications during the First World War and the interwar period (since 1914 for Luxembourg, 1916 for Switzerland, 1926 for Austria, 1929 for Italy, 1932 for Scotland, and 1936 for England and Wales), but deaths occurring later usually do not follow the standard age categories. Only Sweden and Hungary, to our knowledge, have uninterrupted publications of deaths grouped more or less under the standard age categories: less than 1 day (or less than 24 hours), 1–6 days, 7–27 days (7–29 days for Hungary up to 1964) and 28–364 days (30–364 days for Hungary up to 1964).

As a first step, the secular tendencies of the decline in mortality by age were studied by choosing, for each cluster of countries identified during the analysis of infant mortality, a reference country for which statistics were available throughout the study period, 1900–1990. The selected countries are Sweden (Cluster 1), Belgium (Cluster 2), Austria (Cluster 3) and Hungary (Cluster 4). For the highest mortality countries (Cluster 5) no reference country could be selected, because our database is currently quite incomplete for those countries (Figure 1.3).

The evolutions of early neonatal mortality (up to 6 completed days), late neonatal mortality (7–27 completed days) and post-neonatal mortality (28–364 completed days) follow an unchanging pattern for each of the reference countries, whatever the general level of mortality. The rapid fall of post-neonatal mortality is beyond doubt the major

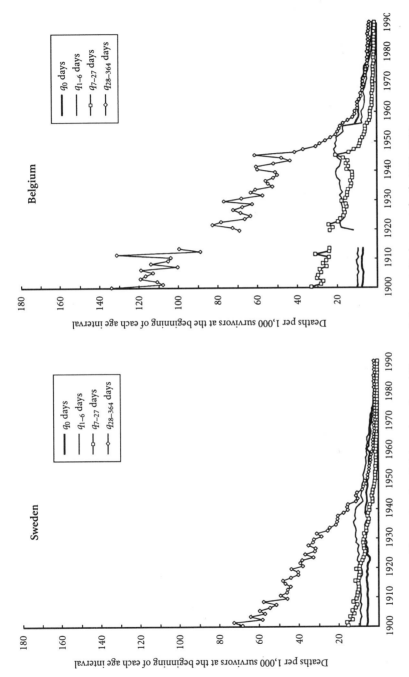

Fig. 1.3. Sweden, Belgium, Austria and Hungary: Infant mortality by age at death, 1900–1990

Source: vital registration.

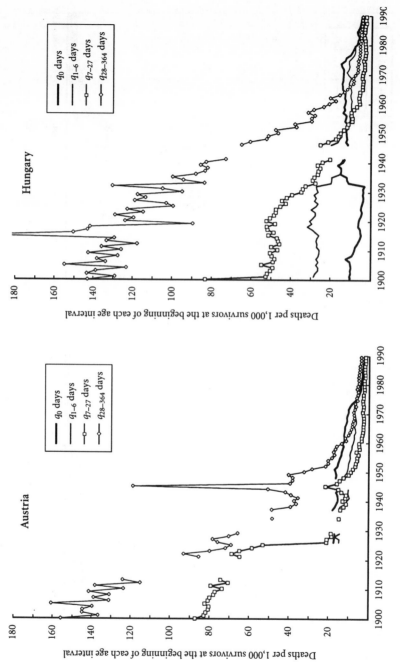

Fig. 1.3. (cont.)

factor in the dramatic decrease in general infant mortality until the beginning of the Second World War in Sweden, until 1955 in Belgium, 1960 in Austria, and 1965 in Hungary. Late neonatal mortality began its decline around 1925 in these four countries, while the first signs of any improvement in early neonatal mortality were observed after the Second World War in Sweden, a little before the end of the war in Belgium and Austria and much later (1975) in Hungary. At the end of those evolutions, the levels of the age-specific risks tended to converge within each reference country. First-day mortality, the remainder of early neonatal mortality, late neonatal and post-neonatal mortality reached almost equivalent levels in 1990.

A more systematic analysis of recent tendencies could be done for the years 1951 to 1990, since it is only after the Second World War that most European countries started to adopt standard publication norms. But this does not automatically imply that strict comparisons of risk measures are possible. There is still some degree of uncertainty about the true definition of first-day mortality: in some cases, the figures truly refer to deaths occurring within the first 24 hours of life, with the length of life being calculated in hours and sometimes minutes (Belgium); in other cases it is calculated by difference in calendar days, with infants whose birth and death occur on the same calendar day being the only ones accounted for. This second method of calculation obviously under-estimates first-day mortality. This underestimation can be illustrated by looking at the case of Czechoslovakia. Before 1985 first-day mortality was calculated using differences in calendar days, and not completed periods of 24 hours, but since 1985 data of both types have been available, allowing for the comparison of the two methods of calculation. In 1989, for instance, 397 deaths were registered according to the difference in calendar days method, while 541 were recorded according to the 24 hours of life method. Given that the precise method of calculation of first-day mortality could not be traced for each country and that differences in administrative definitions of 'registrable' live births exert an influence on the first-day mortality figures, comparative analysis over time and across countries is better based on mortality occurring after the first day of life.

As Figure 1.4 shows, the five groups (clusters) of countries distinguish themselves first of all by their levels of post-neonatal mortality. At the beginning of the study period (1951–1955) this varies from 70 deaths per 1,000 survivors at 28 days (Cluster 5) to 9 per 1,000 (Cluster 1); at the end of the period (1986–1990) it varies from 9 to less than 3 per 1,000. The late neonatal period has been the lowest-risk period in the first three clusters since the early 1950s. The countries belonging to clusters 4 and 5 were only to experience this situation 10 and 20 years later, respectively.

The two components of early neonatal mortality (first-day mortality and mortality from 1 to 6 completed days) show particularly low levels in the countries of Cluster 1. In the first three clusters, the first-day mortality level is almost always higher than the mortality registered during the rest of the early neonatal period. The opposite situation characterizes the countries belonging to clusters 4 and 5. Furthermore, the higher-mortality clusters (3, 4 and 5) have a delayed decline in early neonatal mortality in comparison with the situation of the two lowest-mortality clusters, where a continuous decline in the early neonatal mortality can be observed from the early 1950s.

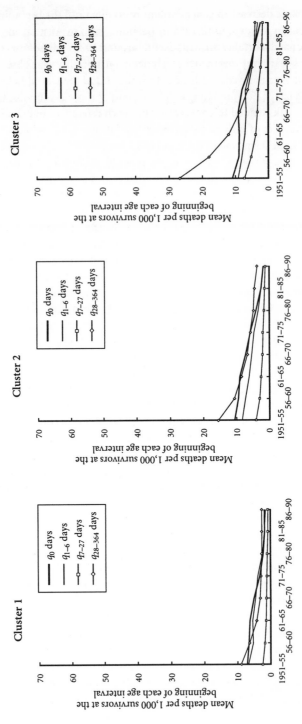

Fig. 1.4. Europe: Infant mortality by age at death, 1951–1990

Source: vital registration.

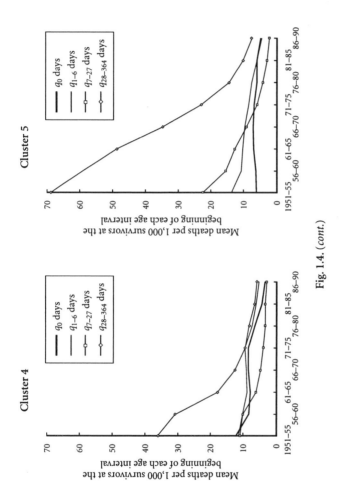

Fig. 1.4. *(cont.)*

The preceding analysis suggests the possibility of a further improvement in the infant mortality level in a large number of European countries. Substantial progress can be made, especially in Central and Eastern European countries. It is nevertheless possible that, given the political changes experienced recently in these countries, the statistics available in the future may obscure any progress made. The survey of the definitions and criteria for birth registration that was done using 1991 as the reference year high-lighted the fact that several countries diverged from the international standards, either in their legal definitions or in their registration practices. The recent adoption of international definitions by most of these countries will doubtless result in an increase in their recorded rates of early neonatal mortality. Results like this have already been published for Lithuania in 1991 (Gourbin and Masuy-Stroobant 1995), and the future removal of the category entitled 'non-viable infants' in Poland should also lead to an increase in the rate of infant mortality of at least 20–25 per cent.

RISK FACTORS AND INFANT HEALTH: TOMORROW'S CHALLENGES

In the Western and Northern European countries, the impressive advances in neonatal intensive-care techniques have contributed significantly to a redefinition of the *de facto* viability criteria and enlarged in practice, and sometimes in the legislation, the criteria for the declaration of births. Improved registration of very preterm or very low birth-weight infants can also contribute to an artificial increase in the level of infant mortality. The solution that has been proposed by the World Health Organization for many years is the production of standardized mortality figures calculated only for children weighing at least 1,000g at birth, which would make international comparisons possible. The 1991 survey showed that of the 27 participating countries, only 12 had the capacity to produce this type of measure, either because the information concerning birthweight appeared on both the birth and the death registration forms, or (when birthweight was recorded at birth) because record linkages were routinely performed between birth and death records.

'Capacity' here refers to the fact that the information was recorded and processed, it does not *per se* imply that the information is published or accessible. Belgium presents an extreme case in this respect: since 1979, birthweight and gestational duration have been systematically collected at birth (live births and stillbirths) and death registration (if death occurs before 3 months of age). To date, this information has never been officially published. In other countries, such as Poland, birthweight categories do not conform to the international recommendations, and in others, such as Italy, birth and infant death statistics are published according to different birthweight categories. In the Scandinavian countries, the decision was taken to organize parallel, independent medical databases, called 'Medical Birth Registries', rather than enrich the vital registration forms with such medical information as birthweight or gestational duration. These medical birth registries are routinely linked with vital registration records. They presently cover almost 100 per cent of births, but usually fail to obtain a similar coverage of infant deaths. Furthermore, differences persist in the objectives, event-definition, contents, access, data-processing systems and publication procedures between the vital registration system and the medical birth registries.

Multiple Deliveries in Europe

The recent development of medically assisted reproduction techniques often produces a higher incidence of multiple conceptions than is the case in natural situations. Infants originating from multiple deliveries are usually born preterm (all the more so in cases of higher-order multiple pregnancies—triple, quadruple or higher) and are also even more subject to the usual risks associated with immaturity, including higher mortality and neurological damage.

For legal reasons (especially matters concerning inheritance) multiple births have usually been recorded at birth since the very beginning of vital registration systems. We therefore had access to long time-series for most of the countries in this study. However, international differences in registration practices are even more important for multiple births than for singletons: multiples experience a greater frequency of preterm delivery and higher risks of foetal death and early neonatal mortality, and are thus highly subject to underregistration or to underscoring of their degree of multiplicity (a twin delivery may be recorded instead of a triplet because one of the babies dies before delivery and does not match the minimum gestational age to be declared as a late foetal death). Practices in this matter vary from one country to another: in Belgium, for example, the published number of infants (including stillborn) resulting from a double, triple or quadruple delivery does not always match the corresponding numbers of double, triple or quadruple deliveries. In this case, both statistics are available for comparison and thus verification is possible. In other cases published figures refer only to the number of multiple deliveries and their order (twin, triple, quadruple, and so on). Another difficulty comes from the inclusion or not of stillbirths in the figures on multiple births or births resulting from multiple deliveries. In general these problems would usually result in an underestimation of the number of multiple deliveries and an underestimation of their order (twin instead of triplet, for example). These inconsistencies led us to prefer statistics on multiple deliveries to the indirect evidence of statistics on births by type of delivery, whenever possible.

The frequency of multiple deliveries has been quite stable over time: in 1950 as in 1900, 1 per 100 total deliveries was a twin delivery, and around 1 per 10,000 was a triplet delivery. The observation of this regularity dates back to ancient times and has even been formalized into a mathematical law: 'If p is the probability of having a twin delivery, p^2 will be the probability of having a triple delivery, p usually being very close to 0.01' (see Zeleny 1921).

Recent studies, however, have shown that the occurrence of multiple deliveries increases with the age of the mother and possibly with her parity—age and parity being closely linked (Tabutin 1977). Hence, the drop in fertility that was observed throughout

Europe from about 1964 to 1975 may be associated with the decrease in twin deliveries observed in this period. But the upward tendency in twin deliveries observed afterwards cannot be explained by an equivalent increase in fertility levels, or by an increase in the average age at motherhood, which only appears to be statistically significant in the mid-1980s. The evolution of triplet deliveries is even more significant (Table 1.3). Triplet and higher-order deliveries are a statistically rare phenomenon that must be analysed with caution. Nevertheless, an upward trend is observed from the mid-1970s in several countries, reaching a maximum of 7 triplet deliveries per 10,000 in Belgium in 1987, and of 6 per 10,000 in the Netherlands in 1990. More generally, a threshold frequency of 2 triplet deliveries per 10,000 deliveries was systematically exceeded in all the Scandinavian countries and in most Western European countries during the 1980s, without any sign of a decline by the end of the decade. However, similar tendencies are

Table 1.3. Europe: Incidence of triplet and
higher-order deliveries, 1960–1990 (per 10,000 deliveries)

	1960	1965	1970	1975	1980	1985	1990
Denmark	1.05	1.44	0.99	2.09	1.05	1.31	2.87
Finland	0.61	1.54	1.71	1.38	1.60	2.25	3.84
Norway	1.29	1.51	0.93	0.53	0.79	1.77	3.81
Sweden	0.39	1.28	0.64	0.77	1.04	0.82	2.71
Austria	0.95	0.61	0.71	0.85	0.88	2.49	1.89
Belgium	0.50	1.09	0.84	1.00	1.69	2.47	5.79
England and Wales	0.97	0.91	1.29	1.35	1.50	1.65	3.06
France	0.94	0.82	0.95	1.26	1.88	2.46	4.33
Federal Republic of Germany	0.93	0.93	1.04	1.02	1.31	2.31	3.41[a]
Republic of Ireland	—	—	—	—	1.62	1.12	1.52
Netherlands	1.04	0.81	0.75	1.58	1.38	1.78	6.01
Northern Ireland	0.95	0.88	0.62	0.00	1.40	1.09	1.90
Scotland	1.56	1.32	1.03	0.44	0.58	1.36	2.64
Switzerland	1.31[b]	0.98	1.01	1.49	2.32	3.55	3.72
Greece	1.46	1.18	1.24	1.47	0.81	—	—
Italy	1.21	0.98	1.04	0.71	1.33	1.53	3.78
Portugal	1.60	1.26	1.25	0.88	1.01	1.15	1.81
Spain	0.83	0.84	0.89	1.00	1.09	1.16	2.28
Bulgaria	0.57	0.32	0.43	0.69	0.70	0.47[c]	1.14
Czechoslovakia	0.55	0.74	1.05	0.94	0.97	1.07	1.15
German Democratic Republic	0.75	0.85	0.84	0.61	0.90	1.13	—
Hungary	1.29	1.13	1.12	0.88	1.42	2.16	2.32
Poland	1.13	0.88	0.73	0.60	0.56	0.74	0.96

[a] 1989 figures instead of 1990.
[b] 1961 figures instead of 1960.
[c] 1986 figures instead of 1985.

Source: vital registration.

not observed in the Central and Eastern European countries (Hungary being an exception) or in the South; but for these regions our series still need to be completed.

Low Birthweight Infants

Information on birthweight (or gestational duration) has only relatively recently been recorded at vital registration in Europe. It first appears in the publications of the Eastern European countries (1956 in Hungary, 1965 in Czechoslovakia and 1975 in Poland) and in Italy (but is in this case limited to births registered from 1959 to 1967). It was made available in the Scandinavian countries with the implementation of the medical birth registries (since 1967 in Norway, 1973 in Denmark, 1982 in Sweden and 1988 in Finland) and it appeared in the national statistical publications of many Western European countries at the beginning of the 1980s.

The number of countries for which it was possible to trace the evolution of the incidence of low or very low birthweight infants for the years preceding the 1980s is therefore rather low: two Scandinavian countries, Norway and Denmark, and three Eastern European countries, Hungary, Czechoslovakia and Poland (Table 1.4).

Table 1.4. Europe: Incidence of very low
birthweight infants, 1970–1990 (per 10,000 live births)

	1970	1975	1980	1985	1990
Denmark[a]		7.7	7.2	8.0	8.1
Finland[a]					6.3
Norway[a]	6.0	6.2	5.9	7.7	8.7
Sweden[a]				6.2	
Austria[b]				8.2	7.7
Belgium[c]			5.4	7.1	
England and Wales[b]			7.4[d]	9.0	9.5[e]
Republic of Ireland[a]				5.2	6.1
Scotland[a]					9.2
Switzerland[b]			5.3	5.8	6.5
Portugal[b]			4.6	5.7	6.3
Czechoslovakia[b]	8.7	8.9	7.6	6.6	7.1
Hungary[b]	18.4	17.4	15.3	15.1	12.9
Poland[b,f]		8.4	8.5	9.0	9.8
		(12.4)	(12.7)	(12.7)	(13.3)

[a] *Source*: medical birth register.
[b] *Source*: vital registration.
[c] *Source*: vital registration, unpublished data.
[d] 1981 figure instead of 1980.
[e] 1989 figure instead of 1990.
[f] Figures in parentheses include births classified as 'non-viable with signs of life' for Poland.

In Norway, the frequencies of low birthweight and very low birthweight infants tended to increase from the early 1980s. No such tendency could be observed for Denmark. The situations of Poland and Hungary are exceptional in many respects: overall the frequencies of very low and low birthweight infants are quite high, with an incidence above 1 per cent for the very low birthweights and more than 8 per cent and 11 per cent for low birthweights in Poland (when the 'non-viable'[7] but in fact live-born infants are taken into account) and Hungary, respectively. The levels reached as well as their evolution place Hungary apart from all simple comparison with other countries. A partial explanation of the high incidence of low birthweights may be found in specific abortion techniques (Hungarian Statistical Office 1972; WHO 1979). The proportion of low and very low birthweight infants in Czechoslovakia is very close to the level of most Western European countries, but, as in the case of Poland, no upward trend can be observed in the most recent years.

For the most recent years in the study (1980–1990), a larger number of countries produce birthweight statistics (Table 1.4), allowing the generalization of the partial observations made above: the incidence of low and very low birthweight infants increased during the 1980s in most Northern and Western European countries. Portugal had a similar evolution, but lack of comparable information for the remainder of the Southern European countries does not permit us to generalize. Once again, the three Eastern European countries depart from this general tendency, showing a quasi-stagnation, if not a decrease. Of note is the very high overall incidence of low and very low birthweight infants in Poland and particularly in Hungary, where it reaches levels that can be twice as high as those observed elsewhere in Europe. There are, however, exceptions to the rules just stated: Denmark is characterized by very stable levels, and the very low levels seen in Finland are probably linked to the recent launch of its Medical Registry, which, at the time, did not ensure complete coverage of births and early deaths.

We observe international variations in the incidence of those low and very low birthweight infants but, if Hungary, Poland and Finland are excluded, the range of observed values is quite narrow: for the 1990 data it varies from 4.2 per cent (Republic of Ireland) to 6.7 per cent (Scotland) for newborns weighing less than 2,500g, and from 0.61 per cent (Republic of Ireland) to 0.95 per cent (England and Wales) for those weighing less than 1,500g. A regional pattern may be sketched, with generally lower levels in the North than in Western Europe. These differences become even more significant if they are viewed in the light of their still high mortality risks. The early neonatal mortality of infants weighing less than 1,500g at birth represented almost 20 per cent of total infant mortality in Western European countries in 1990, and the early neonatal mortality of infants weighing less than 2,500g at birth represented close to 30 per cent of the total infant mortality rate.

Even if birthweight data are collected at birth registration, they are not necessarily

---

[7] At the time of the 1991 survey, a minimum 24-hour survival period was still required in Poland for the official registration of newborns weighing less than 1,001 g. If they did not survive they were registered in a separate category called 'non-viable births with signs of life' and published accordingly, but they were not included in the official infant mortality figures.

Table 1.5. Europe: Early neonatal mortality of very low birthweight infants, 1980–1990 (per 1,000 live births)

	1980	1981	1982	1983	1984	1985	1986	1987	1988	1989	1990
Denmark[a]	310					213	232			261	
Finland[a]								179	180	184	175
Norway[a]		268	255	293	278	253	222		260	187	210
Sweden[a]			202	183	151	190	208	160	191		
Austria[b]						338	311	288	249	259	189
Belgium[c]		262	244	267	266	248	218	243	204		
England and Wales[b]		269	251		240	231	225	216	219	183	
Republic of Ireland[a]					424	388	355	294	336	312	297
Scotland[a]								217			189
Italy[b]				503		457					
Czechoslovakia[b]							424	432	396	360	378
Hungary[b]	567	490	475	456	482	505	499	462	429	394	398
Poland[b,d]						399	384	391	360	354	337
						(574)	(570)	(565)	(545)	(530)	(510)

[a] *Source*: medical birth register.
[b] *Source*: vital registration.
[c] *Source*: vital registration, unpublished data.
[d] Figures in parentheses include births classified as 'non-viable with signs of life' for Poland.

collected at death registration. Furthermore, birth and death record linkages are not routinely performed in every country. In cases where the medical birth registries generally limit their registration to the early neonatal period, it was decided to conduct the comparative analysis on this specific age period, which in the case of low birthweight infants is a crucial one with respect to mortality.

During the period 1980–1990 the early neonatal mortality of very low birthweight infants improved slightly in several countries. It reached about 20 per cent in 1990 in the North and the West of Europe, but significantly exceeded 30 per cent in Eastern Europe. Similar tendencies can be observed for the mortality of low birthweight infants, with levels varying from 4–5 per cent in the North and the West to more than 7 per cent in the East (Table 1.5). Eastern European countries thus combine the disadvantages of a particularly high rate of low birthweight infants with an even higher birthweight-specific mortality among these infants. Czechoslovakia still experiences a high mortality in comparison to its Western European neighbours, but it has a much lower incidence of low birthweight infants than Hungary or Poland. This explains its relatively median position in the general pattern of European infant mortality. Also of note is the very special situation of the Republic of Ireland, where a low incidence of low birthweight infants is associated with a very high birthweight-specific mortality in the context of the rest of Western Europe. Both might be consequences of poor access to neonatal intensive-care units.

CONCLUSIONS

At the end of this broad survey of the evolution of infant mortality in Europe since 1900—unfortunately still a rather elementary exercise because of the limitations of the published data—it seems nevertheless possible to make some concluding remarks.

1. The dramatic decrease in infant mortality throughout Europe during the twentieth century is certainly one of the most extraordinary victories that humanity has known. This spectacular decline followed a typical four-stage pattern, which can be associated with the gradual medicalization of motherhood.

- The two world war periods exerted a positive effect on the organization of maternal and child health care. The crisis created by the First World War is linked to the effective start of maternal and child health systems in many countries, with the first large-scale concerted attempt to organize local child health clinics and, in some countries, to provide nutritional supplements by means of milk depots (Masuy-Stroobant 1984).
- Acceleration of the hospital delivery process became significant in the years following the Second World War, with the spread of social security systems in Europe. Consequently, a sustained and permanent decline in post-neonatal mortality started in the early 1920s, and improvements in maternal mortality and the first signs of a drop in early neonatal mortality were observed in the early 1950s.

- Stillbirth rates began to decline in the interwar period, when antenatal clinics were organized on a more systematic basis.
- More recently, the provision of neonatal intensive-care units during the 1980s led to a further drop in early neonatal mortality.

2. This general four-stage model of decline is obviously limited to an age-specific disaggregation of the evolution of infant mortality. If problems of data quality and the availability of comparable information could be solved, it could be extended to the evolution of European infant mortality by cause of death. But to fit the evolution of each specific country, a time dimension would have to be added to this general model. The observed differences in general infant mortality levels between East and West may be explained if a time-lag is considered. To determine whether this delay is the result of differences in economic and social development levels and process, access to adequate care, or climatic and environmental factors is beyond the scope of this chapter.

3. Geographical and temporal comparisons of infant health or mortality indicators are still difficult to make. Despite a general tendency towards the adoption of common definitions for vital registration of live and stillbirths all over Europe, there are still differences, and their impact on the comparability of the infant mortality figures derived from them is rising. For some countries, inconsistencies in the figures on the evolution of early neonatal mortality have resulted from changes in the registration criteria. Usually these changes mean a widening of the concept of viability and thus bring about an increase in the reported infant mortality figures. More recently, owing to advances in neonatal intensive-care techniques, survival of very small infants has been constantly improving. Consequently, medical viability criteria and legal rules for the registration of births may no longer coincide. The paradoxically low stillbirth rates of the Eastern European countries are not, at first sight, linked to differences in definition, but this situation obviously deserves further investigation.

4. In the present social and political context, the problem of the future should be addressed: the countries with low infant mortality levels are confronted with some of the consequences of the techniques developed in order to improve infant survival and to solve infertility. Medically assisted reproduction techniques and intensive neonatal care demand an enormous amount of human and financial investment. The results are positive in many respects: improved preventive care provided to women with high-risk pregnancies, better organization of transfers to intensive-care units, reduction in the mortality risks of very preterm infants and the widening of the concept of viability. The victories can easily be enumerated. But the assumption that further improvements in survival rates *per se* imply better health in infancy must be discussed: when more and more very small infants are able to survive, are they also free from impairments and disabilities or, more important, the brain damage that is often linked with extreme immaturity?

5. Looking at the East, where the incidence of low birthweight infants and their birthweight-specific mortality are significantly higher than in Western European countries, their backwardness in this respect could be made up for by lowering early neonatal

mortality and by improving specialized care for very small newborns. But could they afford the costs of such highly expensive equipment when we observe today the adverse effects of structural changes and possibly long-term economic crisis, which bring about a lowering of public health expenditure and a widening of social inequalities?

Appendix 1.1

As far as we know, given the information available to us, the following changes occurred in the geo-political borders covered by the published infant mortality figures:

Austria: figures refer to the Austro-Hungarian Empire until 1917; figures for live and stillbirths do not include the Burgerland from 1914 to 1920; figures for infant deaths do not include the Burgerland from 1926 to 1928.

Belgium: until 1921, the figures do not include the eastern Cantons (prior to this time they belonged to Germany).

France: the territory comprised 77 *départements* in 1914–1919, 90 *départements* in 1920–1938, 87 *départements* in 1939–1942, 86 *départements* in 1943–1947, and 90 *départements* from 1948 onwards. The territorial changes concern mainly the Alsace and Lorraine *départements*.

Poland: the National Institute of Statistics did not provide data for the period before 1949, arguing that they are not comparable.

Germany: Germany was divided into two distinct countries from 1946 to 1991. We did not have access to separate retrospective figures for the former Federal and Democratic republics, hence figures before the separation refer to the German Republic, with the following internal territorial changes: the Alsace and Lorraine *départements* (1917–1918), the province of Posen (1919), and various border regions with Belgium, Poland, Czechoslovakia, Denmark and Danzig (1920–1921) were for specific years (indicated in brackets) not included in the published statistics.

Romania: before 1930, the figures refer to the former Romanian Kingdom.

Table 1A.1. Europe: Infant mortality, 1900–1990 (deaths per 1,000 live births)

	1901–05	1906–10	1911–15	1916–20	1921–25	1926–30	1931–35	1936–40	1941–45
Denmark	119.33	108.11	97.20	91.02	81.86	82.32	71.35	59.97	48.35
Finland	131.04	117.00	109.98	113.94	95.61	87.90	72.20	71.75	61.40
Iceland	101.10	118.69	74.39	68.53	52.42	53.26	51.14	36.15	37.65
Norway	79.87	69.31	66.20	61.92	51.69	49.49	44.91	39.38	37.24
Sweden	91.02	78.13	72.20	66.24	59.91	57.56	50.08	41.88	31.01
Austria	215.93	201.50	190.74	153.12	138.29	117.21	99.03	80.68	91.67
Belgium[a]	154.12	147.89	139.21	119.28	106.15	101.24	88.57	84.91	86.45
England and Wales	134.95	117.08	109.56	89.94	76.05	67.88	62.17	55.37	49.50
France[a]	138.86	126.22	124.19	119.78	100.34	94.28	74.33	70.11	81.86
Federal Republic of Germany[b]	199.07	174.20	155.18	129.38	119.25	92.55	73.04	66.43	—
Republic of Ireland	—	—	—	—	—	67.95	67.59	69.23	75.17
Luxembourg	158.83	156.14	146.16	127.76	110.30	107.57	85.55	71.19	87.38
Netherlands[a]	136.40	114.19	99.26	89.65	69.59	56.36	44.53	37.25	50.17
Northern Ireland	—	—	—	—	81.03	78.84	78.35	77.17	73.30
Scotland	119.95	112.42	112.75	99.03	91.75	85.45	80.75	75.80	67.71
Switzerland	134.24	115.06	99.32	82.41	65.11	54.01	48.37	44.97	40.44
Greece	—	—	—	—	87.79	95.97	120.76	113.45	—
Italy	167.41	152.14	139.89	149.55	122.66	119.41	104.73	103.01	110.10
Portugal	142.72	149.06	152.10	170.57	146.31	145.11	145.68	134.98	129.88
Spain[c]	172.39	158.94	152.45	161.44	142.67	123.97	112.20	119.27	109.25
Bulgaria	147.62	160.23	143.86	133.40	155.94	147.08	147.10	142.76	130.45
Czechoslovakia	225.34	205.30	191.27	161.45	155.65	138.56	119.07	127.02	—
German Democratic Republic[b]	199.07	174.20	155.18	129.38	119.25	92.55	73.04	66.43	—
Hungary	213.31	205.80	207.46	205.54	187.29	172.17	156.74	134.42	126.08
Poland	—	—	—	—	—	—	—	—	—
Romania	202.53	172.66	193.07	212.92	232.21	195.82	182.47	177.78	156.69
Yugoslavia	—	—	—	—	144.15	151.18	153.32	137.40	—

Table 1A.1. (*cont.*)

	1946–50	1951–55	1956–60	1961–65	1966–70	1971–75	1976–80	1981–85	1986–90
Denmark	40.18	27.40	22.40	19.64	15.70	11.67	8.99	7.90	7.88
Finland	51.85	32.35	24.59	18.84	14.39	11.16	8.38	6.29	5.95
Iceland	24.40	21.45	16.44	17.24	13.17	11.57	8.25	6.23	6.02
Norway	31.08	22.64	19.85	17.13	13.91	11.63	9.04	8.07	7.89
Sweden	23.95	19.31	16.86	14.77	12.27	10.02	7.71	6.80	5.92
Austria	75.61	51.33	41.04	30.87	26.30	23.91	15.81	12.00	8.86
Belgium[a]	62.77	43.72	33.57	26.37	22.38	18.17	13.30	10.60	8.93
England and Wales	36.33	26.91	22.64	20.61	18.45	16.80	13.18	10.17	8.81
France[a]	62.10	45.11	31.62	24.40	20.14	15.49	10.90	8.99	7.72
Federal Republic of Germany[b]	70.82	48.53	36.21	27.48	23.25	22.06	14.74	10.30	7.93
Republic of Ireland	56.65	40.23	33.07	27.60	22.06	17.86	13.90	9.91	8.41
Luxembourg	57.80	43.04	35.76	27.93	21.41	16.16	12.67	11.61	8.62
Netherlands[a]	31.36	23.73	18.61	15.80	13.53	11.51	9.42	8.23	7.19
Northern Ireland	47.80	36.59	28.25	26.62	24.06	21.14	15.85	11.79	8.46
Scotland	47.31	32.93	27.93	25.02	21.17	18.81	13.69	10.46	8.39
Switzerland	36.03	28.53	22.82	19.85	16.25	12.89	9.34	7.37	6.94
Greece	38.55	42.51	40.53	37.93	32.88	25.25	19.71	14.87	10.80
Italy	76.55	58.44	47.23	38.88	32.24	25.23	17.10	12.31	9.21
Portugal	107.05	90.99	85.14	74.95	59.87	42.67	28.84	19.16	13.33
Spain[c]	76.96	60.33	49.33	41.40	32.42	21.88	15.13	10.75	8.32
Bulgaria	114.73	91.12	58.46	34.89	29.72	25.13	21.24	16.92	14.68
Czechoslovakia	83.22	49.45	28.98	22.89	22.81	21.13	19.15	15.65	12.16
German Democratic Republic[b]	93.90	55.25	43.08	30.02	20.72	16.69	12.99	10.83	8.43
Hungary	98.27	68.63	56.34	42.74	36.50	33.83	25.68	20.14	16.56
Poland	108.03	92.36	69.88	49.57	35.54	26.32	22.63	19.55	16.68
Romania	*150.25*	96.92	77.52	56.40	51.95	37.95	30.71	26.06	—
Yugoslavia	*110.26*	114.50	93.22	78.31	59.18	43.69	34.09	29.53	23.90

[a] An undefined number of early neonatal deaths where birth was registered after death, the so-called 'présentés sans vie', could not be included in the live births or in the infant deaths. This was the case for Belgium for the years 1914–1918, for the Netherlands before 1918, and for France for the years 1900–1919 and 1932–1945.

[b] Before 1945, the figures for the former Federal Republic of Germany and the former Democratic Republic refer to the former Germany (See Appendix 1.1).

[c] Before 1975, infant deaths occuring within 24 hours were counted as stillbirths and thus not included in the live-birth and infant death figures.

Note: Figures in *italics* do not cover the entire five-year period.

Source: vital registration.

Table 1A.2. Europe: Stillbirth rates, 1900–1990 (per 1,000 births)

	1901–05	1906–10	1911–15	1916–20	1921–25	1926–30	1931–35	1936–40	1941–45
Denmark	23.73	23.33	23.42	24.71	24.05	23.30	24.67	25.55	20.72
Finland	24.99	24.43	25.28	25.50	26.48	26.45	26.41	23.00	21.00
Iceland	30.87	30.10	31.09	29.02	24.62	25.55	20.95	20.84	22.70
Norway	23.92	22.51	22.25	22.03	21.28	24.73	24.89	22.57	20.17
Sweden	—	—	—	23.31	24.52	26.12	27.14	27.94	23.13
Austria	26.58	25.29	25.13	30.80	24.80	29.16	27.39	26.43	21.03
Belgium[a]	36.27	36.10	35.80	38.70	38.75	33.57	32.48	29.72	25.09
England and Wales	—	—	—	—	—	39.79	40.97	38.47	30.47
France[a]	45.19	44.81	43.82	42.90	33.02	28.86	32.58	33.58	27.37
Federal Republic of Germany[b]	30.67	29.58	29.54	30.68	32.18	31.42	27.80	23.82	—
Republic of Ireland	—	—	—	—	—	—	—	—	—
Luxembourg	28.94	28.68	32.64	35.01	33.45	33.75	35.44	28.16	24.26
Netherlands[a]	40.81	39.52	37.74	30.36	26.45	25.04	25.09	24.95	19.29
Northern Ireland	—	—	—	—	—	—	—	—	—
Scotland	—	—	—	—	—	—	—	42.18	35.72
Switzerland	34.91	32.90	30.82	28.80	27.60	24.35	22.47	21.04	16.76
Greece	—	—	—	—	11.93	9.41	10.37	9.64	—
Italy	42.87	42.95	40.76	43.42	43.10	36.41	33.76	31.44	28.66
Portugal	15.55	15.23	33.46	40.94	42.39	40.17	42.33	44.06	43.97
Spain[c]	24.95	24.26	24.99	26.71	27.58	30.76	32.04	30.18	26.03
Bulgaria	5.60	6.97	5.82	4.74	5.43	6.50	8.62	11.53	11.84
Czechoslovakia	29.04	27.97	27.53	22.57	23.63	20.86	20.75	23.97	16.33
German Democratic Republic[b]	30.67	29.58	29.54	30.68	32.18	31.42	27.80	23.82	—
Hungary	19.67	19.42	20.33	23.15	26.72	28.33	28.24	27.58	23.18
Poland	—	—	—	—	—	—	—	—	—
Romania	18.60	23.51	26.44	16.94	15.16	18.18	19.86	23.71	24.40
Yugoslavia	—	—	—	13.37	11.83	10.41	10.57	11.03	—

Table 1A.2. (*cont.*)

	1946–50	1951–55	1956–60	1961–65	1966–70	1971–75	1976–80	1981–85	1986–90
Denmark	17.89	18.38	15.05	11.45	8.83	7.17	5.61	4.88	4.83
Finland	18.36	18.03	16.65	12.86	9.81	7.33	4.81	3.97	4.48
Iceland	17.64	15.71	13.19	13.75	11.32	8.84	5.56	3.70	3.16
Norway	17.53	15.25	14.26	12.39	11.14	9.04	7.23	5.70	4.42
Sweden	20.48	17.82	15.31	11.64	8.99	6.85	4.91	3.94	3.79
Austria	21.06	18.87	16.25	12.88	10.70	9.00	7.02	4.97	3.78
Belgium[a]	25.03	19.52	15.84	14.18	12.24	10.56	8.36	6.87	5.85
England and Wales	24.03	22.95	21.44	17.27	14.15	11.56	8.51	5.95	4.89
France[a]	20.44	18.01	17.06	15.80	14.21	11.99	9.49	7.72	6.44
Federal Republic of Germany[b]	21.80	21.08	16.79	13.24	10.89	8.89	6.21	4.62	3.70
Republic of Ireland	—	—	21.39	18.45	14.93	12.32	9.93	8.28	6.88
Luxembourg	24.77	17.27	15.72	16.82	13.49	8.87	6.66	5.82	4.46
Netherlands[a]	19.51	17.68	16.22	14.05	11.59	9.05	7.27	5.92	5.65
Northern Ireland	—	—	—	20.61	15.88	13.90	9.86	7.06	4.99
Scotland	29.22	25.49	22.85	19.11	14.98	12.28	7.98	5.83	5.31
Switzerland	16.40	15.12	12.63	11.33	9.61	7.83	5.92	4.81	4.16
Greece	*10.02*	11.05	13.19	14.72	14.35	12.42	10.39	8.89	—
Italy	31.50	29.79	26.00	21.67	17.20	13.00	9.32	7.23	5.93
Portugal	41.84	39.24	34.70	30.35	28.63	18.73	14.01	12.11	9.67
Spain[c]	25.89	28.68	28.21	24.29	19.37	14.71	9.32	6.68	4.88
Bulgaria	*11.21*	—	*12.08*	10.90	9.70	8.87	7.53	7.05	6.03
Czechoslovakia	16.46	13.83	10.95	8.90	7.58	6.74	6.25	5.25	4.52
German Democratic Republic[b]	23.72	20.02	16.49	14.05	11.35	8.85	7.08	5.80	4.74
Hungary	23.71	17.22	14.37	11.91	10.18	8.98	8.17	7.08	6.06
Poland	*18.19*	14.95	12.78	11.33	10.53	8.52	7.00	6.08	5.53
Romania	25.78	19.83	16.93	15.28	15.54	11.00	9.34	8.34	—
Yugoslavia	12.54	11.06	10.40	10.11	9.59	8.12	7.24	6.49	5.87

[a] An undefined number of early neonatal deaths where birth was registered after death, the so-called 'présentés sans vie', were counted as stillbirths in France for the years 1900–1919 and 1932–1945. For Belgium and the Netherlands, the published figures allow for the distinction between 'true' and 'false' stillbirths.

[b] Before 1945, the figures for the formal Federal Republic of Germany and the former Democratic Republic refer to the former Germany (See Appendix 1.1).

[c] Before 1975, infant deaths occuring within 24 hours were counted as stillbirths and thus not included in the live-birth and infant death figures.

Note: Figures in *italics* do not cover the entire five-year period.

Source: vital registration.

References

BASCH, P., 1990. *Textbook of international health*, New York, Oxford University Press.

DUC, G., 1982. 'Néonatologie 1981, bilan et perspectives', *Revue médicale de Suisse Romande* 102, pp. 399–408.

EVERITT, B., 1980. *Cluster analysis*, 2nd edn, London, Heineman Educational Books.

FRIEDE, A., RHODES, P., GUYER, B., BINKIN, N., HANNAN, M. and HOGUE, C., 1987. 'The postponement of neonatal deaths into the postneonatal period: evidence from Massachusetts', *American Journal of Epidemiology* 127(1), pp. 161–170.

GOURBIN, C., 1991. 'Les pratiques de déclaration des événements "Naissance vivante" et "Mortné" en Belgique', master's thesis in demography, University of Louvain, Louvain-la-Neuve.

—— 1995. 'Critères d'enregistrement des événements "naissance vivante" et "mort-né"', in J. DUCHENE and G. WUNSCH (eds.), *Collecte et comparabilité des données démographiques et sociales en Europe, Chaire Quetelet 1991*, Louvain-la-Neuve, Académia/L'Harmattan.

—— and MASUY-STROOBANT, G., 1995. 'Registration of vital data: are live and stillbirths comparable all over Europe?', *Bulletin of the World Health Organization* 73(4), pp. 449–460.

HERTOGHE, L., DE WALS, P., PIRON, M., BERTRAND, F. and LECHAT, M.-F., 1987. 'Quality of perinatal death registration: a study in Hainaut, Belgium', *European Journal of Pediatrics* 146, pp. 473–476.

HUNGARIAN CENTRAL STATISTICAL OFFICE, 1972. 'The effect of the number of abortions on premature births and perinatal mortality in Hungary', Budapest.

IMHOF, A. E., 1981. *Die gewonnenen Jahre*, Munich, C.H. Beck.

KEIRSE, M., 1984. 'Perinatal mortality rates do not contain what they purport to contain', *The Lancet* 26 May, pp. 1166–1169.

LANTOINE, C. and PRESSAT, R., 1984. 'Nouveaux aspects de la mortalité infantile', *Population* 39(2), pp. 253–264.

MASUY-STROOBANT, G., 1984. *Les déterminants de la mortalité infantile: la Belgique d'hier et d'aujourd'hui*, Louvain-la-Neuve, CIACO.

—— 1995. 'Santé et mortalité infantile: indicateurs et comparabilité', in J. DUCHENE and G. WUNSCH (eds.), *Collecte et comparabilité des données démographiques et sociales en Europe, Chaire Quetelet 1991*, Louvain-la-Neuve, Académia/L'Harmattan.

MUGFORD, M., 1983. 'A comparison of reported differences in definitions of vital events and statistics', *WHO Statistics Quarterly* 36, pp. 201–212.

PELLER, S., 1948. 'Mortality: past and future', *Population Studies* 1, pp. 405–456.

ROLLET-ECHALIER, C., 1990. *La politique à l'égard de la petite enfance sous la IIIème République*, INED, Travaux et documents 127, Paris, Presses Universitaires de France.

TABUTIN, D., 1977. 'Quelques données sur les accouchements multiples en Belgique', *Population et Famille* 40(1), pp. 1–20.

UNITED NATIONS, 1954. *Foetal, infant and early childhood statistics*, vol. I: *The statistics*, ST/SOA/ Series A. Population Studies no. 13.

WOODS, R. I., WATTERSON, P. A. and WOODWARD, J. H., 1988 and 1989. 'The causes of rapid infant mortality decline in England and Wales, 1861–1921. Parts I and II', *Population Studies* 42(3), pp. 343–366 and 43(1), pp. 113–132.

WORLD HEALTH ORGANIZATION 1979. 'Gestation, birthweight and spontaneous abortion in pregnancy after induced abortion', *The Lancet* 20 January, pp. 142–145.
—— 1985. *Having a baby in Europe*, Public Health in Europe no. 26, Copenhagen.
ZELENY, C., 1921. 'The relative numbers of twins and triplets', *Science* March, pp. 261–264.

2

Assessing Change in Historical Contexts:
Childhood Mortality Patterns in Spain during the Demographic Transition

DAVID S. REHER, VICENTE PÉREZ-MOREDA
AND JOSEP BERNABEU-MESTRE

Grappling with the issue of change in any historical context is an often-thorny task, even where basic patterns may appear to be straightforward. The demographic transition in Europe is a case in point. Our common-sense interpretation of this process is that fertility and mortality retreated from high and varying pre-transitional levels to low and fairly constant ones, owing largely to the modernization of society, to medical and scientific advances, to economic improvement and to people coming gradually to base their decision-making process on themselves and their families rather than on often-abstract social and cultural norms. As long as the issue is viewed in this way, there can be little argument: fertility and mortality did decline, and society did modernize. This is evident to anyone who wants to look at historical change from afar and treat it as a simple, straightforward process. If, however, we choose to look at the demographic transition more closely, clarity and linearity prove to be misleading assumptions and rapidly vanish amid a cloud of questions. Historical processes, like life, tend to be heterogeneous, and easy generalizations often founder on the reefs of reality.

The complexity of historical reality, especially the complexity of mortality during the demographic transition, is our theme here. Delving into the causes of demographic change, which is one aspect of the basic question, is beyond the scope of this chapter. Instead, we will discuss the more immediate internal dynamics of demographic change, with particular reference to infant and child mortality between 1800 and 1960. The problems inherent in assessing the heterogeneity of change will be illustrated with the help of unpublished data taken from local Spanish archives. Many of the issues discussed, however, are general ones and deserve greater consideration from historical demographers working on this period.

Research for this chapter was supported by the Dirección General de Investigación en Ciencia y Tecnología (DGICYT) of the Ministerio de Educación y Ciencia (PB92-0022). Alberto Sanz Gimeno and Diego Ramiro Fariñas provided competent and enthusiastic help. Without them an undertaking of this sort would have been unthinkable. Elena Robles coordinated data collection in Alicante. Begoña Gómez Garay and Begoña Cremades provided much-needed help throughout the project.

C.A. Corsini and P.P. Viazzo (eds.) The Decline of Infant and Child Mortality, 35-56.
© *1997 UNICEF. Printed in the Netherlands.*

THE DYNAMICS OF CHANGE

The problems that arise in any attempt to assess the structural dynamics of mortality change relate to the availability of data, pinpointing the timing of change and the appropriate lags and leads of different mortality indicators, estimating the intensity of change, especially with relation to timing, our ability to portray the heterogeneity of change in a convincing manner, and evaluating the demographic (as well as social and economic) implications of change. All of these points represent potential pitfalls for our ability to evaluate mortality change correctly.

Generally speaking, it is very difficult to generate data of sufficient quality to allow for a complex analysis of mortality during childhood. In many countries, time-series data exist only for a few mortality indicators (normally infant mortality rates—IMRs), and begin only with the commencement of vital registration, some time towards the end of the nineteenth century. In some cases, local studies have been able to generate more complex indicators, but the data refer only to local contexts and are generally grouped over relatively lengthy periods. Such data are woefully inadequate for unravelling the dynamics of change. Time-series data are ideal; but if official series appear only after the process of change is under way, they too are inadequate for the task. This is especially true if we want to identify the moment and the context of the onset of change. Spanish data are affected by most of these problems, since published data date from 1900 onwards and even then only enable us to generate time-series for infant mortality. Spain is not alone on this count.

Even though change tends to take place over a relatively prolonged period of time, the onset of the process of change is of key importance. Even with adequate data, pinpointing trend changes can be problematic, mainly because it is impossible to establish a universally acceptable baseline. Many different types of problem can arise:

(i) In some cases, the downward trend comes after a prolonged period of worsening mortality or a particular mortality crisis. Does change date from the moment the decline sets in, or from when previous lower values are surpassed?

(ii) Sometimes two patterns can be present. For a period of time, perhaps 10 or 20 years, mortality declines modestly and then there are interruptions. The net mortality reduction over the entire period, however, may well be substantial. Subsequently, much sharper decline sets in. When does real change take place? Which moment is the most important? While the period of rapid decline is unquestionably important, the earlier gradual mortality reduction may well have brought significant increases in the numbers of surviving children and have paved the way for later decline. It is quite possible that the context of causality was somewhat different during each period.

(iii) Trend changes are almost never irreversible. When a trend change occurs, say, 10 years after the initial onset of decline and is the result of an epidemic lasting 3 years, does it constitute a sufficiently important reversal to negate the significance of the earlier decline?

These are thorny issues that have no straightforward answers. If, however, we are really going to be able to evaluate the social, economic, demographic and epidemiological context of the mortality transition, they must be given serious consideration.

Estimating the intensity of change is another important issue, though perhaps less recalcitrant than the question of timing. There are a number of possible approaches, with varying degrees of sophistication, but none of them is wholly satisfactory. This is especially true when we want to determine the lags and leads in the behaviour of certain mortality indicators. An example is establishing the point of comparison of the intensity of change. What is the correct vantage point for comparing, say, infant and child mortality? Should an appropriate comparison be based on certain periods, or on the years elapsed since the initial trend change of each indicator? Both perspectives are potentially valid.

There is no reason at all to expect mortality change to be a uniform process over the different ages of childhood. It is generally accepted that child mortality ($_4q_1$) began to decline before infant mortality (q_0), and that neonatal mortality came down somewhat later still. It is quite possible, however, that reality was far more complex. During childhood a child went through a number of different stages, all of which posed different types of risk to its health. Risk factors for a child who was being breastfed before teething were different from, say, those for a child who had just been weaned, or for one who was 4 or 5 years old. Over the long run, mortality declined for all of them, but there is no reason to expect all the different risk environments they lived in to have changed necessarily at the same moment. This sort of heterogeneity will be spectacularly visible in the Spanish data presented later in this chapter.

If the onset and intensity of childhood mortality are indeed heterogeneous, the demographic implications of certain patterns will be different from those of others. This issue is especially important in terms of the effects of mortality change on fertility within marriage and on the amount of time that parents invested—and 'wasted'—in children who were eventually going to die. Where high-intensity indicators were the first to decline, their effect on families would be far greater than in those contexts in which relatively less-intense mortality indicators diminished first.

While it is impossible to address all of these issues adequately within the context of this chapter, data will be presented that will offer proof of the heterogeneity of childhood mortality patterns in rural Spain and enable us to evaluate a number of the issues raised here. Appropriate indicators will be generated in different regional contexts, and time-series dating from the early nineteenth century to 1960 will be presented. Lags of as much as 30 or 40 years will emerge and the relative intensity of change will be shown to vary sharply for different mortality indicators. Certain regularities can be observed across regional contexts, which suggests that the patterns observed transcend specific local contexts and are at least in part independent of prevailing mortality levels and other contextual constraints. The results point to a number of substantive issues that are of crucial importance to understanding mortality change and must be addressed in future research.

GENERATING CHILDHOOD MORTALITY INDICATORS IN SPAIN

Comparatively little is known of mortality during childhood in Spain, especially before the beginning of the twentieth century. A number of studies evaluate local mortality patterns, but very few of these have generated time-series over relatively prolonged periods.[1] Much of what we know is summarized in Table 2.1, which indicates that in most areas of the country mortality in childhood was generally high, and that child mortality ($_4q_1$) tended to be relatively high compared with mortality during the first year of life, a pattern that has been observed for other countries of the Mediterranean region.[2] Our knowledge of childhood mortality patterns has improved greatly during the twentieth century thanks largely to the research carried out by Marcelino Pascua (1934), A. Arbelo Curbelo (1962) and Rosa Gómez Redondo (1992).

These three authors generated yearly series of infant mortality rates and corrected for underregistration for Spanish provinces and, in some cases, for capital towns. Despite their significant contribution to our understanding of infant mortality patterns, our knowledge of the parameters and contexts of mortality decline continues to be less than satisfactory. Apart from IMRs, no time-series for other childhood mortality indicators have yet been generated, relatively little is known about the epidemiological contexts of change, and we have no knowledge of subprovincial variation by district, social group, wealth, or migratory or educational status. Perhaps the greatest obstacle to our understanding of the entire historical process is that all of these authors have based their work on published mortality data, which date only from 1900 onwards.[3] Apart from some data from certain local studies, we have no idea when or how infant mortality decline began.

There is a research project currently under way in Spain that promises to remedy some of these problems. One of the project's goals is to generate reliable time-series data on infant and child mortality based on local parish and civil registration data for a limited number of Spanish regions. These time-series start from the date at which systematic registration of death by age began, often as early as 1800. In certain parishes cause-of-death data were also being generated (generally starting in 1838) by parents' occupation and by migratory status. These data will eventually enable us to generate time-series of deaths by age, sex and cause for at least two Spanish regions. The cause-of-death data are still being compiled and will not be used in this chapter.

---

[1] Exceptions can be found in Muñoz Pradas 1990, Reher 1991 and Livi Bacci and Reher 1993.

[2] This pattern of relatively high child mortality can also be seen in life-tables generated for Spain during the early part of the twentieth century, as well as in the Coale and Demeny South model life-tables. See, for example, Instituto Nacional de Estadística 1952, Coale and Demeny 1966 and Caselli 1994.

[3] In 1900, vital statistics based on the Civil Register began to be published yearly in the *Movimiento Natural de la Población*.

Table 2.1. Spain: Infant and childhood mortality between the seventeenth and nineteenth centuries

Place	Source	Date	IMR	$_4q_1$	$_5q_5$	Notes
Santander	a	18th cent.–1815	208			4 parishes
		1820–1860	171			5 parishes
Santiago de Compostela (Galicia)	b	1730–1760	252	316	128	Family reconstitutions, average of different 10-year periods
		1760–1790	201	239	83	
		1790–1810	225	230	60	
Guipúzcoa	c	1790–1799	127	138		Mean of 4 parishes
(Basque Country)		1800–1815	145	173		Mean of 3 parishes
New and Old Castile	d	18th cent.	197			Mean values of several parishes and several 10-year periods
		1780–1803	365			
		1800–1839	265			
Otero de Herreros	d	1820–1849	185	219	56	Mean of several decades
(Segovia, Old Castile)	d	1850–1899	224	235	71	Same
Villacastín (Segovia)	d	1820–1839	262	346	90	Same
Zaragoza (Aragon)	d	1786–1790	210	175	39	Mean of 8 parishes
Los Molinos (Madrid)	e	1620–1729 (male)	323	152	93	
(New Castile)		1620–1729 (female)	242	240	62	
		1620–1729 (total)	282	197	75	
Alameda (Madrid)	e	1652–1685	241			
Pozuelo (Madrid)	e	1676–1699	293			
Cuenca (town) (New Castile)	f	1842–1862	228	240		
Valdeolivas (Cuenca)	f	1818–1837	305	331		
Penedès (Barcelona) (Catalonia)	g	1675–1690	219	347		Mean of several parishes
		1784–1790	196	312		
		1857–1864	178	245		
Palomòs (Girona) (Catalonia)	h	1705–1751	256	284		
		1762–1799	232	283		
		1810–1829	126	186		
Orihuela (general area) (Alicante, Valencia)	i	1850–1870	243			Mean of several decades
		1870–1900	240			
Yeste (Albacete) (New Castile)	j	1879–1900	224			

Note: Based on local data coming mainly from family reconstitutions.

Sources: a: Lanza 1991, 228–242; b: Martínez Rodríguez 1992, 54; c: Piquero 1991, 163; d: Pérez Moreda 1980, 146–167; e: Soler Serratosa 1985, 182–184; f: Reher 1990, 111; g: Muñoz Pradas 1990, 112–124, esp. 113; h: Nadal Oller 1956; i: Olivares and Vinal 1988, 653; j: Martínez Carrión 1983, 259–281.

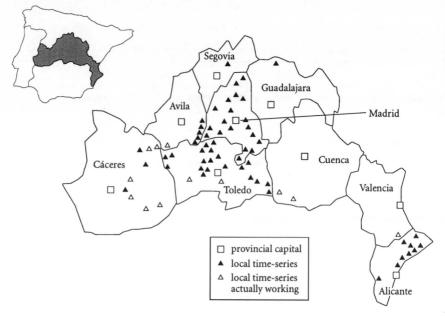

Map 2.1.

Time-series of demographic data of differing lengths have been generated for 49 different communities, located mainly in the central areas of the country and in the province of Alicante along the Mediterranean coast. This comprises 4 places in Avila, 16 in Madrid, 16 in Toledo, 2 in Cáceres, 1 in Guadalajara and 9 in Alicante. All of these places are situated in rural areas, although some of them can be considered small towns. In the interests of clarity, two general time-series have been generated. One of them includes the nine parishes in Alicante, representing a total population of about 20,000 during the early decades of the twentieth century. The other sample is much larger and is made up of all of the different time-series taken from the provinces of central Spain (mostly Madrid and Toledo, although three other provinces are represented as well). For 1900 the sample includes 39 villages and small towns and a total population of nearly 110,000. The reliability of the sample for central Spain is considerably higher than that of the Alicante sample, but some of this latter sample has been retained in order to compare very distinct demographic regimes. A summary description of each series can be found in Appendix Table 2A.1. Only villages with high-quality data were selected, and the reliability of the indicators we have generated appears to be acceptable for the most part (Table 2.2).[4] Map 2.1 shows the places covered by the project as a whole, including those used in this chapter. In 1900 life expectancies in the rural areas

[4] The infant mortality rates we have generated for the sample parishes compare favourably with those stemming from the rural areas of the provinces of Madrid, Toledo and Alicante in 1900. Only in Alicante do we feel that there is some cause for concern, because the indicators generated are lower than official statistics.

Table 2.2. Spain: Infant mortality and life expectancy (e_0)
for rural areas of regions included in the samples, 1900

Region	Infant mortality rate		Life expectancy (e_0) (both sexes)
	Published vital registration data	Sample of villages	
Central Spain[a]	208	210	34.36
Alicante	156	135	38.11
Spain	201		35.22

[a] 'Central Spain' refers to the unweighted average of the rural areas of Madrid and Toledo.

Note: Official data have been adjusted for underregistration owing to children dying in the first day of life. Rural estimates have been derived by subtracting data for provincial capitals from provincial totals. The IMR is based on births and deaths (0 years) in 1900 and 1901. Life expectancy (e_0) refers to rural areas of these provinces and is based on census and vital registration data.

of central Spain were slightly below those obtaining in rural areas of Spain as a whole, and in Alicante they were slightly higher. These areas do not represent the only possible mortality patterns in the country, and so we will not attempt to infer patterns obtaining in the entire country from the data presented here.

Data were collected by sex, by month of death during the first year of life (with those children who died the day they were born being grouped separately), and by exact age of death between 1 and 9 years of age. The death rates and probabilities of death were then calculated as cohort rates. All rates were generated using the equations contained in Appendix 2.1. All childhood mortality indicators were generated annually, but are presented here as five-year moving averages.

ASSESSING THE TIMING, INTENSITY AND SIGNIFICANCE OF CHILDHOOD MORTALITY DECLINE IN ITS EARLY STAGES

The existence of uninterrupted time-series spanning the entire process of the demographic transition with data on a large number of childhood mortality indicators can afford us a unique view of the complexity of the process of change. The forerunners can be identified, as can the laggards. The onset of significant decline in each of them may span as much as three decades or more. Certain cross-regional regularities appear that suggest that the observed patterns are not merely local or a matter of chance.

Many of the issues discussed earlier are brought out in Figures 2.1 and 2.2, which contain basic childhood mortality data for each sample. These figures raise many substantive issues that can be discussed only marginally in this chapter. There are certain common points in both samples, and there is divergence as well. In both areas, pre-transitional child mortality was extremely high, normally between 200 and 300 per

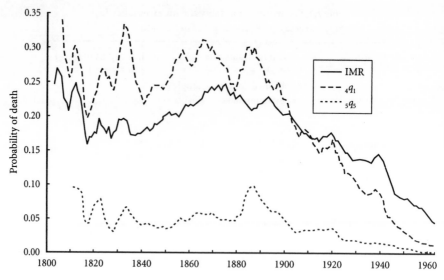

Fig. 2.1. Central Spain: Childhood mortality, 1800–1965 (five-year moving averages)

1,000. By contrast, infant mortality was very high in central Spain, often near 250 per 1,000, but closer to 150 per 1,000 in Alicante. Everywhere, pre-transitional mortality for 5- to 9-year-olds was slightly above 50 per 1,000. Thus, in central Spain, mortality was uniformly high up to 5 years of age, while in Alicante only child mortality was high. The reason for these differences, and especially for the surprising behaviour of Alicante, where mortality was moderately low during the first year of life but extremely high afterwards, is unclear. It is an issue to be addressed in the course of future research.

There are other noteworthy regularities. In both cases, the middle years of the nineteenth century appear to have been ones of worsening mortality. The increase in infant and child mortality was substantial everywhere, though it is most visible in central Spain, where IMRs rose by nearly 50 per cent between the late 1830s and *c.*1870. Child mortality followed the same pattern, though increases may well have set in somewhat later than for infant mortality, perhaps in the 1850s. This mortality pattern at mid-century has been found in other European contexts, and does not appear to be the result of improving registration.[5] It suggests the possibility of worsening living conditions and more widespread childhood diseases. The role of epidemic mortality in this trend, especially for IMRs, appears to have been small. The trend towards increased childhood mortality was prolonged and apparently general. Contrary to many common-sense notions, pre-transitional mortality did not rest on a plateau; the years immediately preceding the secular decline in mortality were ones of sharply worsening mortality conditions.

In both central Spain and Alicante, mortality decline began during the last third of

---

[5] IMRs were already fairly high at earlier dates, as were neonatal mortality rates.

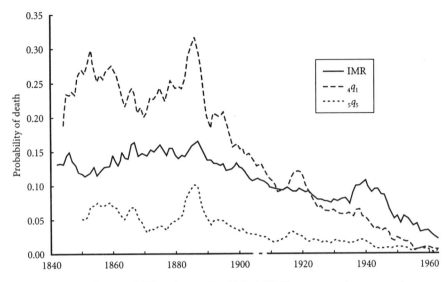

Fig. 2.2. Alicante: Childhood mortality, 1840–1965 (five-year moving averages)

the nineteenth century and by 1900 it had gathered considerable steam. Any analysis of infant mortality based only on data from the twentieth century is bound to be misleading. The earlier data suggest that the final 20 or 30 years of the nineteenth century were crucial to the fundamental patterns of change. It should be kept in mind that the samples used are all basically rural, and that the effects of any economic or social modernization in these areas, although typical of urban contexts during the twentieth century, were modest at best. In other words, the relatively early starting-date of change may well have been a general pattern, quite independent of relative levels of wealth or modernization.

Returning to the general theme of this chapter, from a more methodological standpoint a considerable degree of heterogeneity can be observed within each of the series, as can some continuity across them. In central Spain, and to a lesser extent in Alicante, there appears to have been a period of gradual decline in mortality, characterized by net reductions along with temporary trend reversals, followed by much sharper declines where interruptions were much less significant. This is most noticeable for infant mortality, but can also be seen for mortality at later ages. In central Spain, IMRs started to go down during the mid-1870s and by the late 1880s had declined by about 10 per cent. In Alicante, it was more a period of stability than of decline: IMRs show few trends from the mid-1860s to the mid-1880s. After the late 1880s in Alicante and the mid-1890s in central Spain, the pace of mortality reduction increased substantially, and trend reversals were no longer significant until the influenza epidemic of 1918–1919 and the Civil War and its aftermath (1936–1940).

Much the same happens with child mortality ($_4q_1$)—although the intensity of fluctuations is much more severe than for infant mortality. In central Spain, the high point was reached around 1865 and was followed immediately by a downward trend. By 1880, child mortality had declined by over 20 per cent. Epidemics during the 1880s drove it back up to near its original levels, but this trend reversal was short-lived. Mortality was especially high in 1882, 1883, 1885 and 1887.[6] Had the epidemics of the 1880s not intervened, child mortality levels appear to have been ready to descend below IMRs some time around 1880. As it was, this did not happen until more than 20 years later. In Alicante, the situation seems to have been quite different, since the entire period from 1870 to 1888 was one of steady mortality increase, culminating in the cholera and measles epidemics of the late 1880s. In all of the cases studied, late childhood mortality ($_5q_5$) behaved much like early childhood mortality ($_4q_1$) in Alicante: steady increases throughout the 1870s and a very high peak in the late 1880s. Mortality declined perceptibly only during the last decade of the century, but then it was extremely fast.

A lesson to be learned from these data is that early and late child mortality were far more subject than infant mortality to the effects of epidemic diseases. Trend reversals in both series were much sharper, as was their basic variability. The peaks in central Spain give a basic chronology of child epidemics throughout the period of study: 1811, 1822–1824, 1833–1835, 1855–1856, 1863–1866, 1885–1888, 1897, 1919–1920 and 1937–1940 were all years of readily definable epidemics. With infant mortality, on the other hand, upward swings were much less pronounced—except during the Civil War—and often did not coincide with the peak child mortality years. The protection afforded by breastfeeding in this respect was essential. Once weaning had taken place, normally at a relatively late age, children were pretty much on their own in a world of recurring epidemic disease, against a backdrop of generally poor levels of nutrition and hygiene. This world, however, was more sensitive to improving nutrition and public health than was that of children dependent on their mothers' milk. This helps explain why change came earlier and was more intense among children above 1 year of age than it was for infants.

The importance of the periods of gradual mortality decline for family demography and family economies should not be underestimated. Women who bore children in central Spain between 1870 and 1880, for example, would have had a much different child survival rate from women who had given birth a generation earlier. Even though the sharp subsequent declines tend to attract our attention much more, the earlier decrease may have had pervasive and unsettling effects. The demographic implications of these changes can be estimated quite easily if fertility is held constant at, say, five child-births for each married woman. Under the prevailing mortality conditions in the central part of the country, women would have had 2.7 children surviving to 5 years of age under mortality conditions between 1860 and 1869, 2.76 between 1870 and 1879, 2.83 between 1880 and 1889, and 2.98 between 1890 and 1899. In other words, net reproduction would have increased by about 10 per cent over this period.

---

[6] Some authors have related these years to various measles, diphtheria, smallpox and cholera epidemics. See, for example, Hauser 1902, II: 43, 77.

This increase in child survival took place despite often-contradictory swings in deaths among children at different ages: in some periods, for example, child mortality was declining while IMRs were stable or even rising. These conflicting trends tended to cancel each other out, although they suggest that the ages at which children died and the time mothers spent caring for them were continually changing (Reher 1995). After the mid-1890s, however, both infant and child mortality declined sharply, thus increasing the probability of survival at a much faster pace than before: between 1900 and 1909 a woman with five childbirths would have had 3.38 children surviving to 5 years of age, and by 1920–1929 this figure had increased to 3.72. Much more needs to be discovered about the precise relationship between that original mortality decline and incipient fertility reduction, subsequent mortality decline and the living standards of families.

Despite the general similarity in the timing of the initial reductions in infant and child mortality, the pace of change was often quite different. Once rapid decline became widespread, a decrease of one third in IMRs took, for example, almost 25 years in Alicante, and about 30 years in central Spain. Similar improvement in child mortality was much faster: about 10 years in Alicante and 15 in central Spain. The result of this process was that, even though child mortality dipped below infant mortality for the first time in 1902 in the central part of the country, not until 1912 (or even 1920) was there a clear difference between the two indicators. In Alicante, this crossover did not take place until the early 1920s, mainly because IMRs there were initially so much lower than child mortality.

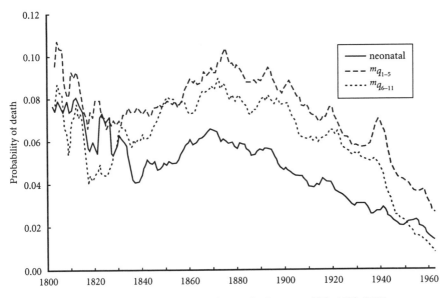

Fig. 2.3. Central Spain: Mortality during the first year of life, 1800–1965
(five-year moving averages)

If we look at mortality during the first year of life, more heterogeneity becomes apparent. Figure 2.3 contains three infant mortality indicators for central Spain, representing different periods of a child's early life. Mortality of children under 1 month of age ('neonat') is largely influenced by congenital defects, birth weight (related to the mother's nutritional status) and certain environmentally caused factors. Between 1 and 5 months of age (early post-neonatal mortality, $^m q_{1-5}$), most children had the more or less full protection of their mother's milk, while between 6 and 11 months (late post-neonatal mortality, $^m q_{6-11}$) supplementary feeding was the norm and teething had begun. As they grew older, environmental factors became increasingly important. Despite the protection afforded by breastfeeding, in most contexts the likelihood of death decreases as the infant gets older. This pattern held in the contexts studied here, though much less so than might be imagined. Late post-neonatal mortality was only slightly below early post-neonatal mortality. In fact, in central Spain mortality between 6 and 11 months of age became significantly lower than mortality in early infancy only after 1940.[7]

The pattern we observed earlier of an initial period of gradual and interrupted decline, followed by significant reductions holds for all our indicators, as does the rise in mortality levels during the middle decades of the nineteenth century. In central Spain, pre-transitional neonatal mortality was around 60 per 1,000; decline started in the 1870s, and the 50 per 1,000 barrier was crossed towards the end of the century. The downward route of neonatal mortality was fairly regular, and between 1870 and 1930 trend reversals were only modest. The variability of other indicators was somewhat higher and decline was much faster than in the case of neonatal mortality. On this count, the reduction in late post-neonatal infant mortality was greatest and began earliest, although the starting-point was often only a few years earlier than for early post-neonatal mortality. Finally, the important trend reversal that took place in all samples during and just after the Civil War is most noteworthy, because once again nearly 'historic' levels of post-neonatal mortality can be observed.

Mortality for older children is also far from uniform. In Figures 2.4 and 2.5, where we have generated probabilities of death for children aged 1 to 6 in central Spain (q_x, where $x = 1$ to 6), this variety of mortality patterns can be readily observed. The most striking heterogeneity is unquestionably shown by the mortality of children 1 or 2 years of age, which underwent very early and significant declines. At higher ages decline did not set in until the latter years of the nineteenth century. In central Spain the earliest childhood mortality rate to decline was that of children 2 years of age (from the mid-1850s), followed closely by that of 1-year-olds (a decade later). Higher-age rates, on the other hand, aborted any incipient downward trend in the late 1880s, and during most of the rest of the century remained at levels that can be considered higher than earlier levels.

These patterns can, in part, be directly attributed to the cholera and measles

---

[7] Given the way in which these indicators were generated, the late post-neonatal death rates substantially underestimate the likelihood of death at that age. Had we been able to weight births acceptably well, late infant mortality would have been considerably higher than mortality between 1 and 5 months of age.

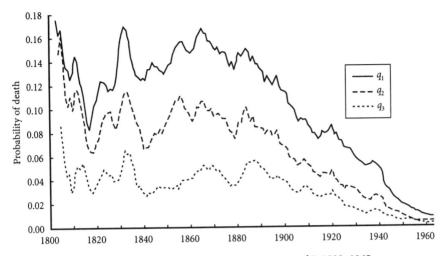

Fig. 2.4. Central Spain: Mortality between ages 1 and 3, 1800–1965
(five-year moving averages)

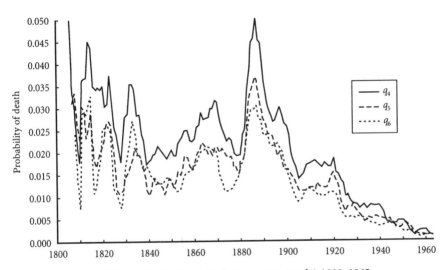

Fig. 2.5. Central Spain: Mortality between ages 4 and 6, 1800–1965
(five-year moving averages)

epidemics of the second half of the 1880s. These epidemics left q_0s, q_1s and q_2s basically
unaffected in central Spain. Mortality at other ages, however, was sharply, even drastic-
ally, affected. The trend reversal for those ages, however, does not appear to have been
only a result of 2 or 3 years of epidemics, since levels were either on the rise or substantially higher than those obtaining earlier for as long as 15 or 20 years. It would be very
risky to speak of any sort of mortality transition at these ages before the very final years

of the nineteenth century. Once decline was a fact of life at all of these ages, however, there were still important interruptions. The most important and lasting of these took place more or less from 1905 to 1920, when declines of all sorts and at all ages slowed, and were even reversed at some ages (especially during later childhood). This reversal is very evident in our data and was certainly not caused by any succession of epidemics. We have yet to find an adequate explanation for it.[8]

Judging from the data presented here, the key mortality decline in both samples occurred among 1- and 2-year-old children and, to a lesser extent, older infants (6–11 months). When mortality began to decline among them, it did so dramatically. In the initial 30 years of decline, q_1s went down by 27 per cent in central Spain and by nearly 50 per cent in Alicante. Since mortality at 1 and 2 years of age was a key component in overall child mortality, the result was to diminish overall $_4q_1$s, despite the fact that at other ages mortality was rising. We have yet to pinpoint the reasons why these ages were the first to fall—although feeding practices, nutritional status and the changing structure of epidemic disease are all potentially important factors. These ages were the pioneers of the mortality transition, pioneers by as much as 30 or 40 years in some cases.

EVALUATING RELATIVE INTENSITIES OF MORTALITY DECLINE DURING EARLY LIFE

In earlier pages we have made numerous references to the differing intensities of mortality change among indicators. Even though our estimates have been crude, the issue is important because of the differences that have appeared. Mortality declined much faster at some ages and in some contexts than others. The key to these differential rates of decline must lie in the specific way in which each age group reacted to changes in feeding habits, nutritional standards, public health measures and living standards or to the varying structure of epidemic disease. There are many different ways of estimating the intensity of mortality decline; some are quite straightforward like the ones used above, others somewhat less so. The method chosen depends on the analytical purpose it is to serve. Up until now, we have used simple measures that have been good only for limited comparisons.

In the following paragraphs, we would like to propose a way of graphically representing the internal dynamics of mortality decline within the samples used so far. We will use general mortality (crude death rates) as our baseline value, and will compare trends in other mortality indicators to the general pattern of overall mortality change. All mortality indicators have been turned into index numbers, with a value of 1.00 for the 1871–1880 period. Subsequently the series of each individual mortality indicator has been deflated by the value of the series of crude death rates indices. The resulting series

---

[8] A fuller explanation of these timing differences in the onset of decline and in trend changes will have to await more detailed cause-of-death analysis, which will be carried out in the course of the research project.

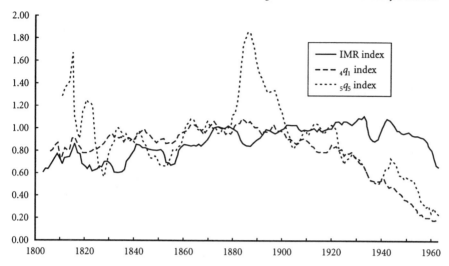

Fig. 2.6. Central Spain: Childhood mortality relative to crude death rates, 1800–1965
Note: Index values of five-year moving averages: 1871–1880 = 100.

will portray the value of a given indicator relative to the crude death rate. If in a particular year the value is 0.75, say, this means that a given indicator has declined by 25 per cent more (or has increased by 25 per cent less) than overall mortality. In other words, once the different indicators have been deflated by the overall mortality index, the line corresponding to 1.00 in the figure represents the detrended performance of the crude death rate.

The results relating to our basic categories of early-age mortality (IMR, $_4q_1$ and $_5q_5$), which can be found in Figure 2.6, are eloquent. The increase in mortality during the middle years of the nineteenth century, which appeared above, was not just part of a generalized mortality increase, but was specific to children. In central Spain, there are indications that between 1855 and the 1880s the share of childhood mortality in general mortality patterns was increasing substantially. The increase was more apparent among children over 5 but affected all ages. A surprising aspect of the data is that declines in IMRs only surpass those of crude death rates at a very late date, if at all. Only after the Civil War are infant mortality declines significant relative to overall mortality trends. The same cannot be said for child mortality, where relative gains already characterized the final decade or two of the nineteenth century. The situation for later child mortality ($_5q_5$) was similar, but gains were never as early or as great as those of $_4q_1$s.

Within the first year of life, the relative position of mortality began to improve for children between 6 and 11 months of age only during the 1930s in the central part of the country (Figure 2.7). Other indicators of mortality during the first year of life showed no decline at all until after the end of the Civil War, and much later in the rural areas of central Spain. In many ways, these data suggest that the transition of infant mortality in this part of the country was incomplete, probably owing to the relatively

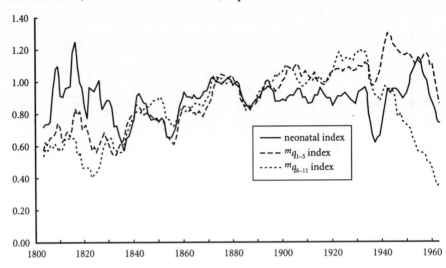

Fig. 2.7. Central Spain: Mortality during the first year of life relative to crude death rates, 1800–1965

Note: Index values of five-year moving averages: 1871–1880 = 100.

lower levels of wealth, maternal education and development of the health system. This differential mortality transition during the first year of life is an important issue for future research.

At higher ages, relative decline started earlier and was much more pervasive (Figure 2.8). Striking regularities can be observed across the different samples. In all cases, q_1 and q_2 are the first to decline, starting in the 1870s and 1880s. After 1920, the rate of decline of higher-age children becomes more prominent. Even though the pioneers of the mortality transition were 1- and 2-year-old children, in the long run mortality decline at higher ages became just as important as that of younger children, or even more important. Infants, however, especially very young ones, lagged behind and mortality gains among them were seldom as pronounced as those for the population as a whole. The general process by which the age structure of childhood mortality became younger as levels became lower was informed by considerable heterogeneity in the trends of individual indicators.

We have been talking about relative gains in mortality at different childhood ages. This does not detract from the fact that mortality among children before their second birthdays showed the sharpest decline in the samples we have used. Once again, children between 6 months and 2 years of age played a leading role, because it was among them that mortality was extremely high—much higher, for example, than in northern Europe—and it was among them that mortality declined first and, at least in its initial stages, most. Consequently, the weight of infant mortality, and especially mortality during the first 6 months of life, became increasingly important during the course of the demographic transition. The rejuvenation of mortality has characterized most

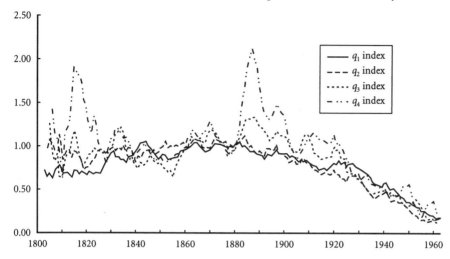

Fig. 2.8. Central Spain: Mortality between ages 1 and 4 relative to crude death rates, 1800–1965
Note: Index values of five-year moving averages: 1871–1880 = 100.

mortality transitions all over the world. We have shown how the routes to lower and younger mortality were mapped out in Spain. Whether or not this was the only route to younger mortality structures in other Mediterranean and non-Mediterranean contexts remains to be seen.

ISSUES FOR DISCUSSION AND FUTURE RESEARCH

A number of conclusions regarding childhood mortality decline can be tentatively advanced in the light of the data presented in this chapter. Some of these are methodological and others are substantive; some are hypotheses that require further research and others merely suggest potential lines of inquiry, some are specifically Spanish while others may well be relevant to geographically wider historical contexts. All of them contribute to deepening and widening our understanding of mortality processes and may well be instrumental in fine-tuning the analytical perspectives we use when dealing with the mortality transition.

The most noteworthy of these conclusions is that the entire process of mortality change has proven to be heterogeneous. Not only have the expected regional differences in the levels and intensity of change appeared, but internal differences have emerged that should caution us against simple blanket explanations of childhood mortality. As a minimum, we must differentiate between infant and child mortality, since the timing and intensity of trend changes for each were quite different. Both of these were composed of other indicators that did not necessarily behave in the same manner. In this way, mortality rates among 1- and 2-year-old children, and to a lesser extent children 6–11 months of age, led the decline, whereas among younger infants and older children the onset of change took place much later. As much as 30 or 40 years separated the trend changes between different indicators. Certain similarities in patterns of behaviour across our regional samples have been noticed. The heterogeneity of mortality is unquestionably common to all societies, though it is unclear whether the specific patterns observed here are applicable elsewhere. We feel that this heterogeneity is highly significant to mortality change and must be taken into consideration whenever possible. To consider infant mortality transitions as a uniform process is to underestimate their inherent complexity and may well make it difficult to pinpoint the constituent contexts that brought them about.

A considerable number of infant and child mortality indicators have been generated, and they have been instrumental in revealing this diversity. Others can and perhaps will be generated, though this may not be necessary. It is unquestionable that without data of this kind it is impossible to assess the complexity of change adequately. Generating yearly time-series has also proven to be very useful because it has enabled us to see cyclical swings and trend changes much more clearly than would otherwise have been possible. In the course of this chapter, we have proposed one way of assessing the relative intensity of mortality change by using crude death rate indices as a baseline value. This is not the only way of evaluating the pace of change, but the results have been illustrative of both the regional and structural differences inherent in the mortality transition. Other ways of looking at these data must still be tried.

The time-span of mortality analysis is crucial. Any coherent explanation of change must include data covering the entire period of transition, along with pre-transitional estimates of basic trends. In this sense, the period of analysis we have chosen for Spain has also proven to be most useful because it has spanned the entire process. Had only published official data been used, it would have been impossible to understand childhood mortality transitions in Spain adequately. Even if the appropriate indicators could have been generated from these data, they would have given a misleading view of a mortality transition that had, in some cases, started three or four decades earlier. In other contexts, it may well be useful to begin mortality analysis at an earlier date.[9]

Spanish data suggest that with some mortality indicators there was a two-step process of decline. During an initial period lasting as long as 20 or 25 years, levels declined very slowly and trend reversals were not uncommon. This was followed by a period of far more rapid decline, one in which interruptions were much less important. Where this pattern does hold, it raises two interesting issues. In the first place, it is plausible that the causes of incipient and of intense mortality declines were quite different and that they may well have been related differentially to such factors as living standards, public health measures and the exact make-up of prevailing disease structures. Second, the implications of each step for the demographic realities of families were certainly different. We feel that incipient change probably had important and measurable effects on the economic and demographic realities of the family reproductive process. It may also

---

[9] Catalonia and the Balearic Islands are examples of Spanish contexts in which earlier starting-points for mortality analysis may be useful.

have been an important factor in paving the way for later and more rapid mortality decline. The extent to which this pattern of two-step decline holds in other historical contexts is a matter of speculation, but may well be worth ascertaining.

A number of substantive issues have been raised in the course of this chapter that will require further research before we are able to evaluate them properly. Examples of these issues are the increase in mortality during the middle decades of the nineteenth century, the halt in the decline between 1905 and the early 1920s, the disruptive effects of the epidemics of the 1880s and the Civil War and its aftermath, the relative importance of epidemics as opposed to 'normal' mortality patterns, the differing mortality structures in Alicante and central Spain, and the differential pace of decline in both regions and within the mortality indicators of each. For all of these issues, we feel that adequate research will be a three-stage process. The basic demographic reconstruction of patterns, much of which has been presented here, is the first one. The second stage will be the reconstruction of reliable cause-of-death series, which will enable us to assess the disease context of mortality change after 1838. Finally, before the dynamics of change can be assessed with the necessary precision and reliability, it will be necessary to generate contextual variables that reflect the social, economic, cultural and health factors involved. The issues are abundant and varied; addressing them with rigour and imagination is of the utmost importance.

Appendix 2.2

Infant mortality rates (IMRs) were generated according to the following formula:

$$\text{IMR} = \frac{D_{0,x}}{(B_{x-1} \times 0.2) + (B_x \times 0.8)},$$

where $D_{0,x}$ = deaths of infants 0 years of age in year x, and B_x = births in year x.

The probabilities of death at different ages were calculated as in the following example:

$$_1q_2 = \frac{D_{2,x}}{B_{x-2} - (D_{0,x-2} + D_{1,x-1})}.$$

For these probabilities, no attempt was made to weight the infant births or deaths, mainly because its effect on the estimations would have been minimal.

Additional indicators were calculated for the first year of life. This was done in a somewhat different way. Neonatal mortality rates (NMRs) were estimated as follows:

$$\text{NMR} = \frac{D_{0m,x}}{B_x},$$

where $D_{0m,x}$ = deaths of infants during their first month of life in year x, and B_x = births in year x.

Different types of post-neonatal mortality were estimated along the lines set out in the following example of mortality rates for children 1 and 2 months of age:

$$\text{TM}_{1-2m} = \frac{D_{1-2m,x}}{(B_x \times 0.833) + (B_{x-1} \times 0.167)}.$$

For the other monthly age groups (3–5, 6–8, 9–11), births were weighted as follows: 0.625 in year x and 0.375 in year $x-1$ for children 3–5 months of age, 0.375/0.625 (6–8 months) and 0.124/0.876 (9–11 months)—weights approximately equal to those existing for the United States in 1965 (Shryock *et al.* 1976: 238). This means that by definition these mortality rates during the first year of life are additive, and their sum is equivalent to the infant mortality rate. In order to simplify the results presented here, we used only three indicators of mortality during the first year of life: neonatal mortality, death rates between 1 and 5 months of age, and death rates between 6 and 11 months. By working in this fashion, the neonatal mortality rate generated is very close to the probability of death for children 0 months of age, whereas the rate for 6- to 11-month-old children is much lower than the actual probability of death would have been had we been able to estimate l_xs (the total number of survivors to exact age x) properly.

Table 2A.1. Spain: Summary description of local time-series used in this chapter

Place	Province	Dates	Source[a]	Population in 1887	Population in 1930
Alicante sample					
Alcolecha	Alicante	1860–1935	P	907	822
Alfaz del Pi	Alicante	1826–1975	P/C	1,200	1,101
La Algueña	Alicante	1866–1975	P/C	(1,526)[b]	(1,565)[b]
Altea	Alicante	1840–1919	P	5,790	5,484
Benidorm	Alicante	1839–1935	P	3,181	3,099
Benilloba	Alicante	1838–1975	P/C	1,392	1,028
Campello	Alicante	1849–1935	P	(2,834)[b]	2,908
Orba	Alicante	1871–1975	C	1,067	1,356
San Juan	Alicante	1871–1975	C	2,973	2,858
Total				20,870	20,221
Central Spain sample					
Bargas	Toledo	1821–1975	P/C	3,320	3,863
Buitrago de Lozoya	Madrid	1871–1950	C	658	787
Cabanillas de la Sierra	Madrid	1871–1950	C	282	326
Cadalso de los Vidrios	Madrid	1838–1975	P/C	1,899	2,289
Calzada de Oropesa	Toledo	1840–1975	P/C	2,246	2,561
Campo Real	Madrid	1887–1950	C	1,427	1,620
Carabaña	Madrid	1800–1970	P/C	1,741	2,393
Cebreros	Avila	1800–1960	P/C	3,878	4,655
Cenicientos	Madrid	1894–1950	C	2,155	2,941
Colmenar de Oreja	Madrid	1871–1941	C	5,813	5,659
Chinchón	Madrid	1838–1970	P/C	4,961	5,044
Escalona	Toledo	1808–1975	P/C	1,188	1,758
Escalonilla	Toledo	1766–1975	P/C	2,880	3,756
Gerindote	Toledo	1680–1975	P/C	1,452	2,079
Hoyo de Pinares	Avila	1840–1975	P/C	1,799	2,878
Jarandilla	Cáceres	1800–1975	P/C	1,819	2,539
Leganés	Madrid	1827–1975	P/C	4,524	5,050
Lillo	Toledo	1821–1975	P/C	2,723	3,748
Loeches	Madrid	1871–1975	C	948	1,041
Méntrida	Toledo	1800–1975	P/C	2,762	2,335
Miraflores de la Sierra	Madrid	1852–1950	P/C	1,494	1,649
Montejo de la Sierra	Madrid	1852–1950	P/C	529	447
Navalcarnero	Madrid	1867–1993	P/C	3,750	5,011

Table 2A.1. (*cont.*)

Place	Province	Dates	Source[a]	Population in 1887	Population in 1930
Navalmoral de la Mata	Cáceres	1815–1975	P/C	4,053	5,550
Oropesa	Toledo	1838–1975	P/C	2,710	4,210
Pozuelo de Alarcón	Madrid	1800–1975	P/C	1,521	4,064
La Puebla de Montalbán	Toledo	1800–1970	P	6,063	7,305
Quintanar de la Qrden	Toledo	1838–1975	P/C	7,443	9,498
El Romeral	Toledo	1871–1975	C	2,250	2,996
San Lorenzo de El Escorial	Madrid	1838–1950	P/C	3,233	6,068
San Martín de Valdeiglesias	Madrid	1852–1971	P/C	4,019	2,343
Santa Cruz de Retamar	Toledo	1841–1975	P/C	2,197	2,555
Sigüenza	Guadalajara	1871–1975	C	4,930	4,850
Sotillo de la Adrada	Avila	1889–1975	C	1,851	2,709
El Tiemblo	Avila	1898–1975	C	2,417	4,258
El Toboso	Toledo	1838–1975	P	1,904	2,985
Torrijos	Toledo	1679–1870	P/C	2,760	4,059
Valdeverdeja	Toledo	1838–1975	P/C	3,455	4,072
Yepes	Toledo	1817–1975	P/C	2,679	3,528
Total				107,733	135,479

[a] P = parish register; C = civil register.
[b] These places were integrated into other municipalities when these censuses were carried out, but kept vital registration records of their own. The population estimates are only approximations.

References

ARBELO CURBELO, A., 1962. *La mortalidad de la infancia en España, 1901–1950*, Madrid, Consejo Superior de Investigaciones Científicas.

CASELLI, G., 1994. 'National differences in the health transition in Europe', working paper, Population Research Institute, Indiana University.

COALE, A. J. and DEMENY, P., 1966. *Regional model life tables and stable populations*, New York: Academic Press (2nd edn 1983).

GÓMEZ REDONDO, R., 1992. *La mortalidad infantil española en el siglo XX*, Madrid, Siglo XXI and Centro de Investigaciones Sociológicas.

HAUSER, P., 1902. *Madrid bajo el punto de vista médico-social: su policía sanitaria, su climatología, su suelo y sus aguas, sus condiciones sanitarias, su demografía, su morbicidad y su mortalidad*, Madrid.

INSTITUTO NACIONAL DE ESTADÍSTICA, 1952. *Tablas de mortalidad de 1900 á 1940*, Madrid.

LANZA GARCÍA, R., 1991. *La población y el crecimiento económico de Cantabria en el Antiguo Régimen*, Madrid, Universidad Autónoma de Madrid and Universidad de Cantabria.

LIVI BACCI, M. and REHER, D. S., 1993. 'Other paths to the past: from vital series to population patterns' in D. S. REHER and R. S. SCHOFIELD (eds.), *Old and New Methods in Historical Demography*, Oxford, Clarendon Press.

MARTÍNEZ CARRIÓN, J. M., 1983. *La población de Yeste en los inicios de la transición demográfica, 1850–1935*, Albacete, Instituto de Estudios Albacetense.

MARTÍNEZ RODRÍGUEZ, E., 1992. 'La mortalidad infantil y juvenil en la Galicia urbana del

Antiguo Régimen: Santiago de Compostela, 1731–1810', *Obradoiro de Historia Moderna* 1, pp. 45–78.

MUÑOZ PRADAS, F., 1990. 'Creixement demogràfic, mortalitat i nupcialitat al Penedès (segles XVII–XIX)', doctoral dissertation, Universitat Autònoma de Barcelona.

NADAL OLLER, J., 1956. 'Demografía y economía en el orígen de la Cataluña Moderna: un ejemplo local: Palamós (1705–1839)', *Estudios de Historia Moderna* 6, pp. 281–309; reprinted in J. NADAL OLLER, 1992. *Bautismos, desposorios y entierros: estudios de historia demográfica*, Barcelona, Ariel.

OLIVARES, C. and VINAL, T., 1988. 'El comportamiento de la mortalidad en los inicios de la transición demográfica (aproximación al caso del Bajo Segura, 1850–1935)', in C. PÉREZ APARICIO (ed.), *Estudis sobre la població del País Valencià*, vol. 2, Valencia, Edicions Alfons El Magnanim/Institut d'Estudis Juan Gil Albert.

PASCUA, M., 1934. *La mortalidad infantil en España*, Madrid, Dirección General de Sanidad.

PIQUERO, S., 1991. *Demografía guipuzcoana en el Antiguo Régimen*, Bilbao, Universidad del País Vasco.

PÉREZ-MOREDA, V., 1980. *Las crisis de mortalidad en la España interior, siglos XVI–XIX*, Madrid, Siglo XXI.

REHER, D. S., 1990. *Town and country in pre-industrial Spain: Cuenca, 1550–1870*, Cambridge, Cambridge University Press.

—— 1991. 'Dinámicas demográficas en Castilla la Nueva 1550–1900: un ensayo de reconstrucción', in J. NADAL OLLER (ed.), *La evolución demográfica bajo los Austrias*, proceedings of the second Congreso de la Asociación de Demografía Histórica, April, vol. 3, Alicante, Instituto de Cultura Juan Gil Albert.

—— 1995. 'Wasted investments: some economic implications of childhood mortality patterns', *Population Studies* 49(3), pp. 519–536.

SHRYOCK, H. S., SIEGEL, J. S. *et al.*, 1976. *The methods and materials of demography*, condensed edn by E. G. STOCKWELL, New York, Academic Press.

SOLER SERRATOSA, J., 1985. 'Demografía y sociedad en Castilla la Nueva durante el Antiguo Régimen: la Villa de los Molinos, 1620–1730', *Revista Española de Investigaciones Sociológicas* 32, pp. 141–190.

3

Differential Mortality Patterns among Infants and Other Young Children: *The Experience of England and Wales in the Nineteenth Century*

ROBERT WOODS, NAOMI WILLIAMS AND CHRIS GALLEY

There is a long-standing convention—almost a general 'rule'—in the demographic literature that the infant mortality rate (IMR or q_0) will normally be higher than the early childhood mortality rate (ECMR or $_4q_1$). All four families of Coale and Demeny's (1983) model life-tables (with the exception of South, levels 1–5) follow this rule and the implications are also adopted, albeit implicitly, in the various editions of UNICEF's *State of the world's children* (see, for example, UNICEF 1994). In this short and preliminary chapter we begin to challenge the assumptions that underpin this convention. Most of our examples are drawn from England and Wales in the nineteenth century, but our arguments and the implications to be drawn therefrom have a wider significance, which we shall attempt to elaborate (see also Woods, Williams and Galley 1993).

We are faced with three tasks: (i) to establish counter-examples to the general demographic 'rule of thumb' that, regardless of life expectancy at birth, ECMR will not exceed IMR, and ECMR will not vary either over time or through space in a way that is substantially independent of IMR; (ii) to suggest reasons why, under certain circumstances, one might expect ECMR to be greater than IMR and for the two rates to vary in a largely independent fashion; and (iii) to draw some implications for work by demographers on high-mortality societies in general.

COUNTER-EXAMPLES TO THE GENERAL RULE

Using the full official English Life-Tables 1–9, Figure 3.1 sketches out the changing relationship between IMR/ECMR and life expectancy at birth in England and Wales between 1841 and 1920–1922. Clearly, infant mortality did not contribute to the general improvement in life expectancy at birth from 40 years to the late 40s, but early childhood mortality did. By the 1870s, ECMR was in full and precipitous decline and life expectancy was poised at levels previously unknown in English history. These low and declining levels of ECMR were subsequently reinforced by the secular decline of IMR. While there were substantial, and only-to-be-expected, differences between male

C.A. Corsini and P.P. Viazzo (eds.) The Decline of Infant and Child Mortality, 57-72.
© *1997 UNICEF. Printed in the Netherlands.*

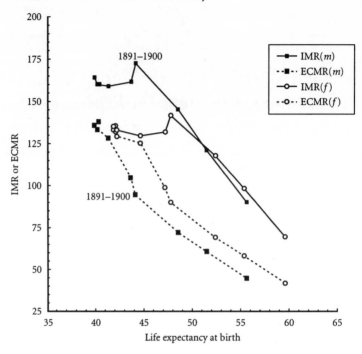

Fig. 3.1. England and Wales: The changing pattern of IMR and ECMR (males and females) related to life expectancy at birth, 1841, 1838–1844, 1838–1854, 1871–1880, 1881–1890, 1891–1900, 1901–1910, 1910–1912 and 1920–1922

Source: English Life Tables 1–9.

and female IMRs, certainly until the 1900s, these differences were far less obvious for ECMRs. Consequently, although IMRs were consistently higher than ECMRs for males, this was by no means always the case for females. Figure 3.1 helps to set the scene for the arguments we wish to present: it illustrates the possibility that IMR and ECMR do not always trend together; that in general—although not always in detail—IMR and ECMR vary inversely with life expectancy at birth; and that there are gender differences in some aspects of early-age as well as overall mortality levels.

However, Figure 3.1 has too many dimensions to make its interpretation a simple matter. Figure 3.2 shows time-series for probabilities of dying by single years of age from 0 (IMR) to 4 years as well as ECMR (1–4 inclusive). The picture is much clearer now. While ECMR began its downward secular trend in the 1850s, IMR stayed at or above 150 deaths per 1,000 live births until the turn of the century. Again the point is reinforced: for the second half of the nineteenth century in England and Wales, IMR and ECMR moved independently, and in 1863 ECMR was actually higher than IMR. The years 1911 and 1918 are also of special note. In 1911 infants, but not other young children, were especially prone to the ravages of 'summer diarrhoea', while in 1918 young children, but not infants, fell victim to the influenza pandemic.

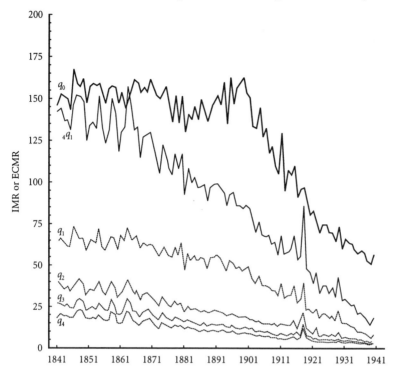

Fig. 3.2. England and Wales: Annual IMR and ECMR series, and q_1, q_2, q_3 and q_4, 1841–1941

Figure 3.3 traces the ratio of IMR to ECMR throughout the period covered by Figure 3.2. It shows that the ratio varied between 1.00 and 1.25 in the middle decades of the century, before beginning a steady increase that was interrupted during periods in which the rate of change of IMR accelerated or decelerated in relation to the rate of change of ECMR. What is emphasized by Figure 3.3 is the rather distinctive—and per-haps peculiar—nature of the relationships between the various components of early-age mortality during the middle of the nineteenth century.

Of course what is not clear from either Figure 3.2 or Figure 3.3 is that, although ECMR was in excess of IMR for only one year when national rates are considered, such averages disguise considerable geographical differences. Figure 3.4 helps us to begin the process of identifying these important spatial patterns, which may reflect considerable epidemiological and environmental variations. It illustrates the association between ECMR and IMR using the 614 districts into which England and Wales were divided for the purposes of civil registration between the 1840s and 1910. The almost-parallel curves represent second-order polynomials that summarize these associations in the 1860s and the 1890s. Clearly, in the 1860s there were certain districts in which ECMR was in excess of IMR, but there were no such districts in the 1890s, because by this time ECMRs had fallen everywhere. Figure 3.4 also traces the association embedded in Coale

Robert Woods, Naomi Williams and Chris Galley

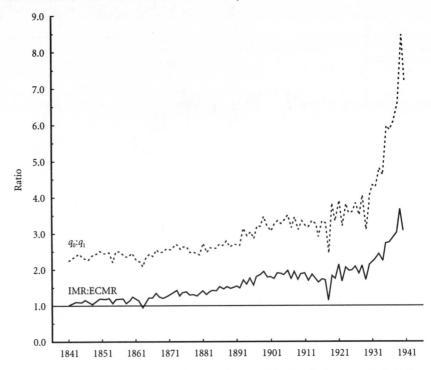

Fig. 3.3. England and Wales: Annual ratios of IMR to ECMR and of q_0 to q_1, 1841–1941

and Demeny's West and North families of model life-tables. The point on the North (N) line at the extreme top right (missing on West) represents the IMR and ECMR appropriate to a life expectancy at birth of 20 years. The next point down towards the bottom left represents 25 years, and so on in five-year increments.

Although nationally and for many of the registration districts one of the two models gives a reasonable approximation of the relationship between ECMR and IMR and the implied level of life expectancy at birth, it is also clear that in the 1890s and especially the 1860s places with high mortality deviated considerably from the model relationships. ECMR was excessive compared to IMR. The places and populations to which this remark applies were not a random cross-section of the total set of districts, however. Figure 3.5 shows that, in the 1860s, 57 of the 614 districts (9 per cent) experienced excess ECMRs, although they contained 28.5 per cent of the total population of England and Wales. Of these 57, 34 (containing 21.9 per cent of the population) also had population densities greater than, or equal to, 1,000 persons per square kilometre (in all there were 66 districts in 1861 with such high and obviously urban population densities, and they contained 31.3 per cent of the population). Although not all the urban districts of England and Wales experienced conditions of excess ECMR in the mid-nineteenth century, many did. One of the principal reasons that urban places were

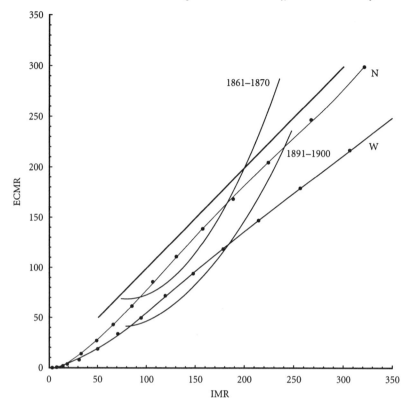

Fig. 3.4. England and Wales: The association between ECMR and IMR
among registration districts, 1861–1870 and 1891–1900

Note: Life expectancies at birth from Coale and Demeny's North (N) and West (W) models are also shown.

likely to experience high mortality was simply that their young populations faced not only high mortality in infancy, but especially high—often even higher—mortality in early childhood. By the last decade of the century the curves in figures 3.4 and 3.5 reveal that ECMR had fallen regardless of the level of IMR; exactly the point being made in Figure 3.2.

Finally, let us for the sake of completeness illustrate the various relationships between IMR and ECMR and population density and how these relationships changed during the last half of the nineteenth century. Figure 3.6 helps in this matter. It shows four regression lines, together with the regression equations, describing the associations between IMR or ECMR and the log of population density for the 1860s and the 1890s. It also gives the distributions for $IMR_{1861-1870}$ and $ECMR_{1891-1900}$. Note the position of the regression lines, the angle of their slopes and the degree of fit given by r^2. Clearly, in each of the four cases there is a strong, statistically significant and positive relationship between mortality in childhood and population density. In the case of $IMR_{1861-1870}$

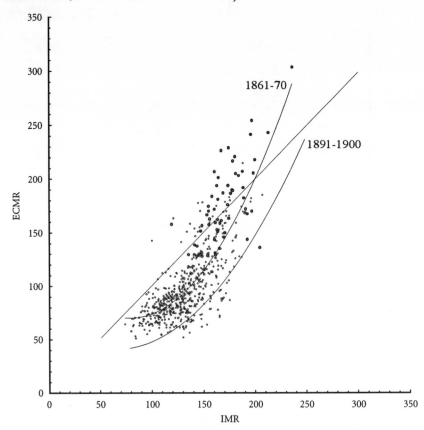

Fig. 3.5. England and Wales: The association between ECMR and IMR
among registration districts, 1861–1870 and 1891–1900

Note: The figure shows the distribution for 1861–1870 in full and emphasizes those 66 urban districts with
population densities over 1,000 persons per km² in 1861.

(line 1) there is a relatively poor fit, with many low-density districts experiencing rather
high IMRs, to the extent that the relationship would be better represented by two curves:
one for below 200 persons per square kilometre and one for above that population
density. For $IMR_{1891-1900}$ (line 3) this is less of a problem; the fit is better and, according
to the slope of the line, there has been some decline in infant mortality at low population densities. ECMR is rather more interesting. The association is particularly strong
for $ECMR_{1861-1870}$ (line 2), but weakens a little for $ECMR_{1891-1900}$ (line 4). Although the
angle of the slope diminishes, reflecting the general decline in ECMR, the reduction is
relatively greater at higher population densities. Line 2 crosses line 1 as one would expect from Figure 3.5.

   In sum, early childhood mortality not only displays a closer association with population density than infant mortality, but unlike infant mortality it also shows substantial

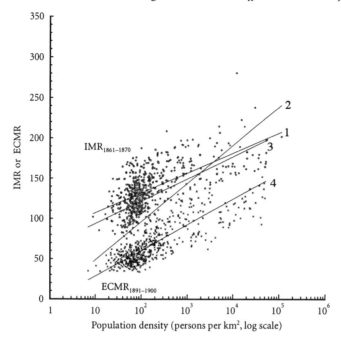

Fig. 3.6. England and Wales: The relationship between IMR and ECMR and population
density (PD) among 614 districts, 1861–1870 and 1891–1900

(1) $IMR_{1861-1870} = 24.100 \log(PD_{1861}) + 83.044$ $r^2 = 0.394$
(2) $ECMR_{1861-1870} = 46.360 \log(PD_{1861}) + 3.937$ $r^2 = 0.717$
(3) $IMR_{1891-1900} = 27.067 \log(PD_{1891}) + 66.850$ $r^2 = 0.500$
(4) $ECMR_{1891-1900} = 30.924 \log(PD_{1891}) - 1.518$ $r^2 = 0.644$

Note: For illustrative purposes the distributions for $IMR_{1861-1870}$ and $ECMR_{1891-1900}$ are shown in detail.

decline over the period, particularly at high levels. Excess early childhood mortality in
the 1860s is confirmed at the upper end of the range of rates and thus at higher population densities.

Figures 3.1–3.6 have, in large part, achieved their objective: they have provided
counter-examples to the general demographic rule that, regardless of life expectancy at
birth, ECMR will not exceed IMR, and ECMR will not vary either over time or through
space in a way that is substantially independent of IMR. Our second task is now to
suggest reasons for these apparent abnormalities.

REASONS

We shall review, in varying degrees of detail, four possible reasons or explanations for
some of the eccentric patterns illustrated above.

First, is it possible that what we have shown for late-nineteenth-century England and

Wales was particular to that place and period? This is a surprisingly difficult question to answer. It is clear that mid-nineteenth-century Sweden experienced a cyclical upturn in ECMR, while the secular decline of IMR was maintained (Fridlizius 1989; Woods 1993). It also seems possible that central Spain was experiencing similar increases in ECMR at about the same time (see Chapter 2 above). In France, ECMR declined from mid-century and before IMR; however, there were no years of excess ECMR, certainly at a national level (Meslé and Vallin 1991, 50).

Second, is it possible that we are exaggerating the general significance of some per-haps isolated examples by emphasizing the importance of short-run fluctuations at the expense of medium- to long-term trends? In other words, are our counter-examples simply temporary aberrations? This is quite possible, since it appears from preliminary results drawn from pooled family reconstitution studies and prepared by Professor E. A. Wrigley and his team at the Cambridge Group for the History of Population and Social Structure that, before the nineteenth century in England, IMR and ECMR did trend together and that the former was always well in excess of the latter. In the larger cities, however, other evidence suggests that ECMRs were more volatile and that similar increases may have occurred during the second half of the seventeenth century (Galley, 1994). Of particular significance, though, is the fact that the period covered in Figure 3.2—approximately that from the mid-nineteenth century to the Second World War—represents one of very considerable change in terms of both mortality and fertility. This was a period of secular change on a scale not previously encountered in European population history. It was also a time of unprecedented urbanization. Although some of the phenomena to which we refer may have been short-lived they certainly occurred in, and had a potentially striking bearing on, that part of our recent past that saw the origins of the contemporary demographic regime in Europe. As such, they occupy a critical position in the first urban-industrial nation's demography and serve to illustrate once again just how non-conformist that demography was in the eighteenth and nine-teenth centuries (see Wrigley 1983).

Third, nineteenth-century England and Wales may have experienced a particular form of epidemiological regime not only as a consequence of their high level of urbaniz-ation, but also because much of that urbanization was concentrated in a relatively small number of very large cities. By 1851, 54 per cent of the total population was urban; a quarter of which was concentrated in just 10 cities of over 100,000 inhabitants (Law 1967). Here, the argument is that rapid urbanization encouraged high mortality from those childhood diseases that are especially responsive to the crowding of susceptibles, such as measles, and that it also perpetuated those urban sanitary conditions that—through water-borne diseases in general and 'summer diarrhoea' in particular—delayed the precipitous decline of infant mortality (Woods, Watterson and Woodward 1988, 1989; Williams and Mooney 1994).

Fourth, and as a development of our third point, what were the underlying epidemi-ological processes that could have created the observed patterns in IMR and ECMR? It is certainly clear from Figure 3.2 that during the 1850s and 1860s ECMR showed violent short-run fluctuations entirely consistent with the activity of epidemics among young

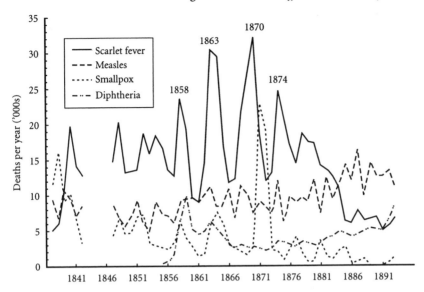

Fig. 3.7. England and Wales: Annual deaths from
scarlet fever, measles, smallpox and diphtheria, 1837–1893

children. Thereafter, these fluctuations subsided somewhat and the secular decline
began. It remains to be seen, however, whether, as in Sweden, this decline was from a
high level reached as a consequence of an earlier cyclical upturn.

In the *Supplements* to their *Annual reports*, the Registrars General of Births, Deaths
and Marriages for England and Wales provided detailed information on the causes of
death of the population disaggregated by age group and district. These data are available
for the decades 1851–1860 to 1901–1910, although the nosology was radically altered
in 1901. The *Annual reports* themselves also provide information on the numbers of
deaths from different causes. These were used by one of Britain's most distinguished
Victorian epidemiologists, Charles Creighton, in his monumental work *A history of
epidemics in Britain* (1894). Creighton illustrated the important epidemiological differences between the major childhood diseases by considering annual fluctuations in
cause-of-death patterns. For example, Figure 3.7 shows annual series of deaths from
smallpox, measles, scarlet fever and diphtheria for England and Wales between 1837
and 1893 using Creighton's statistics. The steady rise of measles and diphtheria, the
near elimination of smallpox, punctuated by some late epidemics (Williams 1994), and
the mid-century dominance, and subsequent decline, of scarlet fever are all clearly represented. However, Figure 3.7 does not consider these various causes of death in an age-
related manner, and this is of special importance for mortality in childhood (Woods
1994). Figure 3.8 considers the under-5 mortality profiles for the same four diseases in
the 1860s and 1890s. Smallpox certainly continued to decline among all young children
during the second half of the nineteenth century, but even by 1861 was already of only

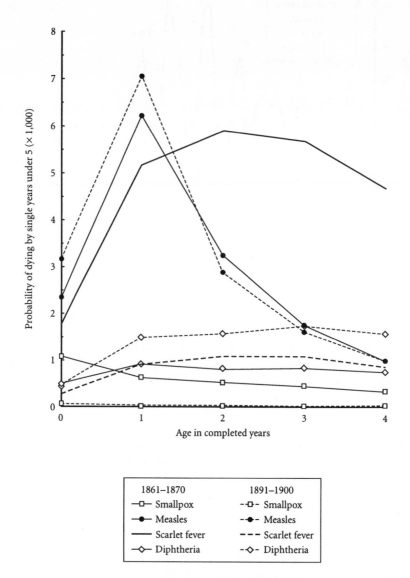

Fig. 3.8. England and Wales: Mortality by single years of age under 5 resulting from smallpox, measles, scarlet fever and diphtheria, 1861–1870 and 1891–1900 compared

minor demographic importance. Measles remained a substantial killer of young children throughout the century—especially of those in their second year—and diphtheria increased somewhat in importance, but was of far less significance than measles (Nelson 1994). However, it is to scarlet fever that most attention should be given, not only because it was the most significant of the four diseases, but also because it mainly affected children aged 1–4 and it declined sharply between the middle and the end of the nineteenth century. For these reasons scarlet fever will be singled out for special attention here.

First, however, it is important to establish the relative positions of causes of death like measles and scarlet fever in relation to ECMR in comparison with those diseases that particularly influence IMR. Figure 3.9 provides some examples. Diarrhoea and dysentery were especially important as causes of death among children in their first and, to a lesser extent, their second years of life. For infants, mortality rates from diarrhoea and dysentery were worse in the 1890s than the 1860s. For 'diseases of the lung' (1860s), which, because of changes in classification, is comparable to 'respiratory diseases' in the 1890s, mortality rates were even higher and they were also worse in the 1890s than in the 1860s, even among children in their second year. Even allowing for the diagnostic problems associated with the reporting of causes of infant deaths (see Williams 1996), figures 3.8 and 3.9 establish convincingly that individual childhood diseases had distinct age-specific mortality profiles; that while some diseases maintained roughly constant mortality rates between the 1860s and the 1890s others—notably smallpox and scarlet fever—declined, and still others increased. While lung and respiratory diseases and diarrhoea and dysentery continued to contribute so substantially to IMR there could be little prospect of substantial decline.

Let us return again to the case of scarlet fever, which appears from Figures 3.7–3.9 to hold a key place in any attempt to explain differential trends for IMR and ECMR and even for occasions when ECMR exceeded IMR, as in 1863 at a national level. Hardy (1993*a*, 990–992) provided a valuable outline of the disease's changing aetiology. Scarlet fever was not properly understood and isolated until the 1920s. The punctate rash on the upper chest and back accompanied by the characteristic raspberry-coloured tongue gave the disease highly distinctive symptoms that were relatively simple to recognize, well before the isolation of the streptococci responsible. A more virulent strain of the disease appeared during the 1820s and 1830s, making scarlet fever the leading cause of death in early childhood until 1875; but in the 1880s and 1890s the disease adopted a milder form. Elsewhere, Hardy (1993*b*, 79) concluded:

The history of scarlet fever in the later nineteenth century cannot convincingly be related to any of the preventive measures taken against it. It is possible that greater awareness of the 'sore throat', assisted by rising diphtheria incidence, led to cases being isolated earlier, thus reducing their infective impact. But the continuing high incidence of the disease, the medical profession's ignorance of its cause and true aetiology, the beginning of its decline before notification and systematic hospitalisation, the statistical evidence of declining case-fatality, and impressionistic evidence of a milder type all contribute to the judgement that preventive measures were largely irrelevant to the declining fatality of the disease after 1870.

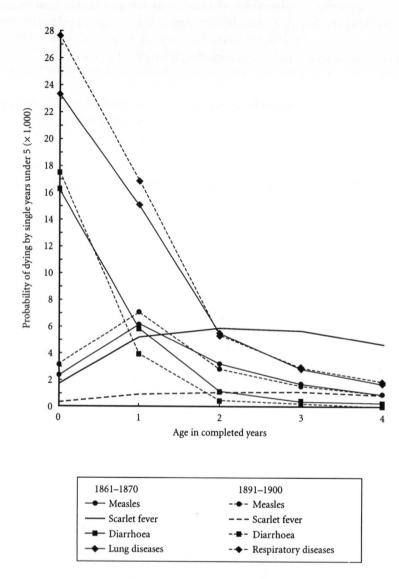

Fig. 3.9. England and Wales: Mortality by single years of age under 5 resulting from measles, scarlet fever, diarrhoea and dysentery, and lung and respiratory diseases, 1861–1870 and 1891–1900 compared

If Hardy is correct in her assertions—and there is every reason to believe that she is—then autonomous changes in the aetiology of scarlet fever had a most important bearing on the decline of ECMR in the late nineteenth century. They may have had a similarly dramatic but opposite effect on ECMR earlier in the century.

However, scarlet-fever ECMRs were not geographically uniform. As one might expect from figures 3.5 and 3.6, mortality rates were at their highest in the largest urban places, which encourages speculation that although aetiological changes may have been autonomous the size of the pool of infectives and the degree of their crowding, both conditioned by urban growth and urbanization, were in some measure responsible for the impact of scarlet fever on ECMR. This point may be partially illustrated using Figure 3.10, which shows the relationship between scarlet fever ECMR and the population sizes of districts in England and Wales in the 1860s and the 1890s. The strong positive association in the 1860s was just as strong in the 1890s, when scarlet fever mortality rates dropped to low levels.

The period in English history during which ECMR declined but IMR did not, and when, as a result of especially high ECMR in the largest urban places, the ratio of IMR to ECMR was remarkably low, may have been short lived, but it none the less offers some interesting insights into the epidemiological impact of urbanization, the autonomous

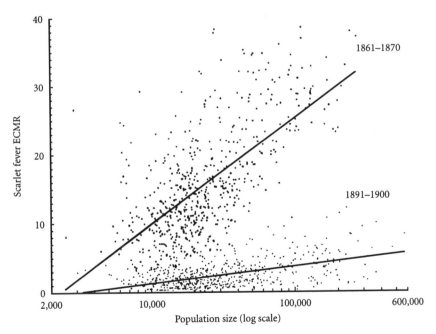

Fig. 3.10. England and Wales: Scarlet fever ECMRs by size of district populations, 1861–1870 and 1891–1900

$\text{ECMR}_{1861-1870}$: $y = 15.468 \log(x) - 51.916$ $r^2 = 0.428$
$\text{ECMR}_{1891-1900}$: $y = 2.463 \log(x) - 8.560$ $r^2 = 0.279$

change in at least one important disease (scarlet fever), the distinctive age-related pro-files of most childhood diseases and the persistence of at least moderate IMRs—even in the face of apparently substantial advances in public health—owing in large part to mortality from, for example, diarrhoea and dysentery and respiratory diseases in general.

IMPLICATIONS

In addition to the obvious points that can be made about the applicability of model life-tables to societies in which life expectancy at birth is less than 50 years, or where one or a number of the components of mortality are undergoing dramatic change, there are several implications to be drawn from the examples and speculations we have presented above.

First, the recent round of Demographic and Health Surveys has brought to light new examples of populations currently experiencing excess early childhood mortality (Sullivan, Rutstein and Bicego 1994). Mali, Senegal, Ghana and Togo—all West African states—have shown evidence of this, and it appears that children in the age group 2–4 years are especially vulnerable to the ravages of malaria and measles. It is also the case that, where the average age at weaning is about 24 months, deaths from diarrhoea-related diseases are especially prominent in the third year of life. In these circumstances both the practice of prolonged breastfeeding and the particular disease environment make it likely not only that early-age mortality will be especially high, but also that many deaths will be postponed from infancy to later years. The role of measles in both the historical European and the contemporary West African cases is particularly interesting, however. In nineteenth-century Europe measles was accompanied by scarlet fever, diphtheria, whooping cough and smallpox, but the average age at weaning was more likely to be 7–8 months than 24 and in some regions breastfeeding was un-common. The general level of child mortality (at 0–5 years) is, therefore, affected by the following factors: the duration, extent and quality of breastfeeding; the prevailing sanitary and pollution environments, which influence the water- and food-borne and respiratory diseases; the prevalence of the infectious diseases of childhood, each of which has its own aetiology and thus epidemiological history; and the extent of poverty, which can turn high levels of morbidity into high mortality. The Mosley–Chen analyt-ical framework for the study of child mortality thus requires some elaboration on these matters (Mosley and Chen 1984).

Second, the complications presented by the childhood diseases may also have in-teresting implications for attempts to use Bourgeois-Pichat's biometric test as a means of assessing the extent of underregistration (Wrigley 1977; Galley, Williams and Woods 1995). Although the test assumes a linear relationship between cumulative IMRs and age at death (transformed by $\log^3(n + 1)$, where n is age in days), significant deviations from linearity have been shown to exist within the first year of life as a result of variations in the extent, frequency and duration of breastfeeding (Knodel and Kintner

1977). Indeed, the timing of weaning is crucial in this respect. Once the immunological protection provided by breastfeeding ends, infants and young children are fully exposed to the particular risks of the epidemiological environment, as reflected in variable ECMRs. Such results suggest that because the biometric test encompasses such a wide margin of error it may be more appropriate to extend the test to cover the first four years of life rather than just the first year of life (Galley, Williams and Woods 1995).

Third, and in broader demographic terms, there are implications for the long and occasionally simple-minded debate on the links between mortality and fertility transitions. It has often been argued that, once infant mortality declines substantially, thereby increasing 'effective fertility', the secular decline of fertility will be initiated (Woods, Watterson and Woodward 1989). However, we have demonstrated in the first part of this chapter that IMR and ECMR represent quite distinct components of childhood mortality that are capable of varying independently. If the decline of marital fertility in late-nineteenth-century Europe was encouraged by the prior decline of mortality, then England and Wales provide yet another counter-example, so that the main component of mortality decline capable of influencing the calculus of rational choice in reproductive behaviour could only have been ECMR. Indeed, it might even be the case that the reduction of high-parity births actually assisted in the subsequent reduction of mortality in the first and second years of life.

Our purpose in writing this chapter has been to set out some preliminary arguments and provide some counter-examples to what demographers have long cherished as general rules. Our points and examples, we suggest, will help to cast a critical light not only on the manner in which mortality has changed its level and structure during the last two centuries, but also the key roles of urbanization, distinct disease environments and the particular aetiologies of individual diseases that have wrought such destruction among young children. Mortality in infancy and early childhood need to be differentiated in all populations with low life expectancy. Many important issues for health policy formation and several important questions that have a major bearing on our understanding of past and present demographies will be ignored if this simple guide is not adopted.

References

Coale, A. J. and Demeny, P., 1983. *Regional model life tables and stable populations*, 2nd edn, New York, Academic Press.

Creighton, C., 1894. *A history of epidemics in Britain*, vol. 2: *From the extinction of plague to the present time*, Cambridge, Cambridge University Press (reprinted 1964, London, Frank Cass).

Fridlizius, G., 1989. 'The deformation of cohorts: nineteenth century mortality decline in a generational perspective', *Scandinavian Economic History Review* 37, pp. 3–17.

Galley, C., 1994. 'A never-ending succession of epidemics: mortality in early-modern York', *Social History of Medicine* 7, pp. 29–57.

GALLEY, C., WILLIAMS, N. and WOODS, R. I., 1995. 'Detection without correction: problems in assessing the quality of English ecclesiastical and civil registration', *Annales de Démographie Historique*, pp. 159–182.

HARDY, A., 1993a. 'Scarlet fever', in K. F. KIPPLE (ed.), *The Cambridge world history of human disease*, Cambridge, Cambridge University Press.

—— 1993b. *The epidemic streets: infectious disease and the rise of preventive medicine, 1856–1900*, Oxford, Clarendon Press.

KNODEL, J. and KINTNER, H., 1977. 'The impact of breast feeding patterns on the biometric analysis of infant mortality', *Demography* 14, pp. 391–409.

LAW, C. M., 1967. 'The growth of urban population in England and Wales, 1801–1911', *Transactions of the Institute of British Geographers* 41, pp. 125–143.

MESLÉ, F. and VALLIN, J., 1991. 'Reconstitution of annual life tables for nineteenth-century France', *Population* (English selection) 3, pp. 33–62.

MOSLEY, W. H. and CHEN, L. C., 1984. 'An analytical framework for the study of child survival in developing countries', in W. H. MOSLEY and L. C. CHEN (eds.), *Child survival: strategies for research*, supplement to vol. 10 of *Population and Development Review*, pp. 25–45.

NELSON, M. C., 1994. 'Diphtheria in late-nineteenth-century Sweden: policy and practice', *Continuity and Change* 9, pp. 213–242.

SULLIVAN, J. M., RUTSTEIN, S. O. and BICEGO, G. T., 1994. *Infant and child mortality, demographic and health surveys comparative studies no. 15*, Calverton, MD, Macro International, Inc.

UNICEF, 1994. *The state of the world's children*, Oxford, Oxford University Press.

WILLIAMS, N., 1994. 'The implementation of compulsory health legislation: infant smallpox vaccination in England and Wales, 1840–1890', *Journal of Historical Geography* 20, pp. 396–412.

—— 1996. 'The reporting and classification of causes of death in mid-nineteenth-century England: the example of Sheffield', *Historical Methods* 29, pp. 58–71.

—— and MOONEY, G., 1994. 'Infant mortality in an "Age of Great Cities": London and the English provincial cities compared, c.1840–1910', *Continuity and Change* 9, pp. 185–212.

WOODS, R. I., 1993. 'On the historical relationship between infant and adult mortality', *Population Studies* 47, pp. 195–219.

—— 1994. 'La mortalité infantile en Grande Bretagne: un bilan des connaissances historique', *Annales de Démographie Historique*, pp. 119–134.

—— WATTERSON, P. A. and WOODWARD, J. H., 1988 and 1989. 'The causes of rapid infant mortality decline in England and Wales, 1861–1921. Parts I and II', *Population Studies* 42(3), pp. 343–366 and 43(1), pp. 113–132.

—— WILLIAMS, N. and GALLEY, C., 1993. 'Infant mortality in England, 1550–1950: problems in the identification of long-term trends, geographical and social variations', in C. A. CORSINI and P. P. VIAZZO (eds.), *The decline of infant mortality in Europe, 1800–1950: four national case studies*, Florence, UNICEF and Istituto degli Innocenti.

WRIGLEY, E. A., 1977. 'Births and baptisms: the use of Anglican baptism registers as a source of information about the numbers of births in England before the beginning of civil registration', *Population Studies* 31, pp. 281–312.

—— 1983. 'The growth of population in eighteenth-century England: a conundrum resolved', *Past and Present* 98, pp. 121–150.

4

Gender Mortality Differences from Birth to Puberty in Italy, 1887–1940

ANTONELLA PINNELLI AND PAOLA MANCINI

Gender mortality differences from birth to puberty (0–14 years of age) vary according to age and over time. Excess male mortality in the first year of life is generalized, whereas in following ages, particularly after the fifth birthday, excess female mortality is more frequent during periods and in countries where mortality levels are fairly high (less than 60–65 years life expectancy at birth) (United Nations 1988*a,b*). As mortality levels decline there is a gradual shift from excess female mortality to a situation of equality, after which excess male mortality becomes increasingly pronounced. To quote Vallin (1988) it could be said that 'females regain their advantage' as maternal mortality falls and gradually disappears almost entirely.

Much attention has recently been devoted to explaining gender mortality differences and how they vary over time. Whereas the tendency previously has been to focus on excess male mortality, a clear contradiction of the fact that men were the stronger sex, recently the tide has turned and excess female mortality is now being examined as an exception to the rule that women have always outlived men.

A recent study by Tabutin and Willems (1994) on trends in gender mortality differences between birth and puberty in some developed countries (England, Spain, Denmark, Greece, Italy, Norway, Sweden, the United States, Australia and Japan) showed that excess female mortality in age groups 5–9 and 10–14 years was found in many countries almost until the outbreak of the Second World War. Furthermore, Tabutin and Willems (1993) showed how excess female mortality after the first birthday is a frequent occurrence in developing countries today. This female disadvantage is found in demographic contexts characterized by varying and considerably different levels of mortality; it vanishes only when youth mortality levels are very low (less than 25 per 1,000)—that is, when life expectancy at birth is above 60–65 years.

This chapter is part of a broader research programme on mortality trends from birth to puberty since the second half of the nineteenth century, coordinated by A. Pinnelli and funded by the Ministero dell'Università e della Ricerca Scientifica e Tecnologica (Fondi 60% Ateneo). This programme aims to undertake an accurate reconstruction of mortality rates by age, sex and cause of death, of children's living conditions and of how change in the social, economic and health sectors may have influenced survival chances. The layout of the chapter was organized by both authors. Specifically, A. Pinnelli drafted the section on gender mortality differences by cause of death and P. Mancini processed the data and drafted the remaining sections.

C.A. Corsini and P.P. Viazzo (eds.) The Decline of Infant and Child Mortality, 73-93.
© 1997 UNICEF. Printed in the Netherlands.

Agreement is lacking on why excess female mortality existed in the past. Many authors have expressed the opinion that in the absence of any sort of biological explanation the cause may be traced to women's status (Eggerickx and Tabutin 1994; Perrenoud 1981; Pinnelli and Mancini 1991; Poulain and Tabutin 1981; Tabutin 1978; Vallin 1988; Waldron 1983, 1987) and their lower economic value (Ginzberg 1994), which may have led to discrimination against young girls. Others find this hypothesis to be groundless since there is no literary or anecdotal, let alone statistical, evidence of such discrimination (Courtwright 1990).

In an interesting review of developing countries, Ingrid Waldron (1987) elaborated two hypotheses to explain this female disadvantage and the shift from excess male to excess female mortality after the first birthday. The first is a biological–structural explanation. Females are less resistant to certain diseases and males to others. As mortality decreases, its structure by cause of death changes. Causes leading to excess female mortality prevail at first, followed by causes of excess male mortality. Thus research focuses, on the one hand, on the circumstances surrounding the epidemiological transition and, on the other, on the whys and wherefores of mortality differences between the sexes for each cause. The biological–structural argument also applies to violent deaths, since the fact that more males die as a result of violence could be traced to hormonal differences. This hypothesis assumes a certain invariability over time in the type and intensity of sex mortality differences by cause.

According to the second hypothesis, the underlying reasons for the shift from excess female to excess male mortality as mortality decreases are of a social nature: excess female mortality is the result of discrimination against girls from the time they are infants with regard to care and nutrition, which gradually disappears as women's status in society improves. Excess male mortality arises and increases with the spread of a type of upbringing that encourages boys to be more aggressive and competitive. This hypothesis presupposes variations in the type and intensity of mortality differences between sexes by cause.

In reality it is not easy to isolate the two hypotheses. The causes of excess female mortality prevail under conditions of high mortality and socio-economic backwardness, where discrimination against girls often exists; whereas the causes of excess male mortality prevail when mortality levels are low and the status of women is improved.

Nevertheless, an analysis of differential mortality trends by sex during infancy and puberty in Italy might well help us to reconstruct an important aspect of living conditions (that is, gender differentials) and provide material on the hypothesized biological differences.

The period considered in this chapter extends from 1887, when the keeping of records of mortality by sex, age and cause of death was generalized throughout the country, to 1940. This was a period of great economic change and social upheaval: industrialization, mass emigration, the First World War, the Great Depression, Fascism, colonial wars and, finally, the lead-up to the Second World War. The health system, too, was completely transformed, with increasing attention being paid to the well-being and health of infants.

DATA

Data regarding mortality rates by age, sex and cause were reconstructed year by year using the National Institute of Statistics databank based on the Fourth Revision of the International Classification of the Causes of Death (Istituto Italiano di Statistica 1958), which has been in force in Italy since 1948, and a reconstruction of deaths and the population by sex and age by Moreno Ventisette.

The causes considered are grouped into the following categories: 'infectious and parasitic diseases', 'diseases of the circulatory system', 'influenza–pneumonia–bronchitis', 'gastroenteritis', 'certain diseases of early infancy', 'ill-defined or unknown causes' and 'accidents'. The group 'infectious and parasitic diseases' was entirely reconstructed cause by cause so that the results could be compared over time. Owing to the difficulties met with, some pathologies were ignored for which only meagre data were available for the period in question or for which classification only began after the start of the study period. These were included under 'other causes' and account for less than 10 per cent of all deaths from infectious or parasitic diseases. The diseases for which there are data available for the entire reference period are tuberculosis, smallpox, scarlet fever, diphtheria, whooping cough, measles, typhoid fever and malaria. Risipola, cerebro-spinal epidemic meningitis, carbuncle, tetanus and syphilis fall under the heading 'other infectious and parasitic diseases'.

MORTALITY TRENDS

Before we discuss gender mortality differences, it is necessary to give a brief overview of infant and youth mortality in Italy from the end of the nineteenth century to the outbreak of the Second World War. Mortality only began to fall towards the end of the nineteenth century, much later than in Northern European countries. At the dawn of the twentieth century, when life expectancy in Denmark, Norway and Finland was more than 55 years for men and between 57 and 59 years for women, in Italy it was still only 40 years or so (Caselli, Meslé and Vallin 1995).

During the years considered in this chapter there was a steady decline in mortality from ages 0 to 14. In fact, mortality in the first year of life fell by 50 per cent; mortality in age groups 1–4 and 5–9 fell by 75–80 per cent, and mortality in age group 10–14 by a little under 70 per cent.

This reduction was halted or reversed at various times by particular events. Mortality after the fifth birthday reached a peak in 1908 and in 1915 as a result of the deaths caused by the Calabria–Sicily earthquake and the Marsica earthquake, respectively (Figure 4.1). Much more perceivable and pronounced for all ages are the consequences of the First World War and the Spanish 'Flu epidemic of 1918–1919. Between 1914, the

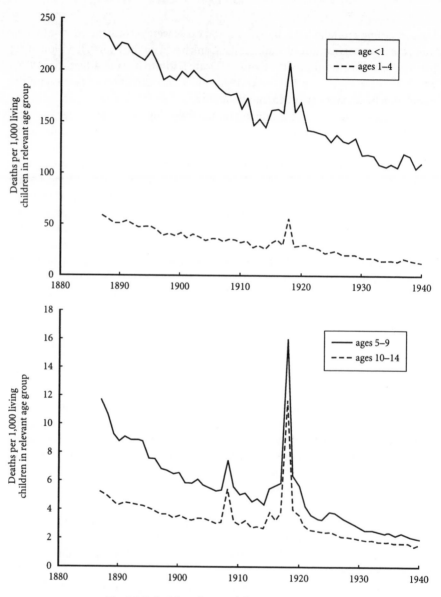

Fig. 4.1. Italy: Mortality trends by age, 1887–1940

Table 4.1. Italy: Relative shares in
mortality decline, by cause of death, 1887–1940

Cause of death	Age group			
	< 1	1–4	5–9	10–14
Infectious and parasitic diseases	26.2	48.1	61.9	62.7
Diseases of the circulatory system	0.9	0.6	1.3	2.8
Influenza–pneumonia–bronchitis	5.1	7.8	6.5	4.3
Gastroenteritis	10.0	18.7	6.1	5.4
Certain diseases of early infancy	25.5			
Ill-defined or unknown causes	3.2	3.5	3.9	4.8
Accidents	0.2	0.5	1.1	2.1
Other causes	28.8	20.8	19.2	17.9
All causes	100.0	100.0	100.0	100.0

year with the minimum mortality prior to the outbreak of war, and 1918, these events raised mortality in the first year by 45 per cent, and mortality at ages 1–4, 5–9 and 10–14 by 118, 272 and 334 per cent, respectively.

The period under consideration witnessed a marked reduction in infectious and parasitic diseases, responsible for as much as 61.9 per cent and 62.7 per cent of the overall reduction in mortality in age groups 5–9 and 10–14 years, and (somewhat less for younger ages) for 48.1 per cent for ages 1–4 and 26.2 per cent in the first year (Table 4.1). Within the category 'infectious and parasitic diseases', some diseases, such as smallpox, scarlet fever and malaria almost disappeared, and others, such as diphtheria, whooping-cough and measles, fell steeply, particularly among children over 5. The fall in mortality from tuberculosis and typhoid fever was only pronounced in the early age groups.

In the period considered, mortality in the category 'certain diseases of early infancy' was halved, accounting for 25.5 per cent of the overall decline in infant mortality. Mortality from gastroenteritis dropped by a third, playing a fairly important role in the decline in mortality at 1–4 years (18.7 per cent). The relatively small decline in mortality from influenza, pneumonia and bronchitis made only a minor contribution to the reduced mortality between birth and puberty. It was only with the discovery and availability of antibiotics and sulphamides after the Second World War that major advances were made in the fight against mortality from respiratory diseases.

There were four principal decisive factors in the decrease in mortality between birth and puberty that resulted especially from the decline in the categories 'infectious and parasitic diseases' and 'certain diseases of early infancy': (i) the spread of pathogenic organisms was controlled by improvements in environmental conditions (sewerage systems, availability of drinking water, improved housing), attention to personal hygiene, more sterile conditions at birth, pest control (of fleas and mosquitoes, for example), and isolation of the sick; (ii) the widespread use of vaccines (against smallpox since 1888 and diphtheria since 1896); (iii) the use of pharmaceutical products (quinine to combat malaria since 1901); and (iv) better infant nutrition (the encouragement of breastfeeding and the distribution of pasteurized milk).[1]

GENDER MORTALITY DIFFERENCES

Along with the all-round decline in mortality over the 50-year period we are looking at, major changes also arose in the differences between male and female mortality risks. The sex mortality ratio (SMR—the ratio of the male mortality rate to the female mortality rate, per 100 deaths) varies with age and time: for children who died before completing their first year of life, the ratio ranged between 112 and 115 during the first part of the period under consideration, increasing to 116–117 in the final years of the period. Variations in subsequent age groups are more pronounced. The SMR at 1–4 years rose from just under 100 (97–98) to over 100 at the end of the First World War. At 5–9 years it was just over 90 at the beginning of the period and rose to over 100 during the 1920s, reaching 109 and 114 in the last two years considered. At 10–14 years the SMR was around 80 in the last years of the nineteenth century, reaching 100 in the 1930s and 114 in 1940 (Figure 4.2).

Thus, the most significant variations occur for children over 4, for whom the fall in mortality was caused almost exclusively by the decline in infectious diseases.

Variations in the SMR were not gradual; they underwent numerous fluctuations and brief phases of real change associated with particular events: the Calabria–Sicily earthquake, the Marsica earthquake, the First World War and, finally, the Spanish 'Flu. During the two earthquakes mortality differences after the first birthday diminished. During the war excess male mortality increased during the first year of life and excess female mortality rose after the fifth birthday. The disadvantage affecting girls aged 5–9 and 10–14 worsened with the Spanish 'Flu epidemic. The underlying reasons for these variations will be described below. Meanwhile, to gain an insight into long-term trends, mortality differences must be analysed in relation to cause of death.

Gender Mortality Differences by Cause of Death

First of all, let us consider whether SMR trends and levels are similar for each cause of death. This, in turn, will allow us to observe whether there are specific causes for female excess mortality and specific causes for male excess mortality and whether gender differences are constant (going back to the biological explanation) or vary with time (according to the social explanation).[2] The results obtained are noticeably hetero-

---

[1] For a more extensive review of factors leading to the decline in infant and youth mortality between the Unification of Italy and the Second World War, see Pinnelli and Mancini 1995a.

[2] It was impossible to calculate SMRs for the category 'certain diseases of early infancy' since categorizations of deaths by sex are only available after 1931. To facilitate a synthetic interpretation of the results on gender mortality differences graphs have been included showing trends in sex mortality ratios by each cause, aggregating the data for the following five-calendar-year groups: 1887–1891, 1896–1900, 1905–1909, 1915–1919, 1922–1924, 1929–1933, 1936–1940.

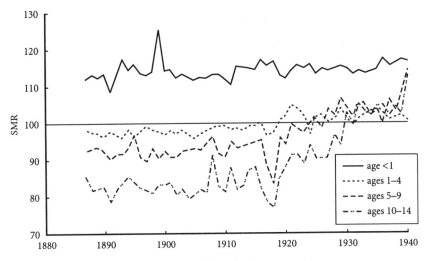

Fig. 4.2. Italy: Sex mortality ratios by age, 1887–1940

geneous. Causes of death can be classified into five groups according to their effect on SMRs (Figures 4.3 and 4.4):

  (i) higher mortality for girls at all ages
 (ii) higher mortality for boys only in the first year of life, and thereafter higher mortality for girls
(iii) excess male mortality until 5 years of age, and thereafter excess female mortality
 (iv) no gender differences
  (v) excess male mortality

The first group includes only whooping cough, a cause that is not very frequent (less than 3 per cent of all deaths before age 5) but is informative. The high risk of death for females at every age was well known even in the past. Another known fact is that for this disease the mother's antibodies offer the child no protection against the disease during either pregnancy or breastfeeding. This fact, which applies only to whooping cough among all of the diseases looked at in the course of this research, may explain the peculiar disadvantage of females even during the first year of life, when excess male mortality is the norm.

The second group comprises typhoid fever, which mainly affects older children, and gastroenteritis, which has a high incidence until the fifth birthday and especially during the first year of life. Since both diseases are strongly linked to hygiene and feeding, nursing practices may explain the composition of this group. The fact that excess female mortality already occurred in the second year of life may be traced back to the fact that children had been weaned. Gini (1919) and Livi Bacci (1980) have stated that children were usually breastfed in Italy more or less until their first birthday. A higher susceptibility of the female organism to diseases of the gastrointestinal tract has been suggested.

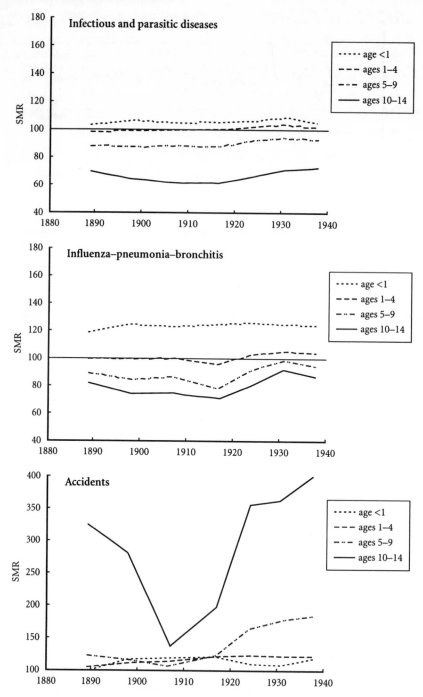

Fig. 4.3. Italy: Sex mortality ratios by age and cause of death, 1887–1940

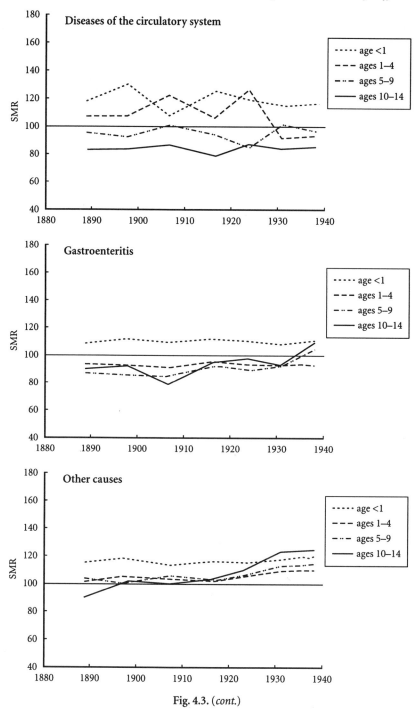

Fig. 4.3. (*cont.*)

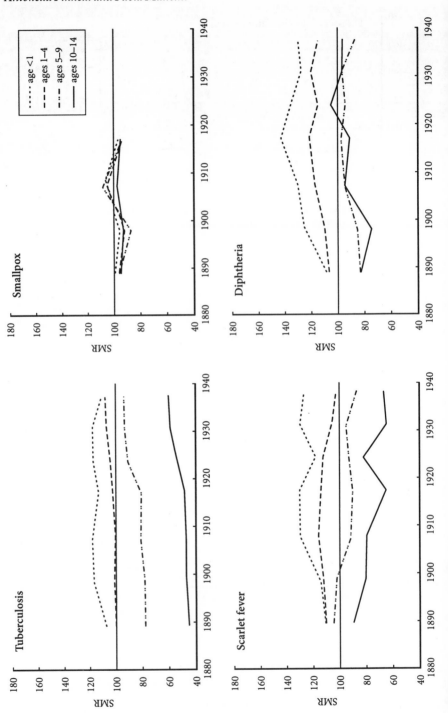

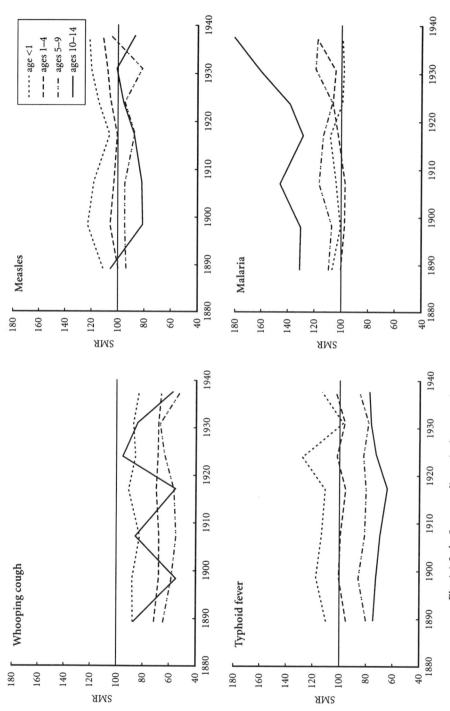

Fig. 4.4. Italy: Sex mortality ratios by age and cause of death, infectious and parasitic diseases, 1887–1940

However, we cannot rule out the possibility that one sex was breastfed for longer than the other or that the quantity and quality of nutrition differed once they had been weaned. Research in developing countries, particularly in those where living conditions are quite precarious, shows that preference towards a son favours breastfeeding practices that are inherently dangerous for the survival of girls, who are, for example, weaned too early or breastfed for too long so that the milk is low in nutritional content (Amin 1990; Arriaga and Way 1987; Das Gupta 1987; Miller 1981).

Likewise, if we look back to when Italy's economy was still largely based on agriculture, as in other developed countries, it is probable that the birth of a son was preferred to that of a daughter. Indirect proof of this is provided by an analysis of the sex ratio at birth according to legitimacy status. Until the early 1900s the sex ratio at birth among illegitimate children was 104–105 males to 100 females, compared with 106 among legitimate children. Perhaps more significantly, for illegitimate children who were later legitimated, the ratio is 108–109 males to 100 females (Figure 4.5), which implies that newborn illegitimate males had considerably higher chances than females of being legally recognized.

The third group includes tuberculosis, diphtheria, scarlet fever, measles, the influenza–pneumonia–bronchitis group and diseases of the circulatory system. Apart from the latter, all are contagious and spread more easily, with more serious consequences, in poorer domestic environments. The health status of children (their susceptibility to becoming ill and their resistance) and their living conditions appear to be determining factors, and it may be hypothesized that from 5 years of age there were already such differences between the sexes in terms of nutrition, care and living habits as would explain higher morbidity and mortality among females. Girls spent most of their day in the home attending to domestic chores and tending to the old and sick, while boys were out in the open air looking after the animals and involved in light agricultural labour. In

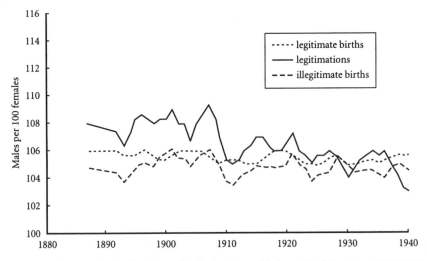

Fig. 4.5. Italy: Sex ratios for illegitimate births, legitimate births and legitimations, 1887–1940

terms of housing conditions (which were not always suitable for humans), where over-crowding was the chief ally of infectious diseases, girls were more exposed to the risk of contact than boys (Giannini 1931; L'Eltore 1947). The effect of proximity on the spread of measles has been confirmed in studies on developing countries (Aaby 1989). Scoliosis, too, was more frequent among girls because of the unnatural position they often assumed when sewing, embroidering or looking after younger children and the use of the corset—all of which also favoured the spread of respiratory tuberculosis (Galli 1899). The fact that each sex is brought up differently may also influence excess female mortality: girls are taught to be more affectionate (they give kisses and are kissed more often) and, for diseases that are easily transmitted, such as those discussed here, this represents another risk of contagion (Courtwright 1990).

Excess female mortality after age 5 for the causes considered in the third group (excluding scarlet fever, which became increasingly rare as a cause of death) was markedly reduced after the First World War. Taking only diphtheria, the disadvantage had already become much less pronounced by the late nineteenth century, almost coinciding with the diffusion of the serotherapy in 1896. Thus, in this health campaign, which in no way discriminated between the sexes, we have a demonstration of the lack of any differential vulnerability to illness.

Smallpox falls into the fourth group. It was very infrequent (1–3 per cent of total deaths) at the end of the nineteenth century, and later became rarer still, almost totally disappearing after the First World War. Once the disease was contracted no cure existed. The fact that there were no gender differences could indicate that neither sex had any particular defence against the disease and that it was not influenced by the living environment and care. As with diphtheria, the fact that there were no mortality differences for smallpox may be attributed to the introduction, in 1888, of compulsory vaccination, which protected both sexes equally well.

In the fifth group we find malaria and accidents. Differences between the sexes are very slight in the first year of life and subsequently increase, becoming quite pronounced in age group 10–14. In this case environment and living habits, by way of different mechanisms, were to the disadvantage of males.

After the reclamation of the areas where malaria had been rife and the campaign for the 'distribution of State quinine', malaria became rare (less than 1 per cent of deaths) and thus any further improvement in the last decades of our study period is bound to be of little importance in explaining young-age mortality. It was only during the First World War that there was a fresh outbreak of the disease, which was a result of the difficulty of making treatment available at a time of such upheaval. The fact that more boys than girls aged 10–14 died at the end of the nineteenth century may be explained by the fact that boys worked and lived out in the open more and were thus more exposed to risk. Since they tended to spend more of their time in the home, girls were better protected: by the end of the nineteenth century mosquito nets were already being widely used by those living in malarial zones.

Accidents fall under the same heading, a cause of excess male mortality at all ages, and especially between 10 and 14 years. Excess male mortality in age group 5–9 and, even more so, age group 10–14 increased under Fascist rule (1922–1943). This was a direct outcome of the different exposure of the sexes to the outside environment in terms of living habits as well as the growing dangers of the urban environment and the different types of education and upbringing—boys trained for the war machine and girls for reproduction.

The analysis made to date allows a number of conclusions to be drawn regarding the presence of biological or social factors in the levels and trends of gender mortality differences.

A biological factor is confirmed only with regard to whooping-cough, the sole cause of death for which gender differences were always to the disadvantage of females and no changes emerged over time. However, since this disease was fairly infrequent it had little influence on overall gender differences.

The SMR was also stable for smallpox, at around 100. This result has already been commented on as showing the absence of any biological gender advantage or disadvantage—a result, perhaps, of state intervention with the introduction of compulsory vaccination to eradicate this disease.

For almost all other causes of death the disadvantage of females shows a downward trend and that of males an upward trend. This would tend to favour a social rather than a biological explanation.

At this point it is necessary to understand whether changes that took place in gender mortality differences are to be attributed to change in the extent and type of gender differences or to a change in the disease structure (that is, the increased role of causes leading to male excess mortality and a decline in those leading to excess female mortality). Thus, using the direct standardization method, for each age group the difference between the SMR for the five-year period 1936–1940 and the SMR for the five-year period 1887–1891 was broken down into two parts, one concerning changes over time of the SMR for each single cause and the other for changes in the mortality structure by cause.[3]

The results in Table 4.2 show that during the first year of life most of the difference between $SMR_{1936–1940}$ and $SMR_{1887–1891}$ was the result of variations in single sex mortality ratios by cause. Thus, the increase in excess male mortality during the first year of life was the result of the widening gap in mortality levels between males and females for all causes and not of the change in the mortality structure by cause.

---

[3] Each SMR may be recalculated as the weighted mean of sex mortality ratios by cause, with weights equal to female mortality rates for the same causes. For example, $SMR_{1887–1891}$ is calculated as

$$\frac{\sum m_i / f_i \times f_i}{\sum f_i}$$

where m_i and f_i are male and female mortality rates by cause of death i. The difference between $SMR_{1936–1940}$ (R′) and $SMR_{1887–1891}$ (R) may be broken down using the following formula: $R' - R = (R' - R'') + (R'' - R)$, where R'' is the weighted mean SMR obtained using as a standard weight female mortality rates by cause obtained as the average of initial (1887–1891) and final (1936–1940) rates.

Table 4.2. Italy: Differences in
sex mortality ratios between 1887–1891 and 1936–1940

Age group	Total difference	Part of difference resulting from:	
		SMR changes	Structural changes
< 1	5	4	1
1–4	5	4	1
5–9	14	9	5
10–14	24	13	11

At ages 1–4 years most of the difference between $SMR_{1936-1940}$ and $SMR_{1887-1891}$ was the result of variations in the sex mortality ratios for each cause of death. The shift from excess female to excess male mortality occurred during the first half of the 1920s and may be traced to the fact that both the 'infectious and parasitic diseases' and the 'influenza–pneumonia–bronchitis' groups changed from being a cause of excess female mortality to being a cause of excess male mortality. A structural effect is unlikely: the two groups considered together were responsible for 53 per cent of total deaths in 1887–1891 and 52 per cent in 1936–1940. Thus, their relative influence did not decrease.

Changes in the disease structure play a greater role at ages 5–9 (accounting for a third of the total variation) and more so at 10–14 (accounting for almost a half), where the shift from a female to male disadvantage occurred between the 1920s and the 1930s.

As time passed, the female disadvantage at 5–9 years from the 'infectious and parasitic diseases' and 'influenza–pneumonia–bronchitis' groups diminished: the percentage of total mortality resulting from these two groups of causes dropped from 63 per cent in 1887–1891 to 46 per cent in 1936–1940. At the same time, there was a steep rise in excess male mortality from accidents (the SMR increased from 124 to 181) and the 'other causes' group, increasing from 25 per cent of total mortality to 41 per cent.

At 10–14 years the structural effect was almost equivalent to the effect of variations in the individual SMRs by cause. In this age group, between 1887–1891 and 1936–1940, excess female mortality for influenza, pneumonia and bronchitis decreased, excess male mortality for accidents increased and there was a gradual shift from excess female to excess male mortality for the 'other causes' (the SMR rose from 90 to 124) and gastroenteritis. It is worth noting that, at the beginning of the period studied, causes of excess female mortality accounted for 95 per cent of total mortality and that this fell to 55 per cent at the end of the period. This is a clear illustration of the importance of structure.

Gender Mortality Diffences at Times of Great Upheaval

As stated earlier, the first two decades of the twentieth century witnessed four major mortality crises of differing intensity and impact—the Calabria–Sicily earthquake of 1908, the Marsica earthquake of 1915, the First World War and the Spanish 'Flu

Table 4.3. Italy: Sex mortality ratios around the earthquakes of 1908 and 1915

Age group	Cause of death	Calabria–Sicily earthquake (1908)			Marsica earthquake (1915)		
		1905–07	1908[a]	1908[b]	1911–14	1915[a]	1915[b]
<1	All causes	112	113	113	113	114	114
	Accidents	115	131	122	115	129	109
1–4	All causes	97	99	98	99	99	99
	Accidents	113	114	113	116	118	127
5–9	All causes	93	97	93	94	95	93
	Accidents	106	109	109	115	108	117
10–14	All causes	81	91	80	84	88	82
	Accidents	248	115	255	323	125	200

[a] Actual SMRs.
[b] SMRs if no earthquake occurred.

epidemic of 1918–1919. Gender mortality differences between birth and puberty changed more during these crises than during periods of calm. An analysis of the reasons further confirms the socio-structural explanation.[4]

During the two earthquakes, the male disadvantage in the first year of life decreased and that of females for the other age groups diminished—only slightly at 1–4 years, steeply at 5–9 and 10–14 years (Table 4.3). The primary explanation for this is that as a result of the earthquakes deaths from accidents rose considerably, thus coming to represent a fairly large proportion of total mortality. In 1908, for example, almost a third of deaths at ages 5–9 and a half at ages 10–14 were from accidents, compared with 7–8 per cent previously. Moreover, earthquakes, by their very nature, do not discriminate by sex or age.[5] In brief, exposure to the risk of death was not significantly different for males and females, thus generating a reduction in gender mortality differences.

During the First World War excess male mortality during the first year of life increased slightly, the female disadvantage at 1–4 years was attenuated, and the excess female mortality at 5–9 and 10–14 years increased sharply (Table 4.4).[6] Infectious diseases, gastroenteritis and the 'influenza–pneumonia–bronchitis' and 'other causes' groups were responsible for the worsening of the status of males during the first year of life; the rise in excess female mortality after the fifth birthday may be attributed to infectious and parasitic diseases (particularly tuberculosis and typhoid fever) and influenza, pneumonia and bronchitis. During the war the gender disadvantage increased for

---

[4] For a detailed description of the methodology used to reconstruct mortality from the two earthquakes and the Spanish 'Flu see Pinnelli and Mancini 1995b.

[5] Both earthquakes were very violent, reaching 10° on the Mercalli scale. They occurred early on a winter's morning when most of the population were still at home (Cavasino 1929; Il Corriere della Sera 14–15 January 1915).

[6] To take into account effects attributable to the war we distinguished between these deaths and those resulting from the Marsica earthquake of 1915 and the Spanish 'Flu epidemic of 1918–1919.

Table 4.4. Italy: Sex mortality ratios,
by age, around the First World War

Age group	1911–1914	1915–1918	1919–1922
< 1	114	116	114
1–4	98	99	103
5–9	94	93	97
10–14	85	82	88

those causes that showed a renewed upward trend in mortality and for age groups in which the gap was already wide prior to the conflict. Thus, those who were already at a disadvantage in peacetime saw their position worsen further. In all likelihood, because the exposure to risk was equal for both boys and girls, morbidity and mortality were even higher for individuals who were in any case more vulnerable.

During the Spanish 'Flu epidemic the male disadvantage increased only ever so slightly during the first year of life, while that of females increased for ages 1–4 and even more so for ages 5–9 and 10–14 (Table 4.5). Thus the position of females at all ages worsened. This may be partly attributed, at least until age 10, to the variation in SMR for influenza, pneumonia and bronchitis to the disadvantage of girls. According to a number of scholars who investigated the problem in the late 1920s, the 'higher frequency of deaths among females from croupy-pneumonia and broncho-pneumonia' during the outbreak of Spanish 'Flu was linked to their lifestyles and duties in the home, which were probably the root cause of increased morbidity and subsequently greater mortality (Boldrini, De Bernardinis and Zingali 1930). The virus is mainly transmitted by direct contact (Crosby 1993) and the contagion depends on proximity and frequency of contact with the infection. Thus, young girls, often relegated to the home and

Table 4.5. Italy: Sex mortality ratios,
by age and cause of death, around the Spanish 'Flu epidemic

Age group	Cause of death	1915–1917	1918–1919[a]	1918–1919[b]
< 1	All causes	116	115	116
	Influenza–pneumonia–bronchitis	128	121	128
1–4	All causes	99	98	101
	Influenza–pneumonia–bronchitis	98	96	102
5–9	All causes	92	87	97
	Influenza–pneumonia–bronchitis	85	78	89
10–14	All causes	81	79	86
	Influenza–pneumonia–bronchitis	68	73	77

[a] Actual SMRs.
[b] SMRs if Spanish 'Flu did not occur.

to the care of the sick, were an easy target. However, the relative overall worsening in the status of women depended still more on changes in the disease structure of mortality. The 'influenza–pneumonia–bronchitis' group, the main cause of excess female mortality, was responsible for 50 per cent of total mortality at 5–9 and 10–14 years, compared with values of 18 per cent and 12 per cent, respectively, in the previous three-year period.

To sum up, it would appear that the variations in the sex mortality ratio during the crises considered in this chapter confirm the importance of exposure factors as well as the structure of mortality by cause of death, and help throw light on the mechanisms underlying these variations.

CONCLUSIONS

We have seen that, during the first year of life, the male disadvantage prevails and increases over time, while for other age groups there is a gradual shift from excess female to excess male mortality that increasingly takes place at later ages over time. The analysis of the causes of death shows that in the first year of life increased male mortality was generally linked to a growing male disadvantage for all causes of death. For subsequent age groups this shift took place for three main reasons: (i) the position of females improved for all causes with time; (ii) many previous causes of female excess mortality then led to excess male mortality; and (iii) the male disadvantage increased further for those causes for which the risk for males had always been higher. Changes in the disease structure are particularly important for children aged 5–9 and 10–14: the impact and number of causes of excess female mortality declined while causes of excess male mortality rose. On the eve of the outbreak of the Second World War females were still at a higher risk of mortality from infectious and parasitic diseases and influenza, pneumonia and bronchitis. However, their unfavourable position was more than counterbalanced by that for males from accidents and 'other causes'.

These results lend credence to the hypothesized existence of a biological basis to excess male mortality (Pressat 1973) present without exception in the first year of life. In the past, this disadvantage was then surpassed by social causes, since the living spaces and lifestyles of the two sexes gradually drew apart with age.

Following the improvements in economic, social and health status at the beginning of this century, the exposure to risk factors, previously responsible for a greater mortality risk for females, gradually declined. The home, for example, where girls spent more of their time than boys, became more habitable and less overcrowded,[7] and the external environment, with growing urbanization, became more and more dangerous. Thus, alongside an improvement in the living conditions of girls, we had a worsening in those of boys. This is also the result of propaganda and paramilitary education

---

[7] It was during the twenty years of Fascist rule that the Institute for Public Housing and Homes for State Employees was founded.

programmes during the Fascist period (Opera Nazionale Balilla): males were strongly conditioned towards aggressive and warlike behaviour and were more at risk of death from accidents. Moreover, with the improvement of women's status, girls were more than likely able to forge a better position for themselves within the home and society.[8] It should also be remembered that during the Fascist era the role of women was re-envisioned as that of future mother responsible for rearing the young, tomorrow's army of the nation. This is borne out by the fact that more and more women became literate and the gap separating them from men narrowed. In terms of illegitimate births, the disadvantaged position of women all but disappeared (Figure 4.5).

In conclusion, going back to the various hypotheses put forward to explain excess female mortality and its gradual disappearance over time, the biological, structural and social hypotheses have all been confirmed. However, changes in the sex mortality ratio are the chief factor underlying the increase in excess male mortality in the first year of life and the fact that excess female mortality disappeared for the following age groups. The biological explanation, which presupposes an invariable sex mortality ratio for individual causes, must thus be played down in favour of the social explanation: the status of girls gradually improved during the period considered. The change in the disease structure was nothing if not the direct consequence of change in the social and health spheres leading to the fall in mortality and gradually improving the living conditions of men and women, boys and girls alike—but particularly girls.

The fact that females were no longer at a social disadvantage brought out the only real biological disadvantage, that of males, which slowly worsened as social transformations took place. Society's encouragement of males to be aggressive and to live dangerously exacerbated, from adolescence onwards, the disadvantage of male young adults and adults.

We cannot take it for granted that the unfavourable position of females was the fruit of neglect, at least in the case of Italy. Most certainly, however, a certain negligence in terms of their being weaned too early and above all the role of women and their different living arrangements, clothing, chores and responsibilities all offer sufficient explanation for the fact that females were at a disadvantage, without having to bring in 'real' forms of discrimination or ill-treatment. An analysis of mortality differences at times of crisis or catastrophe helps confirm this suggestion, since the rise or fall for either sex largely depended on the type of event in question. In the case of earthquakes differences lessened; war worsened the status of the sex that was weaker in peacetime, and the Spanish 'Flu pandemic considerably increased excess female mortality after 5 years of age. If it were true that ill-treatment and discrimination lay at the root of excess female mortality, the picture would have been quite different: in this case during a period of difficulty the mortality of the less-appreciated sex would simply grow rather than change according to circumstances.

---

[8] The year 1903 marked the founding of the Italian National Women's Council, witness to the first stirrings of the women's movement (Benetti Brunelli 1933).

References

AABY, P., 1989. 'La promiscuité, un facteur déterminant de la mortalité par rougeole', in G. PISON, E. VAN DE WALLE and M. SALA-DIAKANDA (eds.), *Mortalité et societé en Afrique au sud du Sahara*, cahier no. 124, Paris, INED.

AMIN, S., 1990. 'The effect of women's status on sex differentials in infant and child mortality in South Asia', *Genus* 46(3–4), pp. 55–69.

ARRIAGA, E. E. and WAY, P. O., 1987. 'Determinants of excess female mortality', *Population Bulletin of the United Nations* 21/22, pp. 45–54.

BENETTI BRUNELLI, V., 1933. *La donna nella civiltà moderna*, Torino, F.lli Bocca Editori.

BOLDRINI, M., DE BERNARDINIS, L. and ZINGALI, G., 1930. 'Demografia, antropometria, statistica sanitaria, dinamica delle popolazioni', in O. CASAGRANDI (ed.), *Trattato italiano di igiene*, Torino, Unione Tipografica Torinese.

CASELLI, G., MESLÉ, F. and VALLIN, J., 1995. 'Le triomphe de la médecine', Dossiers et recherches 45, Paris, INED.

CAVASINO, A., 1929. 'Note sul catalogo dei terremoti distruttivi dal 1501 al 1929 nel bacino del Mediterraneo', in REGIA ACCADEMIA NAZIONALE DEI LINCEI, *Memorie scientifiche e tecniche*, Rome.

COURTWRIGHT, D. T., 1990. 'The neglect of female children and childhood sex ratios in nineteenth-century America: a review of the evidence', *Journal of Family History* 15, pp. 313–323.

CROSBY, A. W., 1993. 'Influenza', in K. F. KIPPLE (ed.), *The Cambridge world history of human disease*, Cambridge, Cambridge University Press.

DAS GUPTA, M., 1987. 'Selective discrimination against female children in rural Punjab', *Population and Development Review* 13, pp. 77–100.

EGGERICKX, T. and TABUTIN, D., 1994. 'La mortalité des jeunes et la surmortalité féminine en Belgique vers 1890: une approche régionale', *Population* 49, pp. 657–684.

GALLI, G., 1899. *Come devo mantenermi sano e prolungarmi la vita?*, Milan, Hoepli.

GIANNINI, G., 1931. 'La mortalità per tubercolosi in rapporto al sesso e all'età', *Maternità e Infanzia* 7(9).

GINI, C., 1919. 'Sulla mortalità infantile durante la guerra', *Atti della Società Italiana di Ostetricia e Ginecologia* 19, Rome, Tipografia Bertero.

GINZBERG, C. A., 1994. 'Sex-specific child mortality and the economic value of children in nineteenth century Massachusetts', Ph.D. dissertation, University of California, Berkeley.

ISTITUTO ITALIANO DI STATISTICA (ISTAT), 1958. *Cause di morte 1887–1955*, Rome.

L'ELTORE, G. 1947. *La tubercolosi in Italia*, Rome, Tipografica Operaia Romana.

LIVI BACCI, M., 1980. *Donna, fecondità e figli*, Bologna, Il Mulino.

MILLER, B. D., 1981. *The endangered sex: neglect of female children in rural North India*, New York and London, Cornell University Press.

PERRENOUD, A., 1981. 'Surmortalité féminine et condition de la femme (XVIIe–XXe siècles): une vérification empirique', *Annales de Démographie Historique*, pp. 89–104.

PINNELLI, A. and MANCINI, P., 1991. 'Différences de mortalité par sexe de la naissance à la puberté en Italie: un siècle d'évolution', *Population* 46, pp. 1651–1676.

———— 1995a. 'Mortality by cause of death from birth to puberty, Italy 1887–1940', in IRP-

CNR, *Contributions of Italian scholars: European Population Conference, Milan 4–8 September 1995*, pp. 191–212.

——— 1995*b*. 'Il declino della mortalità infantile e giovanile in Italia tra fine '800 e inizio '900: un cammino interrotto da periodi difficili', in papers circulated in advance of the fourth Congreso de la Asociación de Demografía Histórica, Bilbao–S. Sebastian, 20–22 September.

POULAIN, M. and TABUTIN, D., 1981. 'La surmortalité des petites filles en Belgique au XIXe et début du XXe siècle', *Annales de Démographie Historique*, pp. 105–117.

PRESSAT, R., 1973. 'Surmortalité biologique et surmortalité sociale', *Revue Française de Sociologie* 14 (special issue).

TABUTIN, D., 1978. 'La surmortalité féminine en Europe avant 1940', *Population* 34, pp. 121–148.

——— and WILLEMS, M., 1993. 'La surmortalité des petites filles dans le Sud des années 1970 aux années 1980', working paper no. 173, Université Catholique de Louvain, Institut de Démographie.

——— 1994. 'Les différences de mortalité entre les sexes de la naissance à la puberté: l'expérience historique de l'Occident (1750–1930)', paper presented at the Chaire Quetelet 1994, 'Santé et mortalité des enfants en Europe: inegalités sociale d'hier et d'aujourd'hui', Louvain-la-Neuve, 12–14 September.

UNITED NATIONS, 1988*a*. 'Variation de la survie, selon le sexe, dans les pays en développement: importance de la distribution régionale e déterminants démographiques', *Bulletin Démographique des Nations Unies* 25, pp. 51–64.

——— 1988*b*. 'Sex differentials in life expectancy and mortality in developed countries: an analysis by age groups and causes of death from recent and historical data', *Population Bulletin of the United Nations* 25, pp. 65–106.

VALLIN, J., 1988. 'Evolution sociale et baisse de la mortalité: conquête ou reconquête d'un avantage féminin', Dossiers et recherches 17, Paris, INED.

WALDRON, I., 1983. 'The role of genetic and biological factors in sex differences in mortality', in A. D. LOPEZ and L. T. RUZICKA (eds.), *Sex differentials in mortality: trends, determinants and consequences*, selections of the papers presented at the ANU/UN/WHO meeting held in Canberra (Australia) 1–7 December 1981, miscellaneous series no. 4, Department of Demography, Australian National University, Canberra.

——— 1987. 'Patterns and causes of excess female mortality among children in developing countries', *World Health Statistics Quarterly* 40(3), pp. 194–210.

5

Infant Mortality in French Cities in the Mid-Nineteenth Century

PATRICE BOURDELAIS AND MICHEL DEMONET

Despite developments in the Statistique Générale de la France, and its many quantitative studies, and the attention given to sanitary and social conditions in French cities from the beginning of the nineteenth century, there exists no reliable information about the pattern of urban mortality during that century. Preston and van de Walle (1978) are the only scholars to have attempted a comparative study of mortality in the three largest French cities, Paris, Marseilles and Lyons. They looked at the three *départements* that contained the majority of their population, Seine, Bouches-du-Rhône and Rhône, respectively. Their results show the magnitude of excess mortality in these very large cities, and enable us to locate more accurately in time the decline of mortality during the second half of the nineteenth century, which in these cities coincided with the construction of sewers and the provision of safe water supplies. Research on child mortality was made more difficult by the practice of wet-nursing in the principal towns, as well as in some smaller cities. Children born in towns were placed with wet-nurses who lived in the country, where many of the children died. This resulted in an underestimate of the mortality of young town-dwellers (Garden 1970; Lachiver 1969). But this methodological difficulty should not be used to disregard the importance of other reasons, more central to French historical research, for this lack of interest. It should be borne in mind that, from the end of the Second World War to the 1970s, it was conditions in the seventeenth and eighteenth centuries that formed the principal interest of both students of historical demography and more general historians in France. Historians tended to be more interested in conditions in the countryside than in those in the towns, as if the search for a national identity in France lay in the country rather than in the towns. However, during the nineteenth century, urbanization and industrialization resulted in changes in the living conditions and in the attitudes of a significant part of the population. Infant and child mortality and changes therein were two essential factors that influenced the levels and characteristics of living standards for many decades. Methodological difficulties and gaps in documentation cannot conceal the fact that urban mortality was a fundamental variable essential to understanding the dynamics of the epidemiological and health transition in France during the nineteenth century.

In this chapter we present the available data, and report the methodological

C.A. Corsini and P.P. Viazzo (eds.) The Decline of Infant and Child Mortality, 95-108.
© *1997 UNICEF. Printed in the Netherlands.*

difficulties that we have encountered. We formulate working hypotheses and set out the preliminary results of a study begun in 1994. Although, we were able to use unpublished material collected by the Statistique Générale de France, and have been successful in unearthing data that make it possible to construct life-tables for several hundred French towns, the results need to be treated with caution because of some technical difficulties, particularly those associated with the definition of the age groups chosen for the study.

THE DATA

Throughout the nineteenth century, but in somewhat irregular fashion, the central authorities of the Statistique Générale de France distinguished between urban and rural data, even though the published figures were often made available only at the level of the *département*. However, between 1853 and 1863 local authorities in the principal place of each *arrondissement* and in all towns with a population of 10,000 or more were required to keep specific statistics. There are more than 400 French towns for which data on births, marriages and deaths are available by age and sex, even though some of them are in reality only very small towns, with fewer than 5,000 inhabitants. Following the censuses of 1856 and 1861, local authorities in these areas were required to provide information on the age distribution of their populations by single years of age, including those who were 'enumerated specially', in particular the military and inmates of religious institutions.

It was therefore possible to construct cross-sectional life-tables by relating deaths that occurred during periods with a census year in the middle (for example, deaths in each year from 1859 to 1863 were related to the population enumerated in the census of 1861). This allowed us to obtain sufficiently large numbers of deaths in the numerator of the ratio to relate to the age structure of the population. However, some difficulties persisted. A preference for round numbers (that is, the tendency for people aged, say, 48 or 53 to declare an age of 50) was often evident both in death registrations and in the censuses. We dealt with this problem by using the methods employed by France Meslé and Jacques Vallin (1989) who found that rounding in the two data sources often provided less unsatisfactory results than did more modern methods of smoothing.

The second difficulty we met was in relating deaths in different years to the population in the middle of the period. Depending on the rate of population growth, and in particular on migration, the age structure could change at very different rates in different towns and this can lead to bias in the construction of life-tables. However, these biases are generally limited over a period of years.

The third difficulty was connected with the changing composition of the age groups suggested by the central administration. In contrast to the practice at the beginning of the century, when quinquennial age groups were clearly defined (5–9 years, 10–14 years, 15–19 years, and so on) the published tables sent to town halls and prefectures contained definitions of age groups that were often ambiguous (for example, 5–10,

10–15 and 15–20). Footnotes specified what was expected: age distributions were to be given by completed year of age, and in each age group the upper bound was to form part of the group. Thus, the deaths of 10-year-olds were to be shown in the age group 5–10; but this is opposite to previous practice, where these deaths would have been related to the 10–14 age group. Judging by the rounded figures, it was concluded that use of the new rules was very patchy (in the majority of cases an individual aged 50 was included in the age group 50–55 rather than in the age group 45–50). As regards census data, when an age distribution by single years of age was required, the headings of the published tables are also ambiguous (1–2 years, 2–3 years, and so on). Nevertheless, in this case it is still simpler to discern the method of grouping used than in the case of quinquennial age groups, when the consequence of the preference for ages rounded to the nearest multiple of 10 must be taken into account.

In terms of infant and child mortality, the practice of wet-nursing can introduce a bias into our figures, since neither the extent nor the geographical distribution of the practice in the mid-nineteenth century is known. This outflow is to some degree compensated for by an inflow of children born elsewhere who migrated into the towns with their parents and ultimately died there. The construction of life-tables for all ages should result in an eventual discontinuity in the series of q-values, particularly around the fifth birthday—but this hypothesis remains to be verified.

THE QUESTIONS

The first problem to be tackled concerns the levels and characteristics of urban mortality in France during the period immediately preceding its decline. Could the mortality patterns in Paris, Lyons and Marseilles be generalized to apply to all French towns, irrespective of their size, function and geographical location? Alternatively, might mortality patterns have been different in industrial cities, garrison towns or towns situated in the South of France? If such differences did exist, how large were they? Is it still possible to speak of 'urban' mortality as a distinct and internally coherent pattern in which similar levels and profiles justify the use of this expression?

Previous research has suggested that mortality in age groups 1–4 and 5–9 years would provide a better means of discrimination than does infant mortality, and can be used to locate the towns in which the situation of children was worst: large towns and new industrial cities (Bourdelais 1984; Bourdelais and Demonet 1996). We would expect comparative study of a larger number of towns to confirm our preliminary results.

The second stage of our study consists of an analysis of the causes of the observed differentials. Since the census contains a number of questions on the socio-economic characteristics of the inhabitants of individual towns, it becomes possible to provide an 'identity card' for each area. Previous studies could yield additional data. As a first step, a study of the rate of growth of different towns during the previous 15 years (Le Mée 1989) provides a better indication of the level and patterns of urban mortality than does their size. Next, we take account of socio-economic conditions in the *arrondissement*, the true hinterland of the towns. Results from the agricultural census of 1852 have made it possible to construct several indicators from which we can choose those that are most relevant for the purposes of our study: price and wage levels, rents, nutrition, the availability of certain amenities, and poverty (Demonet 1990).

Our objective is to disaggregate the effects of factors that indicate the level and patterns of urban mortality and to use multivariate analysis to rank them hierarchically. This will allow us to assess, for example, the effect on mortality of geographical location, size and the rate of growth, as well as socio-economic factors.

A FIRST ANALYSIS

To ensure that such a study is feasible, we chose a group that consisted of 71 towns with more than 2,500 inhabitants, situated in a quarter of French *départements*. (We used the last quarter of the alphabetical list of *départements* because this was the easiest method of choice given the arrangement of the archives.) The selection used the French definition of a town as a commune in which at least 2,000 individuals lived in agglomerations (Table 5.1). The data needed to construct 71 separate life-tables were extracted: annual numbers of births, deaths by age group and sex during the 5 years with the census year as the centre, and the age and sex structure obtained from the census of 1861—a total of some 30,000 numbers. We must again emphasize that the study was purely exploratory and that the methodological difficulties inherent in the data remind us not to pay excessive attention to small differences in mortality between different towns.

Based on the experience of previous research on urban mortality in Belgium (Eggerickx and Debuisson 1990) and in the industrial town of Le Creusot in France (Bourdelais and Demonet 1996) we decided to retain three (and sometimes four) age groups: 0, 1–4, 5–9 (and 10–14) years.

In a comparison of mortality in the selected towns (which varied in size and function) with mortality in the country as a whole, urban excess mortality, measured by the proportion of those in the life-table who survived to their tenth birthday (l_{10}), was found in only half the cases. Urban excess mortality is not, therefore, a universal phenomenon (Table 5.2). Even if there was no relation between a city's size and its child mortality, the rank of towns with fewer than 5,000 inhabitants is not random; 10 out of 15 were among the 18 towns in which mortality at ages below 10 was lowest. By contrast, child mortality in the industrial towns (Le Creusot, Corbeil, Le Havre, Mazamet, Toulon and Elbeuf) at ages 1–4 and 5–9 was particularly high compared with that of the country as a whole, and even with that of Lyons. There was considerable variation between towns situated in the same *département*, and large differences were found even between different towns situated in the same region. In the absence of a more detailed analysis, there appears to be no simple relation between a town's size, its location and the level of child mortality.

Table 5.1. France: Population of the towns studied, 1861 (in ascending order)

	Males	Females	Total
Melle (Deux-Sèvres)	1,174	1,431	2,605
Charolles (Saône-et-Loire)	1,453	1,760	3,213
Neufchâtel-en-Bray (Seine-Inférieure)	1,522	1,855	3,377
Bellac (Haute-Vienne)	1,647	1,886	3,533
Lure (Haute-Saône)	1,685	1,860	3,545
Neufchâteau (Vosges)	1,647	1,987	3,634
St Calais (Sarthe)	1,666	2,006	3,672
Rambouillet (Seine-et-Oise)	2,413	1,812	4,225
Montdidier (Somme)	2,094	2,177	4,271
Péronne (Somme)	2,191	2,272	4,463
Loudun (Vienne)	2,049	2,466	4,515
Tonnerre (Yonne)	2,185	2,368	4,553
Coulommiers (Seine-et-Marne)	2,234	2,382	4,616
Parthenay (Deux-Sèvres)	2,147	2,482	4,629
Doullens (Somme)	2,146	2,752	4,898
Corbeil Essonne (Seine-et-Oise)	2,412	2,642	5,054
Montmorillon (Vienne)	2,702	2,470	5,172
Mantes-la-Jolie (Seine-et-Oise)	2,415	2,791	5,206
Avallon (Yonne)	2,605	2,928	5,533
Mirecourt (Vosges)	2,520	3,038	5,558
Remiremont (Vosges)	2,598	3,050	5,648
Mamers (Sarthe)	2,658	3,071	5,729
Apt (Vaucluse)	2,882	2,870	5,752
Joigny (Yonne)	2,804	3,072	5,876
Brignoles (Var)	3,161	2,991	6,152
La Flèche (Sarthe)	2,858	3,571	6,429
Castelsarrasin (Tarn-et-Garonne)	3,189	3,537	6,726
Les Sables-D'Olonne (Vendée)	3,338	3,658	6,996
Gray (Haute-Saône)	3,655	3,404	7,059
Lavaur (Tarn)	3,501	3,937	7,438
Provins (Seine-et-Marne)	4,066	3,470	7,536
St Yrieix-la-Perche (Haute-Vienne)	3,784	3,756	7,540
Vesoul (Haute-Saône)	4,056	3,526	7,582
Gaillac (Tarn)	3,769	4,066	7,835
Fontenay-le-Comte (Vendée)	3,719	4,240	7,959
Etampes (Seine-et-Oise)	3,763	4,456	8,219
Napoléon Vendée (Vendée)	4,349	3,928	8,277
Yvetot (Seine-Inférieure)	3,938	4,606	8,544
St Dié (Vosges)	4,577	4,977	9,554
Orange (Vaucluse)	4,799	5,081	9,880
Meaux (Seine-et-Marne)	5,087	4,826	9,913
Draguignan (Var)	5,206	4,867	10,073
Moissac (Tarn-et-Garonne)	4,844	5,376	10,220
Mazamet (Tarn)	5,336	5,583	10,919
Sens (Yonne)	5,178	5,913	11,091

Table 5.1. (*cont.*)

	Males	Females	Total
Melun (Seine-et-Marne)	6,766	4,402	11,168
Fontainebleau (Seine-et-Marne)	6,230	5,212	11,442
Epinal (Vosges)	5,808	6,084	11,892
Fécamp (Seine-Inférieure)	6,381	5,735	12,116
Châtellerault (Vienne)	6,973	7,230	14,203
Albi (Tarn)	7,020	7,548	14,568
Auxerre (Yonne)	7,357	7,721	15,078
St Germain-en-Laye (Seine-et-Oise)	7,673	7,620	15,293
Le Creusot (Saône-et-Loire)	8,784	7,310	16,094
Mâcon (Saône-et-Loire)	9,039	8,963	18,002
Dieppe (Seine-Inférieure)	9,218	10,042	19,260
Chalon-sur-Saône (Saône-et-Loire)	9,351	10,359	19,710
Niort (Deux-Sèvres)	9,171	10,706	19,877
Elbeuf (Seine-Inférieure)	9,413	10,573	19,986
Abbeville (Somme)	9,704	10,297	20,001
Castres (Tarn)	10,816	10,654	21,470
Montauban (Tarn-et-Garonne)	12,215	13,766	25,981
Poitiers (Vienne)	14,946	15,693	30,639
Avignon (Vaucluse)	18,548	17,712	36,260
Le Mans (Sarthe)	17,209	19,891	37,100
Versailles (Seine-et-Oise)	24,638	19,261	43,899
Limoges (Haute-Vienne)	25,990	25,069	51,059
Amiens (Somme)	28,264	30,517	58,781
Toulon (Var)	39,815	27,589	67,404
Le Havre (Seine-Inférieure)	34,787	35,972	70,759
Rouen (Seine-Inférieure)	49,060	53,506	102,566

Table 5.2. France: Infant and child mortality, 1859–1863
(in descending order of number of female survivors at age 10)

	q_0		$_4q_1$		$_5q_5$		l_{10}	
	M	F	M	F	M	F	M	F
Neufchâteau[a]	158	99	94	84	34	15	736	812
Coulommiers[a]	168	124	106	79	37	10	716	799
Loudun[a]	187	71	192	125	48	54	626	769
Poitiers[b]	134	106	150	124	44	46	704	747
Montmorillon	116	116	93	133	20	35	785	739
Avallon	175	158	139	110	66	21	664	734
Doullens[a]	176	146	81	107	32	38	733	734
Vesoul	151	118	117	130	65	51	701	729
Lure[a]	165	144	87	106	32	53	738	724

Table 5.2. (*cont*)

	q_0		$_4q_1$		$_5q_5$		l_{10}	
	M	F	M	F	M	F	M	F
Parthenay[a]	176	87	121	141	65	79	677	723
Tonnerre[a]	147	93	160	180	53	29	679	722
Moissac[b]	167	157	114	118	26	35	719	718
Charolles[a]	161	111	125	129	88	79	670	714
Châtellerault[b]	148	110	137	167	48	37	701	714
Bellac[a]	163	145	84	149	37	26	738	708
St Dié	177	149	136	129	43	44	680	708
Le Mans[b]	178	157	99	116	34	51	716	707
Melle[a]	139	133	121	159	70	29	705	707
Sens[b]	238	155	139	126	76	43	607	707
St Yrieix-la-Perche	143	122	145	152	32	52	709	706
La Flèche	184	163	141	133	43	40	671	696
Mantes-la-Jolie	141	166	65	115	34	62	776	693
Gray	190	140	139	162	19	47	684	687
Niort[b]	155	141	231	158	45	52	621	686
Les Sables-D'Olonne	159	151	184	144	57	61	647	683
Mâcon[b]	139	121	145	176	59	58	693	682
Mirecourt	246	177	148	126	37	52	619	682
Remiremont	246	175	132	133	29	47	636	682
France	*180*	*157*	*130*	*130*	*47*	*50*	*657*	*679*
Fontenay-le-Comte	154	116	200	193	56	50	639	678
Draguignan[b]	196	170	143	160	28	33	671	674
Montdidier[a]	187	194	153	158	29	12	669	671
Melun[b]	222	185	128	149	33	35	656	669
Fontainebleau[b]	168	165	157	167	38	41	675	667
Chalon-sur-Saône[b]	165	145	216	169	59	63	616	665
St Germain-en-Laye[b]	190	164	253	157	35	58	584	664
Yvetot	240	184	163	131	53	66	602	662
Lavaur	163	127	205	207	43	49	637	658
Epinal[b]	185	187	143	154	61	46	656	656
Amiens[b]	214	187	166	163	35	39	633	654
Fécamp[b]	234	195	140	148	48	46	628	654
Brignoles	218	174	180	187	32	28	622	653
Lyons[b]	*194*			*174*		*63*		*652*
Auxerre[b]	168	156	172	197	50	43	654	648
Péronne[a]	189	190	142	153	31	56	674	648
Abbeville[b]	224	181	164	171	35	46	626	647
Neufchâtel-en-Bray[a]	232	279	150	61	52	45	620	646
Meaux	232	192	214	162	68	49	563	644
Versailles[b]	205	193	148	173	34	38	655	642
Orange	185	166	244	211	62	25	578	641
Rambouillet[a]	265	187	218	183	140	38	495	640
Joigny	187	218	137	168	72	43	651	623

Table 5.2. (*cont.*)

	q_0		$_4q_1$		$_5q_5$		l_{10}	
	M	F	M	F	M	F	M	F
Castelsarrasin	140	176	145	205	48	58	700	617
St Calais[a]	231	275	113	111	29	43	663	617
Limoges[b]	155	132	261	256	41	47	599	615
Napoléon Vendée	213	179	224	192	86	80	558	611
Gaillac	199	146	257	264	41	30	571	610
Avignon[b]	193	171	267	230	35	49	571	607
Albi[b]	161	138	299	264	47	58	560	597
Apt	154	159	231	262	45	43	621	595
Etampes	204	197	189	204	68	73	601	593
Mamers	303	295	74	126	73	49	598	587
Castres[b]	138	118	279	303	43	50	595	585
Provins	286	246	259	198	42	34	507	584
Elbeuf[b]	271	233	306	218	58	52	477	569
Montauban[b]	217	219	258	263	50	52	552	546
Rouen[b]	322	302	175	180	50	46	532	546
Dieppe[b]	294	264	213	229	28	44	540	542
Toulon[b]	240	199	333	304	63	56	475	527
Mazamet[b]	155	156	312	365	52	47	552	510
Le Havre[b]	290	289	292	250	58	59	474	502
Corbeil (Essonne)	225	282	277	275	54	49	530	495
Le Creusot[b]	263	191	367	369	73	84	432	467

[a] Towns with fewer than 5,000 inhabitants.
[b] Towns with more than 10,000 inhabitants.

In terms of mortality patterns, an analysis of the life-tables for males in the 71 towns that extend beyond the first 14 years of life (Figure 5.1) shows a principal axis that separates those towns in which infant mortality was higher than mortality at ages 1–4 (Mamers, Doulens) from those in which the opposite was true (Albi, Mazamet, Castres). The second axis contrasts the shapes of the survival curves between birth and fifteenth birthday, distinguishing particularly between those towns in which mortality declined steeply after age 5 (Draguignan, Coulommiers) and those where the rate of decline was less steep between ages 5 and 15 (Charolles, Melle). Towns in which infant mortality and mortality rates at ages 1–4 are very similar, but mortality begins to fall at ages 5–9 and continues to do so at ages 10–14, are situated close to the centre of gravity of the cluster of points (Auxerre, Le Havre). Geographical groups are not absent, even though they cannot be used to rank the communities in our sample. Fontainebleau and Melun are near to one another in the figure; by contrast, the pattern in Meaux, another sub-prefecture in the *département* Seine et Marne, is so different that it moves the town to the opposite side of the figure. In some cases, towns belonging to the same *département* are more or less clustered, which reflects their similar mortality patters. Albi,

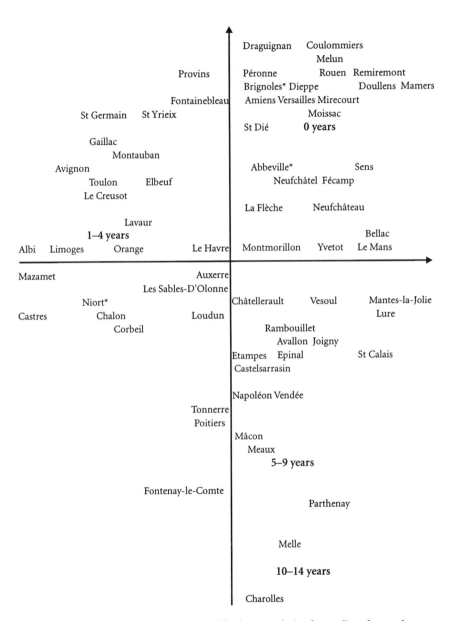

Fig. 5.1. France: The two principal axes of the factor analysis of mortality of young boys

* Montdidier (not shown) would fall in the same place as Brignoles; Gray would fall in the same place as Abbeville; and Apt in the same place as Niort.

Castres and Mazamet (which are in the Tarn *département*) are close to one another in Figure 5.1, and they abut on Limoges, Saint-Germain-en-Laye, Avignon, Toulon, Le Creusot, Niort, Orange and Elbeuf. This does not mean that these cities form a regional group, even though they include numerous towns situated in southern France. An automated classification based on complete life-tables produces six groups, the fifth of which includes Mazamet, Lavaur, Montauban, Gaillac, Castres, Albi, Orange, Apt, Le Creusot and Elbeuf. This confirms the convergence of mortality rates that we have found using only child mortality only as an indicator (see Figure 5.2).

High levels of mortality at ages 1–4 and 5–9 are to be found in some industrial towns in northern France as well as in towns in the South of France, where it has been shown that high summer and autumn temperatures were responsible for many of the deaths of young children. To some extent, such a clustering is indicative of the fact that the industrial environment and living conditions in these northern cities, in which a dangerous habitat goes hand in hand with insufficient or completely absent public health measures, have the same effect in terms of the risks of infectious disease for infants as the hot climate in southern France. This similarity of effect makes it necessary to play down the importance of the hot climate as an explanatory factor in high child mortality. Moreover, seasonal variations in the number of deaths of children under 10 years old in Le Creusot and Elbeuf, as well as the small number of published studies of cause-specific mortality, show that diseases of the digestive system (gastroenteritis and diarrhoea) were the principal causes of death among young children. It is known that these diseases tend to spread in areas where water is contaminated because of inadequate separation of drinking water from sewage, and where household overcrowding prevents the adoption of measures that would improve hygiene. The high mortality of children who live in the so-called 'Mediterranean' towns was, therefore, not simply the result of excessive heat in summer and autumn, but also of inadequate public hygiene measures.

LESSONS LEARNED FROM OUR
PRELIMINARY STUDY

In terms of data and methods, some estimates of mortality levels and certain irregularities in the data suggest the need to check the consistency of statistics of deaths by age and locality. Inconsistencies can be caused by random variations in thinly populated small towns (Charolles, Avallon, Tonnerre, Rambouillet) or by inaccuracies in the source material (Dieppe). The low numbers of deaths in smaller towns are often the cause of 'aberrations', which may lead to faulty results and make them more difficult to assess. We therefore decided to extend our study to include all French *départements* and to cover the entire national territory, but to retain only towns with a population of at least 10,000 (which include 30 out of our original 71). Even in the absence of statistical analysis—the only reliable method—the figures in Table 5.2 clearly indicate a clustering of towns with a population of at least 10,000 inhabitants among the areas most affected by infant mortality. In Figure 5.3, each town is represented as a function

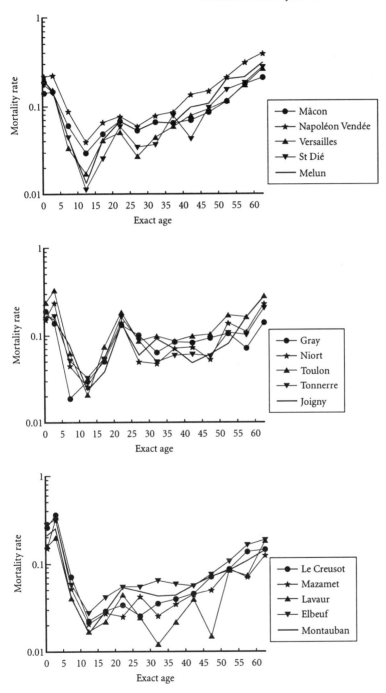

Fig. 5.2. France: Male mortality profiles classed by type, 1859–1863

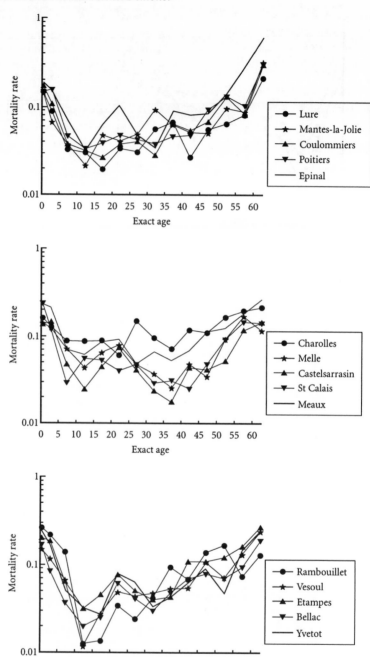

Fig. 5.2. (*cont.*)

of total population (the abscissa) and the number of children who survived to their tenth birthday per 1,000 births (the ordinate).

The proportion who survived to their tenth birthday could be used as the most easily calculated, and possibly the most reliable, indicator of child mortality in a multivariate analysis of the relationship between urban characteristics and child mortality. Differences in the pattern of mortality between the first three age groups can be used in a second stage of the analysis. Moreover, consideration of this indicator (the proportion who survive to their tenth birthday) in Figure 5.3 shows the existence of a relationship between a town's size and its child mortality. This is seen in the negative gradient of the regression line, which remains unchanged when towns with more than 40,000 inhabitants (relatively few) and those with less than 4,000 inhabitants (where random variation and 'aberrations' are most frequent) are excluded from the sample. A town's size will be one, but not the only indicator of the level of child mortality.

Another hypothesis that we have tested—that child mortality at different ages was generally higher in towns than in the country—proves not to be universally true. The number of children who survived to their tenth birthday, which we have used as a summary indicator of mortality in the first three age groups and to remove 'errors' of classification between these groups, is shown in Table 5.2. In 28 out of 71 towns mortality was lower than in France as a whole. Finally, in the industrial towns (Le Creusot, Mazamet, Toulon, Elbeuf) as well as in those sheltered from industry (Rouen, Le Havre, Amiens, Limoges), high excess mortality of children is found (only 432 boys out of 1,000 survived to their tenth birthday in Le Creusot, and 477 in Elbeuf); the experience of Lyons was much more favourable. Before attempting a more profound causal analysis we need to improve the quality of statistics on the socio-economic characteristics of individual towns as another stage of this project.

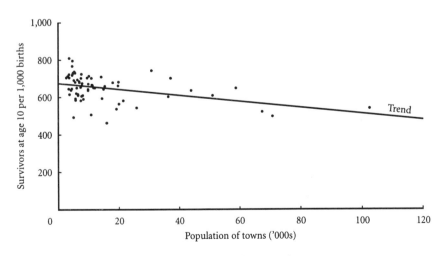

Fig. 5.3. France: Town sizes and infant mortality, 1859–1863

References

BOURDELAIS, P., 1984. 'L'industrialisation et ses mobilités (1836–1936)', *Annales E.S.C.* 5, pp. 1009–1019.

—— and DEMONET, M., 1996. 'The evolution of mortality in an industrial town: Le Creusot in the nineteenth century', *The History of the Family* 1(2), 183–204.

DEMONET, M., 1990. *Tableau de l'agriculture française au milieu du XIXe siècle*, Paris, Editions de l'Ecole des Hautes Etudes en Sciences Sociales.

EGGERICKX, T. and DEBUISSON, M., 1990. 'La surmortalité urbaine: le cas de la Wallonie et de Bruxelles à la fin du XIXe siècle (1889–1892)', *Annales de Démographie Historique*, pp. 23–41.

GARDEN, M., 1970. *Lyon et les lyonnais au XVIIIe siècle*, Paris, Les Belles-Lettres.

LACHIVER, M., 1969. *La population de Meulan du XVIIe au XIXe siècle*, Paris, SEVPEN.

LE MÉE, R., 1989. 'Les villes de France et leur population de 1806 à 1851', *Annales de Démographie Historique*, pp. 321–393.

MESLÉ, F. and VALLIN, J., 1989. 'Reconstitution des tables annuelles de mortalité pour la France au XIXe siècle', *Population* 44, pp. 1121–1157.

PRESTON, S. H. and VAN DE WALLE, E., 1978. 'Urban French mortality in the nineteenth century', *Population Studies* 32(2), pp. 275–297.

6

Urbanization, Infant Mortality and Public Health in Imperial Germany

JÖRG VÖGELE

Life expectancy in Western Europe has more than doubled within the last two hundred years. This can be attributed largely to a substantial reduction in infant mortality. Whereas in historic Germany, for example, only one third of all infants born in some years survived the first year and often only one half of those born in a particular year reached maturity, infant mortality in recent years has been as low as 6.7 deaths per 1,000 life births, and life expectancy is, in fact, higher for infants than for those aged 1 and over (Daten des Gesundheitswesens 1993, 184). The mechanisms of this remarkable decline still remain a puzzle and are vigorously debated. Key explanatory factors cited in recent studies as determining levels and trends of infant mortality include, for example, the legitimacy status of infants, fertility, feeding practices, housing conditions, and parental education, wealth and occupation (Woods, Watterson and Woodward 1988, 1989).

For Germany, levels and trends of infant mortality, as well as social and regional variations, have already been discussed in great detail. Feeding practices have been identified as a major factor in the high infant mortality rates in nineteenth-century Germany (Kintner 1982; Stöckel 1986). Regional differences in infant mortality have been attributed, to a large extent, to different attitudes towards life and death in general (Imhof 1981; Ottmüller 1991). In late-nineteenth-century Prussia, however, regional disparities were diminishing, whereas social differentials were increasing (Spree 1988, 1995). Since these were not identical to class formation, mortality change cannot be exclusively explained in terms of differences in wealth. Recent research has shifted attention towards a systematic analysis of urban–rural differentials in infant mortality, and in particular the levels and trends of infant mortality and causes of death in the cities (Vögele 1994). One major issue in this context is the effect of public health provision on the secular decline in urban mortality. The large urban agglomerations in particular possessed the potential and the innovative power to carry out health-related measures on a large scale. This highlights the active role of the towns in the fight against disease in the dramatic change towards modern health conditions. It is for this reason that the mechanisms behind this development will be investigated in the context of specific urban-industrial living conditions and urban public health measures undertaken to secure or improve health conditions. This chapter attempts to analyse urban infant

C.A. Corsini and P.P. Viazzo (eds.) The Decline of Infant and Child Mortality, 109-127.
© *1997 UNICEF. Printed in the Netherlands.*

mortality change in Germany during the late nineteenth and early twentieth centuries against the background of increasing public health services. As a prerequisite, levels and trends of urban infant mortality and the changing patterns of disease will be analysed. Subsequently, the focus will be on two major elements of sanitary reform—central water-supply and sewerage systems and municipal milk supply—and on the growing infant-care movement. For this purpose, the specific developments in the 10 most populous towns (in 1910) and average conditions in all towns with a population exceeding 15,000 inhabitants will form the core of the following analysis.[1]

CHANGES IN URBAN INFANT MORTALITY IN IMPERIAL GERMANY

The years between unification and the First World War are generally considered to constitute an essential period in Germany's transformation from an agriculturally dominated state and society towards an industrially dominated one. This process was accompanied by rapid population growth and an increasing concentration of the population in urban agglomerations (Köllmann 1974; Matzerath 1985; Reulecke 1985; Laux 1989). In 1871, 36 per cent of the German population lived in communities of 2,000 or more; by 1910 the proportion was 60 per cent (Hohorst, Kocka and Ritter 1975, 44). The big cities in particular registered accelerated growth during this period. Industrialization and urbanization radically changed urban living conditions. High population densities in the cities together with devastating environmental conditions were ideal for the transmission of disease.

It is not surprising, therefore, that death rates in Prussia and in most of the largest German towns reached a peak in the 1860s and 1870s, coinciding with the beginning of Germany's main period of urbanization. In the following decades, however, urban areas registered a strong decline in mortality (Vögele 1991). This trend started in the younger age groups first. But it was infant mortality, which traditionally ran at high rates in the urban environment, that showed the most substantial improvements. In the period under investigation, infant mortality in Germany declined substantially, from 21 deaths per 100 births in 1875 (in Prussia) to 15 deaths per 100 in the German Empire in 1913. It is important to emphasize that the decline in infant mortality started earlier and was more pronounced in towns than in rural areas. Prussian data permit an analysis of aggregate urban–rural infant mortality differentials from 1875 onwards (unfortunately only on the basis of politically defined urban and rural administrative units).[2]

---

[1] The 10 largest towns were Berlin, Breslau, Cologne, Dresden, Düsseldorf, Frankfurt am Main, Hamburg, Leipzig, Munich and Nuremberg. With over 7 million inhabitants, these towns represented 11.1 per cent of the total population.

[2] In 1905, for example, data for rural Prussia include 27 rural communities with over 20,000 inhabitants. Together they comprised 4.43 per cent of all inhabitants of rural Prussia. Unfortunately, there is no further differentiation available. (This figure is calculated from *Preußische Statistik*, an official publication of the Royal Statistical Office in Berlin. Between 1861 and 1934, 368 volumes were published.)

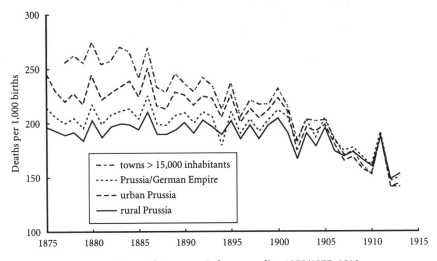

Fig. 6.1. Imperial Germany: Infant mortality, 1875/1877–1913

Note: Prussia 1877–1900; German Empire 1901–1913

Sources: *Preußische Statistik*; Veröffentlichungen des Kaiserlichen Gesundheitsamtes (Beilagen), 1878–1914; Rothenbacher 1982, 396.

At the start of the observation period, urban infant mortality rates were significantly higher than those of rural areas. However, from this high level the trend of urban rates was downward from the beginning of the registration period. In contrast, the decline for rural Prussia and for the whole of Prussia did not begin until the early decades of the twentieth century (Figure 6.1). Consequently, in the course of the twentieth century, the towns showed increasingly lower infant mortality rates than rural areas, and, indeed, the national aggregate. Even the death rate of illegitimate infants—traditionally very high—declined in urban environments, whereas it increased in the countryside (Prinzing 1899, 613). Taking all German towns with over 15,000 inhabitants, infant mortality declined in the last decades of the nineteenth century from a very high level, and this trend accelerated after the turn of the century. In this respect, the towns and especially the large self-governing cities (*Großstädte*), traditionally regarded as being particularly unhealthy, showed significant improvements. In Prussia in 1905/6 life expectancy at birth in the large towns with over 100,000 inhabitants was higher than in medium-sized towns with 20,000–100,000 inhabitants: 42.71 years for males, 48.35 for females in large towns; 42.58 and 47.64, respectively, in medium-sized towns (Ballod 1913, 58).

Causes of Death

A major methodological problem that has to be tackled is how to assess urban infant mortality in Germany. Existing studies have usually collected their data at the level of the larger Prussian administrative units, the *Regierungsbezirke*. In order to establish an urban–rural comparison they have contrasted selected units that they consider to be dominated by industry and agriculture, respectively. There are two problems in such an approach. First, concentration on Prussia might have been acceptable as representative if the focus of the investigation had been social or regional differences within Germany, but in the context of an analysis of urban mortality in Imperial Germany it excluded 5 of the 10 largest towns (Dresden, Hamburg, Leipzig, Munich and Nuremberg). Second, the *Regierungsbezirke* comprised various towns and cities as well as rural areas and were, therefore, heterogeneous units. Even the archetypal industrial unit during that period, the *Regierungsbezirk* Arnsberg, included substantial agricultural elements. Therefore, the analysis has to make use of the specific municipal statistics. A reasonable urban–rural comparison could only be obtained by investigating a specific town and its surrounding rural areas, using demographic data at the level of larger registration areas. For the big cities, however, this is an inadequate procedure since the areas directly surrounding a city were often urban in character as well, or were substantially influenced by central-place functions of the neighbouring city. Furthermore, as the conditions in the largest towns provided a role model, the traditionally applied urban–rural dichotomy would underestimate their primary role within the context of the secular mortality decline (Vögele, forthcoming).

The following analysis will, therefore, focus on the demographic developments in the 10 largest cities and evaluate the urban effect in comparison with other, smaller towns (the average of all towns with more than 15,000 inhabitants). As corresponding data are not available for Germany, the conditions in Prussia will form the comparative framework. This will provide trends rather than exact statistics, since Prussia was becoming increasingly urbanized during the period under investigation. As a consequence, the number of births in urban areas increased despite a significant reduction in urban fertility rates. In Prussia, for example, the proportion of urban live births increased from 33 per cent in 1875 to 42 per cent in 1913 (*Preußische Statistik*).

The available sources differ markedly in the ways that they classify diseases.[3] Health statistics, including statistics on causes of death, were to a large extent decentralized— a matter for individual German states.[4] Even within states the methods of recording causes of death differed between the various municipal statistical offices. In addition, classification changed over time. In order to reconstruct changes in disease patterns over time and to compare different towns, the disease data had to be grouped together and standardized. This revised, unified classification scheme was modelled on the Prussian registration system, since half of the towns in the German sample registered their causes of death according to this scheme, and the development in Prussia serves as a basis for comparison.[5]

[3] For a synopsis of the different schemes see Würzburger 1909–1914, 45–55.

[4] A brief survey of the development of vital statistics and of attempts to create an international causes-of-death registration is offered by Tutzke 1969, 33–110.

[5] Using source material for the large towns offers the opportunity to devise a more detailed classification system than the scheme provided by Kintner, who arranged broad categories for Germany on the national level, derived from the various registration schemes of Saxony, Baden, Hamburg, Bremen, Prussia and Germany for the period 1878–1932. (See Kintner 1986, 45–54.)

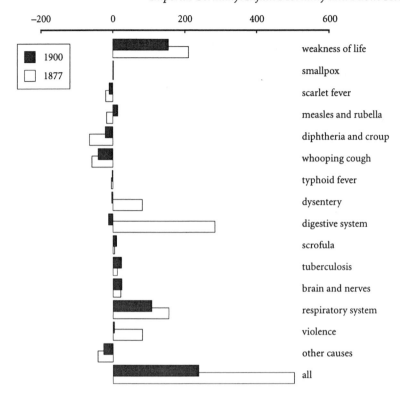

Fig. 6.2a. Imperial Germany: Differences in infant mortality
between the 10 largest towns and Prussia, 1877 and 1900

Note: Since relative figures would unnecessarily emphasize the role of epidemiologically less important diseases, the graph represents the IMRs for the 10 largest towns minus the IMRs for Prussia as a whole.

Sources: statistical yearbooks of the individual towns; *Preußische Statistik.*

The predominant causes of death among infants were gastro-intestinal diseases and *Lebensschwäche* (weakness of life)[6] often linked with *Abzehrung* (emaciation, atrophy), which was probably a result of an illness of the digestive system (Würzburg 1887/1888, 48–52; Flügge 1894, 275; Prinzing 1900, 636–637). In the 10 largest towns of Germany in 1877, over 50 per cent of infant deaths were the result of digestive diseases, and almost 25 per cent the result of weakness.[7] Diseases of the respiratory system followed in third place, with substantially lower rates. In fourth place were 'other causes', followed by diseases of the brain and nerves.[8] Whereas in Prussia as a whole in 1877, when compared

---

[6] Contemporary experts considered convulsions, emaciation, atrophy, and teething as causes of death following digestive sickness, and consequently subsumed those diseases under the digestive disease group (see Prinzing 1899, 577–635). Kintner (1986, 50–51) confirmed this view by applying regression analysis to cause-specific infant mortality rates for various German administrative areas.

[7] These data are derived from the statistical yearbooks of the individual towns and *Preußische Statistik.*

[8] Diseases of the nervous system may also, at least partially, have included intestinal diseases. (See Kintner 1986, 46.)

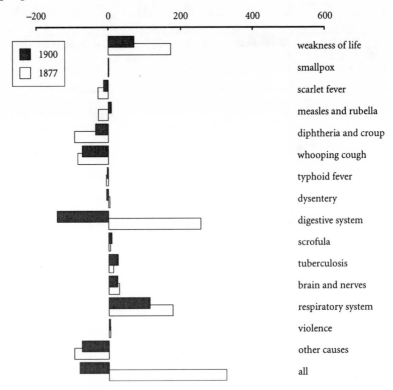

Fig. 6.2b. Imperial Germany: Differences in infant mortality
between the 10 largest towns and rural Prussia, 1877 and 1900
Note: Figures represent the IMR for the 10 largest towns minus the IMR for rural Prussia.
Sources: statistical yearbooks of the individual towns; *Preußische Statistik*.

to the urban sample, mortality from the classic infectious diseases of childhood (scarlet fever, measles and rubella, diphtheria and croup, and whooping cough) was clearly higher, it was mainly the gastro-intestinal disease complex that was responsible for the higher overall urban mortality, followed by weakness and diseases of the respiratory system (Figure 6.2a). Similar patterns can be seen when the sample is compared to rural Prussia (Figure 6.2b). Before 1900 the relative reduction of high infant mortality levels in urban areas was brought about principally by a decrease in gastro-intestinal diseases.[9] Between 1877 and 1907, the decline in digestive diseases was the major component in the reduction of urban infant mortality (Figure 6.3). With this in mind, attention should be paid to changes in the urban environment, particularly during the

[9] Owing to changes in cause-of-death registration in the Prussian aggregate (referring especially to digestive diseases), a direct urban–rural comparison after 1904 is difficult, if not impossible. (See 'Preußen. Erlaß, betr. die Neubearbeitung des Verzeichnisses der Krankheiten und Todesursachen', 1904, *Veröffentlichungen des Kaiserlichen Gesundheitsamtes* 28, 645–651; *Preußische Statistik* 189, 6; Kintner 1986, 47.)

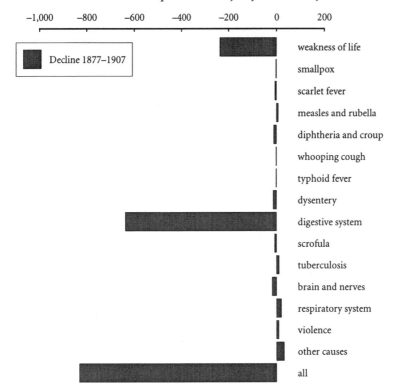

Fig. 6.3. Imperial Germany: Absolute contribution of the various causes of death to the overall decline in infant mortality in the ten largest towns, 1877–1907

Sources: statistical yearbooks of the individual towns; *Preußische Statistik*.

late nineteenth century, because of their potential influence in the decrease in digestive diseases. In this context, I will now concentrate on the influence of sanitary reform on urban infant mortality change.

INFANT MORTALITY AND SANITARY REFORM

Sanitary reform focused on measures to improve the hygiene conditions of the urban environment. Specific measures were carried out in an increasingly systematic manner during the last decades of the nineteenth and the early twentieth centuries. Particular emphasis was placed on central water-supply and sewerage systems, but programmes also selectively included disinfection and control of food and municipal milk supply (Weyl 1904, 1). In the following discussion, the focus will be on central water-supply and sewerage systems as the major component of sanitary reform during the late nineteenth and early twentieth centuries, and on municipal milk supply as a strategy especially designed to reduce infant mortality.

Central Water-Supply and Sewerage Systems

A major factor affecting the urban environment during the second half of the nineteenth century was the installation and expansion of central water-supply and sewerage systems. In the absence of a legislative framework, the initiative was completely in the hands of the traditionally self-governing and powerful local communities. Following the pioneering example of Britain, sanitary reforms spread in Germany during the last decades of the nineteenth century. Major building activities for central water-supply systems were being undertaken in the large towns, particularly in the 1870s and 1880s. By 1900 all large towns had a central water supply, compared with only 47 per cent of the smaller towns (those with 2,000–25,000 inhabitants). There were wide regional differences: 67 per cent of the smaller towns in Prussia and 35 per cent in the other German states still had no central water supply by the turn of the century (Grahn 1904a, 309). Despite the continued dominance of localistic–miasmatic theories about the origins of many diseases, the expansion of sewerage systems came some time after the construction of waterworks: the main period of construction occurred around the turn of the century.

The level and trend of the death rate from typhoid fever is considered to be a classic test for assessing the health impact of these reforms (Otto, Spree and Vögele 1990, 297–301). Given the prevalence of digestive disease among infants, this test should be extended to infant mortality rates—particularly since the decline in urban infant mortality was accompanied by a decline in breastfeeding practices in the large towns of Germany (Prinzing 1906, 294; Kintner 1985, 169–172). In Cologne in 1902, for example, 40 per cent of all mothers breastfed their infants. One generation earlier the rate had been 94 per cent (Selter 1902, 384). In Berlin in 1885, 55.5 per cent of all infants were exclusively breastfed; by 1900 this proportion had declined to 31.4 per cent (Neumann 1902, 795). In the traditionally non-breastfeeding areas, the percentage of infants nourished solely with artificial food was even higher. According to material from the Munich children's hospital, the number of infants never breastfed was 78.3 per cent in 1861–1869, rising even higher to 82.3 (1870–1878) and 86.4 (1879–1886) (Büller 1887, 320; Escherich 1887, 233; Seidlmayer 1937, 29). In view of this development, environmental improvement may have played an increasingly important role in the decline in infant mortality, since artificial food was to a large extent prepared with water, and animal milk was often diluted. This implies that the potential effect of these changes to the public health infrastructure should be measurable in relation to the subsequent development of both death rates from digestive diseases and infant mortality.

Recent research has indicated that sanitary reform played a part in the decline of urban infant mortality in Germany, although the effects were not as strong or coherent as for typhoid fever (Stöckel 1986, 230–231; Brown, forthcoming). This is remarkable in view of the decreasing breastfeeding rates and the increased use of water in the preparation of infant food. The impact of central water supply on the reduction of typhoid fever may, perhaps, have been overestimated, and the disease may have been generally on the retreat.[10] There is, indeed, some support for assuming a relatively restricted potential impact of central water supply and sewerage on health. The quantitative and qualitative state of these facilities left much to be desired. In the nineteenth century they were still generally restricted to the large cities. In many of them, technical standards, particularly with respect to water filtration, were insufficient.

The limitations and successes of infrastructural measures can be demonstrated using the example of Hamburg. The city had an early central water supply (1842), yet failed to install a filter plant. This deficiency contributed crucially to the devastating effect of the infamous cholera epidemic of 1892, which caused 8,616 deaths (Evans 1987). Infant mortality reached a peak during this year. After the installation of a filter plant in the following year, not only did the risk of dying from cholera and typhoid fever decrease, but deaths from digestive diseases were also reduced, increasing the survival chances of infants (Vögele 1994, 411–416). The Hamburg case reveals that central water supply per se had no positive effect on health conditions. In literal terms it simply implied that water was taken from a specific source and distributed throughout the town.

Although a single water source facilitates quality control, in the absence of knowledge about the true origin and spread of disease this advantage remained hypothetical. Supporters of localistic–miasmatic theories denied the need to control drinking-water resources, but the increasingly scientific analysis of water encouraged growing opposition to this theory. With the rise of bacteriology, scientists focused their investigations on a number of unidentified and obscure germs. As scientists were still unable to identify pathogens, it was assumed that the critical value was 1,000 unidentified germs per cubic centimetre of water (Grahn 1904b, 975). This, combined with the belief in self-purification of flowing water, did not help to encourage the development of artificial sand-filtration, adequate sewerage disposal and river conservancy. Without recognition of the fact that all these components contributed to an integrated circulatory water system, which was only as effective as its weakest point, lasting improvements in health conditions were not guaranteed and set-backs were inevitable. A poorly balanced programme of water services, in fact, even increased health problems. Numerous outbreaks of typhoid fever in these places reflected the persistent risk of using drinking water. It is not surprising, therefore, that even as late as 1888 there was only a weak negative correlation in the largest German towns between private water consumption (litres per capita per day) and IMR, indicating the inadequacy and potential risk of the central water supply. After the turn of the century this correlation became slightly stronger.[11] The death rate from acute digestive diseases in the 10 largest cities and the average rate for all towns over 15,000 inhabitants, however, remained at a permanently high level during the last decades of the nineteenth century (Figure 6.4).

---

[10] For an explicit discussion see Vögele 1993, 345–365.

[11] A correlation of daily water consumption per capita and IMR in the largest German towns gives the following results:

1888: $r = -0.2597$, sig (two-tailed) $= 0.500$;

1912: $r = -0.4749$, sig (two-tailed) $= 0.196$.

(*Statistisches Jahrbuch deutscher Städte;* Veröffentlichungen des Kaiserlichen Gesundheitsamtes (Beilagen).)

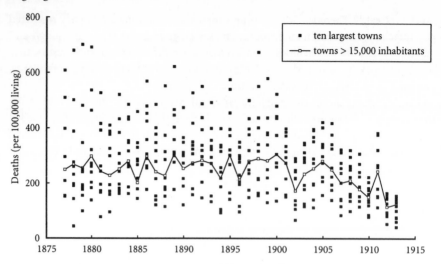

Fig. 6.4. Imperial Germany: Urban mortality from acute digestive diseases, 1877–1913
Source: Veröffentlichungen des Kaiserlichen Gesundheitsamtes (Beilagen), 1878–1914.

Municipal Milk Supply

Although the towns invested substantial sums of money in central water-supply and sewerage systems, the supply and distribution of municipal milk only began after some considerable delay. High infant mortality rates were traditionally considered to be inevitable (Pfaffenholz 1902, 402–403). Declining birth rates, however, raised fears about the nation's economic and military future, and led to a concentration of forces in the battle against high infant mortality. This was reinforced as statistical evidence revealed that Germany ranked badly in an international context, especially when compared to France or England. The case for healthy infant nutrition became more and more the focus of attention, and the supply of adequate animal milk was considered to be a high municipal priority.

In Germany, the sale of pasteurized or sterilized milk commenced in the late 1880s. Complete sterilization was expensive, and therefore rarely applied in practice. As an additional obstacle, milk was not one of the subjects dealt with in the nutrition laws, and in 1900 only three towns (Berlin, Dresden and Munich) had special regulations concerning children's milk. Consequently, there were many complaints about the quality of milk (Flügge 1894, 321). One crucial point was that urban milk provision relied increasingly on an imported supply as cattle-breeding in the towns declined rapidly. Long distances and inadequate transport often led to a deterioration in the quality of milk. In the early years the supply and preparation of milk was completely in the hands of private enterprises and free tradesmen, but by the late nineteenth century many municipalities had established their own management system to deal with milk supply and distribution (Spiegel 1908, 232). Following French models, a handful of towns established municipal milk depots in the first decade of the twentieth century. Many other towns also recognized the importance of regulating milk supply and insisted on certain standards. As a consequence, quality improved. In Düsseldorf in 1895, for example, 23 per cent of the official examinations found the milk to be unsatisfactory; in 1906 only 3 per cent of samples failed to pass the test (Schrakamp 1908, 110). By 1901 police ordinances included regulations about the importation of milk from outside the town. Each consignment of milk had to be sealed before being imported, and its origin clearly identified. Merchants had to register at police stations, so that in the case of irregularities the responsible persons could easily be found (Schrakamp 1908, 110–113). Bacteriological examination, however, remained difficult and, given the expense involved, was hardly feasible in practice (Pfaffenholz 1902, 400). It was for this reason that the amount of specially treated and controlled milk for children available in the towns remained very limited, amounting on average to only 500 litres per 100,000 inhabitants per day. Sold at a price of 50–60 Pfennige per litre, this type of milk was more than twice as expensive as normal milk, and was consequently only an option for well-to-do sections of the population (Pfaffenholz 1902, 404; Spiegel 1908, 229).[12] However, there was growing opposition to even this limited supply. Some elements of the food industry promoted their own artificial products camouflaged with scientific expertise. There were reports from Bonn in 1902 that young families had received a brochure, signed by a paediatrician, recommending the use of powdered infant food (Cramer 1902, 419).

At the time, people were convinced of the success of municipal milk supply in improving the state of health of infants and young children. Recent international research seems to be divided on the question. For Britain it has been argued that the substantial fall in infant mortality after the turn of the century can be attributed mainly to the improved provision of pasteurized milk, the introduction and popularization of dried milk as an infant food, and the widespread use of condensed or evaporated milk (Beaver 1973; Dwork 1987). But more recent studies are sceptical about the impact of municipal milk supply on the decline of infant mortality in Britain. Since breastfeeding remained widespread, the health of infants was more dependent on demographic and socio-economic factors (Woods, Watterson and Woodward 1989, 116–120). Others have suggested that consumption of milk that was often of poor quality contributed to ill health (Atkins 1992, 227), particularly because of its part in infant deaths from tuberculosis and digestive diseases. Since German breastfeeding rates were lower, milk supply was potentially more influential. However, demographic data confirm the generally poor state of municipal milk provision. An adequate and widespread milk supply should have contributed to a decline in mortality from tuberculosis and digestive diseases among infants, as well as reducing climatic fluctuations in the structure of infant mortality. In the German towns, however, the death rate from tuberculosis among infants actually increased from 29 per 10,000 births in 1877 to 44 in 1900; it declined

---

12 In Berlin, Cologne, Düsseldorf, Hamburg, and Frankfurt normal milk was sold at an average price of 22 Pfennige per litre. (See *Statistische Monatsberichte der Stadt Düsseldorf 1910* (Beilagen), 6.)

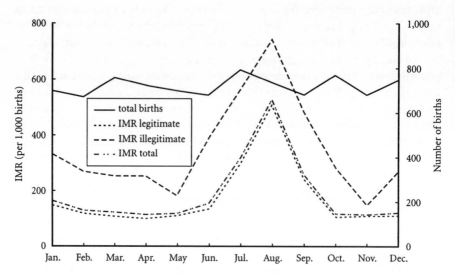

Fig. 6.5. Düsseldorf: Seasonal distribution of infant mortality by births in specific months, 1905

Source: Jahresbericht des Statistischen Amts der Stadt Düsseldorf für 1905, 4–5.

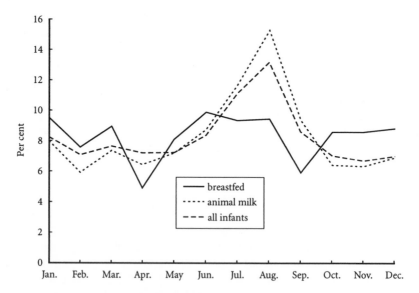

Fig. 6.6. Berlin: Seasonal distribution of infant mortality by feeding practices, 1908

Source: Statistisches Jahrbuch der Stadt Berlin 32, 1913, 183.

only slightly, to 38, by 1907, although it fell constantly in the age groups from 5 years upwards. Death rates from digestive diseases, on the other hand, experienced a strong decline at the beginning of the twentieth century when assessed from average figures for all towns with a population exceeding 15,000 inhabitants and in the 10 largest towns (Figure 6.4). However, climatic dependency remained. The cold summer of 1902 was accompanied by low infant mortality (see Figure 6.1; Spiegel 1908, 225; Kruse 1912, 179), but the hot summer of 1911 registered high infant mortality rates (Kruse 1912, 175–201; Seidlmayer 1937, 20). Seasonal fluctuations persisted, with a pronounced summer peak (Vögele 1994, 420–421; Silbergleit 1896, 454). The case of Düsseldorf shows that this cannot be ascribed to an increased number of births during the summer months (Figure 6.5). Illegitimate infants in particular—the weakest group—registered this peak. Berlin data reveal that summer excess mortality affected artificially fed infants most strongly, whereas breastfeeding provided some protection in the hot periods of the year (Figure 6.6). It was only during the deprivation of the First World War that the summer peak began to vanish (Hecker 1923, 287), which was a result of increased breastfeeding (Seidlmayer 1937, 22–31). Demographic evidence, therefore, confirms the view that a qualitatively satisfactory milk supply reaching a substantial portion of the population (and especially the poor) had still not been developed by the first decade of the twentieth century.

INFANT WELFARE CENTRES

Health-securing measures created in the period under investigation formed an essential basis for a health-preserving way of life. The role of the health-care recipients, however, was of equal importance. The provision of satisfactory hygienic milk, for instance, was of little value if the purchasers stored it in the warmest place in the house (Soxhlet 1886, 255) and neither washed their hands before preparing the milk nor cleaned the bottles after use. In other words, the potential benefits of an improved health-related infrastructure remained underutilized in the absence of a corresponding improvement in personal hygiene. The evolution of a collectively rooted personal-hygiene regime was, therefore, a necessity. This resulted from an increasingly rational approach to life. Corresponding mentalities and norms of behaviour pervaded society from top to bottom. Within this process, medicine increasingly took over the tasks of educating and controlling (Spree 1980; Tennstedt 1981; Labisch 1992). This is said to have made the doctors into 'transmission vehicles' for these new values, which success-fully spread among working-class people and affected contemporary views on hygiene and health.

For the most part, however, nineteenth-century doctors were not given access to sick infants. Doctors complained that they were rarely consulted in a case of infant sickness, or only when it was too late to apply any successful treatment (Stumpf 1886, 438). At the same time, however, the statutes of many general hospitals excluded infants from admission. A revealing indicator concerning medical treatment of infants is the official death certification. Apart from Prussia, this certification was obligatory in the larger German states. However, it was only carried out by a doctor if the person had received medical treatment; otherwise the cause of death was registered according to information proffered by parents or relatives (Prinzing 1899, 634; Prinzing 1906, 323–325). In this sense, the proportion of medically certified causes of death can function as a proxy for medical access. According to the available source material this was rather limited. In Lower Bavaria in 1866–1867, for example, doctors were consulted only in 3 per cent of all cases of infant sickness (Maier 1871, 193). In Württemberg in 1900 only 38 per cent of all dying infants received medical treatment, compared with 70–90 per cent in the higher age groups (Prinzing 1906, 322). In Dresden in 1891–1896, death was not certified by a doctor in 49 per cent of all infant deaths; in the higher age groups this was the case in only 2 per cent of all deaths (Schlossmann 1897, 178). In Saxony, where specific statistical information was recorded from 1873, the percentage of medically certified causes of deaths for all infants rose from 15.8 in 1875 to 39.5 in 1910; even as late as the 1920s the number of medically certified infant deaths only slightly surpassed 50 per cent (Würzburger 1930, 190).

Other attempts to mediate bourgeois elements of hygiene to members of the working class were similarly limited. In urban areas, elementary school education lasted several years—but hygiene matters were not a part of the official curriculum during the nineteenth century. The necessary medical guides and handbooks of infant care were not widely circulated or distributed among working-class families. Similarly, breastfeeding campaigns remained without broad effect during the nineteenth and early twentieth centuries (Stöckel 1986, 252–256). Nevertheless, private expenditure on health and hygiene soared after the turn of the twentieth century (Hoffmann 1965, 676–677). Analysis of the housekeeping books of blue-collar workers, white-collar workers and civil servants indicates, however, that there remained substantial differences in expenditure on health and body care between the classes (*2. Sonderheft zum Reichsarbeitsblatt* 1909, 56–57). This implies that increased private expenditure in this area may simply be a proxy for higher income or improved living standards rather than a reflection of increased hygiene-consciousness.

It was at the beginning of the twentieth century that doctors realized the necessity for an active health-care approach to the population. From 1907 onwards they developed the so-called 'advancing infant care', which enabled medical personnel to be in direct contact with mother and child through house-visits (Rott 1926/1927, 1931; Engel and Behrendt 1927). Indeed, health visiting was started with great enthusiasm. Infant-welfare centres were created by the municipalities (often connected to the local milk depots) or by private associations (*Vereine*) supported by municipal authorities. By 1907 there were 101 infant-welfare centres, 17 of which included health visiting (Trumpp 1908, 119–120). Of our sample, all towns except Nuremberg had such an institution (Trumpp 1908, 120). Regulations were strict. Mothers had to agree to be visited, and they had to present themselves at the centre either once a week or once a fortnight. They had to establish their eligibility for financial support for breastfeeding (*Stillprämien*) by demonstrating the act of breastfeeding in front of the doctor, showing that they had milk and that their babies would suckle. As with the milk depots, however, the success of these facilities was rather limited.

Even in 1927 there were complaints that, despite house visits and financial support for breastfeeding, many mothers could not be dealt with by the local advisory centres. The proudly released figures that 60–80 per cent of all the mothers in a town had been officially contacted must be treated cautiously.[13] Medical experts involved in health visiting conceded that even in the industrial town of Dortmund the rate did not surpass 60–70 per cent, despite very substantial efforts (Engel and Behrendt 1927, 97). Moreover, this figure refers to single visits; it provides no indication concerning the intensity or frequency of the contacts.

The reasons for the limited success are complex. Local practitioners were often opposed to the centres, fearing that the cost-free advice offered would reduce their income (Dietrich 1908, 51; Trumpp 1908, 129). More important, however, was the fact that this approach was based on a significant misconception of working-class living conditions. Even if the mothers accepted these new facilities and values, they could not take full advantage of them. For example, in the big cities a mother's visit to the centre often required long-distance travel and the use of expensive public transport. If there were other children in the family they had to be left alone at home or accompany the mother. Milk was often inadequately handled as a result of a lack of domestic facilities. There was no cool place in the small and often overcrowded working-class tenements to store it. Insufficient heating material prevented the mothers from heating the milk or cleaning the bottles properly. Finally, mothers were overburdened with a multitude of tasks and a restricted family budget. It was only the First World War that brought about a substantial increase in breastfeeding rates in German towns, with a subsequent fall in infant mortality.

CONCLUSION

In Germany the peak of the urban infant mortality rates was reached in the 1860s and 1870s, coinciding with the beginning of Germany's main period of urbanization. Thereafter the trend of urban infant mortality rates was downwards, whereas the decline for the whole of Prussia did not begin until the first decades of the twentieth century. Consequently, after the turn of the century the towns showed increasingly lower rates than rural areas or, indeed, the national aggregate. It was the big cities in particular that led the way in this development. At the same time these cities were forerunners in the implementation of various public health strategies, in particular the installation of central water supply and sanitation, municipal milk supply and advancing infant care. In theory these measures could have contributed to the decline in infant mortality. In practice, however, their effect was often limited or inadequate. Since theories about the origins of disease were still unclear, the systems often did not

---

[13] For a more optimistic view see Frevert 1984, 320–344 and Frevert 1985, 421–446.

satisfy hygiene requirements. The number and capacity of milk depots and infant-welfare centres were relatively small, and, what is more, their acceptance among the working-classes was limited since they were designed to a large extent without regard to actual working-class living conditions. It was only the increased breastfeeding rates during the deprived war years that may have contributed substantially to the continuing decline in infant mortality. In Imperial Germany, the key explanatory factors may rather be in the field of demographic and economic change. During this period, however, high infant mortality rates were increasingly acknowledged to be high and no longer taken as inevitable. The major components that determined the level of infant mortality rates were identified, and strategies to fight these high rates were systematically elaborated. In this sense, the basis was formed for the continuing decline of infant mortality rates during the course of the twentieth century and for the current lowest-ever rates in developed countries. At the same time, the historical case can open new perspectives and provide the tools to combat high infant mortality rates in present-day less developed countries.

References

ATKINS, P. J., 1992. 'White poison? the social consequences of milk consumption in London, 1850–1939', *Social History of Medicine* 5, pp. 207–228.

BALLOD, C., 1913. *Grundriss der Statistik*, Berlin, J. Guttentag.

BEAVER, M. W., 1973. 'Population, infant mortality and milk', *Population Studies* 27, pp. 243–254.

BROWN, J. C., forthcoming. 'Public health reform and the decline in urban mortality: the case of Germany, 1876–1912', in G. KEARNS, W. R. LEE, M. C. NELSON and J. ROGERS (eds.), *Improving the public health: essays in medical history*, Liverpool, Liverpool University Press.

BÜLLER, F., 1887. 'Ursachen und Folgen des Nichtstillens in der Bevölkerung Münchens', *Jahrbuch für Kinderheilkunde* 16, pp. 313–340.

CRAMER, 1902. 'Wichtige Aufgaben der öffentlichen und privaten Wohlfahrtspflege auf dem Gebiet der künstlichen Ernährung der Säuglinge' (contribution to the discussion following Pfaffenholz), *Centralblatt für allgemeine Gesundheitspflege* 21, pp. 417–419.

DATEN DES GESUNDHEITSWESENS, 1993. *Ausgabe 1993*. Schriftenreihe des Bundesministeriums für Gesundheit no. 25, Baden-Baden, Nomos.

DIETRICH, E., 1908. 'Das Fürsorgewesen für Säuglinge', *Zeitschrift für Säuglingsfürsorge* 2, pp. 1–61.

DWORK, D., 1987. *War is good for babies and other young children: a history of the infant and child welfare movement in England, 1898–1918*, London, Tavistock.

ENGEL, S. and BEHRENDT, H., 1927. 'Säuglingsfürsorge', in A. GOTTSTEIN, A. SCHLOSSMANNN and L. TELEKY (eds.), *Handbuch der Sozialen Hygiene*, vol. 4, Berlin, Springer.

ESCHERICH, T., 1887. 'Die Ursachen und Folgen des Nichtstillens bei der Bevölkerung Münchens', *Münchener Medicinische Wochenschrift* 34, pp. 233–235, 256–259.

EVANS, R., 1987. *Death in Hamburg: society and politics in the cholera years 1830–1910*, Oxford, Clarendon Press.

FLÜGGE, C., 1894. 'Die Aufgaben und Leistungen der Milchsterilisierung gegenüber den Darmkrankheiten der Säuglinge', *Zeitschrift für Hygiene und Infectionskrankheiten* 17, pp. 272–342.

FREVERT, U., 1984. 'The civilizing tendency of hygiene: working-class women under medical control in Imperial Germany', in J. C. FOUT (ed.), *German women in the nineteenth century: a social history*, New York, Holmes and Meier.

—— 1985. ' "Fürsorgliche Belagerung": Hygienebewegung und Arbeiterfrauen im 19. und frühen 20. Jahrhundert', *Geschichte und Gesellschaft* 11, pp. 421–446.

GRAHN, E., 1904a. 'Die städtischen Wasserwerke', in R. WUTTKE (ed.), *Die deutschen Städte*, vol. 1, Leipzig, Brandstetter.

—— 1904b, 'Zur Geschichte der hygienischen Beurteilung des Wassers bis Ende 1902', *Schillings Journal für Gasbeleuchtung und verwandte Beleuchtungsarten sowie für Wasserversorgung* 47, pp. 973–982.

HECKER, R., 1923. 'Studien über Sterblichkeit, Todesursachen und Ernährung Münchener Säuglinge', *Archiv für Hygiene* 93, pp. 280–294.

HOFFMANN, W. G., 1965. *Das Wachstum der deutschen Wirtschaft seit der Mitte des 19. Jahrhunderts*, Berlin, Springer.

HOHORST, G., KOCKA, J. and RITTER, G. A. (eds.), 1975. *Sozialgeschichtliches Arbeitsbuch: Materialien zur Statistik des Kaiserreichs 1870–1914*, Munich, C.H. Beck.

IMHOF, A. E., 1981. 'Unterschiedliche Säuglingssterblichkeit in Deutschland, 18. bis 20. Jahrhundert—Warum?', *Zeitschrift für Bevölkerungswissenschaft* 7(3), pp. 343–382.

KINTNER, H. J., 1982. 'The determinants of infant mortality in Germany from 1871 to 1933', Ph.D. dissertation, University of Michigan.

—— 1985. 'Trends and regional differences in breastfeeding in Germany from 1871 to 1937', *Journal of Family History* 10, pp. 163–182.

—— 1986. 'Classifying causes of death during the late nineteenth and early twentieth centuries: the case of German infant mortality', *Historical Methods* 19(2), pp. 45–54.

KÖLLMANN, W., 1974. *Bevölkerung in der industriellen Revolution*, Göttingen, Vandenhoeck & Ruprecht.

KRUSE, W., 1912. 'Was lehren uns die letzten Jahrzehnte und der heisse Sommer 1911 über die Säuglingssterblichkeit und ihre Bekämpfung', *Centralblatt für allgemeine Gesundheitspflege* 31, pp. 175–201.

LABISCH, A., 1992. *Homo hygienicus: Gesundheit und Medizin in der Neuzeit*, Frankfurt-am-Main, Campus.

LAUX, H.-D., 1989. 'The components of population growth in Prussian cities, 1875–1905 and their influence on urban population structure', in R. LAWTON and R. LEE (eds.), *Urban population development from the late-eighteenth to the early-twentieth century*, Liverpool, Liverpool University Press.

MAIER, K., 1871. 'Die Sterblichkeit der Kinder im ersten Lebensjahr in Bayern', *Journal für Kinderkrankheiten* 57, pp. 153–198.

MATZERATH, H., 1985. *Urbanisierung in Preußen 1815–1914*, Stuttgart, W. Kohlhammer/ Deutscher Gemeindeverlag.

NEUMANN, H., 1902. 'Über die Häufigkeit des Stillens', *Deutsche Medicinische Wochenschrift* 28, p. 795.

OTTMÜLLER, U., 1991. *Speikinder–Gedeihkinder: Körpersprachliche Voraussetzungen der Moderne*, Tübingen, edition diskord.

OTTO, R., SPREE, R. and VÖGELE, J., 1990. 'Seuchen und Seuchenbekämpfung in deutschen

Städten während des 19. und frühen 20. Jahrhunderts: Stand und Desiderate der Forschung', *Medizinhistorisches Journal* 25, pp. 286–304.

PFAFFENHOLZ, 1902. 'Wichtige Aufgaben der öffentlichen und privaten Wohlfahrtspflege auf dem Gebiet der künstlichen Ernährung der Säuglinge', *Centralblatt für allgemeine Gesundheitspflege* 21, pp. 393–416.

PRINZING, F., 1899. 'Die Entwicklung der Kindersterblichkeit in den europäischen Staaten', *Jahrbücher für Nationalökonomie und Statistik* 3rd series, 17, pp. 577–635.

—— 1900. 'Die Kindersterblichkeit in Stadt und Land', *Jahrbücher für Nationalökonomie und Statistik* 3rd series, 20, pp. 593–644.

—— 1906. *Handbuch der medizinischen Statistik*, 1st edn, Jena, Gustav Fischer.

REULECKE, J., 1985. *Geschichte der Urbanisierung in Deutschland*, Frankfurt-am-Main, Suhrkamp.

ROTHENBACHER, F., 1982. 'Zur Entwicklung der Gesundheitsverhältnisse in Deutschland seit der Industrialisierung', in E. WIEGAND and W. ZAPF (eds.), *Wandel der Lebensbedingungen in Deutschland: Wohlfahrtsentwicklung seit der Industrialisierung*, Frankfurt-am-Main, Campus.

ROTT, F., 1926/1927. 'Die drei Senkungsperioden der Säuglingssterblichkeit im Deutschen Reiche', *Gesundheitsfürsorge für das Kindesalter* 2, pp. 491–508.

—— 1931. 'Gesundheitsfürsorge für das Kindesalter', in M. v. PFAUNDLER and A. SCHLOSSMANN (eds.), *Handbuch der Kinderheilkunde: Ein Buch für den praktischen Arzt*, vol. 1, 4th edn, Berlin, F.C.W. Vogel.

SCHLOSSMANN, A., 1897. 'Studien über Säuglingssterblichkeit', *Zeitschrift für Hygiene und Infektionskrankheiten* 24, pp. 93–188.

SCHRAKAMP, F., 1908. 'Gesundheitswesen', in T. WEYL (ed.), *Die Assanierung der Städte in Einzeldarstellungen*, vol. 2, sub-vol. 2: *Die Assanierung von Düsseldorf*, Leipzig, Wilhelm Engelmann.

SEIDLMAYER, H., 1937. *Geburtenzahl, Säuglingssterblichkeit und Stillung in München in den letzten 50 Jahren*, Munich, Rudolph Müller und Steinicke.

SELTER, 1902. 'Die Nothwendigkeit der Mutterbrust für die Ernährung der Säuglinge', *Centralblatt für allgemeine Gesundheitspflege* 21, pp. 377–392.

SILBERGLEIT, H., 1896. 'Kindersterblichkeit in europäischen Grossstädten', proceedings of the eighth Congrès International D'Hygiène et De Démographie, vol. 7, Budapest, Pester Buchdruckerei.

SOXHLET, F., 1886. 'Ueber Kindermilch und Säuglings-Ernährung', *Münchener Medicinische Wochenschrift* 33, pp. 253–256, 276–278.

SPIEGEL, L., 1908. 'Kommunale Milchversorgung', *Schriften des Vereins für Socialpolitik* 128, pp. 219–243.

SPREE, R., 1980. 'Die Entwicklung der differentiellen Säuglingssterblichkeit in Deutschland seit der Mitte des 19. Jahrhunderts (Ein Versuch zur Mentalitätsgeschichte)', in A. E. IMHOF (ed.), *Mensch und Gesundheit in der Geschichte*, Husum, Matthiesen.

—— 1988. *Health and social class in Imperial Germany: a social study of mortality, morbidity and inequality*, Oxford, Berg.

—— 1995. *On infant mortality change in Germany since the early 19th century*, Münchener Wirtschaftswissenschaftliche Beiträge no. 95–03, Munich.

STÖCKEL, S., 1986. 'Säuglingssterblichkeit in Berlin von 1870 bis zum Vorabend des ersten Weltkriegs: eine Kurve mit hohem Maximum und starkem Gefälle', *Berlin-Forschungen* 1, pp. 219–264.

STUMPF, 1886. 'Ueber Kindermilch und Säuglings-Ernährung' (contribution to the discussion of F. Soxhlet), *Münchener Medicinische Wochenschrift* 33, p. 438.

TENNSTEDT, F., 1981. *Sozialgeschichte der Sozialpolitik in Deutschland: vom 18. Jahrhundert bis zum Ersten Weltkrieg*, Göttingen, Vandenhoeck & Ruprecht.

TRUMPP, J., 1908. 'Die Milchküchen und Beratungsstellen im Dienste der Säuglingsfürsorge', *Zeitschrift für Säuglingsfürsorge* 2, pp. 119–137.

TUTZKE, D., 1969. 'Die Entwicklung der Geburts- und Sterbestatistik einschließlich der Todesursachenstatistik', *NTM–Schriftenreihe für Geschichte der Naturwissenschaften, Technik und Medizin* 6(1), pp. 33–110.

VÖGELE, J., 1991. 'Die Entwicklung der (groß)städtischen Gesundheitsverhältnisse in der Epoche des Demographischen und Epidemiologischen Übergangs', in J. REULECKE and A. CASTELL (eds.), *Stadt und Gesundheit: zum Wandel von 'Volksgesundheit' und kommunaler Gesundheitspolitik im 19. und frühen 20. Jahrhundert*, Stuttgart, Franz Steiner.

—— 1993. 'Sanitäre Reformen und der Wandel der Sterblichkeitsverhältnisse in deutschen Städten, 1870–1913', *Vierteljahrschrift für Sozial- und Wirtschaftsgeschichte* 80, pp. 345–365.

—— 1994. 'Urban infant mortality in Imperial Germany', *Social History of Medicine* 7, pp. 401–425.

—— forthcoming. *Urban mortality change in Britain and Germany, 1870–1910*, Liverpool, Liverpool University Press.

WEYL, T., 1904. 'Assanierung', in T. WEYL (ed.), *Soziale Hygiene: Handbuch der Hygiene*, vol. 4 (supplement), Jena, Gustav Fischer.

WOODS, R. I., WATTERSON, P. A. and WOODWARD, J. H., 1988 and 1989. 'The causes of rapid infant mortality decline in England and Wales, 1861–1921. Parts I and II', *Population Studies* 42(3), pp. 343–366 and 43(1), pp. 113–132.

WÜRZBURG, A., 1887 and 1888. 'Die Säuglingssterblichkeit im Deutschen Reiche während der Jahre 1875 bis 1877', *Arbeiten aus dem Kaiserlichen Gesundheitsamte* 2, pp. 208–222, 343–346 and 4, pp. 28–108.

WÜRZBURGER, E., 1909–1914. *Die Bearbeitung der Statistik der Bevölkerungsbewegung durch die Statistischen Ämter im Deutschen Reiche*, Allgemeines statistisches Archiv no. 7 (supplement), pp. 45–55.

—— 1930. 'Die Häufigkeit der ärztlichen Beglaubigung von Todesursachen in Sachsen', *Bulletin de l'Institut International de Statistique* 24, pp. 189–203.

2. SONDERHEFT ZUM REICHSARBEITSBLATTE, 1909. *Erhebung von Wirtschaftsrechnungen minderbemittelter Familien im Deutschen Reiche*. Bearbeitet im Kaiserlichen Statistischen Amte, Abteilung für Arbeiterstatistik, 1909, Berlin, Heymann.

7

Locality or Class? *Spatial and Social Differentials in Infant and Child Mortality in England and Wales, 1895–1911*

A L I C E   R E I D

The short period covered by this chapter, 1895–1911, encompasses the sharp downturn in the national infant mortality trend of England and Wales, and is thus an era of particular importance in the history of these countries' health. In the 1880s roughly 140 babies died out of every 1,000 born alive. The chance of death rose during the following decade, reaching a peak of 163 per 1,000 in 1899, after which it declined precipitously (Woods, Watterson and Woodward 1988, 349). It is now generally agreed that it is misleading to concentrate on this 1899–1901 turning point in the national series. Lee (1991) demonstrated the existence of considerable regional diversity in infant mortality at a county level, with evidence of declines in many counties from 1861 or 1871, and Woods *et al.* (1988, 357) showed the importance to the national trend of large towns and cities with pernicious health environments. The concentration of population in such areas meant that they exerted a major (and ever-growing) influence on national infant mortality, and their susceptibility to 'epidemics' of diarrhoea during the long hot summers of the 1890s produced the rise in infant mortality at the end of the century. Williams and Galley (1995) offered a reconciliation between these two observations by comparing a selection of cities and their rural hinterlands. They suggested that the beginnings of the decline in infant mortality can be traced back at least as far as the 1860s but that the 'urban–sanitary–diarrhoeal effect' noted by Woods *et al.* was operating in many large cities to obstruct any fall in the national rate. Relocating the outset of the decline to the mid-nineteenth century prompts a refocusing of the search for its causes. In this context the relationship with fertility decline obviously needs to be addressed. Williams and Galley pointed this out, but at the same time emphasized the difference between the causes of the decline and the influences affecting its differential emergence and pace. They recognized that 'any explanation of infant mortality decline also needs to take into account the factors which facilitated or inhibited its decline' (p. 420). This chapter is an attempt to use a rare and valuable data set to gain some further insight into such factors at the time of maximum diversity in infant mortality levels and trends.

    The authors cited above have tended to concentrate on levels and trends in infant mortality by location. Although the most basic comparison—that between urban and

C.A. Corsini and P.P. Viazzo (eds.) The Decline of Infant and Child Mortality, 129-154.
© *1997 UNICEF. Printed in the Netherlands.*

rural places—provides spectacular differentials, with much dimmer prospects for child survival in urban areas, infant mortality also varied markedly between individual towns. Woods, Williams and Galley's (1993) overview of mortality in a selection of large, medium and small English towns between 1840 and 1910 showed that mortality was not simply a function of the size of the town. Some smaller towns had levels of infant mortality consistently above those of larger cities. 'In a number of small towns,' they wrote, 'including Preston, infant mortality rates during the second half of the nine-teenth century were considerably above those of large cities such as Liverpool and Manchester' (p. 42). They suggested that variation in such factors as housing provision, sanitary arrangements (and especially whether a town was served by privy-middens or water closets) and patterns of female employment could help to explain differences be-tween urban areas (see also Williams and Mooney 1994, 196).

There is no doubt that during the demographic transition there was a gulf of experi-ence in economic, social, cultural and environmental terms between small market towns and factory-dominated manufacturing centres or the crowded metropolis of London. The search for proxy variables to capture the variation that will best explain infant mortality levels and trends has concentrated on urbanization and industrializ-ation. On the basis of her study of the 1911 census, Watterson (1986, 1987) suspected that industrialization was an important factor in child survival chances. This was later confirmed by Lee (1991), who found that almost half the variation in infant mortality rates by county in 1921 could be explained in terms of industrial—and especially mining—concentration (p. 63), and suggested that 'the divergence which characterised regional infant mortality rates during the half-century before the 1920s reflected the high cost of early industrialisation' (p. 64). Williamson (1981, 1990) is another author who considered the role of industrialization. He included a 'dark satanic mill' index in his analysis of infant mortality in 1905, but rejected this out of hand: 'it was not indus-trialisation that generated the disamenities associated with high infant mortality rates, but rather urbanisation ... almost all of the predicted infant-mortality variance within regions can be explained by two forces: crowding within dwellings, and density and size of urban environments within which those dwellings were located' (1981, 246).[1]

Other researchers have heralded social class as the major determinant of infant and child mortality differentials in England and Wales in the late nineteenth and early twentieth centuries (Preston and Haines 1991), based mainly on the evidence of the 1911 census of England and Wales. This included three questions specifically addressed to currently married women, the answers to which enable the estimation of retrospec-tive time-series of infant mortality. These questions were included in the 1911 census as a result of growing worry among the middle classes about the threat of 'race suicide'.

---

[1] Williamson's data set consisted of 72 towns used in the 1905 'Report of an Enquiry by the Board of Trade into Working Class Rents, Housing and Retail Prices, together with Standard Rates of Wages prevailing in certain occupations in the Principal Industrial Towns of the United Kingdom'. Although there was a fair amount of variety in the type of town, the description used in the title, the *principal industrial* towns, does suggest that there may not have been enough industrial variation in the sample to produce differentials in the industrialization factor.

It was felt that the health and intellect of the middle classes, who were having fewer and fewer children, were being diluted by the continued high numbers born into the 'stunted and sickly' working classes. As a consequence, T. H. C. Stevenson, the Statistical Superintendent at the General Registry Office (responsible for analysing the information collected in the 'fertility' census) developed what was to be the precursor of the social class system still used for official purposes today. This 'professional model' relies purely on male occupation to assign status (other more quantifiable variables, such as income, were not recorded on British census forms) and divides workers into various non-manual and manual strata. In 1911 the non-manual strata consisted of the upper and middle classes (class I) and lower-grade white-collar workers (class II). Manual workers were divided into the skilled (class III), the semi-skilled (class IV) and the unskilled (class V). In addition, Stevenson singled out three 'special' occupational groups that demonstrated what he felt was atypical fertility and mortality: textile workers, miners, and agricultural labourers made up classes VI, VII and VIII, respectively. From 1921, the three special classes were reincorporated into classes I to V.[2] Students of fertility and infant and child mortality using the 1911 census have followed the original form of analysis by continuing to use the official class classification despite its shortcomings.

Although Preston and Haines's investigation also threw up geographical variation in infant mortality, they singled out class as the most important factor. Like the proponents of the importance of locality, however, they were unsure what aspects of the variable were able to affect infant mortality. They confessed that they were 'left without a wholly persuasive explanation of why British mortality differentials by social class were so much larger than those in the United States' (1991, 197). While they attributed some of the class effect to income, they admitted that this could not be the entire answer. They speculated that, in addition, 'a higher degree of residential segregation by occupation in England, combined with residentially differentiated public service and weak diffusion of information and practices across places, may be part of the explanation' (ibid.).

The mere identification of variables, such as location and social class, that are associated with large differentials in child survival but could represent a variety of underlying influences does not allow us much of an insight into the inner workings of the infant mortality decline. To assess clearly the meaning of each variable we need to have some idea of which elements affect survival. Moreover, the spatial distribution of classes over environments makes it difficult to gauge the relative impact of each of these factors. Table 7.1, calculated from the data set that will be described in the next section, reveals

---

[2] Although social stratification was an inescapable part of Victorian society, there had previously been little rigorous official analysis of social class. Higgs (1991) pointed out that the occupational groupings out of which social classes were formed were based not on social hierarchies, but on the materials being worked up in productive processes. Thus, the retired and the unemployed, employers and employees were included in the same occupational groups. On the development of the professional model of social classes, which has been much criticized from the start, see Szreter 1984. Szreter suggested that Stevenson used a circular argument in employing occupational fertility and infant mortality levels to create a classification that was used for the analysis of those phenomena.

Table 7.1. England and Wales: Distribution of population
living in households headed by different social classes, by environment, 1911

Social class	Agriculture	Professional	Light industry	Staple industry	All (number)
(a) Percentage of each social class living in each environment					
I	10	48	31	11	8,795
II	23	21	39	17	16,920
III	10	16	57	16	22,378
IV	13	15	32	40	19,441
V	9	14	43	33	14,756
Textile workers	7	3	16	74	1,285
Miners	0	0	1	98	9,019
Agricultural labourers	79	8	10	4	3,141
None	10	20	39	31	7,197
(b) Percentage of population in environments in each social class					
I	6	23	7	3	
II	27	20	17	9	
III	16	20	33	11	
IV	18	16	16	24	
V	9	12	17	15	
Textile workers	1	0	1	3	
Miners	0	0	0	27	
Agricultural labourers	18	1	1	0	
None	5	8	7	7	
All (number)	14,085	18,153	38,242	32,452	

Note: numbers may not sum to 100 owing to rounding.

a concentration of lower-class workers in the unhealthy cities. The table shows that 77 per cent of class V and 72 per cent of class IV lived in areas dominated by industry of some sort (see below for an explanation of the different sorts of place), whereas agricultural areas held only 9 per cent and 13 per cent of these two classes. From a different perspective, in the unhealthiest places (the staple-industry environments) classes IV and V made up 39 per cent of the population, a figure which rises to 70 per cent when textile workers and miners are included. Only 12 per cent belonged to classes I and II. In agricultural environments, on the other hand, 27 per cent of the population lived in households headed by workers from classes IV or V (45 per cent when agricultural labourers are included), but 33 per cent lived in class I or II households. Preston and Haines (1991, 197) recognized that the residential segregation of social classes could help to explain the observed mortality differentials, and Smith (1991) implied that class differences in England and Wales may have been a product of location within neighbourhoods. Smith went so far as to suggest that location was much more important than 'the advantages or disadvantages consequent upon the status of individuals' (p.

236). Given the acknowledged importance of these factors, it is essential to disentangle the influences of locality and class by separating out the independent effects of each in order to assess which is the more important.

The problem cries out for studies into the simultaneous effects of locality and class, but these have been limited by the constraints of data availability. Aggregate data, whether from the 1911 census or from vital registration, is usually all that is available for this period because stringent confidentiality rulings in England and Wales prohibit access to individual records for 100 years. Aggregate data carry the additional risk of falling into the ecological fallacy whereby spatial associations are mistakenly assigned causal links.[3] This chapter takes advantage of privileged access to a set of anonymized individual returns to the 1911 census. These data allow us to explore the interrelations between locality, class and other variables measurable from the census, and also to tailor variables to our own needs. The work is part of a larger enterprise based on this data that looks at demography, household and family around the beginning of the twentieth century.

DATA

The 1911 census data used in this chapter are part of a more substantial data set consisting of anonymized individual returns to the 1891, 1901, 1911 and 1921 censuses, which was given to the Cambridge Group for the History of Population and Social Structure by the Office of Population Censuses and Surveys (OPCS). The data set (hereafter referred to as the 'OPCS data set') consists of transcriptions of the individual returns, without names and addresses, for 53 clusters of enumeration districts encompassing approximately the same spatial areas in each of the four census years. The 53 clusters are in turn distributed across 13 'places'. Each place lies within a registration district, although the clusters making up each place are not necessarily contiguous units on the ground. Map 7.1 shows the 13 Registration Districts (RDs) in 1891 and the abbreviations that we use to refer to the places within them that we studied. In 1911, the year on which this chapter is based, the total population in the OPCS data set was 102,752. This population contained 17,741 married, co-resident couples in which the mother was aged 20–49 and properly answered the special questions that enable the estimation of infant and child mortality. Because age at death of the child is not known, it is possible to estimate child survival only up to certain approximate ages, according to the marital duration of the mother (see below). These approximations can all be converted to infant mortality using an appropriate life-table,[4] but it is important to realize that, even when expressed as infant mortality, the figures really represent child survival.

---

[3] See Williams 1992, 74–75 for a discussion of this problem.
[4] The 1911 life-table for England and Wales is used in this case.

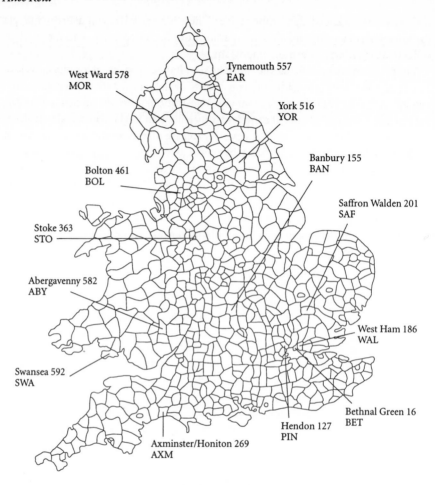

Map 7.1. England and Wales: The location of the
registration districts that contain the OPCS locales

Note: Along with the full name of the registration district in which each locale lies, the map gives the
number of the registration district in 1891 and the three-letter code used to identify the locale.

Source: The author is grateful to Professor R. I. Woods of the Geography Department, University of
Liverpool, for permission to use his outline map of registration districts.

LOCATION AND ENVIRONMENT

A first step towards the better understanding of influences on infant mortality during
transition is a more detailed investigation of geographical differentials. The ability to
assign individuals to units as small and precise as clusters of enumeration districts allows this project much greater sensitivity in spatial classification than is usually possible
using published statistics. The 53 clusters of enumeration districts have been classified

into six categories, which have called 'environments'. The industrial structure (using the working population of both sexes aged 15 and over) is used as a proxy for environmental conditions to produce four main categories, two of which are subdivided:

Agriculture	dominated by agricultural occupations
Professional:	large sections of the population working in the professional and service sectors
Rural	bordering countryside
Urban	well within urban areas
Light industry	with a mixture of industries
Staple industry:	dominated by only a few industries
Manufacturing	textile/pottery/metal manufacture towns or cities
Mining	mining villages in the countryside

While some of the 13 places are fairly homogeneous, with all the constituent districts falling into the same environment, for other places the OPCS selection of enumeration districts includes a range of different environments, and each of these has been grouped with similar districts from other places. Thus the agricultural areas near Abergavenny have been placed with those around Banbury, Saffron Walden and our rural sections of Westmorland, whereas the mining community of Blaenavon, which also makes up part of Abergavenny, has been placed with the pit village of Earsdon (Tynemouth).

The OPCS set of places does not form a representative sample of England and Wales, but it can be viewed as a series of case-studies. Similarly, I believe that the environments into which the clusters of enumeration districts have been grouped can be treated as case-studies of such environments at a broader level. When the whole of England and Wales is classed according to the four basic environments without the subdivisions under professional and staple-industry areas,[5] the vast majority (81 per cent) of the area is still dominated by agriculture, yet this contains only 15.5 per cent of the *population*. In contrast, professional and light industry environments—almost exclusively urban and each with less than 4 per cent of the overall acreage—contain about 21 per cent and 36 per cent, respectively, of the people of England and Wales. Staple areas were in fact less densely populated (with 11 per cent of the area and 27.5 per cent of the population), owing to the rural nature of many mining districts. The North–South divide is strikingly obvious, with the northwestern bias towards staple industry (mining, metal-working, textiles and earthenware). The favourable position of London in terms of mortality may be at least partly explained by its lack of unhealthy staple-industry areas.

I believe that, for the OCPS selection of places, this environmental classification based on very small spatial units is a much more sensitive approximation of a 'spatially-structured disease environment' (Smith 1991, 236) than the geographical divisions available from the published census reports.

---

[5] This could be performed for one year only, 1921, using registration districts, a much larger unit of analysis than that used for the OPCS data. The classification is thus bound to be less sensitive than that applied to the OPCS data, but the general picture remains valid.

ENVIRONMENT, SOCIAL CLASS AND INFANT MORTALITY

One of the most reliable ways of simultaneously assessing the relative effects of different variables, especially with a relatively small data set, is to use multiple regression. Ordinary least squares (OLS) regression was performed on women married for less than 25 years, who had ever had a child, and whose husband was with them on census night. This limited the data set to 10,625 couples. The observations for each woman were weighted by the number of children she had ever borne so that the characteristics of women with more children assume greater importance—reflecting relative contributions to overall levels of child mortality. The dependent variable is the mortality index (the ratio of actual to expected child deaths, calculated for an individual woman, where the expected number of child deaths depends on the woman's marital duration).[6]

The independent variables used are those that could be derived from the census returns and are thought likely to influence early-age mortality. Given the constraints of the data, they tend to be of mostly of a socio-economic nature.[7] Care must be taken in interpreting the coefficients of the included variables since they may well be affected by omitted variables. It is important to bear in mind that variables measured at a point in time (as with the census) may have changed since a previous event such as a the birth or death of a child. They may even have changed as a result of such an event. For example, a woman may leave the labour force because of the birth of a child or return to it if a child dies. Extreme caution must, therefore, be used in the interpretation of results and in the attribution of causal pathways.

Most variables are categorical, represented using dummy variables, with the reference category representing a numerically large group often with extreme experience of child mortality. All variables are calculated for each individual woman, reflecting information about that woman alone. Thus they are all microlevel variables, apart from that denoting environment.

The sixfold environment classification is used, with manufacturing, which exhibits the worst record for child survival, as the reference category. Social class is as defined by the Registrar General in 1911. Each class is represented by a category of the class variable, and there is an additional category for those who are not assigned a class at all. There are thus nine categories, and social class V, which had high (although perhaps not extreme) mortality, is used as the reference category.

---

[6] Expected child deaths equals the number of children ever born to each woman multiplied by the proportion of child deaths to women of that marital duration in the population as a whole, adjusted by the multipliers for the indirect estimation of infant mortality as given in the UN's *Manual X* (United Nations 1983). See Farah and Preston 1982, Trussell and Preston 1982, and Preston and Haines 1991 for similar applications and discussions.

[7] Of course, it is not imagined that the variables included will capture all of the variation in infant and child mortality. There are many factors I suspect to be important that are unavailable from the census (such as parental education, income, weather and so on)—and some that may not even have been identified as important.

Age of wife and age of husband are continuous variables that are expected to act as controls on changing mortality over time. Nativity is a categorical variable, with six categories: born and enumerated in the same county (reference category), born and enumerated in different counties in Great Britain, born in Eastern Europe, born in Ireland, born elsewhere overseas, and birthplace unknown. The Eastern European category was included as a proxy for Jewish mothers, who have been reported to have better child-care practices and thus children with much better survival prospects (Goldstein, Watkins and Spector 1994; Marks 1994).

A wife's labour-force participation has been expanded from a simple working/not working dichotomy to include information about possible sources of child care beyond the mother herself. If a servant or non-working female relative aged over 15 was present in the household, then a potential child-care source was considered to be present.[8] The combination of this with the work status of the wife produces a fourfold distinction, with 'not working with no potential extra child care' used as the reference category. The work variable was expanded in this way because it is plausible that the additional availability of child care would reduce child mortality, particularly for women employed outside the home. Naturally there may be many other forms of potential child care that we cannot see in the census, such as relatives living outside the home or neighbours. The absence of a result should not therefore lead to an automatic dismissal of the hypothesis.

In the husband's unemployment variable, those women whose husband was not working are compared to the reference category of those whose husband was working.[9] The final two variables in the table—one indicating the presence of servants in the household and the other indicating the presence of boarders—measure the contrast with the reference categories where couples do not have servants or boarders living with them.[10]

Finally, the number of rooms in the household was included, since it might have reflected elements of both income and overcrowding. This variable is divided into three categories (1–2, 3–5 and 6 or more rooms), with the middle one as reference category. It is not imagined that it will be a very good measure of either financial resources or overcrowding, since the size of house occupied depends not only on income, but also on the availability of housing and the number of people needing to be accommodated, and the number of people in the household is a crucial factor in overcrowding. The best intuitive measure of overcrowding is persons per room, which one would expect to be positively correlated to the risks of infant and child mortality—that is, a greater number

---

8 The variable was expanded in this way partly to provide comparison with Preston and Haines, but it differs from their variable in that not only did they use 'servant or relative over the age of 16' as a source of possible child care, but they did not restrict relatives as a source of possible child care to those not in work.

9 There may be correlation here with the final class variable (no class), which could confuse results.

10 It is recognized that the child-care element of the women's work variable is highly correlated to the servants variable but the variables were left as they were in order to facilitate comparison with Preston and Haines. Experiments were performed using the women's work dichotomy, care provided by relatives and servants as main effects and with interactions to test both the relationship with the servants variable and the difference between the two types of child-care provision.

of persons in each room increases overcrowding and infant mortality. Both the number of people in the household at the time of census and the number of persons per room can be included, but the relationships that emerge from the data work very strongly in the opposite direction. I suspect that this is due to child death reducing the number of people alive to be enumerated, and thus overcrowding. Thus only 'number of rooms' is included in the analysis reported here.

Table 7.2 shows the parameter estimates for a simple comparison of environment and social class (with wife's age included as a control for mortality decline). The results show that, individually, both environment and social class have marked effects on the prospects for infant survival, confirming conclusions reached by the authors discussed above. From column (1) it can be seen that manufacturing areas are indisputably the most detrimental to child health, and agricultural and professional places near the countryside are the least. In these latter two areas the chances of survival are over 75 per cent higher than in manufacturing places. Mining areas have the next poorest record after manufacturing, despite the fact that they, too, tend to be rural. This confirms my suspicion that the rural–urban divide does not capture all the mortality variation. The distinction between manufacturing and other urban places lends credit to the view that the industrial structure of a place is somehow connected to factors influencing the health of the inhabitants.

Social class differentiation is visible in column (2): there is a clear survival gradient from classes I to V, with class I over 50 per cent better off than class V. Agricultural labourers (class VIII) are even more advantaged, with over 60 per cent better survival, and miners (class VII) among the least well off, with levels very similar to class V. (The small numbers of male textile workers, class VI, render that group a very atypical sample.) Clearly, almost all those returning themselves as agricultural labourers must have lived in the countryside, and miners in mining districts. Similarly, the typology of environments used here means that the higher social classes will be concentrated in professional areas and the lower in other urban districts. It is likely, therefore, that environment and social class differentials in infant mortality are to some extent measuring the same things. It would be valuable to discover the extent to which the effects of environment and social class are independent, and which is responsible for any common variation.

Column (3) helps to answer this by showing the simultaneous effects of both environment and social class. It can be seen that, while the effect of environment is largely unchanged (the coefficients have decreased, but by relatively small amounts), that of social class is substantially lessened by the inclusion of environment. The coefficients here are much smaller, especially among the higher classes and agricultural labourers— those concentrated in the healthier environments. Thus, their favourable position overall is, to a large extent, produced by their location. To a fairly large degree, infant mortality differentials by social class are observed because environment has not been controlled for. The apparent differences emerge from the aggregate data because of the spatial segregation of social classes: the higher social classes tend to live in the better environments, and the lower classes in the poorer environments.

Table 7.2. England and Wales: The effect of environment, social class and other socio-economic variables on infant mortality, *c.*1896–1911 (multiple regression)

Explanatory variables	(1)	(2)	(3)	(4)
R^2	0.0471	0.0256	0.0533	0.0732
Adjusted R^2	0.0465	0.0247	0.0521	0.0707
Intercept	0.7515***	0.6562***	0.8723***	0.6475***
Age of wife	0.0184***	0.0169***	0.0188***	0.0188***
Environment				
Agricultural	−0.7775***		−0.7222***	−0.6476***
Professional–Rural	−0.7725***		−0.6983***	−0.5675***
Professional–Urban	−0.4003***		−0.3622***	−0.3211***
Light Industry	−0.3653***		−0.3367***	−0.3131***
Manufacturing	—[a]		—[a]	—[a]
Mining	−0.2236***		−0.2886***	−0.2732***
1911 social class				
I		−0.5424***	−0.3968***	−0.1994***
II		−0.3267***	−0.2181***	−0.0844*
III		−0.2410***	−0.1845***	−0.1070***
IV		−0.1581***	−0.1706***	−0.0974**
V		—[a]	—[a]	—[a]
VI (textiles)		−0.1697	−0.3892***	−0.3505***
VII (mining)		0.0342	−0.0424	−0.0178
VIII (agricultural labourers)		−0.6360***	−0.2507***	−0.2279***
None		−0.1906	−0.1711	−0.3264***
Nativity				
Same county				—[a]
Other United Kingdom				−0.0749**
Ireland				−0.0359
Eastern Europe				−0.3111***
Other foreign				−0.1245
Not known				−0.1780**
Women's work				
No work, no child care				—[a]
No work, child care				−0.0395
Working, no child care				0.3416***
Working, child care				0.1724*
Number of rooms				
1–2				0.3254***
3–5				—[a]
6+				−0.2025***
Age of husband				0.0038
Unemployment of husband				0.3828***
Servants in household				−0.1322**
Boarders in household				0.0704*

*** significant at 1% level; ** significant at 5% level; * significant at 10% level.
[a] reference category.
Note: The dependent variable is the mortality index per woman, weighted by number of births.

Although environment exerts more influence on infant and child mortality than social class, the latter does continue to have some effect. These variables are handy tools for establishing differentials in infant and child mortality, but it is likely that their effect on survival is produced by some combination of underlying factors. Environment, for example, might affect child health through sewerage, water supply or air quality, and the relevant factors in social class might be income, education, servant-keeping, or child-care availability. Using multiple regression, it is possible to attempt to discover more about what environment and social class represent by the inclusion of additional variables. Column (4) of Table 7.2 shows the results of regression run with additional variables calculated at an individual level from the census returns. It shows that my attempts to isolate other factors that might affect infant and child mortality have met with some success, but none of the factors diminished the importance of the environment or wholly explained social-class findings.

Some survival advantage in financial or social security is confirmed by the analysis: variables that may be thought of as indicating a certain amount of hardship within the household,[11] such as male unemployment, female labour-force participation (especially where there is no source of potential child care within the household) and the presence of boarders, are associated with higher infant and child mortality. Measures of economic well-being, on the other hand, such as a greater number of rooms and (to some degree) the presence of servants, are associated with better prospects of child survival, as is residence in a different county from that of birth.

Such variables, along with social class, can be thought of as reflecting characteristics and practices that may pertain to the individuals belonging to different sections of society. They thus measure the extent to which individuals, according to their identification with different groups, are able to affect the health of their children. The power of individual behaviour, albeit governed by cultural dictates, is demonstrated by the finding that the children of women born in Eastern Europe suffered lower mortality than those of mothers born elsewhere, confirming the hypothesis that the child-care practices of Jewish women enhanced the survival chances of their children. Prolonged breastfeeding and strict religious rulings demanding a high degree of cleanliness in the preparation of food and in personal hygiene are likely to have reduced the risks of artificial food for Jewish infants. Added to this, a better diet among Jews both during weaning and later on in childhood could afford protection against infectious diseases. The resultant low levels of infant mortality among Jewish immigrants in the poorest areas of the metropolis are therefore all the more remarkable (Marks 1994, 43–91).

While environment has the more important influence on infant mortality, socio-economic factors do also have an effect, and Table 7.3 shows that these vary according to environment. Where environment is favourable, as in agricultural and professional–rural areas, there is little difference between the child mortality experiences of different

---

[11] Lower social classes are more likely to be seen with boarders than higher: 12.6 per cent of the couples in social class V used in the analysis had a boarder in their home, whereas less than half as many—only 6.1 per cent—of class I couples did. More dramatically, 32.8 per cent of class I couples had a servant, compared with only 1.1 per cent of class V couples. In addition, more of the lower-class wives were out at work: 12.4 per cent of class V, as opposed to 5.8 per cent of class I.

classes. (The exception is that class V in professional–rural environments is at a distinct disadvantage compared to other social groups.) On the other hand, it is only in manufacturing environments, where the environment itself is not conducive to child health, that a consistent and significant social-class gradient emerges. This suggests that the superior finances, knowledge or other privileges of the higher classes do enable them to preserve the health of their children to a greater degree, but only in those areas. Social class in England and Wales around the turn of the century may, as Preston and Haines wrote, have 'connoted a constellation of factors related to mortality: earnings, education, style of life, housing, security, residential amenities, privilege, empowerment, and so forth' (1991, 196), but it was only where conditions were particularly bad that the possessors of these factors were able to muster them in defence of the health of their children.

While the effect of the presence of servants, boarders and unemployed fathers is fairly uniform over all environments, the effect of the wife working differs not only in magnitude but also in direction. A correlation has often been observed between high levels of women's work and high levels of infant and child mortality, and it has frequently been supposed that the former is to blame for the latter. Indeed, women's work was a particular *bête noire* of those concerned with the problem of infant mortality. The Registrar General believed the 1911 census data to have established the 'evil results of maternal employment' with regard to child health,[12] and H. R. Jones was convinced of the connection several years earlier:

These causes of death [convulsions, diarrhoea, atrophy, and premature birth]—at least the excess in them—must be attributed to the employment of women. The care of the babies is entrusted to others—they are fed artificially almost from birth. A case in point came under my personal observation this week, in which the mother returned to her work on the fourteenth day after her confinement, and 14 days later the child was brought into the hospital suffering from gastric derangement due to improper feeding (1894, 56).

Although a positive correlation between infant and child mortality and women's work does emerge in the entire data set, this is not observed in every place. In those areas where there were plenty of job opportunities for women in the manufacturing sector, a working wife is indeed associated with a higher incidence of child mortality. I have argued elsewhere, however, that a child's death may free a woman to return to work by reducing her workload in the home (Garrett and Reid 1994). This is a prime example of reverse causality, according to which instead of the women's work causing the child's death, the death facilitates the work. Reverse causality must always be borne in mind with such cross-sectional data as the census, especially where independent variables may have changed their value since the event of interest (in this case, a woman may have

12 While previous work had only suggested a relationship between women's work and infant mortality, the Registrar General was satisfied that he was able to place the relationship on a firmer statistical basis: 'Although the evidence has been somewhat contradictory, it has in the main pointed to the evil results of maternal employment, especially outside the home, but it naturally could not provide any such measures of their extent as is now available' (Census of England and Wales 1911, *Fertility of Marriage*, pt. ii, pp. lxxvii–lxxviii).

Table 7.3. England and Wales: The effect of social class and other socio-economic variables on infant mortality in each environment, *c.*1896–1911 (multiple regression)

Explanatory	All	Agricultural	Professional–Rural	Professional–Urban	Light industry	Manufacturing	Mining
R^2	0.0732	0.0317	0.0749	0.0761	0.0649	0.0455	0.0305
Adjusted R^2	0.0707	0.0144	0.0572	0.0415	0.0597	0.0368	0.0107
Intercept	0.6475***	−0.0006	0.2331	0.8374***	0.1063	0.6752***	0.6904**
Age of wife	0.0188***	0.0221***	0.0158**	0.0078	0.0222**	0.0202**	0.0025
Environment							
Agricultural	−0.6476***						
Professional-Rural	−0.5675***						
Professional-Urban	−0.3211***						
Light industry	−0.3131***						
Manufacturing	—[a]						
Mining	−0.2732***						
1911 social class							
I	−0.1994***	0.1492	−0.4445***	−0.4823**	−0.0793	−0.5106***	0.0658
II	−0.0844*	0.0192	−0.3173**	−0.0061	0.0092	−0.3323***	−0.2354
III	−0.1070***	0.0556	−0.2678**	−0.3382**	−0.0645	−0.1647*	−0.1088
IV	−0.0974**	0.0062	−0.2881**	−0.1677*	−0.1420**	−0.0402	−0.3357
V	—[a]	—[a]	—[a]	—[a]	—[a]	—[a]	—[a]
VI (textiles)	−0.3505***	−0.4649	−0.8025	0	−0.1940	−0.3974**	0
VII (mining)	−0.0178	−0.9051	0.7152	−1.1562	0.5309	−0.0633	−0.0633
VIII (agricultural labourers)	−0.2279***	0.0150	−0.6298***	0.1051	−0.6287**	−1.5486	−1.1775**
None	−0.3264***	−0.8737*	−0.8981	0.0689	−0.3823**	−0.1712	−1.1614

Nativity							
Same county	—[a]	—[a]	—[a]	—[a]	—[a]	—[a]	—[a]
Other united kingdom	-0.0749**	-0.0046	-0.0373	-0.0633	-0.1980***	0.0056	0.0848
Ireland	-0.0359	-0.6684	0.2597	0.1852	0.1586	-0.4125	0.3471
Eastern europe	-0.3111***	0	0	-0.1260	-0.3826***	0	0
Other foreign	-0.1245	-0.8886	0.2493	-0.1108	-0.2202	0.0388	-0.5250
Not known	-0.1780**	-0.2222	-0.2937	-0.1999	-0.0973	-0.4324*	0.0616
Wife's work							
No work, no care	—[a]	—[a]	—[a]	—[a]	—[a]	—[a]	—[a]
No work, care	-0.0395	-0.0987	0.0021	-0.2148	-0.0431	0.1182	-0.1798*
Working, no care	0.3416***	-0.1771	0.0092	0.8271***	0.2765***	0.5439***	-0.1265
Working, care	0.1724*	0.3528	0.1411	-0.2278	-0.0149	0.3017	1.0793**
Number of rooms							
1–2	0.3254***	0.1511	0.8660***	0.0455	0.4591***	0.3809***	0.0234
3–5	—[a]	—[a]	—[a]	—[a]	—[a]	—[a]	—[a]
6+	-0.2025***	-0.0407	0.0625	-0.1749	-0.2846***	-0.2352**	-0.2382
Age of husband	0.0038	-0.0037	0.0047	0.0036	0.0063	0.0014	0.0138
Unemployment of husband	0.3828***	0.5272**	0.2017	0.1423	0.2941*	0.9466***	0.1190
Servants in house	-0.1332**	-0.1065	-0.3770***	0.1294	-0.0413	-0.1970	-0.2243
Boarders in house	0.0704*	0.1137	0.0286	0.1190	0.1715***	-0.0138	-0.0387

*** significant at 1% level; ** significant at 5% level; * significant at 10% level.
[a] reference category.
Note: The dependent variable is the mortality index per woman, weighted by number of births.

changed from not-working to working since the death of a child). Married women's work is thus not necessarily detrimental to child health; indeed, in other environments (agricultural and mining), the children of working women appear to have slightly better survival prospects than those of non-working women. This could be because of the type of work predominating in those areas, but may also show the benefits of additional income brought in by the wife (Collet 1898; Dyhouse 1978).

Regression results have disclosed substantial differentials in infant and child mortality at the turn of the century by environment or location, and some advantage to the higher social classes within the least healthy environments. The behaviour of such differentials across the mortality decline—whether they increase or decrease—will help to identify influences that inhibited or encouraged the transition, even if we cannot discover its actual causes.

DIFFERENTIALS ACROSS TIME

Long-term series of infant and child mortality by social class show persistent differentials for a century and a half after 1750, followed by convergence after 1900 (Woods and Williams 1995). Trends since 1921 have proved relatively easy to determine given the regular publication of mortality rates for the relatively stable five social-class groups, but before that date estimates have to be gleaned from various elite groups and small surveys. The 1911 census is thus a particularly valuable source, since it yields not only differentials but trends, if only for a short period. All those who have looked at the pattern of child mortality over time from this source have commented upon the widening of social-class differentials (Woods, Williams and Galley 1993; Woods and Williams 1995; Haines 1995). Haines found that 'social class in England and Wales during the 1890s and 1900s tended to be related to the speed of mortality decline: mortality in childhood declined more rapidly among the higher and more privileged social classes' (1995, 315), and Woods and Williams suggested that 'higher social classes were able to take some special early advantage of the general mortality decline at the turn of the century' (1995, 29).

Unsurprisingly, these patterns in child mortality over time by social class are echoed in our smaller data set. Estimates of infant mortality have been calculated using the demographic techniques of indirect estimation. These techniques were originally developed by William Brass for use in situations where there is no vital registration system to provide numbers of births and deaths (Brass 1964, 1975; Brass *et al.* 1968). They enable the transformation of the ratios of children-dead to children-ever-born of women in standard five-year age- or marital-duration groups into estimates of survival probabilities from birth to various exact ages. These in turn can be used to calculate a time-series of infant mortality for the 15 or so years preceding the survey.[13] The

---

[13] The methods are discussed in the UN's *Manual X* (United Nations 1983). Their use in historic contexts is demonstrated by Watterson 1986, 1987, 1988, and Preston and Haines 1991.

estimates reflect child survival from birth until the late teens, and are thus composite measures of infant and child mortality. It is important to remember that although, as here, such estimates may be expressed as infant mortality rates, they also encapsulate elements of mortality at older ages. Time-series are shown in Figure 7.1, and absolute and relative declines between three approximate dates (1893, 1900 and 1910) are shown in Table 7.4. In absolute terms, infant-mortality decline was concentrated in the second part of the period and little class gradient was visible. But because the better-off were already at an advantage, their relative decline was greater and inequality increased. Figure 7.2 and Table 7.5 show similar measures for the four main environments (only four are used in order to make the numbers larger, and hence more reliable) and tells a similar story, with little decline until the dawn of the new century. Absolute declines are no greater in the healthy than in the unhealthy environments, although their low initial levels mean that they witness the greater relative improvements.

Figures 7.3–7.6 and Table 7.6 show the relative changes in the different classes within each of the four main environments. Concentrating on the latter part of the period, it can be seen that the overall class pattern of larger declines among the higher classes is repeated in staple-industry locations. While the survival of lower-class children did improve, the improvement was relatively smaller than that secured by more privileged children in similar places. This suggests that the decline in infant and child mortality was, to some extent at least, affected by behavioural factors. The enhanced ability of the middle classes to affect the health of their children might be a reflection of the take-up of new ideas by these people, or of the introduction of developments that money could buy.

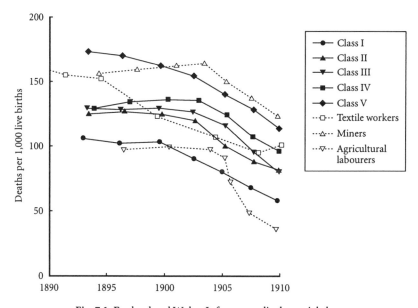

Fig. 7.1. England and Wales: Infant mortality by social class

Table 7.4. England and Wales: Infant mortality change, by social class, 1894–1910

Social class	Infant mortality rates			Absolute change		Percentage change	
	1894	1901	1910	1894–1901	1901–1910	1894–1901	1901–1910
I	106	91	58	–15	–33	–14	–36
II	125	130	82	+5	–48	+4	–37
III	127	128	80	+1	–48	+1	–38
IV	129	141	96	+12	–45	+9	–32
V	173	153	114	–20	–39	–12	–25
Textile workers	160	120	101	–40	–19	–25	–16
Miners	156	165	123	+9	–42	+6	–25
Agricultural labourers	97	95	36	–2	–59	–2	–62

Table 7.5. England and Wales: Infant mortality change, by environment, 1894–1910

Social class	Infant mortality rates			Absolute change		Percentage change	
	1894	1901	1910	1894–1901	1901–1910	1894–1901	1901–1910
Agriculture	81	88	50	+7	–38	+9	–43
Professional	115	110	68	–5	–42	–4	–38
Light industry	139	130	86	–9	–44	–6	–34
Staple industry	165	167	120	+2	–47	+1	–28

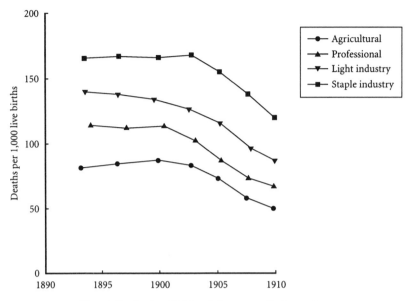

Fig. 7.2. England and Wales: Infant mortality by environment

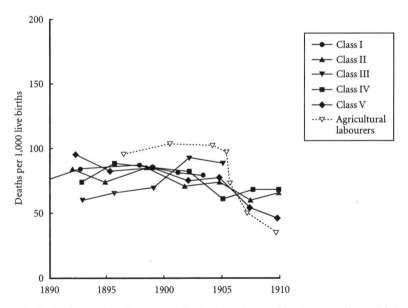

Fig. 7.3. England and Wales: Infant mortality in the agricultural environment, by social class

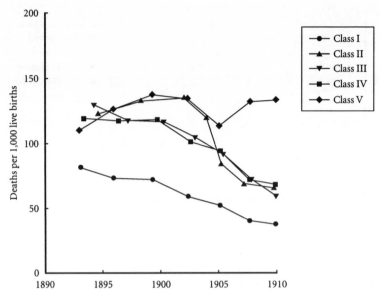

Fig. 7.4. England and Wales: Infant mortality in the professional environment, by social class

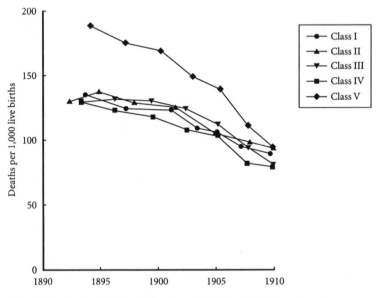

Fig. 7.5. England and Wales: Infant mortality in the light industry environment, by social class

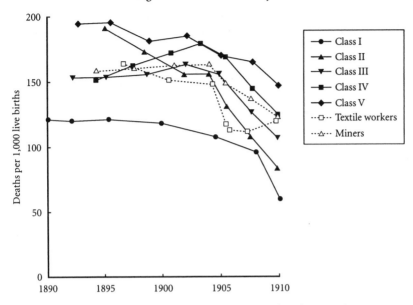

Fig. 7.6. England and Wales: Infant mortality in the staple industry environment, by social class

Table 7.6. England and Wales:
Infant mortality change, by environment and social class, 1894–1910

Social class	Agriculture	Professional	Light industry	Staple industry
(a) Percentage change 1894–1901				
I	−16	−19	−24	−21
II	+15	+16	−5	−26
III	+49	−22	−3	+10
IV	+11	−6	−9	+21
V	−13	+21	−20	−13
Textile workers				−33
Miners				+4
Agricultural labourers	+5			
(b) Percentage change 1901–1910				
I	+62	−44	−14	−37
II	−32	−54	−24	−40
III	−19	−42	−35	−36
IV	−17	−39	−33	−31
V	−45	0	−37	−13
Textile workers				+10
Miners				−25
Agricultural labourers	−65			

In poor environments, where the threat posed by infant and childhood diseases was high, superior resources and knowledge were able to offer some protection in the early years of life. The advantages of the better-off were increasing at the turn of the century—the time when advances in medical knowledge and theories of disease causation were growing apace (Fee and Porter 1992). This prompts the suggestion that improvements in medical and health knowledge, as they affected child health, were important influences in the increase in the survival chances of the young. Growing class differentials imply that changes in recommended practices, preventions and treatments either seeped down through society in a class-specific way or were only able to be put into practice by those with more money, space or other resources.

In agricultural and professional environments, where the environment did not present such a virulent attack on the health of the young, improvements in mortality were not manifested in a class-specific way. The meagre resources of the lower classes offered as effective a defence as the greater ones of the middle classes. Several possible scenarios could account for this. The information network may have been more effective in such environments, with knowledge gained by all at a similar rate; but this does not seem very plausible. Alternatively, in the healthier areas, where the middle classes were concentrated, they might have used their newly gained knowledge in pressing for improvements, such as to sewerage or water supply, that would have enhanced the health of the whole community. Their greater numbers in such places would have lent them more political clout than in heavily industrial locations, where they were a smaller group in society. A third possibility, as mentioned above, is that the middle classes' superior resources and access to information may not have constituted much of an advantage because the environment represented less of a threat to their children's health. For example, the knowledge that long-tube feeding bottles were likely to harbour infection and cause diarrhoea could reduce diarrhoeal deaths; but this would only have a dramatic impact where infants and children were particularly at risk from the environment, and then only when those who had that knowledge were also armed with the resources to purchase and sterilize more suitable receptacles. Where there was less risk of bottles becoming infected, as in places where sanitation was better or where clean water was a commonly enjoyed convenience, money and knowledge had little impact.

CONCLUSIONS

Using the 1911 census to calculate trends and differentials in infant and child mortality for the 15 or so years leading up to 1911, I have attempted to reveal more about this feature of the demographic transition in England and Wales. I have no quarrel with recent suggestions that the decline was well under way in some areas of the country by the 1860s (Williams and Galley 1995). Indeed, the very low levels of mortality I have found in agricultural communities support those arguments. Although this early start to the decline means that I have not been able to investigate its causes, I do believe that the analysis of differentials and of the behaviour of those differentials over time provides more insight into inhibiting and enabling factors in the fall in mortality among various groups in society.

Analysis of the aggregate results from the 1911 census suggests that a child's chance of survival was strongly conditioned by who its parents were, or, more precisely, by what job its father did (Watterson 1988; Preston and Haines 1991). Using individual records from the same source I have demonstrated that, once other factors are controlled for, the largest differentials in infant and child mortality were associated with where the child lived. The ability to classify environment for small areas shows not only that the conventional rural–urban divide is important in affecting life chances, but that the heavily industrial environments (whether urban–manufacturing or rural pit-villages) are the most pernicious to health. The relationship between social class and infant and child mortality that emerges in the aggregate picture is primarily a product of location within spatially structured health environments. The fact that a macrolevel variable emerges as the most important is revealing. It suggests that early-age mortality around the turn of the century was less a matter of individual behaviour, which might be picked up through the measurement of individual characteristics, and more a question of the circumstances—particularly locational circumstances—in which people found themselves. Class did, however, retain some effect, especially in the 'worst' environments, where the children of the higher classes were advantaged in terms of health.

My attempt to discover more about which elements of environment and social class affect infant mortality has met with limited success. I can only make suggestions as to the influences that might be at the root of environment. Certainly, provision of sanitation and the quality of water and air must be major candidates. My analysis has suggested that social class seems to be a proxy for such factors as wife's work, number of rooms, husband's unemployment, servant-keeping and migration status. In turn, these could be proxies for income or education. Unfortunately, the anonymization of the OPCS data set prevents further exploration of such possibilities within the current project.

Suggestions about inhibiting and enabling factors in the decline of infant and child mortality can be derived from the experiences of infant mortality decline of the different social classes within each environment. The precipitous fall after 1901 in most environments lends weight to a suggestion that climatic conditions were important in retarding the decline of mortality in many large towns and cities. The long hot summers of the 1890s combined lethally with disgraceful standards of sanitation and over-crowded conditions to produce diarrhoeal deaths of epidemic proportions. Woods, Watterson and Woodward (1988, 362) demonstrated this 'urban–sanitary–diarrhoeal' effect in major cities, and it is likely that it was a particularly dangerous force where mortality was highest—in those areas dominated by a few industries (textiles, earthenware, metal manufacture and mining).

It was only in such dangerous places that the middle classes were able to create a significant health advantage for their children. And when the factors behind mortality were better understood the middle classes were able to capitalize and therefore to forge the greatest improvements in health. In *Fatal Years*, Preston and Haines used the lack of social-class differentials in mortality in the United States to argue that lack of know-how rather than lack of resources was 'principally responsible for foreshortening life'. They implied that rapid developments in the understanding of infectious-disease processes and related innovations, leading to increased public knowledge in the twentieth century, were behind the later emergence of differential childhood mortality by social class (1991, 209). On the other hand, Woods and Williams argue that although 'know-how influenced the sharp downward trend of mortality . . . resources conditioned the persistent differentials and social class gradient' (1995, 130).

On the basis of my findings it does seem more likely that the turn-of-the-century decline of mortality in the industrial heartlands was facilitated by developments in knowledge about disease-causation and health. Government and public health initiatives to bring such measures to the people probably played a part in diffusing new knowledge. It is also probable that social-class differentials were influenced by both know-how and resources. Where there was a very high risk of early death some aspects of know-how would have been of little use to those who could not afford to act upon it, and money is not much good at protecting health unless it is targeted at the right objects. Moreover, it is necessary to add the important qualification that superior knowledge and resources only secured survival benefits in the most unhealthy environments. Where the threat to infant and child life was smaller, any differences in behaviour between the classes paid few dividends. But there were still substantial declines in such areas, suggesting that there was some increase in know-how that was accessible and implementable by the whole population, whatever resources they had at their disposal. Alternatively, there may have been some aspect of the mortality decline that was based on environmental change not behavioural change. Drawing attention to the role of rapidly improving sanitation in the late nineteenth and early twentieth centuries in England, Haines (1995, 315) supported this idea when he found that social class was less important in accounting for trends than in explaining differentials. It is likely that in each place a unique cocktail of influences reacted with infant and child mortality to enhance or retard its decline. The next step in analysis must be more-detailed studies of the factors affecting small areas.

References

BRASS, W., 1964. 'Uses of census or survey data for the estimation of vital rates', paper prepared for the African Seminar on Vital Statistics, Addis Ababa, 14–19 December.
—— 1975. *Methods for estimating fertility and mortality from limited and defective data*, Chapel Hill, NC, Carolina Population Center.
—— *et al.*, 1968. *The demography of tropical Africa*, Princeton, NJ, Princeton University Press.
CENSUS OF ENGLAND AND WALES 1911. 13: *Fertility of marriage*, part i (1917) and part ii (1923).
COLLET, C., 1898. 'The collection and utilisation of official statistics bearing on the extent and

effects of the industrial employment of women', *Journal of the Royal Statistical Society* 61(2), pp. 219–270.

DYHOUSE, C., 1978. 'Working class mothers and infant mortality in England 1895–1914', *Journal of Social History* 12, pp. 248–267.

FARAH, A. A. and PRESTON, S., 1982. 'Child mortality differentials in Sudan', *Population and Development Review* 8, pp. 365–383.

FEE, E., and PORTER, D., 1992. 'Public health, preventive medicine and professionalization: England and America in the nineteenth century', in A. WEAR (ed.), *Medicine in Society*, Cambridge, Cambridge University Press.

GARRETT, E. M. and REID, A. M., 1994. 'Satanic mills, pleasant lands: spatial variation in women's work, fertility and infant mortality as viewed from the 1911 census', *Historical Research* 67, pp. 157–177.

GOLDSTEIN, A., WATKINS, S. C. and SPECTOR, A. R., 1994. 'Childhood health-care practices among Italians and Jews in the United States, 1910–1940', *Health Transition Review* 4, pp. 45–62.

HAINES, M. R., 1995. 'Socio-economic differentials in infant and child mortality during mortality decline: England and Wales, 1890–1911', *Population Studies* 49, pp. 297–315.

HIGGS, E., 1991. 'Disease, febrile poisons, and statistics: the census as a medical survey 1841–1911', *Social History of Medicine* 4, pp. 465–478.

JONES, H. R., 1894. 'The perils and protection of infant life', *Journal of the Royal Statistical Society* 57, pp. 1–103.

LEE, C. H., 1991. 'Regional inequalities in infant mortality in Britain, 1861–1971: patterns and hypotheses', *Population Studies* 45, pp. 55–65.

MARKS, L., 1994. *Model mothers: Jewish mothers and maternity provision in East London, 1870–1939*, Oxford, Clarendon Press.

PRESTON, S. and HAINES, M., 1991. *Fatal years: child mortality in late nineteenth-century America*, Princeton, NJ, Princeton University Press.

SMITH, D. S., 1991. 'Mortality differences before the health transition', *Health Transition Review* 4, pp. 235–237.

SZRETER, S. R., 1984. 'The genesis of the Registrar General's social classification of occupations', *British Journal of Sociology* 35, pp. 522–546.

TRUSSELL, T. and PRESTON, S., 1982. 'Estimating the covariates of childhood mortality from retrospective reports of mothers', *Health Policy & Education* 3, pp. 1–36.

UNITED NATIONS, 1983. *Manual X: indirect techniques of demographic estimation*, New York.

WATTERSON, P. A., 1986. 'Role of the environment in the decline of infant mortality: an analysis of the 1911 census of England and Wales', *Journal of Biosocial Science* 18, pp. 457–470.

—— 1987. 'Environmental factors in differential infant and child mortality decline in England and Wales circa 1895–1910', unpublished Ph.D. thesis, University of London.

—— 1988. 'Infant mortality by father's occupation from the 1911 census of England and Wales', *Demography* 25, pp. 289–306.

WILLIAMS, N., 1992. 'Death in its season: class, environment and the mortality of infants in nineteenth-century Sheffield', *Social History of Medicine* 5, pp. 71–94.

—— and GALLEY, C., 1995. 'Urban rural differentials in infant mortality in Victorian England', *Population Studies* 49, pp. 401–420.

—— and MOONEY, G., 1994. 'Infant mortality in an "Age of Great Cities": London and the English provincial cities compared, c.1840–1910', *Continuity and Change* 9, pp. 185–212.

154   *Alice Reid*

WILLIAMSON, J. G., 1981. 'Urban disamenities, dark satanic mills and the British standard of living debate', *Journal of Economic History* 41, pp. 75–83.

—— 1990. *Coping with city growth during the British industrial revolution*, Cambridge, Cambridge University Press.

WOODS, R. I., WATTERSON, P. A. and WOODWARD, J. H., 1988 and 1989. 'The causes of rapid infant mortality decline in England and Wales, 1861–1921. Parts I and II', *Population Studies* 42(3), pp. 343–366 and 43(1), pp. 113–132.

—— and WILLIAMS, N., 1995. 'Must the gap widen before it can be narrowed: long-term trends in social class mortality differentials', *Continuity and Change* 10, pp. 105–137.

—— —— and GALLEY, C., 1993. 'Infant mortality in England, 1550–1950: problems in the identification of long-term trends and geographical and social variations', in C. A. CORSINI and P. P. VIAZZO (eds.), *The decline of infant mortality in Europe, 1800–1950: four national case studies*, Florence, UNICEF and Instituto degli Innocenti.

8

Infant Mortality in Greece, 1859–1959:
Problems and Research Perspectives

VIOLETTA HIONIDOU

Studies of historical infant mortality have gained pace in recent years. The identification of long-term trends, the reasons for the observed levels, and the timing and the causes of the decline were among the first issues to be addressed. For countries that possess good-quality long-term sources, such as Sweden and England, many of these basic questions have been answered. However, for some other European countries, including Greece, the study of infant mortality is still in its very early stages. The reasons behind this scarcity of studies are varied, but include a lack of continuity in the published statistics and, according to Greek demographers, the poor quality of the nineteenth- and twentieth-century vital registration statistics. Because of the continuity problem in the published statistics, this chapter concentrates on infant mortality for the population of Mykonos, for which data are continuously available for the period from 1859 to 1959. The discussion consists of three parts. In the first, the sources and the methodology that were used are briefly presented, together with an assessment of the data quality. In the second part, the changes over time are examined, and in particular the timing of infant mortality decline and its possible causes. In the final part, a comparison between infant mortality for the island population of Mykonos and that for the whole of Greece is made and an agenda for future research is set.

DATA SOURCES USED IN THE STUDY OF MYKONOS

Two sets of sources have been employed in this study: civil registration certificates provide the demographic basis and 28 in-depth interviews with elderly members of the Mykoniati community offer the basis for the qualitative analysis.

The civil registration certificates cover the whole population of the island of Mykonos[1] and have been available on the island continuously since 1859. The reporting of

The research upon which this chapter is based was originally funded by a research studentship from the University of Liverpool and later by an EEC Human Capital and Mobility Fellowship. I would like to thank Bill Gould, Graham Mooney, David Siddle, Chris Wilson and Bob Woods, who provided helpful comments on earlier drafts of this chapter. I would especially like to express my gratitude to Naomi Williams, who went through the final draft of this chapter thoroughly, offering invaluable advice.

C.A. Corsini and P.P. Viazzo (eds.) The Decline of Infant and Child Mortality, 155-172.
© *1997 UNICEF. Printed in the Netherlands.*

births, deaths and marriages was first made compulsory in Greece in 1836, when a decree was passed concerning the 'Maintenance of the civil registration books' by the mayors (or suitable persons) and the submission of an annual report of all vital events to the Central Statistical Office in Athens (*Statistiki tis fisikis kiniseos tou plithismou* [*KTP*] 1956, XIII). Although some communities began registration from this date,[2] in the majority of Greek communities the decree was never enacted. In 1856 the same decree was passed, again making mayors responsible for registering vital events. This time, however, it allowed the employment of a registrar, a clerk specifically responsible for civil registration (*KTP* 1869, 2). Yet, according to the director of the Statistical Office in Athens, the literacy level of the appointed registrars was too low to allow them either to understand the purpose of the collection of vital statistics or to fulfil their duties effectively. So, a new approach was suggested in 1869. This involved the reporting of vital events to the registrars both by the family or relatives concerned, and independently by priests (*KTP* 1869, 3). The involvement of the clergy was considered essential: priests were informed of a birth soon after its occurrence in order to give the first blessing, they were the only persons authorized to conduct marriages, and they also offered the last blessing prior to a burial (ibid.). This new approach had been legalized by 1873.[3] Thus, data concerning the vital events for the whole country were collected and published annually for the years 1860–1885, with the exception of 1862 and 1863.[4] From 1885 the system for collecting annual totals collapsed even though registration continued, at least in some areas, such as Mykonos and Hermoupolis. Therefore, there are no official publications of vital statistics for the period 1886–1920. In 1921, the collection of data by the Central Statistical Office from the towns and communities that had continued registration was resumed and statistics were published for the period 1921 to 1938, with gradually improving coverage.

With Greece's entry into the Second World War in 1940, the collection of the statistical forms collapsed once again. Even though the war officially ended in 1945, the civil war that then ensued did not come to an end until 1949. The collection of data was only resumed in 1955.

---

[1] Mykonos is one of the Cycladic islands. It is situated in the Aegean sea and covers an area of approximately 124 square kilometres. There is one main population settlement, the town of Mykonos, where the island's port is also situated. During the period of the study, the rest of the population resided in rather isolated farmhouses. During the period 1861–1961, the population was 4,782 at its height in 1861 and 3,530 at its lowest level in 1961.

[2] Communities that began registration in 1836 include, for example, those on Mykonos and in Naupleion. For Mykonos lists of reported births, deaths and marriages have survived for various years between 1836 and 1858 (National Archives of Greece, Athens, Archive of Mykonos, community archive 411, sub-folder III). Also, summary statistics of births, deaths and marriages were already being sent quarterly to the Prefect by 1847 (Folk-lore Museum of Mykonos, Archive of Mykonos 1846, folder 16, sub-folder 19).

[3] On Mykonos priests were involved with civil registration from a much earlier date. In 1847, for instance, three priests were reprimanded in Mykonos for performing baptisms and burials without seeking the necessary permit from the municipal authorities. They also received a warning that, if this was repeated, they would be discharged from their duties as priests (Folk-lore Museum of Mykonos, Archive of Mykonos 9 October 1847, folder 16, sub-folder 19, register number 639).

[4] In 1863–1864 the collection and publication of the statistics was interrupted by political unrest (*Kinisis tou plithismou en Elladi* 1866, Introduction).

Thus, the principal demographic sources for this study are the civil registration data that are continuously available in Mykonos from 1859 on. These consist of birth, death and marriage certificates. The study comes to an end in 1959 because an increasing number of births started taking place in the maternity hospitals of Syros and Athens and these births were not registered on Mykonos.[5] A wealth of information is usually available in the certificates, even though the amount of information provided differed over time. For example, almost all birth certificates provide the father's full name and the mother's full name including her maiden name; in more than 75 per cent of them both the paternal and the maternal grandfathers' names are also given. In the death certificates, apart from the full name and the age of the deceased person, in many cases the father's name or even surname is also provided (Hionidou 1993, 26–31). Family reconstitution was employed in order to avoid problems of age-misreporting and also problems linked to the effects of migration (Hionidou 1993, 97–120).

Twenty-eight in-depth interviews were conducted with older members of the Mykoniati community in order to complement the demographic material, to compensate for the relative absence of secondary sources about Mykoniati society and, most importantly, to provide an insight into aspects of, and attitudes towards, childbirth, infant feeding practices and child care. No special effort was made to select a representative sample, since it is impossible to draw up a list of the existing population by name and age. Rather, I relied on my existing connections, mainly through the employees of the municipal authority and the community office. Five of the informants were males and the rest females. Their ages ranged from 70 to 93, with a mean age of 83.0 and a median of 84.5. Thus, their memories refer essentially to the first half of the twentieth century.

The majority of the informants resided in the town at the time of the interview. Nevertheless, they had not necessarily lived in the town of Mykonos throughout their childhood or their adulthood. Some informants had lived in Athens for a number of years, while some had never left the island. Overall, the informants seem to cover almost all the possible alternatives of residence, marital status, migratory moves, and occupational and social-status groups.

The life history of the informants was recorded in the interviews including the number of children ever born, children who died, and infant feeding practices. There were questions concerning the informant's and his/her siblings' education as well as questions about public health measures on the island. Even though a basic questionnaire was devised, the interviews were open-ended and the informants' answers were followed up.

The following sections discuss the problems concerning the quality of the data and the rules adopted within family reconstitution for the calculation of the various rates. Then the trends of infant, neonatal and post-neonatal mortality will be presented and the possible causes that triggered the changes over time will be explored.

---

[5] Even though only births that took place up to 1959 are examined here, the data referring to the deaths of these children or of their parents later than 1959 were also utilized.

PROBLEMS OF MEASUREMENT AND DATA QUALITY

In family reconstitution studies the continual presence of a family needs to be ascertained so that families that might have temporarily migrated and possibly experienced the birth or the death of a child elsewhere, for example, are excluded. In selecting the families to be included in the calculation of the infant mortality rates, the rules proposed by Henry and adjusted by Wrigley have largely been followed (Hionidou 1993, 122). Only legitimate births were included, although the inclusion of illegitimate births would not change the overall picture, since illegitimacy affected only 1.1 per cent of all births in the period 1859–1959.[6]

The distribution of dummy births (Table 8.1) gives a broad indication of the quality of the data.[7] Certainly, in the first half of the period, when underregistration was most likely, more than half of the dummy births were traced through a marriage and not a death. Among the deaths, only 30 per cent involved infants. Birth registration shows a gradual improvement.[8] According to all the female interviewees, a priest would visit the house of the newborn child very soon after the birth had taken place to offer the first blessing.[9] The timing of the visit varied from 'within a few hours' (four informants) to 'within 24 hours' (nine informants) and 'within three days' (four informants).[10] Thus, the priest—who would also report the birth—was informed of the birth of a child very soon after delivery, which suggests that, at least in the case of Mykonos, live-born children who survived only for the first few hours were regularly registered. It was also clear from the interviews that stillbirths were not reported either as births or as deaths and were buried informally by the parents rather than in the municipal graveyard. According to an interview with a midwife who practised on Mykonos from the 1940s onwards, infants who died within a couple of hours of the delivery could also be treated as stillbirths and thus were not registered. However, in cases where the infant survived

---

[6] It is rather difficult to establish levels of illegitimate infant mortality: unless illegitimate children died in early infancy it is very difficult to trace them in later life, since the birth certificates gave only their first names. For 51 out of the 157 illegitimate births registered on Mykonos a death certificate was found. Of the 51 cases, 42 were infant deaths.

[7] Dummy marriages, i.e. families for which a marriage certificate was not traced, were included in the analysis since they overwhelmingly represented those who married before 1859. Dummy births were excluded from all calculations of infant mortality.

[8] Using the method described by Henry (1980, 46–47), no sex-specific birth underregistration was traced, except in the first decade. Henry provides acceptable limits for the values of the sex ratio for a specific number of births. For approximately 1,600 births, as was the case in Mykonos for every decade in the period 1859–1928, the limits of the sex ratio are 100 to 110.5. For the same period the decadal sex-ratio values for Mykonos varied between 98 and 108.

[9] The priest was invited and accompanied to the house by a member of the household or by a close relative.

[10] The other answers were 'within a couple of days' (three informants), and 'soon/after a few days' (two informants). Among the three males who were asked whether the priest would offer a first blessing and when, the answer was negative in one case and no answer was given in the other two cases. All three male respondents showed an ignorance of the details surrounding childbirth and the customs, mainly linked to the Church, concerning the newborn.

Table 8.1. Mykonos: Distribution of dummy births,
by origin and proportion of dummy births among all births, 1859–1959

Period of birth	Dummy births from marriages	Dummy births from deaths	Dummy births from infant deaths	Percentage of dummy births
1859–1868	101	75	17	10.8
1869–1878	47	50	14	5.1
1879–1888	70	90	18	9.0
1889–1898	80	73	28	7.8
1899–1908	53	34	8	4.4
1909–1918	33	22	7	3.2
1919–1928	19	24	10	2.5
1929–1938	11	26	8	2.6
1939–1948	1	23	14	2.4
1949–1959	0	2	2	0.3

Note: 'Dummy births' are the unrecorded persons whose death was registered at a reported age of less than 15 or whose marriage was recorded on Mykonos. In both cases it was necessary that their parental family could be traced among the reconstituted families. The year of birth was estimated from the reported age at death or the age at marriage.

Source: Family reconstitution data.

more than a few hours (more than five hours according to the same informant) a hastened baptism would take place and a proper burial would follow. Registration had thus been ensured.

While estimates of the probable degree of underregistration of deaths and, more specifically, of infant deaths similar to those of birth-underregistration cannot be made, there are no reasons to suppose that underregistration of infant deaths exceeded that of births or that it was serious for long periods of time. Clon Stefanos (1884, 450) maintained that the coverage of death-registration was better than that for births in nineteenth-century Greece. Again, the only probable source of 'loss' of both births and infant deaths was in the case of infants who died within a few hours of birth.

The timing of baptism is not as important as it is for the users of, for example, English parish registers. Unbaptized children were not offered the last blessing by the church. Although that should not have affected the registration of births, since the registration of baptisms was a separate procedure altogether, it may have affected the reporting of deaths of unbaptized children. From the years when dates at both baptism and birth are available (1860, 1920, 1929 and 1938), no general pattern in the interval between birth and baptism can be detected. Although the interval could be as short as a couple of days in some cases, it could also extend to a few months. In most cases the interval was less than a month, although baptisms could also be concentrated during specific religious festivals. The responses from the interviewees confirmed that there was no established sense of when the appropriate time for baptism should be. Although many suggested it should take place either within the first week of life or approximately 40 days after birth, others suggested a period of a few months or even longer, perhaps a year. Nevertheless, most informants indicated that whenever the death of an infant was imminent, a hastened baptism often took place at home, performed either by a lay person (*kantilo-vaftisma*) or by a priest. Therefore, even though the official practice was not to offer a blessing to a dead unbaptized infant, every precaution would be taken to avoid this situation.

Finally, a match was made among the respondents' family histories and the existing records of births and deaths of their children. For all the infant and child deaths that were reported in the interviews, a death certificate was available in the Mykonos database. The same applied to the births that took place on Mykonos. Three of the respondents had had some of their children born in Athens and therefore these births were not registered on Mykonos.

To summarize, there are no indications of serious underregistration of infant deaths, with the probable exception of deaths occurring during the first day, and it seems that the registration of births was improving over time.

LEVELS AND TRENDS OF INFANT MORTALITY OVER TIME

The evolution of decennial infant mortality rates, as calculated from the family reconstitution data set, is shown in Figure 8.1 and Table 8.2. Overall levels of infant mortality remained remarkably low throughout the period and did not exceed 135 per 1,000. The relative stability of neonatal mortality (deaths in the first month of life) is particularly striking when considered alongside the long-term trend of post-neonatal mortality, which closely mirrored the pattern for total infant mortality. Even so, neonatal mortality comprised a not-insignificant fraction, between 23 and 32 per cent, of overall infant mortality.[11] Its decline started in the 1930s but at a much slower rate than for post-neonatal mortality. Therefore it contributed only a small percentage to the overall decline of infant mortality, at least during the initial stages. This is in accordance with other European experiences, where the major contributor to the decline of infant mortality in the late nineteenth and twentieth centuries was the decline of post-neonatal mortality (for England, see Woods, Watterson and Woodward 1988, 351; for Belgium, see Morel 1991, figure 11.1).

Post-neonatal mortality, on the other hand, showed a gradual increase until 1918, a sharp rise between 1919 and 1928, and an uninterrupted steep decline thereafter. In our attempt to explore the reasons behind this trend, we should start by asking whether the increasing rates up to 1929 are genuine. If neonatal mortality is assumed to have been 28 per 1,000 live births (the average of the period 1879–1918), then the infant mortality

---

[11] Its low value in the first two decades and its stability thereafter, until 1918, lead us to accept the existence of a small degree of underregistration of early infant deaths at the beginning of the study period. Nevertheless, because of the very low levels of neonatal mortality compared with the post-neonatal component, even if we inflate neonatal mortality to a value of 28 (the average value of neonatal mortality in the period 1879–1918), the impact on the overall infant mortality rate would be negligible.

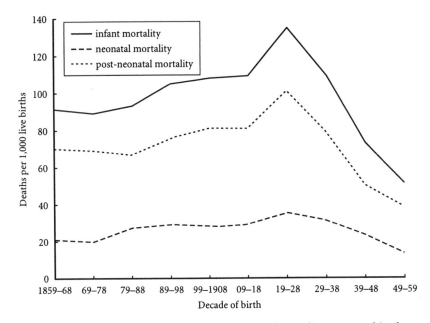

Fig. 8.1. Mykonos: Infant, neonatal and post-neonatal mortality, sexes combined, 1859–1959 (family reconstitution results)

Table 8.2. Mykonos: Neonatal, post-neonatal and infant mortality, by sex, 1859–1959 (family reconstitution results, deaths per 1,000 live births)

Period of birth	Neonatal mortality	Post-neonatal mortality	q_0			Number of births
			Total	Males	Females	
1859–1868	21	70	91	84	99	1,215
1869–1878	20	69	89	85	94	1,532
1879–1888	27	67	93	98	89	1,307
1889–1898	29	76	105	116	93	1,553
1899–1908	28	81	108	114	103	1,633
1909–1918	29	81	109	122	96	1,403
1919–1928	35	101	135	145	125	1,382
1929–1938	31	78	109	121	96	1,104
1939–1948	23	50	73	65	82	735
1949–1959	13	38	51	57	45	449

Source: Family reconstitution data.

rates in the first two decades of our study become 99 and 97, respectively. This inflation of the early values of infant mortality rate reduces the range of its values to 17 per cent in the period 1859 to 1918. The most likely reason for the gradual rise of the infant mortality rate is the well-known decline of the island's economy since the mid-nineteenth century. Stott (1982, 16) indicated that

[T]he success of all aspects of the local economy, including sea-trade, was declining by 1861. The island once had been an important sea-port, but was becoming decreasingly significant by the mid-nineteenth century, as steam-powered vessels did not make the frequent stops that the sailing vessels formerly required.... sea-trade also was declining as a source of direct income and employment on the island, as locally owned, sail-powered ships failed to compete with faster vessels. The island's once substantial production and export of wine was reported as having seriously declined by the mid-nineteenth century. Farmers suffered as trade declined, and unemployment and economic hardship reduced local markets for produce.

[T]his trend of general economic decline continued during the latter decades of the nineteenth century and beginning of the twentieth century.

In addition, Tsoucalas pointed out that the island ports experienced an economic decline from 1853 onwards, which accelerated after 1880 (Tsoucalas 1977, 171). In 1884 a contemporary observer stated that, while the island had been quite prosperous only a few years earlier, the decline suffered by the sailing industry in the preceding decade had driven a large proportion of the Mykoniati population into poverty (Stefanos 1884, 555). Thus, the increase in infant mortality on Mykonos over time appears to be genuine. It is unfortunate that a comparison cannot be made with the experience of other Greek communities, owing to the lack of similar studies for this period.

The sharp rise in infant mortality in 1919–1928 deserves special attention. This period was characterized by the arrival in Greece of more than a million refugees from Asia Minor. Their arrival was associated with an increase in mortality rates throughout the country (Valaoras 1939, 21–22). Even though some refugees temporarily settled on Mykonos, and thus experienced some vital events that were also registered (especially deaths), their inclusion in the calculation of infant mortality rates for this chapter was very limited because of the rules imposed by family reconstitution. Thus, the registered rate refers almost exclusively to the Mykoniati population and is independent of the experience of the refugee population.

The timing of the substantial increase of infant mortality in the decade 1919–1928 suggests that it may have been associated with the influenza pandemic of 1918. However, when annual infant mortality rates are considered, it becomes clear that the whole decade from 1919 to 1928 was characterized by high mortality. A major peak occurred in 1924—the largest in the whole hundred-year series, with the exception of the 1941–1942 famine peak. This indicates the absence of any major impact of the influenza pandemic on the infant population of Mykonos. According to the reported causes of death for 1919–1928, 34 per cent of infant deaths were due to diarrhoea. Among the remaining causes, atrophy and debility dominated and none was due to contagious diseases.

Although the lack of published data before 1921 prevents extended comparisons, Mykonos does not seem to have been exceptional in experiencing the peak in the infant mortality rate in the early 1920s. For example, in Athens the infant mortality rate rose from 201 per 1,000 births in 1907 to 258 in 1922–1924 (Hatzivasileioy 1935, 809; Kanellakis 1955, 136).[12]

In exploring reasons for the increase in mortality in the 1920s, increased urbanization, which has often been associated with surges in levels of mortality, must be considered a possible factor. However, increased population concentration cannot be the explanation in this case, since there was a gradual decline in the population residing in the town of Mykonos.[13] So, while there were as many as 4,025 inhabitants in 1861, by 1889 this had fallen to 3,382, and to 2,866 by 1920. By 1928 there were only 2,836 inhabitants.[14] Therefore, we cannot speak of increasing population density. In addition, the significant increase in mortality during the 1920s was not confined to infants; it affected the whole population of Mykonos (Hionidou 1993, figure 2.6). Moreover, in a review of public health in Greece, Kopanaris (1925, 204; 1933) pointed out that, between 1912 and 1923, Greece experienced the most serious outbreaks of epidemics due to the war and the mobilization and the arrival of the refugees. For Mykonos, the reasons stem principally from the effects of the very long period of almost continuous war from 1912 to 1923 and the economic disruption that resulted from it. The long absence of men certainly disrupted agricultural production. Food imports, upon which the country relied heavily, were seriously affected by the economic embargo imposed for political reasons upon the Greek government in 1920 by the *Entente*.[15] The importation of foodstuffs, which increased substantially during the war because of the decline in domestic production, was obstructed by the devaluation of the drachma in 1919 (Agianoglou 1982, 305). The magnitude of the prevailing rate of inflation is evident from the massive increase in the consumer price index, which rocketed from a basis of 100 in 1914 to 1,181 in 1923 and 1,858 in 1928 (Soldatos 1993, 364). A 37.5 per cent increase was registered in only two years, 1920–1921 (Riginos 1987, 160). Moreover, the financial situation in the country did not improve during the 1920s; the need

---

12 Part of the increase in Athens can be attributed to its rapid growth and the crowded conditions that accompanied this. In 1907–1920 annual population growth reached 5 per cent for the first time, while gross population density almost doubled between the two dates. Leontidou (1990, 64–65) attributed the population increase exclusively to migration. Increased poverty and a decline in the living standards of the Athenian population in the period immediately following the Balkan Wars were also mentioned by Leontidou (1990, 46, citing Mavrogordatos 1983). Furthermore, the arrival of refugees in the early 1920s, a significant proportion of whom settled in the capital, almost certainly accentuated the existing problems.

13 Apart from the population of the town, the administrative unit of the town of Mykonos (*Dhemos Mykonoy*) included those residing in its outskirts. In 1920, for example, the population of the town was 2,031 and the population living in the outskirts was 835. Unfortunately, in most census years only the total population of the administrative unit is given.

14 The data were derived from the published censuses, with the exception of the 1861 figure, which was calculated from the census enumerator's book.

15 The reasons for the economic embargo can be found in Svoronos (1990, 124). An earlier naval embargo, imposed in 1916 by the English and French upon the 'Old Greece' (i.e. Greece within the boundaries of 1828, of which Mykonos is part), also resulted in a severe shortage of food supplies.

to import foodstuff continued because domestic production did not increase enough to cover for the substantial numbers of refugees who arrived in the early 1920s (Agianoglou 1982, 305–306). So, it seems legitimate to believe that the significant increases in infant mortality in the 1920s were largely a reflection of, and were determined by, external circumstances.

The consistent downward trend in infant mortality in Mykonos from the end of the 1920s was very steep and abrupt. Again, using the scattered information that is available for Greece we can attempt to place the timing of infant mortality decline in a broader context and assess whether it was exceptional.[16] Using published data and dividing Greece into 10 major departments, Kanellakis (1955) showed that for the department of Central Greece/Euboia (including Athens and Piraeus) infant mortality—starting from high levels—declined from 1925 onwards. The remaining departments, which were dominated by rural areas, showed an increase until the beginning of the 1930s and a decline thereafter.[17] In the individual departments the decline started between the years 1931 and 1933.[18] Nevertheless, it seems that an increase in infant mortality followed by decline was experienced by most areas of Greece, including Mykonos, within a decade, thus suggesting a similar causality.

But what were the reasons for the infant mortality decline? In their attempt to explain the rapid decline of the infant mortality rate in England and Wales after 1900, Woods, Watterson and Woodward (1989) singled out the following major factors: infant feeding practices, fertility decline, women's education and poverty. The factor identified by the authors as the most important was the preceding fertility decline. Fertility decline can affect the survival chances of an infant both directly (that is, its personal chances of survival after birth) and indirectly through improvements in the mother's health. Among the direct reasons that can be included are the increased amount of the mother's time that can be devoted to the child, since there are less young children to be looked after, the reduced risk of catching infectious diseases in a household with fewer children, the lowering of the child's parity and the lengthening of birth intervals. Woods *et al.* also recognized the possible positive effects of improvements in women's education and, finally, the positive effect of sanitary improvements, the increasing availability of fresh water and the improvements in the quality of milk supply.

If we turn to the case of Mykonos and explore the possibility of the impact of significant improvements in public health, the available scattered evidence suggests that no major changes were made throughout the study period. In 1854 Ragavis (vol. 3, 122) noted that a large well was the principal source of water for the population of the town of Mykonos. Presumably, small ones scattered around the island provided the necessary water to the rest of the population. In 1933 Kopanaris (p. 345) indicated that,

---

[16] In Greece, civil registration was enforced, once more, at the beginning of the 1920s, and by the end of the decade coverage was considered satisfactory.

[17] Although the initial increase until the early 1930s is entirely attributed by some Greek demographers to better registration, it is also accepted that by 1929 registration was complete and, therefore, that part of the increase in infant mortality is genuine.

[18] At a smaller geographical level, more variability in the timing of the start of the decline was observed for at least some of the departments (Kanellakis 1955, 77).

although most of the Greek towns had obtained a central water supply by 1930, no changes had taken place in the countryside. He added that the government Public Health Service had made recommendations to the local authorities and passed laws that made the construction of sewers compulsory. However, although these recommendations were followed by the majority of the towns during the 1920s, there were few changes in the rural areas.[19] This is clear when it is considered that only 16 per cent of the rural population were served by any kind of water-supply system in pre-Second World War Greece (Cherry and Mangun 1954, 478). The only improvements Kopanaris mentioned for Mykonos were repairs to the wells and the water-tank in Ano Mera and the installation of pumps in three of the wells. In 1954 the publisher of the newspaper *Nea Mykonos* questioned the local government plans to build a water-tank that would provide only a fraction of the town's population with water. The rest of the population, he added, would continue to obtain water from the uncovered wells, and he then suggested that the wells should be covered and systematically chlorinated in order to protect the health of the population (*Nea Mykonos* April 1954). The exclusive use of the wells by the Mykoniati population for obtaining drinking water until well after the Second World War was substantiated by all interviewees.[20] By 1957 there were two water-tanks available in the town of Mykonos. It seems that by 1961 most of the population was provided with drinking water from the available water-tanks, since, according to the census, only 6 per cent of the households were provided with water from a well. Still, at the same date, 40 per cent of the households did not posses a water-closet.

The interviews offer a further insight into the prevailing situation concerning the availability of water-closets from the 1920s onwards. A quite clear distinction was made between the situation in the rural areas and that in the town. In the former case, almost all the informants indicated, usually with sympathetic laughter, that there were no such facilities, at least not before the Second World War. In some cases they indicated that hovels were used; in all the other cases the surrounding open spaces were used. Only 3 out of the 15 interviewees who lived in rural Mykonos indicated that a water-closet had been built earlier than the mid-1940s.[21] The situation was more progressive in the town, as the informants themselves indicated. Overall, it seems that in the 1920s a high, and ever-increasing, proportion of houses contained a water-closet.[22] Nevertheless, this

---

[19] Nevertheless, the recommendations made by the Public Health Service in the 1930s were not totally ignored. On 20 September 1934 the newspaper *H Mykonos* mentioned that the local authority had removed the pigs from the houses to a communal yard situated on the borders of the town—although it was still very close to houses.

[20] All 19 informants who answered the question 'where did you obtain your drinking water?' gave identical answers. Some of the town-dwellers indicated that they bought water that used to be brought to them by a well-owner. Some of the informants still used water from wells for their drinking requirements at the time of the interview.

[21] In all cases, the addition of a water-closet took place when a new house was built, i.e. only through individual initiative. The three informants who built a water-closet in rural areas prior to the Second World War did so in 1938, approximately in 1927 and in the 1920s, respectively. I should also note that those who lived on the islands of Dheles are considered rural.

[22] Of the 13 informants who resided in the town in the 1920s, 12 indicated that either their parents' house

was not universal and there were also references to the common use of pots that were emptied into the sea, holes in the town or the nearby open spaces. Even where a water-closet was available, water was rarely, if at all, used.

So, although an increasing number of houses in the town had water-closets in the 1920s, there were still significant numbers of inhabitants who did not have access to one. Moreover, almost no one in the rural areas possessed a water-closet until the end of the Second World War. Thus, no major public health improvements seem to have taken place before or during the 1930s.

The information collected about infant feeding practices points to widespread use of breastfeeding, at least in the rural parts of Greece. This can be inferred from a number of sources. In 1860 the author of an article in a journal called *O iatros tou laou* ('The doctor of the people') suggested that, for breastfed infants, whenever breastmilk was insufficient and the need for additional artificial food arose, cornflour pap instead of the commonly used flour or semolina pap should be used by their mothers (Anon. 1860, 265–267, cited in Soutzoglou-Kottaridi 1991, 416–417). In several newspaper articles from the 1830s to the early 1860s, a strong disapproval of mothers who used wet-nurses and 'thus avoid[ed] their primary obligation to their children following what fashion dictates' is also evident (Soutzoglou-Kottaridi 1991, 428–433). We should note, however, that all the newspapers were published in the towns (Athens, Syros, Naupleion) and were therefore addressed to urban populations, and certainly to the upper classes since the high cost of wet-nursing was constantly stressed. In Mykonos, wet-nursing was used at the beginning of the study period and at least until the beginning of the twentieth century for foundlings.[23] The 1861 census book lists a wet-nurse who was residing in the same house as the nursling child. However, the existence of only a single case indicates that the wet-nursing of legitimate children was very restricted in Mykonos and was probably limited to upper-class families.[24] Again this is confirmed by the oral evidence, in which only one of the informants, who came from a wealthy family, mentioned that her mother employed wet-nurses for her children.[25] All the other informants, without a single exception, stated that they themselves breast-fed, just as their mothers had done. While there was some variation in the reported duration of breastfeeding, 12 months could be considered as a minimum average.[26]

or their own house possessed a water-closet. The informants mentioned that either they moved to town and there was a water-closet in the house or that their parents built one in the mid-1920s. In the case of the wealthiest the answer was invariably that there had been a water-closet in their parents' house. In most cases this was a Turkish-style water-closet with a cesspool, which, according to all informants but one, was never emptied.

[23] This is clear in a number of documents concerning the payments of wet-nurses by the municipal authorities (Folk-lore Museum of Mykonos, Archive of Mykonos 1870, folder 22, sub-folder 2; 1882, folder 39, sub-folder 3; 1890, folder 50, sub-folder 5; 1901, folder 60, sub-folder 2; 1905, folder 63, sub-folder 2).

[24] The fact that the family that used a wet-nurse was clearly a member of the elite is indicated by the house-hold head's occupation (merchant) and the fact that a servant was included in the household.

[25] She indicated that employing a wet-nurse was the only alternative to breastfeeding considered. The reason she gave for her mother's not breastfeeding was that she did not have enough milk. She also indicated that the wet-nurse did not reside with them, because she had a baby of her own to look after.

[26] Four of the informants stated that they breastfed their children for a minimum of between 7 and 12 months, and another 17 of the informants stated a duration between 12 and 24 months and sometimes longer. (Two of the female informants did not bear any children.)

Breastfeeding was not scheduled, but would take place on demand and supplementation rarely started prior to the fifth month. Moreover, the post-partum non-susceptible period for women married between 1859 and 1918 was estimated to have been as high as 12 months, indicating even longer periods of breastfeeding (Hionidou 1993, table 8.15). Thus, any further lengthening of the breastfeeding period could not have made a significant contribution to a reduction in infant mortality in the 1920s and 1930s.

Improvements in education, and especially that of females, can affect levels of infant mortality in a number of ways. In historical populations, it is believed that women with some years of schooling were able to read newspapers and leaflets concerning infant-care practices. Caldwell (1981) argued that educated women in developing countries are not only more likely to seek medical help and be better informed about child-care issues but are also more likely to challenge the authority of the older generation in all aspects, including traditional infant-care practices.

On Mykonos, a substantial increase in female school-attendance occurred only in the late 1920s, when school enrolment and attendance became obligatory according to a law that was passed in 1926. The improvement in school enrolment was immediate and obvious. In 1924 there were 255 male pupils and 80 female pupils in primary schooling (Kyriazopoulos 1924), and a further 70 students of both sexes who were enrolled in the secondary school. In 1933 the total number of pupils enrolled in school had grown to 838 (*Mykoniatika Chronika* 21 January 1934). No significant changes occurred prior to the 1920s, although a gradual improvement in the school enrolment of boys was evident (Hionidou 1993, 38–40). These findings were confirmed by the informants. Among the wealthy Mykoniati families, boys and girls attended school for approximately the same number of years; for the rest of the population, prior to 1925, a clear distinction between the necessity of education for boys and that for girls was made. This was repeatedly mentioned by the informants themselves and was also shown in the numbers of boys and girls who enrolled and graduated in 1912–1913 in a primary school situated outside the town of Mykonos: 42 boys and 9 girls were enrolled, while 14 boys and 2 girls graduated (Folk-lore Museum of Mykonos, Archive of Mykonos 1912–1938, folder 84, sub-folder 1). The significance of the 1926 law becomes evident in that it had an immediate impact upon the schooling of the female informants, and especially those from rural areas: six out of the nine rural informants who were born prior to 1915 were never enrolled at school, and those who were attended for an average of three years. Of those who were born after 1915, all six attended school, for an average of four years. It should be noted that among the town-dwellers all female informants but one attended school. So, substantial improvements in the education of females started only in the late 1920s on Mykonos. Any improvements in female education in the 1920s would concern the potential mothers of at least 10 years later (the late 1930s). However, the effect of the first 'educated' cohort was most probably concealed for some years, since it coexisted with that of the older, 'less-educated' cohorts. Therefore, improvements in female literacy could not have had any significant impact on infant mortality until, at the earliest, the 1940s, a time when infant mortality decline was already well under way.

An additional issue here is whether, even in the case of widespread literacy, there were adequate sources of information in the form of newspapers, radios and leaflets. Although a limited number of newspapers devoted to Mykonos were published in Athens in the 1930s, and were presumably available on the island, they contained no information about infant-care or fertility practices. Access to other newspapers published in Athens and Syros was occasional and probably restricted for the overwhelming majority of the Mykoniati population prior to the Second World War. The first radio arrived in Mykonos in 1933 (*Mykoniatika Chronika* 31 December 1933). Assuming that some years elapsed before a significant proportion of the population had access to a radio, it is clear that there could be no association between the availability of a radio and the onset of infant mortality decline.

Therefore, it seems unlikely that public health improvements, increased female literacy, or changing breastfeeding patterns could have initiated the infant mortality decline that took place in the 1930s. The main alternative hypothesis left is the possible effect of a preceding decline in marital fertility on the survival chances of infants.

The various fertility–infant mortality interrelations are complex and bidirectional. Declining fertility may stimulate infant mortality decline through the reduction of high-parity births, which are known to experience above-average mortality, and through the extension of birth intervals. The lengthening of this interval ensures that the child receives more attention than it would if another child was born soon after. It also ensures the avoidance of the so-called 'maternal depletion' syndrome, where repetitive childbearing at short intervals leads to the birth of low-weight babies (Hobcraft, McDonald and Rutstein 1983, 585).

Infant mortality can also affect levels of fertility. The replacement effect may operate, where the death of an infant or child is followed by its deliberate 'replacement' by the parents, thus increasing fertility. It should be stressed, however, that the replacement effect can function only in a controlled-fertility setting. The interrelationship of infant mortality and fertility is further complicated by the association with breastfeeding. Prolonged breastfeeding can contribute substantially to low infant mortality because of the partial immunity it offers to infants in the first critical months of their lives. Breastfeeding beyond the first month also prolongs the non-fecund post-partum period and thus defers the next pregnancy. This has an effect on the length of the birth interval and therefore on infant mortality. In contrast, the death of an infant results in the stopping of breastfeeding, the shortening of the post-partum anovulatory period and, finally, the increase of fertility.

In establishing which of these relationships were in operation, and in which direction, in the case of Mykonos, we should start by reiterating that prolonged breastfeeding (a minimum average of 12 months) was practised throughout the study period. Breastfeeding was responsible for the low levels of infant mortality on Mykonos. In terms of the link between infant mortality and fertility we should expect a positive relationship (that is, increasing infant mortality leading to increasing fertility); however, this unequivocally was not the case on Mykonos. The long-term increase in infant mortality did not have any effect on the levels of fertility, since fertility remained largely stable for the marriage cohorts up to 1918 (Hionidou 1993, 205–222). At exactly the time when

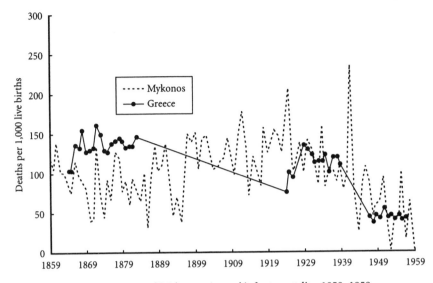

Fig. 8.2. Greece and Mykonos: Annual infant mortality, 1859–1959

Sources: Mykonos database; *Kinisis tou plithismou en Elladi* 1864–1884; *Statistiki tis fisikis kiniseos tou plithismou* 1921–1938, 1956–1960.

infant mortality experienced a substantial increase in 1919–1928, the restriction of marital fertility was initialized among the couples married in the same decade. In contrast, the decline of fertility that was initialized in the 1920s seems to have had a significant effect on infant mortality, the decline of which started within 10 to 15 years of the fertility decline.[27] The effect of fertility decline on infant mortality is evident in both components of infant mortality: neonatal and post-neonatal (Figure 8.1). The decline in neonatal mortality after 1929 suggests that fertility decline had a direct impact on the health of the mother. This is also evident in the rapid decline of maternal mortality from 1929 onwards (Hionidou 1993, table 6.9).

MYKONOS IN A NATIONAL CONTEXT

Figure 8.2 shows Mykonos in a national context. The rates for Greece are from the published data, while those for Mykonos have been calculated from the death certificates according to the reported age at death.[28] The lack of continuity in the published statistics for Greece, which has essentially prevented studies of infant mortality in Greece, is evident. However, a number of points can be made. First, while the rates are

---

[27] The decline of infant mortality is considered to have started in the late 1930s, since the decline experienced between 1929 and 1938 was, in part, only a return to the earlier levels.

[28] The reported age at death was used for Mykonos in order to obtain rates comparable to those calculated for Greece from the published sources.

in close agreement at the end of the period, there are greater discrepancies at the beginning. Part of the explanation for this stems from the fact that, while the population of Mykonos was rural and semi-urban, the urban centres included in the population of Greece inflated the rates for the country as a whole. The fact that mortality in general, and especially that of infants, was high in the urban centres was evident even to contemporaries.[29] For example, the area of Attica, which includes Athens as well as some rural areas, had an infant mortality rate of 319 per 1,000 live births in 1868–1878, while Syros's infant mortality rate was 242. An additional reason for the excess infant mortality in the major urban centres of Greece, such as Athens and Syros, was the existence of foundling hospitals. There, mortality was outstandingly high. In the Athens Foundling Hospital, for instance, the infant mortality rate in 1915 was as high as 650 deaths per 1,000 admitted infants (Anon. 1920, 37). As late as 1931–1932, the infant mortality rate of Athens was substantially inflated by the mortality of the foundlings, from a value of 98.8 to a value of 129 (Hatzivasileioy 1935, 815).

So, the infant mortality rate of Mykonos was most probably representative of that of Greece if the major urban centres are excluded. For the urban centres, additional research is needed to establish their levels and trends of infant mortality and the specific problems they had to face.

CONCLUSIONS

The main observations of this study are the extremely low levels of infant mortality in late-nineteenth- and early-twentieth-century Mykonos, and their close association with long periods of breastfeeding. Moreover, the primary factor in the infant mortality decline was the decline in post-neonatal mortality. The decline of infant mortality does not seem to have been associated with the introduction of public health measures, since even at the time of the decline water supplies remained poor, and systems of excrement-removal rudimentary, for the majority of the population. Rather, infant mortality decline seems to have been the result of the decline in fertility.

In addition, the Mykoniati pattern of infant mortality seems to have been representative of that of Greece if the major urban centres are excluded. Additional research is needed to establish the levels and trends of infant mortality in urban centres such as Syros, where sources similar to the ones used for Mykonos are available. Moreover, research concerning illegitimacy and foundlings should be an essential part of the study of infant mortality in urban centres because of their potential for inflating rates of mortality to excessive levels. Finally, a study of the coverage and the quality of published statistics in Greece—sources that remain largely unused to the present day—should precede any attempts to study the long-term trends of infant mortality.

---

[29] Maccas (1911, quoted by Kanellakis 1955, 31) attributed the high infant mortality rate of the towns to the lower prevalence of breastfeeding in comparison with the rural areas. In addition, Stefanos (1884, 543) observed that diarrhoea was more prevalent in urban areas.

References

AGIANOGLOU, P., 1982. *To perasma apo tin feoudarchia ston kapitalismo stin Ellada*, Athens.

ANON, 1860. 'Amilon–marantamilon', *O iatros tou laou*, IZ(A), 1 September, reprinted in SOUTZOGLOU-KOTTARIDI 1991.

ANON, 1920. *To Dhmotikon Vrefokomeion Aqhnwn kata ta eth 1916–1919*, Athens, I.B. Bartsou.

CALDWELL, J. C., 1981. 'Maternal education as a factor in child mortality', *World Health Forum* 2(1), pp. 75–78.

CHERRY, R. L., and MANGUN, C. W. Jr, 1954. 'Technical assistance in public health: the 6-year program in Greece', *Public Health Reports* 69(5), pp. 475–486.

HATZIVASILEIOY, G., 1935. 'H vrefiki thnisimotis en Athinais', *Asklipios* 6, pp. 809–833.

HENRY, L., 1980. *Techniques d'analyse en demographie historique*, Paris, INED.

HIONIDOU, V., 1993. 'The demography of a Greek island, Mykonos 1859–1959: a family reconstitution study', Ph.D. thesis, University of Liverpool.

HOBCRAFT, J., MCDONALD, J. W., and RUTSTEIN, S., 1983. 'Child-spacing effects on infant and early child mortality', *Population Index* 49, pp. 585–618.

KANELLAKIS, A., 1955. 'Symvoli eis tin meleti tis vrefikis thnisimotitos en Elladi', Ph.D. thesis, University of Athens.

KINISIS TOU PLITHISMOU EN ELLADI, Athens, National Press (published annually 1860–1861, 1863–1885, 1889–1890).

KOPANARIS, F., 1925. 'Greece', in *International Health Year-book*, Geneva, League of Nations.

—— 1933. *H dimosia ygeia en Elladi*, Athens, Chronopoulos.

KYRIAZOPOULOS, G. D., 1924. 'Ekthesis peri tis georgikis kai ktinotrofikis paragogis tou teos demou Mykonou kai ton kinotiton Mykonou kai Ano Meras', unpublished manuscript, Mykonos.

LEONTIDOU, L., 1990. *The Mediterranean city in transition*, Cambridge, Cambridge University Press.

MACCAS, G. N., 1911. *H thnisimotis tis paidikis ilikias en Elladi: aitia kai mesa pros peristolin*, Athens.

MAVROGORDATOS, G. T., 1983. *Stillborn republic: social coalitions and party strategies in Greece, 1922–1936*, Berkeley, CA, University of California Press.

MOREL, M.-F., 1991. 'The care of children: the influence of medical innovation and medical institutions on infant mortality 1750–1914', in R. SCHOFIELD, D. REHER, and A. BIDEAU (eds.), *The decline of mortality in Europe*, Oxford, Clarendon Press.

RAGAVIS, I. P., 1854. *Ta Ellinika, itoi perigrafi geografiki, istoriki, arxaiologiki kai statistiki ths Arxaias kai neas Ellados*, 3 vols, Athens, K. Antoniadis.

RIGINOS, M., 1987. *Paragogikes domes kai ergatika imeromisthia stin Ellada, 1909–1936*, Athens, Idryma Ereynas kai Paideias tis Emporikis trapezas.

SOLDATOS, G. T., 1993. 'The inter-war Greek economy: income inequality and speculation', *European History Quarterly* 23(3), pp. 359–379.

SOUTZOGLOU-KOTTARIDI, P., 1991. *Paidi kai ygeia sta prota xronia ths aneksartitis Elladas 1830–1862*, Athens, Dodoni Press.

STATISTIKI TIS FISIKIS KINISEOS TOU PLITHISMOU, Athens, National Press (published annually 1921–1938, 1956).

STEFANOS, C., 1884. 'Grèce, Géographie médicale', in A. DECHAMBRE (ed.), *Dictionnaire Encyclopédique des Sciences Médicales*, vol. 2, series 4, Paris, G. Masson and P. Asselin et Gie.

STOTT, M., 1982. 'The social and economic structure of the Greek island of Mykonos 1860–1978: an anthropological perspective', Ph.D. thesis, London School of Economics.

SVORONOS, N. G., 1990. *Episkopisi tis neoellinikis istorias*, 12th edn, Athens, Themelio.

TSOUCALAS, K., 1977. *Eksartisi kai anaparagogi: o koinonikos rolos ton ekpaideutikon mixanismon stin Ellada (1830–1922)*, Athens, Themelio Press.

VALAORAS, V. G., 1939. *To dimographiko provlima tis Ellados kai i epidrasis ton prosphigon*, Athens.

WOODS, R. I., WATTERSON, P. A. and WOODWARD, J. H., 1988 and 1989. 'The causes of rapid infant mortality decline in England and Wales, 1861–1921. Parts I and II', *Population Studies* 42(3), pp. 343–366 and 43(1), pp. 113–132.

9

Life Histories of Lone Parents and Illegitimate Children in Nineteenth-Century Sweden

ANDERS BRÄNDSTRÖM

In 1993 UNICEF launched what it described as an 'important and provocative new series' of annual reports on *The Progress of Nations*. According to UNICEF, 'it is time that the standing and prestige of nations were assessed less by their military and economic prowess and more by the protection they provide for the lives, the health, the growth and the education of their children.' Special emphasis was put on infant and child survival, since the reduction of mortality rates in these age groups is 'a measure of all things'. The level of infant and childhood mortality in a population is directly influenced by 'the income and education of the parents, the prevalence of malnutrition and disease, the availability of clean water and safe sanitation, the efficacy of health services, and the health and status of women' (Arrigoni and Himes 1993, 7).

Although infant and childhood mortality is such an excellent measure of the maturity of a society, it is also very difficult to disentangle the different components that contribute to the mortality level. Some positive factors, such as clean water and safe sanitation, might be counteracted by the low status of women in a society. Historically, the prevalence of breastfeeding in a population often counterbalanced negative effects of social class and bad sanitation (Brändström 1984; Corsini and Viazzo 1993b, 12). Consequently, many of the underlying causes of infant mortality decline in Western countries between 1750 and 1950 are still very poorly understood. Industrialization often meant proletarianization, bad sanitation, overcrowded housing conditions and the spread of such infectious diseases as tuberculosis and diarrhoeal diseases. Behavioural norms changed and the influence of the Church decreased. The illegitimacy ratio increased steadily in most countries, alongside an increase in the working-class population. At the same time, almost as a contradiction, mortality decreased even among illegitimate children and the poor. To quote from Reher and Schofield (1991): 'it would only be a small exaggeration to say that our understanding of historical mortality patterns, and of their causes and implications, is still in its infancy.'

In most analyses of the secular decline in infant and childhood mortality, children born out of wedlock record the highest mortality rates and the lowest life expectancies. This is so whether studies are based on national statistics or on family reconstitutions at the micro level. Whatever religion dominates an area, illegitimate children have the shortest life expectancies. Comparison between different economies and modes of

A longer version of this paper appeared in *History of the Family* 1(2), published by JAI Press Inc., Greenwich, CT, and London.
C.A. Corsini and P.P. Viazzo (eds.) The Decline of Infant and Child Mortality, 173-191.
© *1997 UNICEF. Printed in the Netherlands.*

production reveals the same familiar pattern: being illegitimate, with a few rare exceptions, equates to facing a much higher mortality rate than being legitimate. The same pattern is found regardless of whether the comparison is made at the local, regional or international level (Corsini and Viazzo 1993a; Mitterauer 1983).

The influence of legitimacy on the chances of survival is also underlined in research based on longitudinal and/or cohort studies. With multiregression techniques, such as logistic or Cox-regression analyses, legitimacy often produces p-values close to zero. Indeed, the importance of legitimacy for the level of infant mortality is often so predictable that it is generally left out of the discussion by historical demographers! Perhaps it is for this reason that our knowledge about the living conditions of lone parents is so limited. To what degree did their social situation affect their chances of survival? What role did different religious beliefs play? What consequences did different forms of inheritance system have on their situation? To what degree did variations in family and household formation influence the acceptance or the rejection of illegitimate children? How was work organized in different settings, and could the illegitimate child be seen as an important production unit in this context? The questions are many. They cannot be isolated from each other, but must be brought together in a single analysis, as pointed out by Mitterauer (1983, 81).

As noted in many other studies, the illegitimacy ratio increased in most European countries during the nineteenth century. In Sweden, approximately 62 per 1,000 births were illegitimate in 1811–1820. By 1851–1860 this number had increased to 90 per 1,000 births, and, by the turn of the century, to 110 per 1,000 births. Illegitimacy was mainly an urban phenomenon in Sweden, at least when we look at sheer numbers. Illegitimacy rates in towns often went above 200 per 1,000 births. Although the countryside displayed comparatively low ratios, illegitimacy was still considered to be a large problem by both the medical profession and, of course, ministers of the Church.

The increase has been interpreted in many ways. According to Edward Shorter (1973, 612), there was a relationship between economic changes (mainly the introduction of capitalism) and the increase in the illegitimacy ratio. Women, especially from the lower classes, were drawn into a new monetary economy; they were no longer restricted to the family or the household as their main workplace. Now, they could seek their fortunes on an open labour market. They experienced an increased degree of freedom because they were less dependent upon parents and husbands for their existence. With personal freedom came sexual liberation. With sexual liberation, where emotions played an increasing role in the selection of marriage partners, came an increase in prenuptial conceptions. Shorter has been the subject of much criticism, mainly because he lacked relevant empirical evidence. According to Tilly, Scott and Cohen (1976, 461), salaries for women were so low that they could hardly have contributed to their economic independence. Instead, the increase in the illegitimacy ratio was a result of traditional values colliding with a rapidly transforming society. High geographical mobility and economic uncertainty forced women to turn to the traditional form of security—the marriage. However, in a society where they lacked the stability normally found in the family or in the presence of kin, illegitimate births were often the unwanted result. Moreover, most illegitimate births took place among the less fortunate classes in society.

Peter Laslett (1980, 217) put forward a completely different explanation. According to him, the increased illegitimacy ratio was mainly due to the emergence of a subculture among lower classes in society that generally looked upon 'official' social norms with suspicion. With the sense that they had little to gain from society came the notion that there was nothing to gain from following the rules and norms of that particular society, including the bourgeoisie's championship of restrained sexuality. Naturally, belonging to the lower social classes in society did not necessarily lead to a promiscuous lifestyle, but many found a new identity in a 'deviant' way of life. According to Laslett, the increase in illegitimate births was not the result of an increase in the *number of women* who gave birth to these children. Instead, a subculture of lower class women gave birth to *more* illegitimate children.

In Sweden, some contemporary debates blamed industrialization and urbanization for the increased number of illegitimate children. According to them, the result of these processes was that social norms and traditional religious values were no longer valued by working-class men and women. The lack of patriarchal guidance and the high consumption of alcohol contributed to a promiscuous lifestyle.

The ethnologist Jonas Frykman (1975) reached a conclusion similar to Shorter's. The reason behind the increase in illegitimacy in Sweden was mainly to be found in a clash between capitalism and old social norms. Traditional values upheld by the Church played a less significant role in the changing economy of the late nineteenth century. Instead, emotions came to be more influential in the selection of marriage partners. Both women and men experienced a new kind of freedom when they were no longer dependent upon succeeding to a farm for their existence. In a rapidly changing society, old traditions such as 'night courtship' collided with increased geographical mobility.

According to another Swedish ethnologist, Orvar Löfgren (1969), 'night courtship' was an almost institutionalized form of social interaction between young, unmarried men and women. They met in situations that were potentially very sexual, but social norms and Christian values kept restraints on the couple. When a young woman became pregnant, social control ensured that she could still count on marriage with the man in question. Consequently, children born under such prenuptial circumstances were often recorded as *betrothal* by the clergy, seldom as *illegitimate*.[1] However, when social control was weakened and geographical mobility increased, traditional night courtship resulted in a rapid increase in the number of illegitimate births. The father was usually no longer locked into the local culture and could avoid parental responsibilities by migrating. The woman, who was often still part of the traditional value system, was condemned by local society as a whore and could only avoid social degradation by migration (Frykman 1977).

In the eyes of the Swedish Protestant Church, the mother of an illegitimate child was not 'pure' and could not take part in normal religious activities. She had to be purified

---

1 Mitterauer (1983) discussed night courtship within the wider context of northern European culture.

according to the Church Law of 1686. Initially, the purification process was official: the unwed mother had to face the parishioners in the church, admit her sins and receive forgiveness. This was changed into solitary purification in 1741, when she was obliged to face only the minister. Mercantilist Sweden was alarmed by the high death rates among illegitimate infants, since the children might otherwise have grown up to become important contributors to the wealth of the nation—'An illegitimate child knows no other master than the State', as was frequently stated in the contemporary debate concerning foundling homes and workhouses. It was hoped that a change in the Church Law would contribute to lowering the social stigma of an illegitimate birth and increasing the population. Purification was officially abolished in 1855, although it continued on the local level for several decades. Illegitimacy was still a crime according to the State Law of 1734. The punishment was usually a fine, which the man, too, had to pay if his guilt could be proven in court. The law was changed in 1864, after which cases of illegitimacy could be brought to court only if the woman pressed charges against the putative father (Andersson 1993).

From 1865, illegitimacy was no longer a *true* crime in the eyes of the Protestant Church and the Swedish government. However, written laws are one thing and public opinion another. Differences in infant mortality between legitimate and illegitimate children were still considerable, which would suggest that the situation for lone mothers improved in some areas, but was pretty much the same in others (Figure 9.1).

Traditionally, historical demographers have analysed legitimacy with the newborn child as the sole object. Life expectancy for the child has been measured and paired with such explanatory variables as social class (reflected in the occupation of its mother or its grandfather), breastfeeding duration, sex, parity and the locality. As mentioned

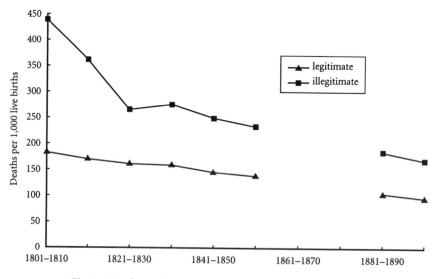

Fig. 9.1. Sweden: Infant mortality, 1801–1900 (decadal averages)

earlier, these results have pointed in a clear direction. Illegitimacy equated to a decreased life expectancy, even after controlling for factors such as social class. Usually, this has meant the end of further investigations into its specific nature.

Why take only the child as the object? If Peter Laslett is right—setting aside his causal argumentation—we should focus our attention much more on complete reproductive histories of single mothers. Who were these women and in what circumstances did they live? Were they to an increasing degree part of a subculture, with more illegitimate conceptions per woman than previously? Or was single parenthood just a stage in some women's life cycles? Was it something unfortunate that happened to them when they were young, but still allowed them to settle down and marry? Did all this change in times of industrialization and modernization when, presumably, social values and norms changed? What effect did all this have on the illegitimate children? If it was a life-cycle phenomenon for their mothers, to what extent are high death rates explained by simple age and parity effects? The illegitimate child would most probably be the first child of a very young mother and consequently suffer from a combination of negative age and parity effects.[2] If increased death risks among children of single mothers were mainly the result of a lack of parental care, what happened to children of the same mother once she married?

THE MATERIAL AND THE COHORT

The research drew 2,569 complete reproductive life histories from the registers of 16 parishes surrounding the town of Sundsvall in the county of Västernorrland (Map 9.1). These parish registers cover the period 1800–1895, although four of the parishes (Lögdö, Galtström, Lagfors and Svartvik) existed only for a shorter period of time or were part of other parishes. These four parishes started as foundries and were turned into large sawmills during the second half of the nineteenth century. They are part of the analyses in this chapter, but will commonly be included in the larger parishes that surrounded them. The analysis of the town of Sundsvall is restricted to the second half of the nineteenth century. All parish registers before 1860, except the church examination register, were destroyed in a large city fire in 1888. Since the church examination register fails to include newborn children, it cannot be used for studies on infant mortality.

The town of Sundsvall, 400 kilometres north of Stockholm, was a small local port-town before 1850, serving what was largely a rural area. As a result of the availability of marginal arable land and work opportunities at some iron foundries in the region, the surrounding parishes showed relatively small indications of overpopulation. A combination of technological changes—the invention of the steam-powered mill and an

---

[2] The effects of age and/or parity on chances of survival commonly display a U-shaped or an L-shaped curve. Risks are highest at young ages and at low parities. Risks decrease considerably by parity two and tend to increase again at parity above four or five. Similarly, death risks are highest among infants born to young mothers, and they decrease gradually down to age group 25–29, after which they slowly start to increase again.

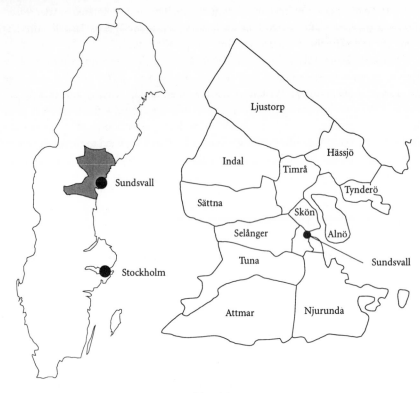

Map 9.1.

increased demand for sawn timber in Europe—quickly turned Sundsvall into the fastest growing industrial region in Europe in the 1860s and 1870s. The population grew rapidly. In 1803 the town of Sundsvall reported a population of 1,775. By 1850 it had reached 2,859. With the expansion of the sawmill industry in the region, it suddenly expanded, registering 6,515 inhabitants in 1870 and 14,831 by the end of the century. Most of the expansion was accomplished by a net inmigration of 2–4 per cent and a natural growth rate that increased from 0.5 to 1.5 per cent per annum. However, unrecorded seasonal and short-term migration was very high in the Sundsvall region. Consequently, the *de facto* population was much larger than the *de jure* population during certain periods of the year. Short-term fluctuations in net migration rates were influenced by the economic development within the forestry industry, attracting people during good years and repelling them during recessions. Sundsvall's positive migration rates suddenly ended in 1890, when the forestry industry could no longer expand at the same rate as before. The golden years of the timber industry in Sweden were over forever.

Migration to the Sundsvall region was characterized by the long distances from which people came. This was especially true during the initial phase of industrialization. The degree to which immigrants adapted to the region was quite high, especially among those who came to the town of Sundsvall. More than 80 per cent of those who married, and 61 per cent of the unmarried, stayed in the town for a minimum of five years. Marriage was a key factor, alongside the obvious importance of job opportunities, in a decision to remain in the town. As a result, the natural population growth in the town of Sundsvall was relatively high in comparison with other urban areas. However, the majority of the population of the Sundsvall region lived in the countryside, where the large sawmills were established. In 1870 they numbered almost 50 along the coast. At the time Sweden was one of the least urbanized countries in Europe. Urbanization started in the 1840s, but at the turn of the century still only some 20 per cent of the population lived in towns (Brändström, Sundin and Tedebrand 1994).

The town of Sundsvall played two roles during the industrialization period. It was the centre of trade, commerce and administration in the region. Consequently, it attracted young, unmarried women to work in the service sector. It also functioned as a staging post for the sawmill industry, attracting large number of men who stayed briefly in the town and then sought employment in the sawmills. Therefore, the female surplus in Sundsvall never reached the high levels found in most other Swedish towns. Women could also find employment in the sawmill industry, especially in the harbour areas, where they unloaded ballast and sapwood, but it was essentially a world with job opportunities mainly for men.

This chapter examines life expectancies among infants born to women who had experienced the birth of an illegitimate child at least once in their reproductive life history. A cohort of women has been followed continuously, despite their geographical mobility within the Sundsvall region. Constant observation ensures that no birth might have gone unrecorded, allowing for a large set of complete reproductive histories. A total of 2,569 women were followed between around 1800 and 1895, during which time they gave birth to a total of 9,282 children. Such explanatory variables as sex, social class, the parish of birth, parity, age of the mother at the birth of each child and marital status have been recorded for the child and the mother.

This study will look at legitimacy as a life-cycle phenomenon. Women who gave birth to illegitimate children at some point in time were followed from the birth of their first child to that of their last child, or age 50 if their histories are somehow truncated. Usually, the illegitimate birth, or births, are the initial ones in the reproductive history. However, the analysis also includes cases where women who were widowed went on to give birth to illegitimate children. Primarily, the study will focus on comparative mortality rates for children born illegitimate and those later born as legitimate. The investigation will rely on techniques based on collective event histories, such as logistic and Cox-regression analyses. Each child will be followed, in relation to its mother, to compare those who died as infants to those who survived infancy. Each new child in the family, illegitimate or legitimate, forms a new record in the analysis. The method is not free of complications. To some extent it disregards the fact that several children are related, even though we know that infant mortality is highly family dependent (Brändström 1984; Greenhouse and Lynch 1994). Statistically, it is difficult to include such dependence in an analysis of this kind, but the problem will be addressed later in the research project. To compensate partially for family dependence, some 'family' variables relating to the complete life history of the mother have been attached to every child, such as parity and the total number of legitimate and illegitimate births in the family.

THE RESULTS

As elsewhere in Sweden, and in Europe for that matter, illegitimacy increased in the Sundsvall region during the nineteenth century. This was especially the case in the town of Sundsvall, where more than 200 per 1,000 births where recorded as illegitimate in some periods.[3]

From Table 9.1 we can see that in the course of the nineteenth century there was a general tendency for the illegitimacy ratio to increase in all parishes in the Sundsvall region, with the exception of industrialized Njurunda and Timrå and the agrarian parish of Indal. However, these three parishes already displayed high numbers during the early period. All other parishes show increases in their ratios (for the town and the former foundries we have only one point of observation), but there are no correlations between the size of the increase and whether the parish was industrialized or remained agrarian. There was a sudden jump in the illegitimacy ratio in the period 1870–1879, which was the most intense period of industrialization. This 'crisis' seems to have affected all parishes, but it is more pronounced in many industrializing parishes. After that 10-year period, rates went down to 'normal' again. Industrialization alone cannot explain high ratios of illegitimacy, since the parishes of Indal, Timrå, Skön and Njurunda, which nevertheless display relatively high illegitimacy ratios, could hardly be counted as industrialized parishes before 1850. The town, with its very high rate, is almost to be considered as a special case in the region.

The analysis of the complete reproductive histories from the Sundsvall region does not lend support to Peter Laslett's theory of subcultures within the population giving birth to an increasing number of illegitimate children. Table 9.2 displays statistics for the number of illegitimate children per woman in three regions: the town of Sundsvall, industrialized parishes and agricultural parishes. Time is divided into three periods: pre-industrial (1800–1859), rapid industrialization (1860–1879) and stabilization (1880–1896). The mean age of women at the birth of their first child was 23.2 years in the town of Sundsvall, 23.1 in the industrialized parishes and 24.0 in the agrarian parishes, which means that women born in 1840 had their first children around 1863–1864. If the town of Sundsvall is separated from the industrialized parishes, we find very small changes in the number of illegitimate children per woman in these age cohorts. The first phase of industrialization caused a temporary increase in the number

---

[3] The admittedly scant statistical evidence available for the late eighteenth century indicates that in the period 1779–1801 the illegitimacy ratio was as low as 38 per 1,000 births, compared with 225 in 1860–1879 and 185 in 1880–1892.

Table 9.1. Sundsvall region: Number of illegitimate births, 1810–1895 (per 1,000 births)

	Alnö[a]	Attmar	Galtström[a]	Hässjö	Indal	Lagfors[a]	Ljustorp	Lögdö[a]
1810–1819	16.4	28.0	190.5	69.8			7.6	41.7
1820–1829	32.5	38.8	89.3	56.2			10.8	
1830–1839	53.9	17.6	16.4	20.3	166.7		14.9	42.6
1840–1849	60.3	37.6	26.7	62.3	93.1		46.4	18.2
1850–1859	45.2	56.1	65.0	65.7	75.6		37.1	25.6
1860–1869	66.2	85.1	71.4	90.6	38.4	47.6	39.6	44.1
1870–1879	114.3	110.2	182.9	99.1	88.3	120.7	90.7	55.6
1880–1889	67.7	88.4	31.2	82.4	78.0	122.0	65.6	
1890–	43.0	68.8	41.1	100.3	103.6	100.0	44.1	90.1

	Njurunda[a]	Sättna	Selånger	Skön[a]	Svartvik[a]	Timrå[a]	Tuna[a]	Tynderö
1810–1819		64.2	59.8	81.6		69.6	68.8	49.4
1820–1829	57.1	49.2	63.4	65.9		56.3	35.1	35.0
1830–1839	33.7	41.0	19.0	79.4		62.9	48.6	54.8
1840–1849	69.2	77.4	57.9	78.6		57.4	61.1	79.1
1850–1859	71.9	74.5	72.2	82.5		45.3	81.1	39.8
1860–1869	53.0	49.3	78.9	114.7	53.0	69.7	73.5	108
1870–1879	102.7	97.4	96.1	108.8	71.4	74.9	107.8	78.6
1880–1889	62.1	72.5	73.6	88.7	34.5	59.4	92.1	77.2
1890–	48.8	61.7	30.0	74.4	23.8	44.4	77.0	99.5

[a] Industrialized after 1850.

Source: The Demographic Data Base, Umeå University.

Table 9.2. Sundsvall region: Descriptive statistics for the number of illegitimate children per woman, 1800–1896

	Sundsvall (N=927)			Industrial (N=3,984)			Agricultural (N=4,308)		
	1800–1859	1860–1879	1880–1896	1800–1859	1860–1879	1880–1896	1800–1859	1860–1879	1880–1896
Mean	—	2.53	2.24	1.59	1.90	1.63	1.51	1.75	1.75
Median	—	2.00	2.00	1.0	1.0	1.0	1.0	1.0	1.0
5% trim	—	2.35	2.10	1.44	1.67	1.46	1.37	1.52	1.49
Variance	—	3.10	2.23	1.11	2.61	1.41	1.14	2.21	2.37
Standard deviation	—	1.76	1.49	1.05	1.61	1.19	1.07	1.49	1.54
Minimum	—	1	1	1	1	1	1	1	1
Maximum	—	5	8	10	10	10	9	10	10

Note: The numbers do not sum to 9,282 because we lack information on locality in 63 cases.

Source: The Demographic Data Base, Umeå University.

of illegitimate births per woman in the town, but the number decreased slightly in the last period. Again, the town is different from the rest of the parishes in the region. It is primarily in the urban area that we find women who gave birth to several illegitimate children.

The agrarian parishes recorded much smaller numbers of illegitimate children in comparison with the town, but they hardly differed from the industrialized parishes. Neither the industrialized nor the agricultural parishes seem to have been much affected by the expansion of the sawmill industry, and we can hardly speak of growing subcultures as proletarianization sets in. Our conclusion must be that there are few indications of a subculture in the Sundsvall region; otherwise we would expect the effect of industrialization to have been an increase in the number of illegitimate children per woman.

CHANCES OF SURVIVAL FOR THE CHILDREN

As frequently mentioned in this chapter, infant mortality is comparatively high among illegitimate children. This pattern is found, for instance, in the town of Sundsvall, where it ranged from 217 per 1,000 live births in 1860–1879 to 216 in 1880–1892. The increase in their risk of dying was 70–80 per cent over legitimate children (Edvinsson 1993, 172). Clearly, lone parenthood meant that children could not be looked after properly, or were deliberately neglected. However, we are really comparing mothers in two different kinds of situation. Will we get the same picture if we compare chances of survival within the same families, that is, between children born before and after marriage?

In Figure 9.2 the survival function, or the cumulative number of deaths, is plotted for the three main geographical areas in the Sundsvall region. There are clear differences between the chances of survival for illegitimate and legitimate children, even when we restrict the analysis to women who at some time in their lives had given birth to illegitimate children. Mortality was highest in the town of Sundsvall, where only 25 per cent of illegitimate children remained alive after 5 years. The first months after birth were the most dangerous, but we find surprisingly little difference depending on legitimacy. Only during the second to the fifth month do we find a slight increase in the death risk for illegitimate children. The curves for the industrialized parishes look quite different. The overall mortality is lower, and approximately 40 per cent were still alive after 5 years. The two curves show large differences between illegitimate and legitimate children. The differences have already appeared during the first month after birth, and they have reached their maximum by 18 months. The level of mortality in the agrarian parishes shows a similar pattern. Some 40 per cent or more are still alive after 5 years. Differences in the survival function have already appeared after the first days of life and have reached their maximum before the children are 1 year old. However, the gap between the two curves is much larger than for the industrialized parishes, and it opens up more quickly.

Clearly, the chances of survival for the children of lone mothers depended on legitimacy. It was also very important *where* the children were born. In the town, the

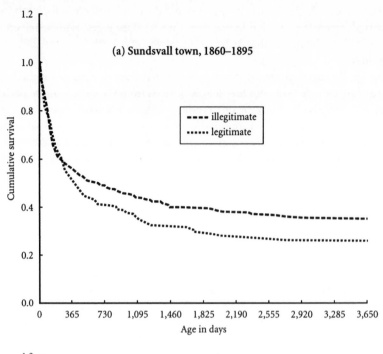

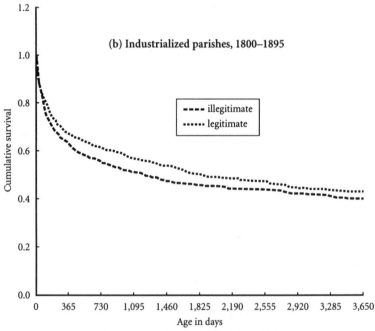

Fig. 9.2. Sundsvall region: Survival functions

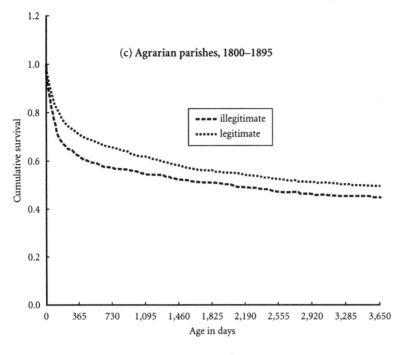

Fig. 9.2. (*cont.*)

negative effects of location are noticeable regardless of whether the children were legit-imate or illegitimate, and the effects lasted for a longer period. In the industrialized and agrarian parishes, the negative effects of location were less severe and almost entirely concentrated in the first year after birth. If children survived this period, their chances of survival did not vary according to whether or not they were born legitimate.

The question is to what extent these results depend on social circumstances, such as social class, and to what extent they depend on more 'biological' factors, such as the age of the mother and the parity of the birth. From Table 9.3 we learn, as expected, that most illegitimate children in these families were born as the first or the second child. From Table 9.4, we can also see that their mothers tended to be young, with an average age at first birth of *c*.23 years for all women in the cohort.

To some extent the differences among the three types of parish could be explained by what we have learned from the previous figures and tables. Each mother in the town tended, generally, to give birth to *more* illegitimate children than women who lived in industrialized or agrarian parishes. They seem to a much higher degree to have been locked into a behaviour, or a social situation, that continued even after they married. Urban mothers were also less fortunate in finding marriage partners—only 63.3 per cent of them managed to find a husband, compared with 80 per cent in the industri-alized parishes and 72.8 per cent in the agrarian parishes. The evidence points to a

Table 9.3. Sundsvall region: Parity among legitimate and illegitimate children, by locality, 1800–1895 (%)

Parity	Illegitimate			Legitimate		
	Sundsvall	Industrialized	Agrarian	Sundsvall	Industrialized	Agrarian
1	51.0	65.5	66.9	0.6	0.5	0.6
2	23.0	18.4	17.4	18.1	19.3	21.4
3	12.3	7.2	6.4	20.1	20.1	20.9
4	5.7	3.9	4.0	16.0	16.8	16.8
5	3.1	2.0	2.1	12.9	13.5	13.0
6	1.7	1.1	1.3	12.6	10.1	9.2
7	1.5	0.8	1.0	7.4	7.4	6.6
8	0.6	0.5	0.6	6.0	5.2	4.9
9	0.6	0.3	0.2	3.2	2.9	3.2
10 or more	0.6	0.3	0.1	3.2	4.2	3.4
Total number of children	522	1,604	1,783	349	2,307	2,237

Note: In 480 of our 9,282 cases we lack the necessary information on either siblings or locality.
Source: The Demographic Data Base, Umeå University.

Table 9.4. Sundsvall region: Age of mother at
birth of first illegitimate child, by locality, 1800–1895 (%)

Age	Sundsvall	Industrialized	Agrarian
15–19	4.5	4.0	3.2
20–29	62.0	55.1	51.1
30–39	29.1	34.2	38.0
40 and over	4.5	6.7	7.8

Source: The Demographic Data Base, Umeå University.

situation where we find in the town the more 'extreme' families with multiple illegitimate births by relatively young mothers and shorter birth intervals. Their social situation
probably did not change that much after they married, or they were weakened by
poverty and many deliveries. In the agrarian and industrialized parishes children were
born under 'safer' biological circumstances. The fact that most children died while very
young in these parts of the region also left the stronger children alive to face the hazards
of later life. However, this is mere speculation. We need more information before we
can reach solid conclusions.

LOGISTIC REGRESSION ANALYSIS

One way of controlling for age and parity is to analyse our cohort with logistic regression: each child will be followed until it dies as an infant or is truncated for other reasons,
or while it continues to live. A number of explanatory variables are included in the
model, each of which may—directly or indirectly—have affected the child's chances of
survival.

The full model tested in this chapter consist of the *age* of the mother at the time of
the child's birth, the *parity* of the child, the *social class* of the mother, the *locality* in the
region, the *sex* of the child, *legitimacy*, mean *birth intervals* and a *time* effect. Also included in the model are tests for effects of the interactions between legitimacy and
parity, legitimacy and age, and parity and age. The explanatory variables, or covariates,
are removed from the model one by one, by testing the probability of the likelihood-
ratio statistics based on the maximum-likelihood estimates (Table 9.5).[4]

Six covariates remain in the model when it has been reduced: legitimacy, locality,
social class, mother's age, mean birth intervals and the time effect. The risk of dying as
an infant increased by 32 per cent for the illegitimate children when we control for the
other variables. There was an increased death risk of approximately 39 per cent when

---

[4] An excellent and detailed description of this technique can be found in the documentation for SPSS,
Advanced Statistics (Release 6.0).

Table 9.5. Sundsvall region: Logistic regression analysis of complete reproductive histories

(a) Variables in the equation

Variable (Reference category)	B	S.E	Wald.	df	Significance	R	exp(B)
Legitimacy	0.2806	0.0798	12.3512	1	0.0004	0.0447	1.3239
Location (Agrarian)			22.1204	2	0.0000	0.0591	
Sundsvall	0.3290	0.0701	22.0387	1	0.0000	0.0621	1.3896
Industrialized	-0.1507	0.0519	8.4359	1	0.0037	-0.0352	0.8601
Social class (Lower)			6.7699	2	0.0339	0.0231	
Upper	0.1275	0.0496	6.6098	1	0.0101	0.0298	1.1360
Middle	-0.0959	0.0604	2.5148	1	0.1128	-0.0100	0.9086
Mother's age (40 and over)			9.5844	3	0.0225	0.0263	
15–19	0.2909	0.1262	5.3138	1	0.0212	0.0253	1.3376
20–29	-0.1457	0.0653	4.9819	1	0.0256	-0.2040	0.8644
30–39	-0.1813	0.0732	6.1361	1	0.0132	-0.0282	0.8342
Period (1850–1895)	0.1592	0.0553	8.2969	1	0.0040	0.0348	1.1726
Mean birth interval	-0.2426	0.6580	13.6094	1	0.0002	-0.0473	0.7846
Constant	-1.2229	0.2083	34.4514	1	0.0000		

(b) Model if term removed

Term removed	Log-likelihood	-2 log LR	df	Significance of log LR
Legitimacy	-2558.712	12.312	1	0.0005
Locality	-2562.989	20.866	2	0.0000
Social class	-2555.966	6.821	2	0.0330
Mother's age	-2555.114	9.116	3	0.0278
Period	-2556.524	7.938	1	0.0048
Mean birth interval (Longest)	-2559.609	14.106	1	0.0002

Note: Event = infant death. Reduced model after backwards stepwise selection based on the probability of the likelihood-ratio statistic based on the maximum-likelihood estimates.

Source: The Demographic Data Base, Umeå University.

the birth took place in the town of Sundsvall, and a decrease of 14 per cent when the child was born in an industrialized parish in comparison with the rural parishes.

As expected, the age of the mother at the time of the birth was also important. Children born to very young mothers had the largest risks of dying: here it increased by 34 per cent in comparison with the oldest mothers. The age groups between these two extremes were in the most favourable situation. Mothers aged 20–29 had a decreased death risk among their children of 14 per cent, and those aged 30–39 a decrease of 17 per cent. Period was important. Risks of dying decreased during the century by approximately 17 per cent. Children from families with longer mean birth intervals had better chances of survival. An increase in mean birth intervals of one year increased the chances of survival for the infants by approximately 22 per cent.

The class of the mother was also important. The lowest social stratum (unskilled workers, agricultural labourers, and so on) is compared to the upper classes (factory owners, higher officials, farmers, and so on) and the middle classes (white-collar workers, farmers, skilled workers, crofters, and so on). The result is unexpected: it turns out that children born to mothers from the upper social stratum in the Sundsvall region had higher risks of dying very early than children from the lowest social stratum. Death risks increased by approximately 14 per cent. The middle social stratum was more fortunate: these children had a death risk approximately 10 per cent lower than the lowest social stratum.[5]

At a first glance, this might surprise us. Normally, we would expect mothers from the lower social classes to have been in the least favourable situation. They came from rather poor backgrounds. They probably had to work quite hard to earn their living. The birth of an illegitimate child ought to have worsened their situation considerably. However, it was mothers from the higher ranks in society whose children had the highest death risks. Again, we return to Peter Laslett's theory of subcultures within the lower classes. The logistic regression analysis of these reproductive histories seems, at least partially, to support his theory. Could there be higher degree of acceptance towards illegitimate children in the working class? To give birth to an illegitimate child was, most likely, a great burden, but the lone mothers of the working class could handle the situation. Finding jobs in Sundsvall might have been easier for them, so that they could support themselves without the direct aid of family and kin.

In this sense, women from the upper classes experienced a worse situation. Their lone parenthood might have been less accepted in their circles of society. To a much larger degree they had to seek employment without their normal social network. Also, they lacked experience of manual labour, which restricted their chances of finding positions where they could support themselves *and* an illegitimate child. With much more to lose, it would be a lot more tempting for them to neglect or abandon an unwanted

---

[5] The same explanatory variables were also entered into a Cox-regression model. The logistic regression tells us about the risk of dying *if* an event is going to happen. The Cox-regression considers the time and analyses *when* an event is likely to happen, that is, whether an infant will die very young or at a later stage. Once again, however, the model produced the same four explanatory variables as the most important. The two results point to the importance of infant mortality for total life expectancy.

child. It is a challenging line of reasoning that merits further study. We need to invest-igate the exact work that these women were involved in and also their closeness to family and other social networks. When they finally married, did they also experience a higher degree of downward social mobility than the other social groups in the Sundsvall region?

CONCLUDING REMARKS

The basic idea behind this tentative study has been to look at legitimacy as a life-cycle phenomenon. Women who gave birth to illegitimate children at some point in time have been followed from the birth of their first child to that of their last child. The study has focused primarily on comparing risks of dying for children born illegitimate with those for later, legitimate children. It has raised more questions than it has answered. Clearly, our knowledge about the living conditions of lone parents and how these conditions affected the lives of their children are limited. The analyses could provide only partial support for Peter Laslett's theory of subcultures within certain layers of the population. Industrialization only temporarily affected the illegitimacy ratio, but the effect was obvious even in agrarian parishes. The number of illegitimate children per woman remained relatively stable over time, except in the town of Sundsvall. It was more common in the urban environment to give birth to several illegitimate children. Mortality was also higher among these infants, but the negative effects of locality struck both legitimate and illegitimate children equally. Even though illegitimate births were more common in the town, there was no clear trend over time to suggest the existence of subcultures.

In the industrialized and agrarian parishes differences in chances of survival were found only during the first year after birth. Besides having fewer illegitimate children in their reproductive histories, women in these areas also managed to find husbands more frequently than urban women. Between 70 and 80 per cent of them married, while the corresponding figure for the town was 63 per cent. Most illegitimate births were experienced by very young women and it was usually their first conception. However, the logistic regression showed that the risk of an infant death was not directly related to parity. Only the age of the mother, and to some extent mean birth intervals, were im-portant among the 'biological' factors. Instead, the decisive factors in infant mortality were mainly 'social': legitimacy, the ecological environment in which the child was born and the social class of the mother. Interestingly, it was children born to women from the upper ranks in society who experienced the highest death risks.

Several aspects need to be studied closer. First, the cohorts need to be extended by adding a cohort of women with the same social background, living in the same parishes, and giving birth to approximately the same number of children, but who have not experienced illegitimate births. We need to look more closely at why children in the town were only affected by (il)legitimacy between the ages of 1 and 5 months, and why this effect was so very modest. Could it simply be explained by the facts that their mothers were relatively young, had shorter birth intervals and experienced relatively more illegitimate births each? There were most likely also social factors involved. The working conditions and the social networks of these women need to be investigated. We have seen that the location where the child was born was very important to its survival. We also know that these women were highly mobile. To what extent did changes in location affect their social situation—their marriage opportunities, for instance. What effect did such changes have on their children's chances of survival? True life histories of lone parents must be the future basis for such an analysis.

References

ANDERSSON, K., 1993. *Ogifta mödrar i Östersund under 1800-talet*, unpublished essay, Department of History, Umeå University.

ARRIGONI, F. and HIMES, J. R., 1993. 'Preface', in CORSINI and VIAZZO 1993a.

BRÄNDSTRÖM, A., 1984. '"De kärlekslösa mödrarna": Spädbarnsdödligheten i Sverige under 1800-talet', dissertation with an English summary, Umeå University.

—— SUNDIN, J. and TEDEBRAND, L.-G., 1994. 'Two cities: urban migration and settlement in 19th Century Sweden', paper presented at the World Economic History Association conference, Milan, 11–16 September.

CORSINI, C. A. and VIAZZO, P. P. (eds.), 1993a, *The decline of infant mortality in Europe, 1800--1950: four national case studies*, Florence, UNICEF and Instituto degli Innocenti.

—— —— 1993b, 'The historical decline of infant mortality: an overview', introduction in CORSINI and VIAZZO 1993a.

EDVINSSON, S., 1993. 'Urban health and social class', in A. BRÄNDSTRÖM and L.-G. TEDEBRAND (eds.), *Health and social change: disease, health and public care in the Sundsvall district 1750–1950*, Umeå University, The Demographic Data Base.

FRYKMAN, J., 1975. 'Sexual intercourse and social norms', *Ethnologia Scandinavica* 20, pp. 1–41.

—— 1977. *Horan i bondesamhället*, Lund, Liber.

GREENHOUSE, J. B., and LYNCH, K. A., 1994. 'Risk factors for infant mortality in nineteenth-century Sweden', *Population Studies* 48(1), pp. 117–133.

LASLETT, P., 1980. 'The Bastardy prone sub-society', in P. LASLETT, K. OOSTERVEEN and R. M. SMITH (eds.), *Bastardy and its comparative history*, London, Edward Arnold.

LÖFGREN, O., 1969. 'Från nattfrieri till tonårskultur', *Fataburen*.

MITTERAUER, M., 1983. *Ledige Mütter: zur Geschichte unehelicher Geburten in Europa*, Munich, C.H. Beck.

REHER, D. and SCHOFIELD, R., 1991. 'The decline of mortality in Europe', in R. SCHOFIELD, D. REHER and A. BIDEAU (eds.), *The decline of mortality in Europe*, Oxford, Clarendon Press.

SHORTER, E., 1973. 'Female emancipation, birth control and fertility', *American Historical Review* 3, pp. 605–640.

TILLY, L., SCOTT, J. and COHEN, M., 1976. 'Women's work and European fertility patterns', *Journal of Interdisciplinary History* 3, pp. 447–476.

10

Mortality among Illegitimate Children in Mid-Nineteenth-Century The Hague

JAN KOK, FRANS VAN POPPEL AND ELLEN KRUSE

In the nineteenth century, the Netherlands had one of the lowest rates of illegitimate births in Europe (Shorter, Knodel and van de Walle 1971, 377). As was the case in other European countries, the judicial position of unwed mothers was very vulnerable. Traditional Dutch law, which had granted pregnant women rights to force the putative father to support the infant and even to marry the girl, was abolished under French occupation. In its place, the French introduced 'recognition', which was intended to create legal ties between the child and its biological father. Although recognition was voluntary on the part of the father, it improved the legal status of the illegitimate child to a certain extent. The father confirmed his obligation to support the child. In addition, the child could inherit from its father, albeit only a third of what it would have received if it had been legitimate. Recognized children could be legitimated by the subsequent marriage of their parents: at that point they became equal to legitimate children in all respects (Kok 1991, 34–37).

As a result of societal prejudices, and because illegitimate children usually lacked the care of their fathers, poverty and misery were the lot of mother and child. Nineteenth-century observers considered the high infant mortality rate and the high stillbirth ratios in particular to be prominent indications of the weak position of these children (*Rechtstoestand* 1898). Dutch national data for the period 1885–1940, presented in Figure 10.1, show that illegitimate children had a large excess mortality.

Although infant mortality in both groups of children decreased over time, during the whole period illegitimate children continued to experience a mortality rate that, for all but two years, was more than 40 per cent higher than that of legitimate children. Even in the 1930s illegitimate children could experience a death rate that was more than 70 per cent higher than that of legitimate children. In addition, illegitimate children were overrepresented among stillbirths (CBS 1975). Whereas illegitimate children made up

An earlier version of this chapter was presented at the 1994 Social Science History Association, Atlanta, Georgia, 13–16 October 1994. We wish to thank Chris Stijnen for his help in collecting the data for this study and Erik Beekink for his assistance with the various computer programs that we have used. We are also very grateful for the support given to us by the staff of the Municipal Archive of The Hague.

C.A. Corsini and P.P. Viazzo (eds.) The Decline of Infant and Child Mortality, 193-211.
© *1997 UNICEF. Printed in the Netherlands.*

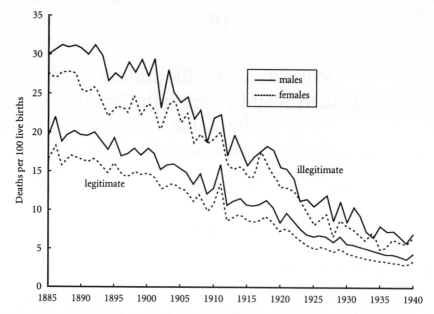

Fig. 10.1. The Netherlands: Infant mortality by legal status at death and sex of the child, 1885–1940

only around 3.2 per cent of all live births in the 1880s and around 3.0 per cent in the 1890s, illegitimate stillbirths made up 5.5 per cent of all stillbirths in these decades.

Studying mortality among illegitimate children is not, however, without problems. First of all, some illegitimate children were legitimated between birth and death by the marriage of their parents. Thus, the numerator and denominator of the illegitimate infant mortality rate did not relate to the same children, and consequently the real mortality rate of this group has been underestimated (Westergaard 1901, 134; Heady and Heasman 1957, 7). An additional problem when studying infant mortality for one particular town or region is that many illegitimate children may have left the city soon after birth, if the mother had gone to the city specifically to give birth to her child in a hospital.

A more fundamental criticism of the use of infant mortality rates by legal status of the child was raised by the Dutch lawyer Bommezijn and by the statistician Westergaard (1901, 347–350). In the opinion of Bommezijn (1899, 138–139), the mortality rate of illegitimate children would always be higher than that of legitimate children: 'When one could compare the mortality rates of legitimate children of prosperous and of poor parents, one would also find a large differential. And it is a fact that by far the largest portion of the mothers of natural children come from the poor and destitute.'

But the excess mortality of illegitimate children may not only be a consequence of the proletarian background of many of these mothers; the relatively low age and inexperience of the mothers may also have played a part. Nineteenth-century Dutch statistical data do not offer the scope to reach definite conclusions on this point. Available data refer only to the legal status of the infants who died, not to other factors that might have played a role.

To find out to what extent illegitimately born children were exposed to higher health risks than children born during marriage, and to ascertain to which factors this excess mortality might be attributed, use has to be made of other data sources and more refined methods of analysis. For this purpose, we studied infant and childhood mortality of children born in the 1850s in the Dutch city of The Hague, making use of the population register and the vital registration system. We followed a cohort of children over time on a day-by-day basis, noting as far as possible all the relevant socio-economic and demographic characteristics of the environment in which legitimate and illegitimate subjects were born and grew up. To investigate the relative impact of these intervening variables on infant and child mortality, a multivariate method of analysis was used.

Using these data sources has the further advantages that one can take into account the fact that (il)legitimate children pass out of the field of observation not only by death but also by migration, and that they can lose their status of illegitimate child by legitimation. If information is available on the number of live-born children who survived at given ages, and on the number who had migrated at each age, life-table procedures can be applied to these data. This makes it possible to study mortality in an unbiased way. A last advantage of the data sources we used is that children might be followed beyond their first year of life. In this way it is possible to ascertain whether legal status at birth had a longer-term effect on the child.

In collecting information on factors responsible for the excess mortality among illegitimate children, we have drawn our inspiration from the framework developed by Mosley and Chen (1984). Mosley and Chen identified five groups of factors (called proximate determinants or intermediate variables) that could directly influence the risk of morbidity and mortality of children: *maternal factors, environmental contamination, nutrient deficiency, injuries* and *personal illness control*. It is through these factors that all social and economic determinants that affect child survival must operate. The problem is that even the sources that we used provide very little information on these intervening variables, apart from the age of the mother. What we can do is to indicate that the (unobserved) intermediate variables are clustered in certain groups, defined for example by the socio-economic group to which the child belonged, the urban background of the mother, the household situation and, last but not least, the legal status of the child. This social clustering of the intervening biomedical variables may provide important clues as to their nature (United Nations 1985, 2).

During the 1850s, The Hague was the political and administrative centre of the Netherlands. In 1850, the city had around 72,200 inhabitants, a number that had increased to 90,300 by 1870. The presence of the Royal Court, of Members of Parliament, foreign diplomats, government bodies, leading civil servants, higher military, and courts of law attracted domestic servants and artisans. In 1850, around 42 per cent of the labour force were employed in the service sector, of which domestic service (22 per cent) and public service (11 per cent) were the most important components. Between 4 and 5 per cent of the total labour force worked in the primary sector; within this sector, the fishing industry, located in Scheveningen, was by far the most important part, and horticulture ranked second. In 1850, 34 per cent of the labour force were employed in industry. The construction sector, clothing and shoe industries were the pillars of industrial activity. A relatively high proportion of the labour force worked in trade and transport (Stokvis 1987). The Hague was characterized by a relatively high frequency of illegitimacy as well as by a very high infant mortality rate. The illegitimacy ratio (the number of illegitimate births per 100 live births) in The Hague around 1850 was 11.2. That level was a little higher than that in Amsterdam and Rotterdam and much higher than in the rural areas of the western Netherlands (Van Poppel 1984). In the period 1850–1859, infant mortality in The Hague was 231 per 1,000 live-born children (compared with 204 in the country as a whole), and it increased during the period 1860–1874. The mortality pattern of the city was severely affected by its location in the delta area; large parts of the surface and groundwater were brackish or severely contaminated. The canals were also used for the discharge of waste and the sewer system was directly connected to them. The better-off could use rainwater or buy surface water of better quality, but the masses used water from the canals for household purposes without treatment or precaution (Vogelzang 1956, 73–74).

DATA-COLLECTION STRATEGY

Two main sources were used in our study: the vital registration system and the population registers. As far as the first is concerned, suffice it to say that on the birth certificate the names and marital status of the parents had to be registered in such a way that the legal status of the child was clear. If the child was illegitimate, then the information concerning the father (including his age) was only notified if he had recognized the child. Later changes in the child's legal status—for example, when a (recognized) child was legitimated because its parents married—had to be recorded in the margin of the birth certificate. Whenever the birth of a child who had died before a birth certificate was made out or who was stillborn was reported, the Registrar was not allowed to make out a birth (or, for that matter, a death) certificate. Nevertheless, a specific certificate for a child who had died before registration was made out and entered in the death register. This certificate did not state if the child had been born alive.

The starting-point for the continuous keeping of population registers in the Netherlands was the census of 1849, the returns of which were copied into the population register. In this register, each household was entered on a double page, with the head of the household first; the head's name was followed by that of his wife (if the head was a married male), children, relatives and other members of the household. Date and place of birth, relation to the head of the household, sex, marital status, occupation and religion were recorded for each individual. All changes occurring in the household in the next decade were recorded in the register. New household members who arrived after the registration had started were added to the list of individuals already recorded, and those no longer resident—as a result of death or migration—were deleted, with a reference to place and date of migration or date of death. Thus, families and individuals can, in principle, be followed on a day-by-day basis for a long period. In most municipalities, registers cover a time span of 10 years between censuses.

To create a data set of illegitimate children we selected all birth certificates from the 891 illegitimate children born in 1850–1852 in The Hague. This means that our database does not contain children who were stillborn or who died before notification. To compare the life histories of our illegitimate children with those of children born within a marriage, we used data from an existing database, the Historical Sample of the Population of the Netherlands (HSN) (Mandemakers 1993). The HSN is a huge historical database built by a group of Dutch researchers from a number of disciplines. The main objective of the HSN is the construction of a random sample of 0.5 per cent of all men and women born in the Netherlands between 1812 and 1922 and subsequently the collection of data concerning their life-course. From this database, we took the data on legitimate children born in The Hague in the period 1853–1879—a sample of 382 individuals.

In the second stage of our data-collection, the population register of The Hague for 1850–1861 was used to acquire information on social and demographic characteristics of the children and their parents. Information was recorded on the type and size of the household in which the children were born, on occupation, religion, date and place of birth of the parents, and on date of death or migration of the children. To collect information on children and mothers who could not be traced directly, the register of the municipal administration for poor relief, the census returns of 1850 and the population register for the period 1861–1879 were consulted. In addition, the death certificates up to 1862 were checked to find out whether children had died in their first 10 years of life without their deaths being mentioned in the population register.

During the collection of these data, several problems had to be solved, the most important of which was the identification of the household in which the child was born. The earliest registers did not give information on the relationships between the members of the household and the head of the household. Moreover, although all households were entered on a separate page when the register started, as time went on this rule was no longer applied. As a consequence, it is difficult to identify which members belong to which household at a particular moment in time. Furthermore, the date of registration was not mentioned for each individual household, so it was often impossible to determine whether a household has been included in the register since 1850 or had been registered later. An additional problem was that many movements from one house to another within the city were not dated.

Owing to these problems, it is hardly possible to be certain about the composition of the household in which a child was born and raised during the first years of life.

ILLEGITIMATE CHILDREN AND THEIR MOTHERS IN THE HAGUE

In several respects, the circumstances in which illegitimate children were born and raised clearly differed from those of legitimate children. The first point to be noted is that there were remarkable and statistically significant differences between illegitimate and legitimate children in terms of the time that elapsed between their births and the notification of their births. Notification occurred on the day of birth or on the day following birth for 42 per cent of illegitimate children, compared with 51 per cent of legitimate births. More than 14 per cent of illegitimate births were notified three or more days after the date of birth; for legitimate births, this was true in only 9 per cent of cases. This difference in the time between birth and notification may be one of the reasons why we found a higher proportion of illegitimate children notified as stillborn.

The second point is that the mothers of illegitimate children tended to be much younger than those of legitimate children, a difference that may have had an effect on the mortality risks of the children. Mothers who bore an illegitimate child were on average 27.9 years old when they gave birth, whereas mothers who were married were on average 32.3 years old. More than 25 per cent of all illegitimate children were born to mothers who had not yet reached 25; this figure was less than 9 per cent for legitimate children. On the other hand, only 13 per cent of all illegitimate children and almost 40 per cent of legitimate children were born to mothers aged 35 and over.

Many illegitimate children acquired legitimate status later in life: 38 per cent were legitimated by a later marriage between the mother and 'father' (that is, a man who, prior to the wedding, had recognized his paternity of the child). Almost 15 per cent of the children were legitimated within three months of their births.

As we mentioned above, the household situation of the newborn babies could not be determined with certainty from the register for 1850–1861. In almost 40 per cent of the cases, information on this subject was completely lacking. Nevertheless, from what we can determine, among illegitimate children four household situations seem to have dominated. Slightly more than 20 per cent of the illegitimate children were born into a household that consisted only of the mother. Almost 15 per cent were born while their father and mother made up a household together, and another 10 per cent lived in a household consisting of the mother and a male household head who was probably not the father of the child. Finally, almost 10 per cent were born into a household that consisted of the mother and one or both grandparents; and in another 2 per cent of the cases the father was also a member of such an household. The predominant household category for legitimate children was, of course, the conjugal unit: almost 87 per cent of the legitimate children were raised in a household unit consisting of the child and both parents.

When comparing mortality risks of illegitimate and legitimate children, the socio-economic position of the mother and child is extremely important. For legitimate children, the information on the occupation of the father, given in the birth certificate or the population register, could be used to classify children according to the socio-economic group to which they belonged. As far as illegitimate children are concerned, the situation is less clear. Almost 14 per cent were notified by a man who later in life legitimated them. Many illegitimate children were notified by their grandmother or grandfather, and in this case, too, the occupation of the notifier gives a reasonable indication of the socio-economic status of the family to which the child belonged. In many cases, where information on occupation of the father was completely lacking, the notifier was not related to the mother but was a member of the medical profession (midwife, surgeon, obstetric doctor or head of a lying-in hospital or other institution) who had assisted in the delivery of the child. All these cases were coded separately under the heading 'Medical notifier'. We may assume that when someone belonging to this professional group had to notify the birth of a child, the health risks for the child were in general higher. For example, male obstetricians were called in only to attend at pathological and protracted deliveries, and institutional deliveries were regarded by Dutch women as the last resort (Van Lieburg and Marland 1989, 313). Moreover, notification by a professional birth attendant implied that the unwed mother had no relative or friend available to perform this task, and thus indicated that she could not fall back on other people for social support.

LIFE-TABLES FOR ILLEGITIMATE AND LEGITIMATE CHILDREN

The available information on the life histories of the children is characterized by what is known in statistical literature as 'censoring'. The main cause of censoring in our case is migration of children out of The Hague. In standard calculations of death rates, information on these children is likely to be eliminated from the denominator, which implies that no use is made of the considerable amount of information that lies in the fact that certain children have *not* died in the period between birth and the moment after which they can no longer be located. Life-table procedures make it possible to utilize information from these 'censored' observations.

The information that is used in calculating the life-table is the time between birth and last observation. For those who die, this time is the survival time; for those who migrate, it is the time between birth and departure (date of censoring); and for those who stay alive during the period covered by the population register, it is the time between birth and the closing date of the register. Figures 10.2 and 10.3 give an overview of one of the life-table quantities for the first year of life and for the first 5 years: the number of survivors, for legitimate and illegitimate children separately, for one-month intervals. Three life-tables are given: one for legitimate children, one for all illegitimate children, and one referring only to illegitimate children who were not legitimated. In this last table, illegitimate children were included among the survivors as long as they were not legitimated and legitimations were treated as censoring events. Differences between the sexes were very small and therefore were not included in the figures.

Differences between legitimated and illegitimate children during the first month of

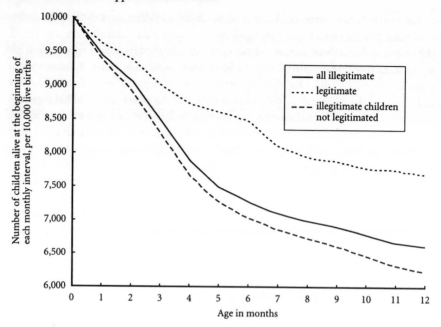

Fig. 10.2. The Hague: Child survival for the first year of life, by legal status, 1850–1879

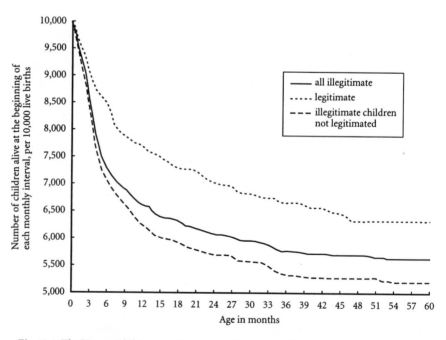

Fig. 10.3. The Hague: Child survival for the first five years of life, by legal status, 1850–1879

life were practically non-existent, but they increased very strongly after the first three months. It is notable that survival is indeed higher among the total group of illegitimately born children than among the group who were never legitimated. After one year, 38 per cent of illegitimate children who were not legitimated had died, whereas among the total group of illegitimate children 34 per cent had died, and among legitimate children only 23 per cent. A number of mothers of (later) legitimated children probably received some kind of support from their future husbands, which enhanced their children's chances of survival. For the first year of life as a whole, statistical tests (the log-rank test for homogeneity χ^2) indicate that differences in mortality between legitimate and illegitimate children are significant ($p < 0.0001$).

During the second year, differences between legitimate children and the total group of illegitimates still went in the same direction as in the first year of life. After the second birthday, however, survival chances among legitimate children were lower than among both groups of illegitimate children. Probabilities of survival between age 1 and age 5 reached 85 per cent among the total group of illegitimate children, almost 84 per cent among children born illegitimately and never legitimated, and 83 per cent among legitimate children. Differences were not statistically significant, but differences in survival between boys and girls did exist: girls had higher death risks than boys. These results correspond with what one would expect, given earlier historical and contemporary studies (Roberts 1976; Westergaard 1901, 391). After the first year of life, a child's vulnerability generally decreased, partly because it was much less dependent on its mother's ability to breastfeed. For that reason alone, one might already expect smaller differences in mortality between illegitimate and legitimate children. In fact, the relationship between mortality and the legal status of the child even reversed. Selection effects may have created such a negative relationship between mortality conditions in the first year of life and mortality in age interval 1–5. If conditions in a cohort were such that more of the genetically 'frail' individuals failed to survive for a full year, then the mortality of that group in age range 1–5 should have been lowered relative to a group in which more of the 'frail' individuals survived. A negative correlation may also have been produced by acquired immunity: children who survived an attack of an infectious disease may have acquired partial or complete immunity to that disease later in life (Elo and Preston 1992). Furthermore, many mothers of legitimate children gave birth to another child after a shorter interval than was usual among the mothers of illegitimate children. As a result of the weaning and neglect of the earlier child, this might have lead to increased mortality risks for legitimate children in the second year of life.

FACTORS INFLUENCING INFANT AND CHILDHOOD MORTALITY: AN OVERVIEW

The main question that we wanted to answer is whether the legal status of the child still had an effect on infant and child mortality when other health-related variables distinguishing illegitimate children from legitimate children (age of mother at birth, socio-economic status, working status, household situation, place of birth of the mother, and religion) were simultaneously taken into account.

One might expect that the legal status of the child as such, aside from all other factors related to unwed motherhood, might seriously affect the mortality risks of a child (Harmsen 1969). In the nineteenth century, the birth of a child outside wedlock was a violation of social mores, the dishonourable consequences of which had repercussions not only for the mother herself but also for the entire family. Shame and social exclusion, loss of job and income, social anxiety and hostility faced the mother. As a consequence, her child was often unwanted. One could imagine, as many contemporaries did (Jonkers 1902, 1905), that strong motives and external circumstances could lead many pregnant unwed women to wish that something would happen to remove the child. It was but a hair's breadth from the conscious wish that something would happen to the thought of doing something to get rid of the unwanted child. When women made unsuccessful attempts to abort the foetus, there could be physiological damage to the child, eventually leading to bleeding toxaemia or prematurity. When the unwanted child could not be 'disposed of' easily, the woman might develop strong hostility towards it, resulting in sometimes unconscious underinvestment in care, feeding and response to illnesses (Scrimshaw 1978).

Many studies have shown that the age of the mother at birth is strongly correlated with perinatal mortality (the number of stillbirths and deaths in the first week of life per 1,000 births). The results of an international comparative study organized by the World Health Organization (1978) in the early 1970s can serve as an example. Mortality was in general lowest among children born to mothers in the age groups 20–24 and 25–29; thereafter it increased to a maximum among the children of women aged 40 and over; it also increased in the youngest age group. One has to realize that the interpretation of the relationship between infant and child mortality and age of the mother at birth is complicated by the fact that age of the mother at birth is closely associated with other known risk factors such as parity, large numbers of children in the family and short birth intervals.

At the level of the household, a variety of goods, services, and assets correlate with child mortality, such as availability of food, quality of water, clothing and bedding, size and quality of housing, supply of fuel for cooking and means to purchase materials needed for hygiene and preventive care. Variations in income and wealth greatly determine the opportunities people have in this area. Recent research explained the higher child mortality in families of single mothers, widows, and divorced mothers by their low socio-economic status compared to married women (United Nations 1985). Data on income were not available in our study; as a substitute, we used information on the socio-economic group to which the child belonged. For this purpose, the occupation of the notifier was used.

In the Netherlands in the nineteenth century, mothers had almost complete responsibility for child care and the time they could spend in food preparation, feeding children, washing clothes, bathing the child, cleaning the house and caring for sick children had a direct influence on child survival. Most mothers of illegitimate children worked away from home during pregnancy and were not able to stop working until very shortly before delivery of the child. They were not allowed or did not dare to ask for breaks and consequently experienced high levels of fatigue and exhaustion. This could play a decisive part in determining the outcome of the pregnancy and the vitality, weight and other characteristics of the infant. After the birth of the child, the mother's time was again required for economically productive activities because there was no husband present to provide support, and so women had to resume work soon after the delivery and could spend less time on maternal activities. Employment away from home could result in neglect or in care by less-skilled older children; infants had to be left alone for long periods of time, succumbing to accidents and illness. Most authors have argued that the absence or the shortening of the period of breastfeeding, in particular, were responsible for the negative effect of the labour-force participation of women on the mortality of their children (Vandenbroeke, van Poppel and van der Woude 1984; Pinnelli 1993; Graham 1994). An important problem in analysing the relationship between working status of the mother and child mortality is that it is not unilateral. Since the death of a child may allow a woman to re-enter the labour market, one may also expect child mortality to have an effect on labour-force participation. This holds especially for unwed mothers because in general when they lose a child they have no other children to care for at home and are free to return to work. The death of a married woman's child, however, may not directly affect her decision to return to work because of other child-care needs within the family. A further problem is that the quality of the historical information in the population register on women's participation in the labour force is usually very poor. We do not know when exactly the mother worked during the child's early days of life. Nevertheless, we used the working status of all women in the analysis (occupation given or not in the population register around the time the child was born).

The effect of the labour-force participation of the mother was partly dependent on the availability of a kinship network (Blom 1991; Tilly and Scott 1978, 36–43). Mothers who could rely on kin were generally much better off, and one might expect that the risks of infant and child mortality would be lower. Members of the family could assume child-care responsibilities and could assist with housekeeping, with care during illness and with shopping. To indicate whether or not a mother could fall back on the support of members of her family, we first of all included the household situation of the mother in our analysis. We distinguished mothers living alone with their child from all other household situations.

Relatives could still, of course, be called upon when they did not live in the same household; however, when immediate or constant care was necessary, distance between the unwed mother and child and the other family members really mattered. The accessibility of the family network was naturally much greater if most of the members lived in the same area than when the mothers were a long distance from home. Native-born women from The Hague thus enjoyed an advantage: they had better access to work and housing and to relatives, neighbours, fellow workers and acquaintances. To indicate the distance between mothers and children and the family network, we used the place of birth of the mother. We differentiated between women born in The Hague and adjacent villages, women born in other municipalities in the province of South Holland and women born outside the province.

Traditions, norms, and attitudes are factors that shape and modify the economic choices and health-related practices of individuals. The most important elements in this category are the value that is attached to children, beliefs about disease causation, and culturally conditioned patterns of dietary intake among mothers and children during pregnancy, lactation, weaning and illness. Nineteenth- and twentieth-century Dutch researchers realized that religion in particular exerted a strong influence on the attitudes of many people towards sickness and on their lifestyle, and was therefore partly responsible for differences in health. Various studies dating from the beginning of the twentieth century showed that Dutch Catholics had a particularly high infant mortality. Factors mentioned in this respect were the low incidence of breastfeeding, the Catholic belief that a child's soul went directly to heaven (which made death something that caused less disturbance) and the greater vulnerability to popular cults, involving distorted sacramental acts, which lead to more interest in extra-medical treatment of illness (Thornton and Olson 1991; Fauve-Chamoux 1981; van Poppel 1992). To take the effect of religion into account, we differentiated the mothers in our sample into three groups: Dutch Reformed, Roman Catholic, and other or unknown religion.

In one part of our analysis, we also included a variable indicating whether the child had been legitimated by the subsequent marriage of the parents, which made children in all legal respects equal to legitimate children. Consensual unions were strongly disapproved of socially and were consistently opposed. Studies of infant health have observed higher infant and child mortality for children of mothers in consensual unions than for those with mothers in legal marriages. Desai (1991; see also Carvajal and Burgess 1978) explained this in terms of differences in the degree of anticipation of marital dissolution: if one expects that consensual unions are less enduring than formal marriages, it seems likely that one or both partners would choose to hold on to their personal income and invest less in the marriage and children than partners in unions based on a greater degree of commitment. When analysing mortality between ages 1 and 5, we therefore included a variable indicating whether or not the child had been legitimated before reaching age 1.

MULTIVARIATE ANALYSIS OF THE MORTALITY OF ILLEGITIMATE CHILDREN

To analyse the mortality history of legitimate and illegitimate children, use was made of an elaboration of life-table methodology increasingly used in the study of life course, namely hazards analysis. This method combines the strengths of life-table and regression analysis. It allows the formulation of equations relating independent variables to the hazard function (the risk of dying), analogous to conventional least-squares regression (Allison, 1985).

The hazard function $h(t;z)$ defines the probability of death at time since birth t, for a child with k independent variables z. The relationship between the hazard function and the independent variables at each duration since birth is written as an equation in which a set of regression-like coefficients, b_x ($x = 1$ to k), indicates the effect of the independent variables in shifting a time-varying, baseline hazard function, $h_0(t)$, associated with a baseline group of births upwards or downwards:

$$h(t;z) = h_0(t) \bullet \exp(b_1 z_1 + ... + b_k z_k)$$

The model is called a proportional hazards model because one assumes that the effect of a variable on the baseline is the same at each time t, so that there are no interactions between covariates and age. There is an underlying hazard function that varies by age but does not depend on the values of the covariates and therefore is the same for all births. The covariates lower or raise the underlying hazard by a multiplicative factor that is constant at all ages. A value of the coefficient $\exp(b)$ of 1.0 means that the variable has no effect; values greater than 1.0 indicate that live-born children with this characteristic are more likely to experience death. Values less than 1.0 have the opposite interpretation.

The assumption of the proportionality of the hazards is in fact contrary to the theory that environmental variables affect mortality more at later ages than at earlier ages. For that reason, the regression equations were estimated separately for two age intervals: the first year of life and the early childhood period, from the twelfth to the sixtieth month.

The results of the multivariate analysis of the effects of characteristics of mother, father and child on mortality are shown in Tables 10.1 and 10.2. The first table deals with the factors differentiating between illegitimate and legitimate children; the second tries to identify factors related to differences in mortality *within* the group of illegitimate children.

The tables give the risk (or hazard) of dying relative to a baseline hazard. A relative risk greater than 1.00 indicates that the mortality rate for the category in question exceeds the mortality rate in the reference category. Children leaving the status of illegitimate child by legitimation were censored.

For the first year of life, Table 10.1 shows that the variable in which we are interested most, the legal status of the child, did indeed have a clear effect on the risk of death; when the child was illegitimate, the risk that he or she would die before reaching age 1 was 30 per cent higher than for children born to married parents.

The factor that was most strongly correlated with infant mortality was the socio-economic group to which the notifier belonged. A clear class divide was visible: the highest socio-economic group had lower death risks than the lower-middle class, and much lower risks than the working class and the petty bourgeoisie. Notifiers without an occupation or with unknown occupations were also associated with high mortality risks. The most remarkable outcome, however, was that when a person belonging to the medical profession notified the birth of the child, mortality risks were more than twice as high as in the highest social class.

The place of birth of the mother also had a very clear effect on infant mortality. In

Table 10.1. The Hague: Proportional hazards coefficients
for infant and childhood mortality, all births, saturated model

Variable	Relative risk	
	Infant mortality	Childhood mortality
Legal status of child		
Legitimate	1.00	1.00
Illegitimate	1.31*	0.85
Sex of child		
Female	1.00	1.00
Male	1.01	0.74
Religion of mother		
Dutch Reformed	1.00	1.00
Roman Catholic	0.83	0.88
Other and unknown	0.88	1.26
Age of mother at birth		
Less than 23	1.37**	0.99
23–34	1.00	1.00
35 and older	1.42**	2.06***
Socio-economic group of notifier		
Upper class and middle class	1.00	1.00
Lower-middle class and skilled manual workers	1.48	6.01*
Petty bourgeoisie	1.71	3.88
Unknown or without occupation	1.83	3.32
Casual and unskilled labourers	1.54	4.64
Notified by medical professional	2.21**	5.64*
Working status of mother		
Working	1.14	0.88
Not working or unknown	1.00	1.00
Place of birth of mother		
The Hague and surroundings	1.00	1.00
Other parts of province	1.31**	1.73**
Elsewhere or unknown	1.64***	1.86**
Model χ^2	69.85***	40.41***
N	1,273	769

*** Significant at 1% level; ** Significant at 5% level; * Significant at 10% level.

those cases in which the woman originated from The Hague or the adjacent municipalities mortality was clearly lower. When she originated from other parts of the province, mortality risks were more than 30 per cent higher. Women originating from outside the province had 64 per cent higher risks.

The age of the mother at birth was also very important for the risk of child mortality. The hazard rate for women who gave birth at ages below 23 was almost 40 per cent higher than for those who gave birth at ages 23–34. Infants of older women had nearly the same excess mortality risk as those born to young women.

Children whose mother had entered the labour force also had higher death risks than children of women who were not employed. Although it is known that these women worked around the time their child was born, it is generally not known whether they were in the labour force at the moment the child died or re-entered only after the death of the child. The direction of the causality is thus not perfectly clear.

The religion of the mother had an effect in an unexpected direction: the lowest risks were found among Catholics. The sex of the child had only a marginal effect on death risks.

For mortality between ages 1 and 5, the same variables were included in our analysis. Table 10.1 shows that illegitimacy now had the opposite, decreasing effect on the risk of death: illegitimate children had a risk of dying between age 1 and 5 that was 15 per cent lower than that for children born to married parents.

The sex of the child had a clear effect on death risks in this age group, and in the expected direction: boys were characterized by lower death rates (Tabutin 1978). The risk of dying between ages 1 and 5 was still strongly dependent on the age of the mother at birth. In particular, children born when the mother was 35 or older had a high excess mortality risk compared with children of younger women.

Again, the socio-economic group to which the notifier belonged had a very strong influence on childhood mortality. All lower and middle social classes had much higher childhood mortality than the upper class. Notification by a medical professional was once more strongly associated with excess mortality.

The place of birth of the mother again had a strong influence on mortality. Women born in other parts of South Holland, but especially women originating from outside the province, had much higher death risks than 'native' women.

Children whose mother had entered the labour force now had lower death risks than children of women who were not employed. The religion of the mother had an effect in an unexpected direction: again the lowest risks were found among Catholics.

Table 10.2 repeats the above procedures, but now only for the group of illegitimate children. The table includes one new variable, the household situation of the mother. Two categories were distinguished: mothers who could be ascertained with more or less complete confidence to be living alone with the child, and all other women, including unknown household situations.

The table generally shows the same tendencies as among the total group of infants. One important difference, however, was that the socio-economic position of the mother had a much stronger influence on the death risks of children than was the case

Table 10.2. The Hague: Proportional hazards coefficients for
infant and childhood mortality, all illegitimate children, saturated model

Variable	Relative risk	
	Infant mortality	Childhood mortality
Sex of child		
Female	1.00	1.00
Male	1.02	0.83
Religion of mother		
Dutch Reformed	1.00	1.00
Roman Catholic	0.87	1.06
Other and unknown	1.10	1.08
Age of mother at birth		
Less than 23	1.09	1.31
23–34	1.00	1.00
35 and older	1.37*	3.44**
Socio-economic group of notifier		
Upper class and middle class	1.00	1.00
Lower-middle class and skilled manual workers	5.36*	1.79
Petty bourgeoisie	5.07	0.88
Unknown or without occupation	6.42*	1.28
Casual and unskilled labourers	4.24	1.95
Notified by medical professional	7.12*	2.23
Working status of mother		
Working	1.14	0.88
Not working or unknown	1.00	1.00
Household situation of mother		
Mother alone	1.00	1.00
Other or unknown	0.88	1.08
Place of birth of mother		
The Hague and surroundings	1.00	1.00
Other parts of province	1.37*	1.38
Elsewhere or unknown	1.64**	1.33
Child legitimated before age 1		
Yes		1.57
No		1.00
Model χ^2	55.93***	32.50***
N	891	534

*** Significant at 1% level; ** Significant at 5% level; * Significant at 10% level.

among illegitimate and legitimate children combined. Furthermore, the household situation of the mother, weakly measured as it may have been, exerted the expected influence on the death rates of illegitimate children: children living alone with their mothers had higher death rates than other children.

In the same table, the analysis is repeated for mortality between ages 1 and 5. Again a new variable is introduced, the actual legal status of the child. Children who were legitimated before age 1 were juxtaposed with those who were not legalized before that age. Surprisingly enough, legitimated children were characterized by higher death risks. Differences between both groups were not statistically significant; nevertheless they were reasonably strong. In the light of our earlier analysis (Table 10.1), in which it was shown that the legal status of the child no longer had an increasing effect on mortality after age 1, this result no longer comes as a surprise.

In comparison with the results of the analysis of mortality among the total group of children, sex of the child had a stronger effect on death risks. The age of the mother at birth now had by far the largest effect: children of women who gave birth at age 35 and over had mortality rates more than three times higher than children of younger mothers.

The socio-economic group to which the notifier belonged now had much less influence on childhood mortality. Notification by a medical professional still had an effect on mortality, but the differences between lower and middle social classes and the upper class were much smaller.

The effect of the place of birth of the mother was still present when only illegitimate children were studied. Once again, children whose mothers had entered the labour force had lower death risks than children of women who were not employed. The religion of the mother now worked in another direction: Catholics no longer had the lowest risks; Dutch Reformed took over this position. The household situation of the mother had a small effect on death risks: children of women living alone at the moment of birth now had lower mortality risks than children living in other household forms.

CONCLUSIONS

Our analysis showed that, in the middle of the nineteenth century, illegitimate children had very little chance of surviving infancy and childhood. When children had reached the age of 1 month, mortality among illegitimate children became very high compared with that among our reference group. Multivariate analysis showed that this excess mortality was caused by a set of factors, the most important being the age of the mother at birth, regional background, and the socio-economic group to which the notifier of the birth belonged. On the other hand, it appeared that, even excluding other factors that differentiated unwed mothers from the 'standard' household consisting of husband and wife, legal status *per se* had an effect on infant mortality. Combining the different factors gives us a picture of the types of unwed mother most likely to lose a child in its first year of life. These women were young or very old, born outside the city, and their child's birth was notified by a professional (midwife or medical doctor), indicating that family or friends were not in the proximity. They lived alone with their child and were obliged to resume work to support themselves and their child. The (lack of) opportunity to breastfeed may have played a key role in this constellation of factors.

It is remarkable that, from their first until their fifth birthday, illegitimate children had lower death risks than legitimate children. Selection effects may have played a role in this, as may the fact that the reference group came from a later period characterized by a somewhat higher mortality. It is highly likely that the effects of being born out of wedlock gradually disappeared during the life course.

References

ALLISON, P. D., 1985. *Event history analysis: regression for longitudinal data*, Beverly Hills, CA, Sage.

BLOM, I., 1991. 'The history of widowhood: a bibliographic overview', *Journal of Family History* 16, pp. 191–210.

BOMMEZIJN, A. B., 1899. *Het onderzoek naar het vaderschap*, Leiden, Eduard Ijdo.

CARVAJAL, M. and BURGESS, P., 1978. 'Socio-economic determinants of fetal and child deaths in Latin America: a comparative study of Bogota, Caracas and Rio de Janeiro', *Social Science and Medicine* 12, pp. 89–98.

CBS, 1975. *Buitenechtelijke geboorte 1840–1973*, 's-Gravenhage, Staatsuitgeverij.

DESAI, S., 1991. 'Children at risk: the role of family structure in Latin America and West Africa', in *Proceedings of the Demographic and Health Surveys World Conference, Washington, D.C. 1991*, vol. 2, Columbia, MD, IRD/Macro International, Inc.

ELO, I. T. and PRESTON, S. H., 1992. 'Effects of early-life conditions on adult mortality: a review', *Population Index* 58, pp. 186–212.

FAUVE-CHAMOUX, A., 1981. 'Les aspects culturels de la mortalité différentielle des enfants dans le passé', in proceedings of the International Population Conference, Manila 1981, vol. 2, Liège, Ordina.

GRAHAM, D., 1994. 'Female employment and infant mortality: some evidence from British towns, 1911, 1931 and 1951', *Continuity and Change* 9, pp. 313–346.

HARMSEN, H. L. F., 1969. 'Social pressure as decisive factor in the high mortality in infants born out of wedlock', unpublished paper presented at the International Population Conference, London.

HEADY, J. A. and HEASMAN, M. A., 1959. *Social and biological factors in infant mortality*, London, HMSO.

JONKERS, E. J., 1902. *Iets over kindervoeding en kindersterfte, meer speciaal in het 1e levensjaar*, Groningen, Wolters.

—— 1905. 'Données statistiques de la mortalité infantile dans les Pays-Bas', in *Proceedings of the International Congress of Hygiene*, Bruxelles.

KOK, J., 1991. *Langs verboden wegen: de achtergronden van buitenechtelijke geboorten in Noord-Holland 1812–1914*, Hilversum, Verloren.

MANDEMAKERS, K., 1993. 'New approach to the study of migration in the Netherlands during the 19th and 20th century: first results of the Historical Sample of the Netherlands', in G. JARITZ, I. H. KROPA and P. TEIBENBACHER (eds.), *The art of communication*, proceedings of the eighth International Conference of the Association for History and Computing, Graz, Austria, 24–27 August, Akademische Druck-U. Verlagsanstalt. Graz.

MOSLEY, W. H. and CHEN, L. C., 1984. 'An analytical framework for the study of child survival in developing countries', in W. H. MOSLEY and L. C. CHEN (eds.), *Child survival: strategies for research*, supplement to vol. 10 of *Population and Development Review*, pp. 25–45.

PINNELLI, A., 1993. 'The condition of women and the health and mortality of infants and children', in N. FEDERICI, K. OPPENHEIM MASON and S. SOGNER (eds.), *Women's position and demographic change*, Oxford, Clarendon Press.

RECHTSTOESTAND VAN ONECHTE KINDEREN: *Vaderschap-Afstamming: Wetsontwerp en memorie van toelichting*, 1898, 's-Gravenhage, Gebr. Belinfante.

ROBERTS, G. W., 1976. *Fertility and mating in four West Indian populations*, Kingston, University of the West Indies.

SCRIMSHAW, S. C. M., 1978. 'Infant mortality and behaviour in the regulation of family size', *Population and Development Review* 4, pp. 383–404.

SHORTER, E., KNODEL, J. and VAN DE WALLE, E., 1971. 'The decline of non-marital fertility in Europe 1880–1940', *Population Studies* 25, pp. 375–395.

STOKVIS, P. R. D., 1987. *De wording van modern Den Haag*, Zwolle, Waanders.

TABUTIN, D., 1978. 'La surmortalité féminine en Europe avant 1940', *Population* 33, pp. 121–148.

THORNTON, P. A. and OLSON, S., 1991. 'Family contexts of fertility and infant survival in nineteenth-century Montreal', *Journal of Family History* 16, pp. 401–418.

TILLY, L. A. and SCOTT, J. W., 1978. *Women, work and the family*, New York, Holt Rinehart and Winston.

UNITED NATIONS, 1985. *Socio-economic differentials in child mortality in developing countries*, New York.

VANDENBROEKE, C., VAN POPPEL, F. and VAN DER WOUDE, A.M., 1984. 'Le développement séculaire de la mortalité aux jeunes âges dans le territoire du Bénélux', *Annales de Démographie Historique*, pp. 257–289.

VAN LIEBURG, M. J. and MARLAND, H., 1989. 'Midwife regulation, education, and practice in the Netherlands during the nineteenth century', *Medical History* 33, pp. 296–317.

VAN POPPEL, F., 1984. *Stad en platteland in demografisch perspectief: de Nederlandse situatie in de periode 1850–1960*, intern rapport 29, Voorburg, NIDI.

—— 1992. 'Religion and health: Catholicism and regional mortality differences in 19th century Netherlands', *Social History of Medicine* 5, pp. 229–253.

VOGELZANG, I., 1956. *De drinkwatervoorziening van Nederland voor de aanleg van de drinkwaterleidingen*, Gouda, Quint.

WESTERGAARD, H., 1901. *Die Lehre von der Mortalität und Morbilität*, Jena, Gustav Fischer.

WORLD HEALTH ORGANIZATION, 1978. *A WHO report on social and biological effects on perinatal mortality*, vol. 1, Budapest, Statistical Publishing House.

11

Childhood Mortality in High-Risk Groups: *Some Methodological Reflections Based on French Experience*

CATHERINE ROLLET

Public services are often provided for particular groups of the population who are known to be vulnerable, fragile, or at 'high risk'. In nineteenth-century France there was concern first about the high mortality among abandoned children, later about the mortality rate of children given out to be wet-nursed, and finally about that of bottle-fed children. The animated debate during the 1860s about the high mortality of nurslings and the most appropriate methods to reduce it was kept going by continued controversy about the mortality of different types of nursling: those whose placement to be fostered by wet-nurses was arranged by a public authority set up by the city of Paris, those whose wet-nurses were selected by their parents, those placed by the public-assistance authorities in Paris, and lastly the natural children of wet-nurses who came to live in towns with the parents of their nurslings (Rollet 1990, 71–97).

The debate was fuelled by the fact that the methods used to calculate mortality rates had not been fully developed. Even the definition of infant mortality (the ratio of deaths of children in their first year of life to the number of births) was not free from problems (Rollet 1990, 27–38). What was to be the denominator of the fraction—births, or the population aged less than 1? Since different methods were used to estimate them, the rates quoted at the time and used for international comparisons could give erroneous results. Although agreement was reached to continue to use numbers of births as the denominator of the mortality rate, some problems remained: should stillbirths be included or excluded from the calculations, or should only some infant deaths be included (those where the child had breathed after delivery)?

Measuring the mortality of specific groups of the population was a complex operation that could be even more liable to error. At the time no generally accepted rules existed, and the inherent difficulties were barely recognized. Some problems about the length of the period of observation remained: should only infant deaths be used in the calculations, as had been the practice in measuring infant mortality, or should deaths that occurred during the first two years of life be included? How should new entrants to observation be treated, given that children entered observation—perhaps by child protection agencies—at different ages (3 days, say, or 3 months)? How should those

C.A. Corsini and P.P. Viazzo (eds.) The Decline of Infant and Child Mortality, 213-225.
© *1997 UNICEF. Printed in the Netherlands.*

who left observation be treated (infants lost from sight or those whose destinations were not known)?

These problems raise tricky methodological questions, the importance of which was not fully appreciated before the end of the nineteenth century, and which became prominent as a consequence of progress in demographic analysis, particularly the dual classification of events by time-period and individuals' ages.

MORTALITY OF CHILDREN IN CARE: A MODEL INQUIRY IN 1889

We begin our analysis by using data from a survey carried out shortly before 1889, which can be regarded as a model for surveys during the period. The Director of Public Assistance in the Ministry of the Interior, Henri Monod, wanted to provide an accurate measure of the mortality of children in care, a category that included foundlings (children abandoned in the streets or other public places), children who had been legally abandoned by their natural parents and poor orphans. Dissatisfied with the statistics available at the time he arranged for the records kept in each *département* to be studied and to follow the lives of children taken into care between 1857 and 1866. The survivors in that group would have attained their majority by 1887 at the latest.

In 1889, he presented the results of this longitudinal study at a session of the Congrès International d'Assistance (Monod 1889, 216–246). He showed that in 12 *départements* the quality of the records was too poor for them to be used because the registers were badly kept or incomplete.[1] In the Seine *département* the records were complete, but unfortunately had been kept in a way that made it impossible to follow the life courses of members of different cohorts, and had, therefore, to be excluded from the study. Finally, for 11 *départements* partial records had to be used (either for specific periods only, or records from particular children's homes).[2] Altogether, complete usable records were available for only 63 *départements*.

The data were ultimately checked by Monod himself. Having examined the death rates for each *département* he decided not to use figures from *départements* in which the mortality of children in care was lower than the rate for France as a whole in his estimates of national rates. He thought that such a situation was improbable, given the origins of the children and their standards of living. Low mortality could be explained in part as the result of incomplete or late registration of deaths. Monod's decision resulted in the elimination of the figures relating to a further seven *départements*[3] where the mortality of children in care was lower than the national average, which Dr Jacques Bertillon had estimated to be 32 per cent.

Monod presented the following summary results: of 75,136 children taken into care

---

[1] Hautes-Alpes, Alpes-Maritimes, Aube, Belfort, Calvados, Creuse, Ille-et-Vilaine, Haute-Loire, Morbihan, Savoie, Haute-Savoie and Vosges.

[2] Aisne, Alpes (Basses-), Ariège, Cantal, Corse, Gers, Isère, Jura, Marne, Tarn-et-Garonne and Vaucluse.

[3] Doubs, Indre, Lot-et-Garonne, Meurthe, Meuse, Haute-Saône and Yonne.

between 1857 and 1866, observed in 1887, 23,720 (31.57 per cent) were discharged or attained their majority (21 years), and 51,416 (68.43 per cent) died before their twenty-first birthday, compared with Bertillon's corresponding figure of 32 per cent for all children.

The difference between the mortality of children taken into care and that of the general population was considerable: mortality in the former group was more than twice the average. Moreover, the estimate is a minimum: children were not taken into care at birth, so that no account is taken of deaths during the first weeks of life, when mortality is high. These results led Monod to study the ages of children at the time they were admitted into care. It proved impossible to trace particulars for all the 75,136 who were admitted into care. He therefore examined the ages of 3,477 children taken into care in 1887. More than half (55.6 per cent) were admitted when they were more than a month old. To adjust the calculated proportion of deaths in care (68.4 per cent), he would have had to take into account the mortality risks of children before they were taken into care. That is, he would have had to obtain a 'correction multiplier'.

This calculation would have had to be carried out for each *département* separately, in order to take account of differences in admission practices, to which the figures bear witness. (Rates in different *départements* ranged from 90.98 per cent in the Loire-Inferieure to 33 per cent in Aveyron and Gers.) Monod admitted that he did not have the information needed for such an adjustment and therefore proposed to use the unadjusted percentages as minimum estimates. The very high excess mortality was, according to him, related to the previous history of the children (congenital deficiencies, difficult labour and poor conditions in very early life) and also to the circumstances in which these children had been reared. Monod stressed the importance of the second group of factors and the urgent need for reform in order to 'make use of the social forces that these children represent, and that is so often lost' (Monod 1889, 246). In the same year Parliament passed a law to control child abuse and thus completed the judicial system for child protection.

Towards the end of the century, Monod carried out a new survey to show that children in care were not as badly treated by the social services as public opinion believed (Monod 1898, 1899). According to him, the child-care system had been much improved, but he could not comment on what had happened to mortality, since different measurement methods had been used in different *départements*: 'I cannot make a general statement on the level of child mortality in our system' (Monod 1899, 653). He thus confined himself to providing a summary of the physical and social environment of children in care who had attained their majority. He considered the situation of 4,135 children who had attained their majority in 1893. From that number he deducted those who had been lost to observation, as well as the mentally ill and handicapped, which left him with a study population of 3,854 young people. According to his calculations the conduct of the vast majority (84.8 per cent) was classed as 'satisfactory', and that of fewer than 4 per cent as 'unsatisfactory'. A few were turned down as unfit for military service, but more were passed fit. They were mainly employed in agriculture and domestic work, but an appreciable number became craftsmen or artisans.

PROBLEMS ASSOCIATED WITH THE
USE OF ANNUAL STATISTICS

In addition to these critical surveys based on a long tradition of registration and follow-up of children in care, a study of the life histories of so-called 'protected' children (those given out to be wet-nursed, but who were supervised by public authorities) shows the difficulties we discussed earlier.

Routine data, such as information about date of death, age and method of feeding were, in principle, supposed to be collected in accordance with the provisions of the law of 1874. However, it took a long time to establish the system of mortality statistics for nurslings required by the new law (Rollet 1990, 425–432).

The early results were quite deceptive. They constituted a third attempt after the first two had failed. The results were based on data for a limited number of *départements* (11) in which registers of births, deaths and child protection at early ages were available. The data related to children born in January 1881 who were followed up until January 1883 (their second birthday and the upper limit of age for public supervision). According to a contemporary observer, the results were 'practically worthless'. In an official report, an inspector merely noted that the average mortality of children in their first two years of life was available in this survey and came to 3 per cent (Bucquet 1887)! Since infant mortality at the time amounted to between 17 and 18 per cent, a figure of 3 per cent for children given out to be wet-nursed is highly improbable and difficult to accept. Moreover, in one *département* in which the prescribed methods were adhered to (Eure-et-Loire), much larger values were found. Of 2,779 infants born in 1881 and placed with wet-nurses, 803, or 29 per cent, died: the proportion was 21 per cent for children who were breastfed, compared with 34 per cent for children who were bottle-fed. Since no reason could be found to explain the difference between the figures in the sample and those in this *département*, one can only conclude that the statistics were incomplete and/or that the prescribed method of calculation had not been strictly followed.

Dr Jacques Bertillon, well known for his work in helping to establish the International List of Causes of Death, agreed to examine the situation and to provide a scientifically correct method that could be used by local government employees. Bertillon was fully aware that an accurate method would only be of interest when it could be applied by the local authorities.

In a paper of 18 pages (Bertillon 1887), Bertillon began by explaining general principles (and problems), followed this by proposing a rapid and 'rigorously exact'[4] application, and finally suggested a method to evaluate mortality during the first year of life. His suggestions took account of the principles established by such statisticians as Lexis (he used Lexis diagrams) and made careful use of life-tables. Construction of life-tables

---

[4] That is, a method that takes account of both entries into and discharges from care (equivalent to immigrants and emigrants).

Table 11.1. France: Infant mortality among wet-nursed
children accepted into care in 1900, by legitimacy (deaths per 1,000)

	Children in care	Entire population
Legitimate children	186	152
Illegitimate children	316	272
All children	222	162

Table 11.2. France: Mortality between 10th and 365th day of life
among wet-nursed children taken into care in 1900 (deaths per 1,000)

	Children in care	Entire population
Legitimate children	179	127
Illegitimate children	301	240
All children	214	132

permits a correct comparison between the mortality of children in care and that of children in the population as a whole.

Bertillon's method was used for the first time at the end of the 1890s. It thus took 10 years for the authorities to apply identical and scientifically correct methods to the study of the mortality of wet-nursed children at a time when no information on the mortality of children in care was available. A major study of the lives of 96,670 children taken into care by the authorities in 1900 revealed that the mortality of wet-nursed children in care was 37 per cent higher than that in the general population (Table 11.1). This excess is even larger (56 per cent) when the study is restricted to mortality between the tenth day and the end of the first year of life (Table 11.2).

Figures that include those children who entered observation during their first few weeks of life fit in well with the results obtained in a comparison of 'daily' mortality in the two populations. The calculations in Table 11.3 relate to 1898.

Before the tenth day of life, the mortality of children in care is lower than that of all children; this is the result of the large number of children admitted into care between the beginning and the end of each age interval. Thus, the comparison is vitiated for the earliest age groups, in which mortality is high. Figure 11.1 clearly shows the very low values of daily death rates of children in care during their first 10 days of life, followed by excess mortality in the same group of children during the remainder of their first year.

The excess mortality of wet-nursed children in care is obvious: on average mortality of children in care is twice as high as that for all French children after the tenth day of life. It would be useful to know whether this excess has been falling over time, possibly as a result of the protection for children in care provided by the law of 1874. Analogous statistics (that is, statistics constructed in accordance with Bertillon's principles)

Table 11.3. France: Mortality of
children in care and of all children, by age group, 1898

Age (days)	Children in care	Entire population
0–4	0.67	3.75
5–9	1.38	1.80
10–14	3.10	1.84
15–29	2.57	1.23
30–90	1.16	0.65
91–180	0.71	0.43
181–364	0.39	0.28

remained available until the Second World War. The results may look surprising. The mortality of children in care, including that of illegitimate children, was declining in parallel with that in the general population (Figure 11.2). The fate of those at risk had, therefore, been improved.

However, the improvement among children in care was not as rapid as that in the population as a whole: in other words, the gap between the mortality of these two

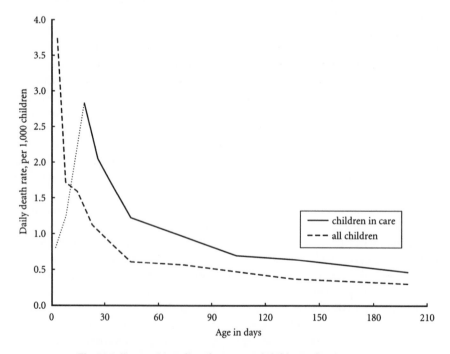

Fig. 11.1. France: Mortality of wet-nursed children taken into care under the provisions of the law of 1874 and of all children, 1897

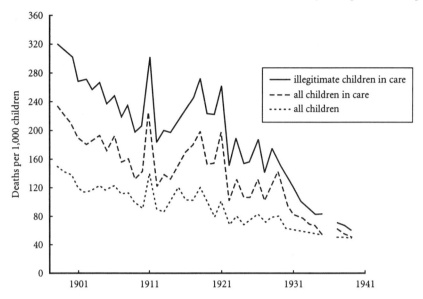

Fig. 11.2. France: Mortality of children in care and of all children, 1898–1939

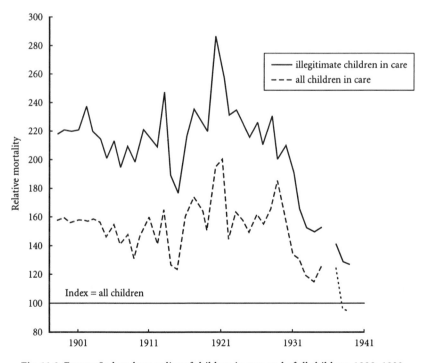

Fig. 11.3. France: Indexed mortality of children in care and of all children, 1898–1939
Note: Index value: all children=100.

groups had been maintained, and even increased. When a comparative index of mortality is calculated, it is apparent that there had been no significant improvement in the situation of children in care relative to that of all children before the end of the 1920s, a time when it became less common for children to be put out to wet-nurses (Figure 11.3).

The excess mortality of wet-nursed children in care remained nearly unchanged during the whole of this period, and reached a peak towards the end of the First World War, when excess mortality was a high as 60 per cent, rising to between 100 and 120 per cent for illegitimate children. Differential mortality between different groups of children persisted until just before the beginning of the Second World War. This shows the complexity of the factors that determine children's welfare and their mortality. A similar situation was apparent among all illegitimate children in the Netherlands. Progress was slow.

ASSESSMENT: THE EXPERIENCE OF DR BUDIN

Use of demographic criteria for the assessment of such welfare measures as we have presented above has a long history. When medical practitioners—paediatricians, obstetricians, and general practitioners—began to participate in the work of infant health consultancy and *gouttes de lait*,[5] which gave priority to those 'at risk' (poor families, town-dwellers, and bottle-fed children), they immediately looked for proof that these protective services were yielding satisfactory results. They were prepared to believe that these services were responsible for a good deal of the decline in infant mortality.

Dr Pierre Budin (1846–1907) was one of the pioneers of this movement (see Rollet 1995). He mentioned three methods to 'prove' the effectiveness of medical advice for infants. As an example, we shall examine the proofs he put forward in the last lecture he gave, in Marseilles in 1907 (Budin 1906–1907). He began by comparing mortality in the population studied with that in a standard population. For premature children admitted to the Tarnier clinic, he compared survival rates of those who were given medical advice and those who were not. Among those who received medical advice, 2 out of 98 died; the figure for those not given advice was 93 out of 859, a mortality rate of 10.8 per cent. The difference in favour of those who had received medical advice was enormous.

For the second method, Budin compared infant mortality before medical advice became available with the situation that followed its adoption, in order to study infant mortality in Paris between 1890 and 1905. He divided this period (rather arbitrarily) into three parts: 1890–1895, when the average proportion of those who died came to 134 per 1,000; 1896–1902, when it was 115 per 1,000; and 1903–1905, when it was 106 per 1,000. On the diagram that he published the arrow indicates the trend and links the two averages of 134 and 106 (Figure 11.4).

---

[5] The *gouttes de lait* were advice centres promoted throughout France to provide mothers with information on effective infant care and to distribute sterilized milk. The first French institutions offering protective services were founded between 1892 and 1894.

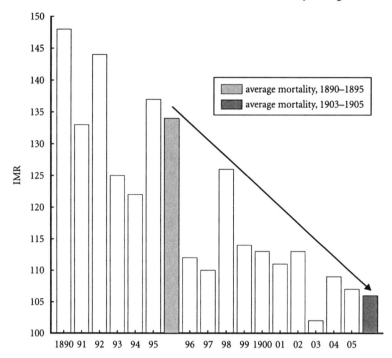

Fig. 11.4. Paris: Infant mortality, 1890–1905

Source: Budin 1907, 261.

Another example is provided by the application of the method to Saint-Pol-sur-Mer, a small town in northern France. The infant mortality rate was high (288 per 1,000) between 1898 and 1903, before services were provided and when infant deaths accounted for half the total number of deaths in the town. A physician from Lille, Dr Ausset, set up a clinic in 1903. In that year mortality was already as low as 209 per 1,000, and in 1904 it fell to 151 per 1,000 (Figure 11.5)

The third method was geographical. It consisted of a comparison of infant mortality in communes in which medical advice was available with that in communes in which such a service was not provided. One example is the town of Auxerre in the Yonne *département*. In 1898 infant mortality was 205 per 1,000; in 1904 (after clinics were provided) it fell to 120, despite the occurrence of heatwaves in that year; and in 1905 it fell further, to 60 per 1,000. Very few of the children who had been examined died (fewer than 30 per 1,000). By contrast, in three neighbouring communes where clinics did not exist, mortality in 1905 varied between 120 and 214; at a minimum it was double that in Auxerre (Figure 11.6).

Many of the methods suggested were imperfect. For instance, Budin analysed the statistics relating to Paris without taking account of the out-migration of infants who had been placed with a wet-nurse; the periods he used in his study were established arbitrarily, and did not recognize the fact that his sample of neighbouring communities

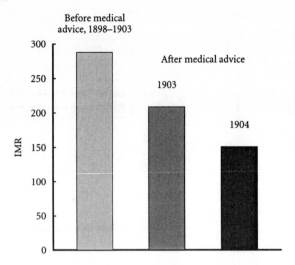

Fig. 11.5. Saint-Pol-sur-Mer: Infant mortality, 1898–1904

Source: Budin 1907, 263.

did not necessarily provide a good standard population to use for comparisons; all the parameters needed to be controlled. Nevertheless, at the time, the results obtained by Budin and others seemed sufficiently convincing to cause public authorities (municipalities and prefectures) to take the initiative to increase the provision of clinics and *gouttes de lait*. These decisions were taken at the beginning of the century, a time when there were few legal obligations for local authorities to provide services for children, except those in specific groups (for example, those given out to be wet-nursed). Vaccination against smallpox did not become compulsory in France until 1902.

A question that occupied the attention of many contemporary writers but was not tested statistically concerned the effects of feeding methods: for instance, under what circumstances did bottle-feeding constitute a larger risk than breastfeeding. This effect was difficult to measure: even if statistics on the number of deaths were available separately for breastfed and bottle-fed children, no figures were available for the population at risk. The lack of a denominator prevented an accurate assessment of mortality by type of feeding. There were also other important factors, such as education and standards of living, that needed to be taken into account.

Some local studies point to severe excess mortality among bottle-fed babies before the Pasteur era. Thus, a physician who studied the situation in the *département* of Calvados for children born in 1865 found that infant mortality had been almost three times higher among bottle-fed babies than among those who had been breastfed (31 per cent compared with 11 per cent: Denis-Dumont 1867, 716–718). In the mid-1880s mortality of infants given out to be wet-nursed varied between a quarter and a half, depending on whether the infant was breastfed or bottle-fed (Lagneau 1896). Paradoxically, even bigger differences were found later—an indication of the approximate nature of this

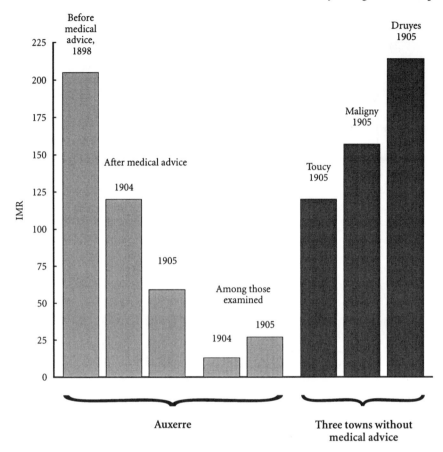

Fig. 11.6. Auxerre and three other communes: Infant mortality, 1905
Source: Budin 1907, 267.

type of measure. In a practice in Rouen the difference was nearly fivefold at the beginning of the century: fewer than 8 per cent of breastfed children died, compared with 36 per cent among the bottle-fed (Budin 1907, 15). Statistics from the Netherlands and above all from Germany confirm the existence of such differences, revealing ratios of 1 to 5, 6 and 7 (or more) at the beginning of the twentieth century. The example of Berlin is the most illuminating because breastfeeding was more common among the poorer groups of the population. In 1900, 7 per cent of breastfed babies died, whereas the death rate of bottle-fed babies amounted to 37 per cent, more than five times as high. Between 1890 and 1905, when the beneficial effects of the sterilization of milk became apparent, the excess mortality of bottle-fed babies fell from 6.8 to 4.1 (Methorst 1909).

To support his demonstration of the urgent need to counsel mothers while they were still breastfeeding and also those who bottle-fed their children, Budin presented a

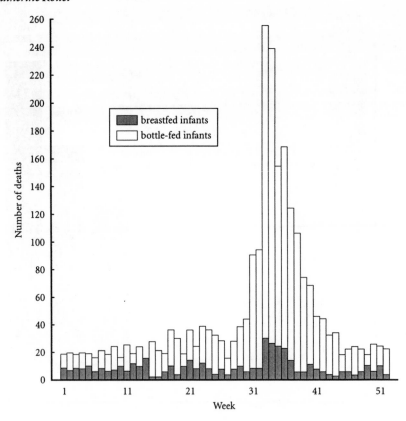

Fig. 11.7. Paris: Weekly deaths from diarrhoea, 1898

Source: Budin 1907, 155.

histogram of the weekly distribution of deaths from diarrhoea in Paris in 1898. He commented that its shape resembled the outline of the Eiffel Tower, and demonstrated the much greater vulnerability of bottle-fed children during the heat of summer (Figure 11.7).

CONCLUSION

This brief summary and evaluation of the methods used in France to measure the mortality of high-risk groups shows the progress that was achieved (which was not linear) and its limits. We note that data that would make it possible to carry out computations similar to those made by Monod exist and could be used in statistical studies. The imperfections in the statistical measures did not prevent contemporary observers from feeling that the excess mortality in the vulnerable groups was too large, and their views were confirmed by the results obtained in scientific surveys. In other words, the conviction that existing conditions were unjust united a majority of members of parliament, the medical profession and local community leaders and provided the motive force for the adoption of new laws and the creation of infant-health consultation centres. This conviction was based on a variety of factors in which statistics played a part, but not the only part.

References

BERTILLON, J., 1887. 'Calcul de la mortalité des enfants du premier âge', *Bulletin du Conseil supérieur de la statistique, deuxième session de 1886*, April, Imprimerie nationale.

BUCQUET, P., 1887. 'Rapport concernant [la protection des enfants du premier âge] par M. Paul Bucquet, inspecteur général honoraire des services administratifs du ministère de l'intérieur', *Journal Officiel* 2 December, pp. 5716–5721.

BUDIN, P., 1906–1907. 'La mortalité infantile dans les Bouches-du-Rhône', *Revue Philanthropique* 29, pp. 549–592.

—— 1907. *Manuel pratique d'allaitement*, Octave Doin.

DENIS-DUMONT, 1867. 'Lectures (Mémoire relatif à l'influence de l'allaitement artificiel du biberon sur la mortalité des nouveau-nés dans le département du Calvados)', *Bulletin de l'Académie de médecine* 21 May, pp. 716–718.

LAGNEAU, G., 1896. 'Combien d'enfants . . . sont privés des soins de leur mère?', *Bulletin de l'Académie de médecine* 14 January, pp. 30–44.

METHORST, H.-W., 1909 and 1911. 'Mortalité aux Pays-Bas', *Bulletin international de statistique* 18, pp. 64–81 and 19, p. 162.

MONOD, H., 1889. 'Rapport de M. le directeur de l'Assistance publique à M. le président du Conseil, ministre de l'intérieur', *Exposition universelle de 1889, Congrès international d'assistance, 28 July–4 August*, vol. 1, Paris.

—— 1898 and 1899. 'Les enfants assistés de France', *Revue Philanthropique* 3, pp. 545–570, 673–703 and 4, pp. 23–40, 139–159, 283–298, 408–419, 542–557, 649–670.

ROLLET, C., 1990. *La Politique à l'égard de la petite enfance sous la Troisième République*, Presses Universitaires de France/INED.

—— 1995. 'De la fièvre puerpérale à la consultation de nourissons: itinéraire d'un accoucheur, Pierre Budin, *"L'heureux événement": une histoire de l'accouchement'*, Musée de l'Assistance publique de Paris, pp. 85–99.

12

A Special Case of Decline: *Levels and Trends of Infant Mortality at Florence's Foundling Hospital, 1750–1950*

PIER PAOLO VIAZZO, MARIA BORTOLOTTO
AND ANDREA ZANOTTO

It is appropriate, we believe, to start this final chapter by remarking that our research on the long-term evolution of infant mortality at Florence's foundling hospital (the Spedale di Santa Maria degli Innocenti) between the middle of the eighteenth century and the Second World War was spurred, and largely shaped, by some of the general indications that emerged from the first Seminar on the Decline of Infant and Child Mortality in Europe, hosted by the Istituto degli Innocenti in 1992.

A survey of the extensive literature on the Innocenti Hospital (Bortolotto 1991) had shown that, while much had been written on its origins and subsequent institutional development, very little was known about levels and trends of infant mortality. Such evidence as could be gleaned from published sources was either vague or fragmentary. From time to time, rather self-satisfied administrators had declared that mortality had greatly declined as a result of measures they had recently introduced in order to regulate the flow of admissions or to improve medical standards and hygiene. More often than not, however, the figures they provided to support such claims turn out to be either difficult to interpret or plainly unreliable: hence our decision to start a research project specifically devoted to the study of infant mortality. The two main aims were (i) to contribute to a better understanding of infant mortality in foundling homes—a subject that appeared (rather surprisingly) not to have received sufficient attention—and (ii) to ascertain whether infant mortality displayed the same trends among Florence's foundlings as among the rest of the Italian, Tuscan or Florentine infant population.

To be sure, we did not actually expect the timing (and the causes) of decline to have been exactly the same. It is widely maintained (see, for example, Ransel 1988, 111; Da Molin 1993, 95–97) that a strong correlation existed between levels and trends in

Research for this chapter was made possible by grants from the Regional Government of Tuscany and the Banca Toscana. The project on the decline of infant mortality at Florence's foundling hospital was part of a wider research programme on the historical evolution of forms of child welfare assistance in Tuscany, promoted by the Istituto degli Innocenti of Florence. We are grateful to Carlo Corsini, who supported this project from the very beginning and has followed its development through its various phases.

foundling mortality and variations in the number of hospital admissions, and that in most European foundling homes mortality dropped significantly during the second half of the nineteenth century as a result of reforms that greatly reduced the annual inflow of abandoned infants. In the case of the Innocenti, it seemed reasonable to expect that the closure of the 'wheel'[1] in 1875, which brought about a drastic decline in the number of admissions (from nearly 2,500 per year to less than 1,000), had entailed a correspondingly marked decline in mortality. It was also well known that, from 1890 onwards, the Innocenti Hospital had made considerable efforts to improve hygiene and medical standards, specifically with a view to reducing infant mortality (Bruscoli 1900, 169–229). Therefore, we expected to pinpoint signs of further decline around the turn of the century—a development more in keeping, perhaps, with the general downward trend displayed by overall national and regional figures.[2] In short, our stated objectives were, first, to locate one or possibly more turning-points in the pattern of infant mortality among the Innocenti foundlings and, second, to assess the impact and relative weight of legislative and medical innovations.

The study of infant mortality in large foundling hospitals, however, immediately poses a basic methodological dilemma. It should be appreciated that the number of infants admitted to European foundling homes varied enormously from one establishment to another. Small hospitals received 50 or fewer infants per year. Large hospitals, on the other hand, could in certain periods receive well over one or two thousand infants per year—and in some extreme cases (Moscow, St Petersburg, Paris, Vienna and Milan) over five, ten or even fifteen thousand.[3] Though not quite in this latter class, the Innocenti Hospital was definitely a very large foundling home: in the two hundred years between the mid-eighteenth century and the Second Word War, more than 230,000 infants and young children were admitted, with an annual average of nearly 1,200 and a peak of 2,500 in the third quarter of the nineteenth century. The very size of these hospitals has led many students of child abandonment to concentrate on selected 'admission cohorts' (see, for example, Corsini 1976, 1984, 1991a,b; Hunecke 1989; Kertzer and White 1994). This approach allows analysis at the level of the individual, the possibility of following individual life-courses, and some sophisticated

---

[1] The 'wheels' were revolving cradles whereby infants could be anonymously introduced into foundling homes. Proposals to abolish the wheels became increasingly frequent in the first half of the nineteenth century. By 1853 most French wheels had been shut, and in the second half of the century the French example was to be followed all over Europe. In Italy, where wheels were closed in rapid succession between 1867 and 1875, much emphasis was placed on the fact that wheels allowed large numbers of unentitled legitimate infants to be 'smuggled' into foundling homes. An overview in English of the Italian debates over the closure of the wheels has been provided by Kertzer (1993, 154–169).

[2] On the evolution of infant mortality in Italy between the mid-nineteenth century and the Second World War, see Mitchell 1980, 138–141 and especially the recent discussion in Del Panta 1994. For Tuscany, see Breschi 1988. We are grateful to Marco Breschi for supplying us with his series of annual infant mortality rates for Tuscany from 1818 to 1985, which was published in his 1988 essay only in graphic form.

[3] In 1890 admission figures reached the startling levels of 16,587 in Moscow and 9,593 in St Petersburg (see Ransel 1988, 307). On admission figures in Vienna and Milan, see Pawlowsky and Zechner 1992 and Hunecke 1989, respectively. On the evolution of child abandonment in Paris and, more generally, on the differences between 'small' and 'large' foundling homes, see Hunecke 1991, 27–38.

demography. The alternative research strategy consists in first establishing the total number of infant deaths recorded in a series of calendar years (or suffered by a sequence of annual admission cohorts) and then relating these aggregate mortality figures to the corresponding admission figures in order to calculate either period or cohort rates of infant mortality.

Mixed research strategies can of course be devised, as will be shown below (pp. 236–243). We would like to emphasize, however, that we have invested time and resources mainly in the reconstruction of a long series of infant mortality rates. For some periods, our work has been facilitated by the availability of manuscript or, more rarely, published statistical sources;[4] for others, it has been necessary to engage in the highly time-consuming task of extracting the data directly from the ledgers in which details about each foundling's admission and subsequent fate were meticulously recorded.

LEVELS AND TRENDS OF INFANT MORTALITY IN THE SECOND HALF OF THE NINETEENTH CENTURY

For various reasons, we decided to concentrate initially on the period between the middle of the nineteenth century and the First World War. This was partly a matter of expediency, since we discovered a source that could, if properly treated, allow us to reconstruct fairly rapidly a series of 'period' rates of infant mortality for over fifty years, from 1838 to 1892. More importantly, we were aware that it was in this period that the wheel had been closed, that the Pasteurian revolution had taken place and, more generally, that the secular decline in infant mortality had started in most European countries, including (albeit still rather timidly) in Italy.

The main results of this initial phase of our research have been presented in Viazzo, Bortolotto and Zanotto 1994*a*. More detailed information about sources, methods and findings, as well as on the Innocenti Hospital and its history, can be found in that article. Here it will suffice to draw attention to Figure 12.1, which shows (i) that between 1838 and 1892 infant mortality was, in general, scarcely correlated with admissions; and, in particular, that the closure of the wheel in 1875 did not entail a noticeable and lasting mortality decline;[5] (ii) that at the end of the nineteenth century the level of infant

---

4 Official statistics were available in print only for the few years between 1896 and 1903, virtually buried in half-forgotten annual reports published by the Innocenti Hospital, and then again for some thirty years from 1919 to 1948 (Guidi 1938, 1948). The most helpful manuscript sources providing aggregate data have been two series of tabular compendia (*Dimostrazioni*), which cover the periods 1777–1824 and 1838–1892: Archivio dell'Ospedale degli Innocenti di Firenze (henceforth AOIF), XLIV, Dimostrazioni e Ristretti mensuali and Dimostrazioni ... del Movimento di Famiglia. Vital information has also come, for 1750–1774, from the statistical evidence assembled in AOIF, Affari Generali, LXXVIII, 66. Two books of *Introduzione ed esito* covering the two decades 1774–1794 have furnished the data on survival rates at age 2 presented in Figure 12.6.

5 The mortality figures represented in this graph are not strict IMRs. They were calculated following the traditional method used in many nineteenth-century foundling hospitals (including the Innocenti), which related a numerator made up of all infants deaths recorded in a calendar year to a denominator consisting of all infants admitted in the same calendar year plus all infants alive on the first day of the same year. As can be

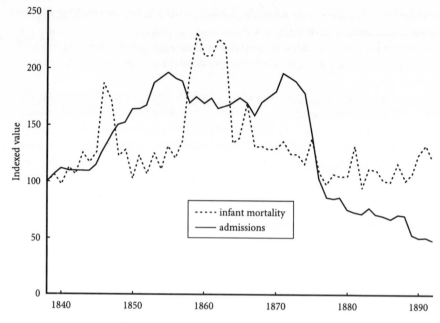

Fig. 12.1. Spedale degli Innocenti: Infant mortality and annual number of admissions, 1838–1892

Note: Index value: 1838=100.

Source: Viazzo, Bortolotto and Zanotto 1994*a*, 254.

mortality was, in fact, very much the same as around 1840, suggesting that scientific progress and improvements in hygiene had little, if any, impact;[6] and (iii) that despite this long-term stability, a number of violent fluctuations can be detected, most notably a major crisis between 1858 and 1863, when infant mortality rates consistently exceeded the level of 500 per 1,000.

As we have shown elsewhere (Viazzo, Bortolotto and Zanotto 1994*a*,*b*), the increased mortality between 1858 and 1863 was a result neither of epidemics nor (at least directly) of any social or economic crisis, but rather of a sudden, largely unpredictable and unusually prolonged shortage of wet-nurses. In this respect, it is necessary to recall some basic points about the functioning of the foundling system. Most general accounts (for example, Fildes 1988, 144–158; Viazzo 1991, 28–29; Kertzer 1993, 123–153) simply report that abandoned infants were first fed in foundling homes by 'internal' wet-

seen by comparing Figure 12.1 with Figures 12.2 and 12.3, this method tended to dampen short-term fluctuations.

[6] Two qualifications are in order. It should be noted, first of all, that mortality risks were increased by an 1887 order of the Italian Ministry of Interior that required all foundlings even remotely suspected of having syphilis to be fed artificially (see Viazzo, Bortolotto and Zanotto 1994*a*, 258–259). Second, the closure of the wheel in 1875 caused changes in the composition of the foundling population that affected the rates of infant mortality.

nurses and that, after a few days or weeks, they were then sent to 'external' wet-nurses, mostly living in the countryside, where they stayed until it was time to be weaned. This is basically correct. But clearly it made a difference whether placement with a wet-nurse took just a couple of days, or a couple of weeks, or perhaps a couple of months. Our findings (Viazzo, Bortolotto and Zanotto 1994*b*, 436–437; 1995) confirmed what Corsini (1991*a*, 96) had suggested on the basis of his analysis of the 1841 admission cohort, namely that by the late 1830s the Innocenti Hospital officials had apparently perfected an extremely efficient organizational procedure whereby approximately 80 per cent of all foundlings were placed with external wet-nurses between one and three days after admission. A remarkable feature of this organizational machine was that it remained quick and efficient even when, from about 1845 onwards, the number of admissions began to rise rapidly. It may nevertheless be surmised that such a rise made the hospital, and the children's lives, increasingly vulnerable to the effects of inadequate supplies of external wet-nurses. The fact that this was indeed the case is demonstrated by the crisis of 1858–1863: the effects were an enormously increased interval between admission and placement with a wet-nurse (nearly two weeks on average), a correspondingly enormous increase in mortality due to overcrowding, and massive recourse to artificial feeding. A substantial increase in the external wet-nurses' salary proved to be the decisive remedy, although this entailed a considerable financial burden on the Innocenti. It seems plausible that the closure of the wheel in 1875, and the subsequent fall in the number of admissions, lessened such vulnerability, and thus contributed indirectly to the stabilization, if not to a clear reduction, of mortality.

POST-WAR DECLINE, 1919–1940

The dangers posed by inadequate supplies of wet-nurses were not yet over, however. If we turn to Figure 12.2, we see that since the beginning of the twentieth century three major crises stand out: the serious worsening of infant mortality in the period 1907–1909, when rates once again approached values close to 400 per 1,000; the astounding peak of the First World War years, which dwarfs even the exceedingly high levels reached in 1858–1863; and, finally, the greatly increased mortality of the Second World War years. All these crises are essentially explained by lack of wet-nurses (Viazzo and Bortolotto 1994*a,b*; Viazzo, Bortolotto and Zanotto 1994*a*).

One important point to be stressed is that the disastrous mortality experienced by the foundlings in Florence (and in most other Italian cities) during the First World War accelerated a process of change that was to revolutionize the whole foundling system in Italy. For centuries, one of the fundamental tenets of this system had been that foundlings had to be immediately separated from their mothers and entrusted to wet-nurses, both for the sake of public morality and for the good of the children themselves (Kertzer 1993, 131–133; see also Viazzo, Bortolotto and Zanotto 1994*a*, 260–262). It was well known that the foundlings' survival chances would have greatly increased had

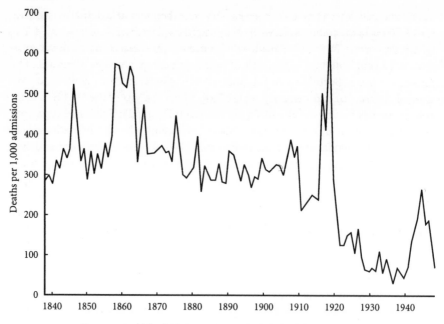

Fig. 12.2. Spedale degli Innocenti: Infant mortality, 1838–1948

they been left with their mothers, yet proposals for a shift from a system based mainly on 'mercenary' nursing to a system relying predominantly on maternal breastfeeding were consistently resisted. After the carnage of the war years, however, when the inability of foundling homes to recruit enough wet-nurses to keep the babies alive became patent, a shift to the maternal system became imperative (Viazzo, Bortolotto and Zanotto, forthcoming).

In Florence maternal breastfeeding was at first strongly encouraged, and then made compulsory, through a series of resolutions passed during or immediately after the war. As a result, the proportion of maternally breastfed foundlings rocketed to 71 per cent in 1920, 84 per cent in 1921 and 91 per cent in 1922. The effects on infant mortality, as shown in Figure 12.2, were striking. In 1920, despite an increased number of admissions, infant mortality fell below the 200 per 1,000 mark for the first time. No less impressively, in 1921 it went down to just 125 per 1,000, a value that compared favourably with the rate of 129.3 per 1,000 for the Italian infant population as a whole. In the 1930s the rate of infant mortality among Florence's foundlings was reported to be roughly on a par with the rate recorded for legitimate children in Tuscany (around 65 per 1,000) and well below the national level, which was in the region of 100 per 1,000.

As we shall see briefly below (pp. 241–243), these figures must be read with some caution. There can be no doubt, however, that the early 1920s and the shift to a pattern of widespread maternal breastfeeding marked a decisive turning-point in the evolution of infant mortality among the foundlings assisted by the Innocenti Hospital. It is also worth noting that in 1923 a national law made breastfeeding of foundlings by their un-wed mothers compulsory for the whole Italian territory, and it is to be hoped that future research will establish the extent to which the case of the Innocenti is representative of wider national trends.[7]

Before moving back to the eighteenth and early nineteenth century, it may be useful to add that, rather paradoxically, although the aim of both central and local authorities was to achieve one hundred per cent maternal breastfeeding, in Florence proportions began slightly to decline after the promulgation of the national law. Thus, in the 1930s about one third of the Innocenti foundlings were still placed with wet-nurses. At the outbreak of the Second World War, wet-nurses suddenly vanished and once again it was necessary to resort to artificial feeding, though clearly on a less massive scale than during the First World War. The dearth of wet-nurses was once again the principal factor accounting for the last great mortality crisis experienced by Florence's foundling home.

EXTENDING THE INVESTIGATION BACKWARDS: INFANT MORTALITY SINCE THE 1750S

If some of the main problems that had spurred our research had largely been solved, other important questions remained unanswered. We had found that, in the late 1830s, the level of infant mortality was already as low as it was to remain until the early twen-tieth century, or indeed until the crucial shift from mercenary to maternal breast-feeding in the early 1920s. What we did not know was when this relatively low level had been attained.

A study of infant mortality between 1445 and 1466, the first two decades of the hospital's welfare activities, reported levels in the region of 450 per 1,000 (Gavitt 1990, 212–222).[8] Evidence pieced together from several published works and manuscript documents suggested, however, that throughout the seventeenth and eighteenth cen-turies, and indeed until 1805, IMRs were exceedingly high (perhaps over 700 or even 800 per 1,000). Mortality was dramatically halved through the implementation of a set of ameliorative measures put in place on 7 December 1805 by the central government of the then Kingdom of Etruria and applied to all Tuscan foundling hospitals.[9]

---

[7] The data reported by Somogyi (1967, 143–144, 191–193) suggest that in the 1930s the average level of infant mortality among foundlings was substantially higher in Italy as a whole than in Florence. They also point, however, to some broad similarities in trends.

[8] These findings are basically in agreement with the figures published by Trexler (1973, 275–277) in his pioneering and highly influential study of foundling mortality in Florence between 1445 and 1451. However, new data recently published by Gavitt himself (1994, 72) for the period 1467–1485 reveal an upward trend from IMRs lower than 500 per 1,000 in the early 1460s to rates exceeding 800 per 1,000 in the early 1480s.

[9] The Kingdom of Etruria was one of the states into which Italy was subdivided during the Napoleonic period. It included most of the territory of present-day Tuscany and lasted from 1801 to 1807, when it was annexed to the French Empire. The decree (*motuproprio*) of 7 December 1805 was deemed by contempor-aries to mark a shift from the 'Old System' of foundling care to a radically different 'New System'.

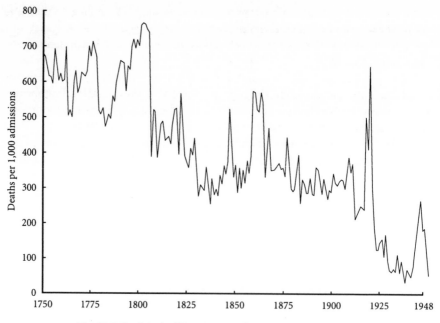

Fig. 12.3. Spedale degli Innocenti: Infant mortality, 1750–1948

Since this evidence appeared to be highly fragmentary and often severely flawed, and in any case far from conclusive, we thought that it was worth trying to extend our series backwards into the eighteenth century. The use of very helpful and previously virtually unknown archival sources has allowed us fairly rapidly to stretch our series back to the year 1750. In this chapter we present for the first time what is arguably the longest infant mortality curve ever reconstructed for large foundling homes (Figure 12.3). We cannot claim that the very long time-series we have put together is completely homogeneous and faultless.[10] Nevertheless, we trust that it provides a far more telling general perspective on the long-term evolution of infant mortality among Florentine foundlings than was available before.

We will briefly mention only two issues. First of all, Figure 12.3 confirms that the enactment of the 1805 legislation did in fact mark a major turning-point, since it led to a sudden and very pronounced fall in infant mortality. In respect of this legislation, it should also be observed that, while considerable emphasis was placed on medical and

---

10 It should be noted, in particular, that annual IMRs for 1750–1776 are cohort rates, those for 1777–1948 are period rates, and those for 1949–1950 are again cohort rates. Moreover, values for 1750–1778, 1786–1805 and 1949–1950 have been estimated by various methods according to the nature of the available information, while those for 1779–1785 and 1806–1948 have been derived directly either from the sources mentioned in footnote 4 above or from the admission registers. Finally, IMRs for 1750–1888 have been calculated by relating annual numbers of infant deaths to total annual numbers of admissions (and are, consequently, slightly underestimated), and IMRs for 1889–1950 are the ratios of annual numbers of infant deaths to annual numbers of children who were less than 12 months old on admission.

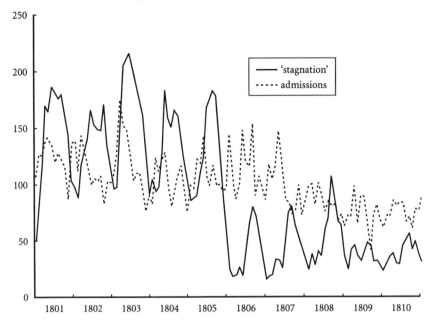

Fig. 12.4. Spedale degli Innocenti: Monthly level of admission and 'stagnation', 1801–1810

hygienic improvements, the key provision was in all likelihood the substantial increase in the external wet-nurses' salary—a measure that had to be counterbalanced by the shortening of the nursing period from 15 to 12 months. This was to prove a crucial step towards the creation of the highly efficient organizational process referred to above. Until 1805, the daily number of babies 'stagnating' (to use the contemporary term) in the hospital and waiting for placement with external wet-nurses typically ranged from about 100 during the winter months to 200 or more during the summer, when the recruitment of external wet-nurses was more difficult. The number of internal wet-nurses could be raised to 70 during the summer, but the ratio remained unfavourable. All this changed radically immediately after the issuing of the ordinances of December 1805, as Figure 12.4 shows. Around 1840, the number of sucklings to be found in the hospital at any point in time ranged only between 10 and 20, without any obvious sign of seasonal variation (see Figure 12.5), and they were fed by a roughly similar number of internal wet-nurses (Bortolotto and Viazzo, forthcoming).

The second point we would like to underline is that long time-series of aggregate figures offer, for all their deficiencies, some notable advantages over studies that concentrate on a limited number of admission cohorts. The most recent, and probably most sophisticated, of these cohort studies is the one conducted by David Kertzer and his associates on eight annual cohorts of infants admitted to Bologna's foundling home between 1809 and 1870. In a 1994 article, Kertzer and White reported infant mortality rates of 706 per 1,000 for 1809–1810, 566 per 1,000 for a period of 20 years centred on

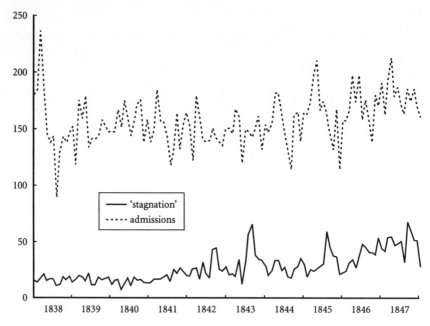

Fig. 12.5. Spedale degli Innocenti: Monthly level of admission and 'stagnation', 1838–1847

1840, and 372 per 1,000 for 1869–1870. Such findings led them to suggest that infant mortality among Bologna's foundlings declined monotonically. If we plot these values against our long-term curve, we discover that the rates estimated for Bologna match almost uncannily the ones found in Florence in roughly the same years, and yet one could hardly argue that in Florence the decline of infant mortality was monotonic.

RELATIONSHIPS BETWEEN
INFANT AND EARLY CHILDHOOD MORTALITY

As we remarked above, analysis at the level of the individual makes it possible to study in much finer detail many important aspects of foundling mortality: the changing structure of infant mortality and the weight of neonatal mortality, for instance, or the varying length of the interval between admission and placement with a wet-nurse.

Another important and largely neglected topic that can be most fruitfully investigated through individual analysis is the relationship between infant and early childhood mortality.[11] Indeed, one of the most valuable findings to emerge from Carlo Corsini's

---

[11] In some places and periods, however, foundling mortality beyond 1 or possibly 2 years of age can prove exceedingly difficult to measure because many foundlings simply disappear from observation. This was the case in both Florence and Milan (two cities where very high proportions of foundlings consisted of legitimate

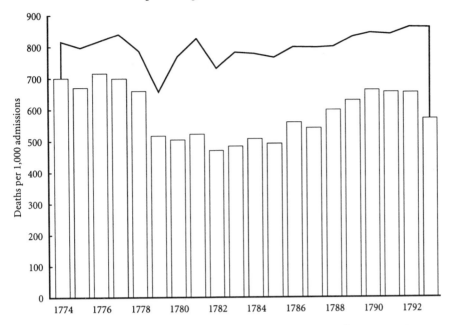

Fig. 12.6. Spedale degli Innocenti: Mortality under 12 and 24 months, 1774–1793
Sources: Books of *Introduzione ed esito* 1774–1794.

cohort analysis of infant mortality among foundlings admitted to the Innocenti in the years 1762–1764 (when babies were breastfed throughout the first 15 months of their lives) and 1809–1811 (when breastfeeding duration had been shortened to 12 months) was that the improvement in the mortality rate achieved by the latter cohort during the first year tended to be cancelled out—or reversed—in the second year. At 15 months, survival rates were very much the same for both cohorts (Corsini 1991*b*, 78–79).

The lesson to be learned is that gains in mortality could be more apparent than real. In this respect, it is relevant to mention that we have recently discovered that the reforms of 1805 had a short-lived, but highly instructive, precedent. In 1779 the Innocenti officials, who had been assured by a committee of distinguished medical men that no serious adverse effects could be expected from a three-month shortening of the nursing period, decided that in order to reduce intolerably high levels of infant mortality the wet-nurses' pay was to be raised and breastfeeding shortened from 15 to 12 months. As Figure 12.3 shows, this measure had an immediate impact on infant mortality, which dropped by nearly one third. Interestingly enough, however, only seven years later the same officials raised the breastfeeding period back to 15 months, since it was felt that

children) towards the middle of the nineteenth century. Data provided by Corsini (1991*a*, 105–107) and Viazzo, Bortolotto and Zanotto (1995) for Florence, and by Hunecke (1989, 160–172) for Milan, indicate that in those years between a third and a half of all foundlings who survived their first year of life were returned to their parents soon after the external wet-nurses had completed the compulsory breastfeeding period.

too many foundlings died because weaning came too early and abruptly. Aggregate data drawn from various sources and presented in Figure 12.6 demonstrate that the Innocenti officials' concern was not unfounded. Despite the spectacular fall of infant mortality, between 1779 and 1786 survival rates at age 2 had hardly increased.[12]

SOME DIFFERENTIALS IN INFANT MORTALITY

What our long-term curve hides is the existence of significant differentials in infant mortality: between males and females, between foundlings of legitimate and illegitimate birth, and even between different categories of legitimate and illegitimate children. One of our aims in constructing a long time-series of infant mortality rates irrespective of gender and legitimacy status has been to provide a yardstick, however crude, against which the results of more detailed future research can be measured. We have, never-theless, already explored a few aspects of differential mortality among Florence's foundlings. In the following sections, we will briefly touch on four such aspects, partly because of their exemplary value and partly because they provide information of relevance to a correct interpretation of the pattern presented in Figure 12.3.

Legitimate/illegitimate

As we have mentioned elsewhere, a distinctive feature of the mode of infant abandon-ment in Florence was that many or most of the infants admitted to the Innocenti Hospital were legitimate (Corsini 1976, 1006–1007; see also Kertzer 1991, 5–6; 1993, 81–84; Viazzo 1994, 40–41). In the years prior to the closure of the wheel in 1875, their number certainly exceeded that of illegitimate children. The main reason why the wheel was shut was precisely in order to curb the abandonment of legitimate children. After 1875 legitimate children continued to be admitted, but their proportion declined substantially.

A study of differential mortality between these two categories of foundling can be conducted most neatly for the 30 years from 1889 to 1918, largely because old defini-tional ambiguities had just been dissolved (from 1889 onwards legitimate and illegiti-mate children were registered in different books) and new ones had not yet appeared. As Table 12.1 shows, infant mortality was considerably higher among the foundlings born out of wedlock (336.2 per 1,000 against 292.8). This finding confirms what could easily be suspected, namely that the apparent absence of infant mortality decline in the late nineteenth and early twentieth centuries was partly due to the compositional changes brought about by the closure of the wheel. However, infant mortality rates also remained very high among foundlings of legitimate birth.

---

[12] On the 1779 reforms and their repeal in 1786, see AOIF, Affari Generali, LXXX, 23; XCII, ff. 29ʳ–31ᵛ. Survival rates at age 2 are provided by the two books of *Introduzione ed esito* mentioned in footnote 4 above. The fact that mortality between 12 and 15 months greatly increased after the 1779 reforms is also confirmed by the first results of an ongoing individual-level analysis of the 1777 and 1782 admission cohorts.

Table 12.1. Spedale degli Innocenti: Differential
mortality of legitimate and illegitimate infants, 1889–1918

	Legitimate	Illegitimate	All
Number of admissions[a]	6,611	18,509	25,120
Number of infant deaths	1,936	6,222	8,158
IMR	292.8	336.2	324.8

[a] Children who were less than 12 months old on admission.

Sources: AOIF, XVI, XVII (*Registrazione delle creature introdotte*).

Males/females

Although the significance of the legitimacy component for mortality cannot be denied, it should also be noted that between 1889 and 1918 differences between legitimate and illegitimate infants were slightly less pronounced than differences between males and females (347.7 per 1,000 for males against 301.1 for females). The data assembled in Table 12.2 indicate that male foundlings had already suffered higher infant mortality in the half century from 1838 to 1888, as we have shown in greater detail elsewhere (Viazzo, Bortolotto and Zanotto 1994*b*, 427–428), and also in the late eighteenth and

Table 12.2. Spedale degli Innocenti: Differential
mortality of male and female foundlings, 1786–1815 and 1838–1918

	Males			Females		
	Number of admissions	Number of deaths	IMR	Number of admissions	Number of deaths	IMR
1786–1790	2,594	1,802	694.7	3,087	1,979	641.1
1791–1795	2,920	2,147	735.3	3,408	2,292	672.5
1796–1800	3,039	2,485	817.7	3,356	2,542	757.4
1801–1805	3,301	2,804	849.4	3,500	2,927	836.3
1806–1810	2,731	1,248	457.0	2,670	1,173	439.3
1811–1815	2,687	1,253	466.3	2,789	1,216	436.0
1838–1888	45,950	18,248	397.1	45,514	16,660	366.0
1889–1918	12,734	4,428	347.7	12,386	3,730	301.1

Notes: For the periods 1786–1815 and 1838–1888, admission figures refer to the total number of admissions; for the period 1889–1918, they refer only to children who were less than 12 months old on admission. For the period 1786–1805, mortality figures refer to mortality under 15 months; for all other periods, to mortality under 12 months.

Sources: 1786–1805: AOIF, XLIV (*Dimostrazioni e Ristretti mensuali*); 1838–1888: AOIF, XLIV (*Dimostrazioni . . . del Movimento di Famiglia*); 1889–1918: AOIF, XVI, XVII (*Registrazione delle creature introdotte*).

early nineteenth centuries. It is interesting to observe that differences seem to disappear only in the very first years of the nineteenth century, when infant mortality was at its highest.

Subsidized/unsubsidized

From 1815 to 1837, any mortality differential to be found along legitimacy or gender lines is overshadowed by the huge differences that can be detected between those infants we might term 'proper' foundlings and the new category of 'subsidized' foundlings. Probably as a form of relief to families affected by the economic crises and by the famine that struck Tuscany in the second decade of the nineteenth century, the Innocenti Hospital began to grant breastfeeding subsidies to children born of poor families, who were formally admitted to the foundling home but actually returned to their own mothers for nursing.

Table 12.3. Spedale degli Innocenti: Number and proportion of 'subsidized' foundlings, 1814–1837

	Admissions	Subsidized	%
1814	1,180	0	0.0
1815	1,512	253	16.7
1816	1,636	281	17.2
1817	1,757	357	20.3
1818	1,415	319	22.5
1819	1,486	298	20.1
1820	1,495	295	19.7
1821	1,391	293	21.1
1822	1,402	308	22.0
1823	1,420	278	19.6
1824	1,296	244	18.8
1825	1,304	251	19.2
1826	1,395	287	20.6
1827	1,385	314	22.7
1828	1,430	330	23.1
1829	1,387	336	24.2
1830	1,492	459	30.8
1831	1,576	458	29.1
1832	1,700	557	32.8
1833	1,636	507	31.0
1834	1,718	518	30.2
1835	1,720	510	29.7
1836	1,819	545	30.0
1837	2,104	820	39.0

Sources: AOIF, XVI (*Balie e bambini*); Bruscoli 1900, 292.

As Table 12.3 shows, the proportion of 'subsidized' foundlings was very high. Indeed, in the mid-1830s they became so numerous that from 1833 the Innocenti officials decided that it was time to list them in different registers from the rest of the foundlings and, from 1839, to produce separate statistics. For about 20 years, however, subsidized infants were registered along with the other foundlings, and the mortality figures that can be immediately derived from official statistical sources include both categories. Since the resulting distortions were too serious not to be corrected, we have disaggregated the mortality figures for subsidized and unsubsidized infants (see Table 12.4).[13] The rates plotted on Figure 12.3 refer to the latter category only.

Recognized/unrecognized

A somewhat similar problem is encountered around a century later, in the 1920s and 1930s. This time, however, difficulties arise from a subdivision introduced in 1921, and reinforced in 1927, between two categories of illegitimate children admitted to the Innocenti Hospital: those who were not legally recognized by their mothers and were mostly placed with wet-nurses, and those who were recognized and mostly breastfed by their own mothers.

Individual-level analysis of a number of cohorts of foundlings admitted to the Innocenti between the two world wars has shown that infant mortality was higher among unrecognized foundlings. At the same time, it has revealed that differences were not as marked as they would appear to have been at first glance. This is explained by a major change in the pattern of child abandonment, which also partly accounts for the suspiciously low levels of infant mortality reported by official Innocenti publications (Guidi 1938, 1948).

For nearly five centuries, Florence's pattern of infant abandonment was characterized by the fact that the vast majority of foundlings were between a few hours and 4 weeks old on admission (Viazzo, Bortolotto and Zanotto 1995). In the 1920s and 1930s, unrecognized foundlings still conformed to this traditional pattern. Thus, over 98 per cent of the 228 unrecognized foundlings who entered the Innocenti in 1936 were under 30 days old on admission. By contrast, only about 60 per cent of recognized foundlings (who accounted for about two thirds of all admissions) were that young. What is more, cases of recognized foundlings admitted when they were 6, 8 or 10 months old were by no means unusual (Viazzo and Bortolotto 1994*b*, 18–22). It is worth remembering that in the period between the two world wars infant mortality rates for foundlings were calculated by relating the number of infant deaths recorded in a calendar year to the number of children under 12 months of age admitted in that same year (Guidi 1938,

---

[13] Infant deaths for 'subsidized' foundlings are certainly underreported (it appears that officials were not interested in recording their fates as precisely as those of the other foundlings) and IMRs are consequently underestimated. The essential aim of our exercise in disaggregation was, however, to establish correct mortality rates for 'proper' foundlings. For the sake of comparison, it may be useful to note that infant mortality rates for the whole Tuscan population ranged between 240 and 300 per 1,000 in the period 1809–1812 (Corsini 1966, 192–194) and between 204 and 240 per 1,000 in the period 1818–1838 (Breschi 1988, 97).

Table 12.4. Spedale degli Innocenti: Differential mortality of 'subsidized' and 'unsubsidized' foundlings, 1815–1832

	Unsubsidized			Subsidized			All		
	Admissions	Deaths	IMR	Admissions	Deaths	IMR	Admissions	Deaths	IMR
1815	1,259	565	448.8	253	(34)[a]	—[a]	1,512	599	396.2
1816	1,355	576	425.1	281	71	252.7	1,636	647	395.5
1817	1,400	679	485.0	357	78	218.5	1,757	757	430.8
1818	1,096	573	522.8	319	46	144.2	1,415	619	437.5
1819	1,188	625	526.1	298	51	171.1	1,486	676	454.9
1820	1,200	475	395.8	295	43	145.8	1,495	518	346.5
1821	1,098	624	568.3	293	50	170.6	1,391	674	484.5
1822	1,094	549	501.8	308	56	181.8	1,402	605	431.5
1823	1,142	450	394.0	278	48	172.7	1,420	498	350.7
1824	1,052	395	375.5	244	52	213.1	1,296	447	344.9
1825	1,053	378	359.0	251	52	207.2	1,304	430	329.8
1826	1,108	460	415.2	287	46	160.3	1,395	506	362.7
1827	1,071	421	393.1	314	57	181.5	1,385	478	345.1
1828	1,100	489	444.5	330	53	160.6	1,430	542	379.0
1829	1,051	355	337.8	336	67	199.4	1,387	422	304.3
1830	1,033	287	277.8	459	61	132.9	1,492	348	233.2
1831	1,118	348	311.3	458	68	148.5	1,576	416	264.0
1832	1,143	346	302.7	557	73	131.1	1,700	419	246.5

[a] Subsidies were first granted (to 253 children) in 1815. The number of these subsidized foundlings who died below age 12 months in 1815 (34) is given in parentheses because it includes no infants admitted in 1814 who died below age 12 months in calendar year 1815. Thus, it is not statistically comparable to the other period infant mortality rates in the table.

Note: IMR = period infant mortality rates.

Source: AOIF, XVI (Balie e bambini).

46–47). Clearly such rates were significantly lowered by the peculiar age distribution at admission displayed by the numerically predominant category of recognized foundlings. It should nevertheless be recognized that the decline of infant mortality signalled by Figure 12.3 was not simply a statistical artefact. This is demonstrated by a study of perinatal, neonatal and post-neonatal mortality among Florence's foundlings in 1939 (Noccioli and Montalenti 1959) and confirmed by the rates we have calculated for the most disadvantaged category of infants admitted to the Innocenti:[14] the 1936 cohort rate for unrecognized foundlings was as low as 83.7 per 1,000, well below the national rate of infant mortality for legitimate children.

CONCLUDING REMARKS

The reason why we have shaped this chapter very much as a sort of chronicle of our own research experience, rather than as a chronological or systematic discussion of infant mortality trends at the Innocenti Hospital, is that such a format brings out more clearly some relationships between this piece of research and a number of methodological and substantive issues of central importance to the overarching project on the decline of infant and child mortality in Europe over the last two hundred years. In this connection, we would like to make a few concluding remarks.

Our first remark has to do with one such central issue, namely whether research strategies relying on aggregate or those using individual-level data should be preferred. This is a dilemma every student of foundling mortality has to face. Since we were interested in assessing the impact of the closure of the wheel, which took place on 1 July 1875, our first round of research was focused mainly on the nominative study of the three annual admission cohorts centred on 1875 (Bortolotto and Zanotto 1993, tables I–XXI). However, some obvious shortcomings of this approach convinced us that it was necessary to invest rather more heavily than we had originally expected in the collection and analysis of aggregate data. Nevertheless, we have repeatedly gone back, whenever necessary and possible, to individual-level analysis in order to study the changing structure of infant mortality, for instance, or to assess the reliability of the aggregate figures we have derived from manuscript or printed sources.[15]

Our second remark concerns the adoption of a long-term perspective. We hope that this chapter has demonstrated that the gradual extension of the time-span covered by our investigation has proved highly rewarding. Though not necessarily wrong, the provisional conclusions reached at the end of each phase of our research now appear to us

---

14 In the years between the two world wars, children admitted to the Innocenti Hospital were divided into three categories: *esposti* (unrecognized illegitimate children), *illegittimi riconosciuti* (recognized illegitimate children) and *legittimi* (legitimate children).

15 So far we have collected, and partly analysed, individual-level data for 31 complete annual admission cohorts (23 from the twentieth century). These cohorts have mostly been selected in order to study in detail the effects of major organizational reforms in foundling care and admission practices and the structure of crisis mortality during the two world war periods. The total number of individual records is now close to 24,000. See Bortolotto and Zanotto 1993; Viazzo, Bortolotto and Zanotto 1995.

to tell only part of the story. Our decision to extend our research back into the eighteenth century is still yielding increasing returns.

Our third and final remark concerns representativeness. The timing and the causes of the decline of infant mortality at Florence's foundling home were clearly not the same as for the rest of the infant population. Moreover, even if we assume that the case of the Innocenti is fairly representative of what happened in many or most foundling hospitals in other parts of Italy and in other European countries, the fact remains that foundlings only accounted for a modest, even negligible proportion of the total infant population. Yet, it would probably be unwise to dismiss what we might term 'foundling studies' as something quite marginal to the mainstream of research on the decline of infant and child mortality in Europe. We have argued elsewhere (Viazzo, Bortolotto and Zanotto 1994*a*) that an accurate investigation of the functioning of foundling hospitals provides a unique vantage point to assess the effects of medical, organizational and legislative innovations aimed at improving the survival chances of infants and young children—a thematic area of increasing interest to students of historical infant mortality (Garrett and Wear 1994).

The role of such measures within the context of general demographic policies—from the late eighteenth century, when European governments began investing in human capital, up to perhaps the mid-twentieth century—should not be underestimated. Italy certainly offers an instructive example. As is well known, in the early decades of the twentieth century Italian rates of infant mortality declined more slowly than did those of other European countries. This was seen as a loss to the nation and was definitely a source of embarrassment to Italian governments. Accordingly, a fundamental task of the demographic policy launched in the years between the two world wars was the reduction of infant mortality. It is significant that a primary target were the mothers of illegitimate child (Ipsen 1997, ch. 4). The newly established National Board for Maternity and Child Welfare, whose fundamental mandate was to reduce infant mortality through the encouragement of maternal breastfeeding, was specifically entrusted with providing assistance for those mothers who recognized and nursed their illegitimate children. Indeed, the financial burden of foundling care proved so heavy that it distracted the Board from its more general objective.

It seems justified for us to conclude this chapter by saying that, although we have illustrated an admittedly special case of decline, a study of the evolution of foundling mortality may shed light on far wider processes. It was in foundling homes that the waste of human lives—in the 1930s as well as in the second half of the eighteenth century—was at its most visible and most urgently called for public intervention.

References

BORTOLOTTO, M., 1991. 'Lo Spedale di Santa Maria degli Innocenti: una rassegna storico-bibliografica', research report, Florence, Istituto degli Innocenti.

—— and VIAZZO, P. P., forthcoming. 'Assistenza agli esposti e declino della mortalità infantile allo Spedale degli Innocenti di Firenze nella prima metà dell'800', in C. A. CORSINI (ed.), *La famiglia toscana dell'800*, Florence, Centro Editoriale Toscano.

—— and ZANOTTO, A., 1993. 'Livelli e tendenze della mortalità infantile allo Spedale degli Innocenti di Firenze nella seconda metà dell'Ottocento', research report, Florence, Istituto degli Innocenti.

BRESCHI, M., 1988. 'L'evoluzione della mortalità infantile', in C. A. CORSINI (ed.), *Vita, morte e miracoli di gente comune: appunti per una storia della popolazione toscana fra XIV e XX secolo*, Florence, La Casa Usher.

BRUSCOLI, G., 1900. *Lo Spedale di Santa Maria degl'Innocenti di Firenze dalla sua fondazione ai giorni nostri*, Florence, Ariani.

CORSINI, C. A., 1966. 'Aspetti demografici dell'Italia nel periodo Napoleonico: la mortalità infantile', *Genus* 22, pp. 185–223.

—— 1976. 'Materiali per lo studio della famiglia in Toscana nei secoli XVII–XIX: gli esposti', *Quaderni Storici* 11, pp. 998–1052.

—— 1984. 'Structural changes in infant mortality in Tuscany from the 18th to the 19th century', in T. BENGTSSON, G. FRIDLIZIUS and R. OHLSSON (eds.), *Pre-industrial population change*, Stockholm, Almquist and Wiksell.

—— 1991a. ' "Era piovuto dal cielo e la terra l'aveva raccolto": il destino del trovatello', in J.-P. BARDET *et al.*, *Enfance abandonnée et société en Europe, XIVe-XXe siècle*, Rome, Ecole Française de Rome.

—— 1991b. 'Breastfeeding, fertility and infant mortality: lessons from the archives of the Florence Spedale degli Innocenti', in S. F. MATTHEWS GRIECO and C. A. CORSINI, *Historical perspectives on breastfeeding*, Florence, UNICEF International Child Development Centre and Istituto degli Innocenti.

DA MOLIN, G., 1993. *Nati e abbandonati: aspetti demografici e sociali dell'infanzia abbandonata in Italia nell'età moderna*, Bari, Cacucci.

DEL PANTA, L., 1994. 'Mortalité infantile et post-infantile en Italie du XVIIIe au XXe siècle: tendences à long terme et différences régionales', *Annales de Démographie Historique*, pp. 45–60.

FILDES, V., 1988. *Wet nursing: a history from antiquity to the present*, Oxford, Blackwell.

GARRETT, E. and WEAR, A., 1994. 'Suffer the little children: mortality, mothers and the state', *Continuity and Change* 9, pp. 179–184.

GAVITT, P., 1990. *Charity and children in Renaissance Florence: the Ospedale degli Innocenti, 1410–1536*, Ann Arbor, MI, University of Michigan Press.

—— 1994. ' "Perche non avea chi la ghovernasse": cultural values, family resources and abandonment in the Florence of Lorenzo de' Medici, 1467–85', in J. HENDERSON and R. WALL (eds.), *Poor women and children in the European past*, London, Routledge.

GUIDI, G., 1938. *Regio Spedale degli Innocenti: rendiconto statistico-clinico per gli anni dal 1928 al 1936*, Empoli, Noccioli.

GUIDI, G., 1948. *Istituto degli Innocenti di Firenze: rendiconto statistico-clinico riassuntivo dal 1923 al 1947*, Florence, Vallecchi.

HUNECKE, V., 1989. *I trovatelli di Milano: bambini esposti e famiglie espositrici dal XVII al XIX secolo*, Bologna, Il Mulino.

—— 1991. 'Intensità e fluttuazioni degli abbandoni dal XV al XIX secolo', in J.-P. BARDET *et al.*, *Enfance abandonnée et société en Europe, XIVe–XXe siècle*, Rome, Ecole Française de Rome.

IPSEN, C., 1997. *Demografia totalitaria: il problema della popolazione nell'Italia fascista*, Bologna, Il Mulino.

KERTZER, D. I, 1991. 'Gender ideology and infant abandonment in nineteenth-century Italy', *Journal of Interdisciplinary History* 22, pp. 1–25.

—— 1993. *Sacrificed for honor: Italian infant abandonment and the politics of reproductive control*, Boston, MA, Beacon Press.

—— and WHITE, M. J., 1994. 'Cheating the angel-makers: surviving infant mortality in nineteenth century Italy', *Continuity and Change* 9, pp. 450–480.

MITCHELL, B. R., 1980. *European historical statistics 1750–1975*, 2nd rev. edn, London, Macmillan.

NOCCIOLI, G. and MONTALENTI, G., 1959. 'Contributo statistico allo studio della mortalità perinatale', *Minerva Nipiologica* 9(5–6), pp. 99–103.

PAWLOWSKY, V. and ZECHNER, R., 1992. 'Verwaltete Kinder: das Wiener Findelhaus (1794–1910)', *Wiener Geschichtsblaetter* 47(3), pp. 129–148.

RANSEL, D. L., 1988. *Mothers of misery: child abandonment in Russia*, Princeton, NJ, Princeton University Press.

SOMOGYI, S., 1967. *La mortalità nei primi cinque anni di età in Italia, 1883–1962*, Palermo, Edizioni Ingrana.

TREXLER, R., 1973. 'The foundlings of Florence, 1395–1445', *History of Childhood Quarterly* 1, pp. 259–284.

VIAZZO, P. P., 1991. 'Breastfeeding, wet nursing and the organization of child care in the past: the case of Florence's Spedale degli Innocenti', Uppsala, *News on Health Care in Developing Countries* 5(3), pp. 28–31.

—— 1994. 'Family structures and the early phase in the individual life cycle: a southern European approach', in J. HENDERSON and R. WALL (eds.), *Poor women and children in the European past*, London, Routledge.

—— and BORTOLOTTO, M., 1994a. 'Andamento e caratteristiche della mortalità infantile allo Spedale degli Innocenti dal 1889 al 1909', research report, Florence, Istituto degli Innocenti.

—— —— 1994b. 'Andamento e caratteristiche della mortalità infantile allo Spedale degli Innocenti dal 1910 al 1948', research report, Florence, Istituto degli Innocenti.

—— —— and ZANOTTO, A., 1994a. 'Child care, infant mortality and the impact of legislation: the case of Florence's foundling hospital, 1840–1940', *Continuity and Change* 9, pp. 243–269.

—— —— —— 1994b. 'Penuria di balie e mortalità degli esposti a Firenze, 1840–1920', in G. DA MOLIN (ed.), *Trovatelli e balie in Italia, secc. XVI–XIX*, Bari, Cacucci.

—— —— —— 1995. 'Continuity, change and chances: a long-term perspective on child abandonment in Florence, 1445–1995', paper presented at the international conference 'Nobody's children: anthropological and historical perspectives on child abandonment', Durham, UK, 28–30 September.

—— —— —— forthcoming. 'Crisi di mortalità e riorganizzazione dell'assistenza all'infanzia abbandonata a Firenze, 1915–1945', in M. C. GIUNTELLA and I. NARDI (eds.), *Le guerre dei bambini: da Sarajevo a Sarajevo*, Naples, Edizioni Scientifiche Italiane.

Index